THIS GREAT LITTLE NATION
THE A–Z OF IRISH SCANDALS & CONTROVERSIES

THIS GREAT LITTLE NATION

The A–Z of Irish Scandals & Controversies

GENE KERRIGAN

AND

PAT BRENNAN

GILL & MACMILLAN

Gill & Macmillan Ltd
Goldenbridge
Dublin 8
with associated companies throughout the world
www.gillmacmillan.ie
© Gene Kerrigan and Pat Brennan, 1999
0 7171 2937 3

Print origination by
Carrigboy Typesetting Services, County Cork
Printed by
Caledonian International Book Manufacturing Ltd, Glasgow

This book is typeset in Goudy 10pt/12pt.

A CIP catalogue record for this book is available from the British Library.

3 5 4 2

This book is dedicated
to
Helena, Sean and Donal Lock — GK
and to
Fran and Jim Brennan — PB

Contents

CONTENTS

Introduction

The idea was to bring together in one volume as many as possible of the scandals and controversies that have shaped or reflected this great little nation. Some are well known, some are still unfolding, others barely registered on the scale of media and public interest at the time. Some are in danger of getting buried in the torrent of details that rushes daily through our lives. One of the functions of journalism is to accumulate and preserve hard-won information, to act as a kind of communal memory.

We confined the choices to the post-independence era, ruling out classic scandals of the Parnell type. We confined it to the South. If this unbalances the book, the inclusion of the scandals arising from the northern conflict would have unbalanced it in a different way. No doubt there are other omissions, events that should have been included. That is in the nature of such a project.

The line between scandal and controversy can shift as we gain perspective on events. In some of these matters what was alleged to be a scandal turned out to be relatively innocent. In some cases the scandal was in the false allegation of scandal.

Thanks are due first to our families: to Noel Murphy and Julie Lordan for their support; and to Kate Murphy and David Murphy, and to Cathleen Kerrigan, for their patience.

As ever, thanks to the staff of Dublin Corporation's invaluable newspaper library, in Pearse Street, and to RTÉ's excellent library. Thanks to lawyers Eoin McCullough and Conor McDonnell, to Fergal Tobin and D Rennison Kunz at Gill & Macmillan, and to copy editor Angela Rohan.

Special thanks to Gerald Barry, and thanks to all our colleagues in journalism, without whom there would be fewer scandals but a lot more unsubstantiated rumours.

Gene Kerrigan and Pat Brennan
August 1999

A

Aer Lingus Holidays

I f a company goes belly-up, and there are unexpected losses of millions of pounds, it might not be unreasonable to expect that someone be made accountable. In 1989 Aer Lingus Holidays appeared to be a modestly profitable subsidiary of the airline company. A few months later, in May 1990, the Minister for Tourism and Transport, Séamus Brennan, had to tell the Dáil that not only was the company not profitable, it had undisclosed trading losses of £7.2 million, property losses of £2 million and unaccounted-for borrowings of over £700,000. Aer Lingus Holidays was insolvent.

So, who was held accountable for the debacle? No one, really. The final chapter in the saga ended eight years later in Dublin Circuit Criminal Court, when the trial of two men accused of conspiring to defraud the company collapsed and the men were acquitted. The taxpayer picked up the final bill for the losses, the wind-up of the company, the garda investigation, and the thirty-four-day trial.

Aer Lingus Holidays (ALH) was set up in 1983 to group together five Aer Lingus travel companies: Sunbound, Stephen's Green Travel, Blueskies, Cara and Enterprise. Cathal Mullan, later chief executive of Aer Lingus, came in from Blueskies to become the new company's chairman. Malachi Faughnan, from Aer Lingus, became chief executive. Peter Noone was financial controller, Peter Keely assistant financial controller. These last two — along with Desmond Flynn, who was solicitor to the company — would later feature in a fraud investigation.

Aer Lingus became concerned that all was not well with the subsidiary when, in the summer of 1989, ALH had trouble paying for the aircraft it had chartered from the parent company. Given the apparently healthy state of the accounts, this shouldn't have been a problem. Aer Lingus asked accountant Niall O'Neill to have a closer look at the books. His initial report showed staggering losses that had not been recorded in the accounts. Aer Lingus called in the accountancy firm of Craig Gardner & Co. for a full investigation. When the accountants were done, in June 1990, they reckoned the accounts showed a deficit of £15 million.

How did it happen? Former chief executive of the company Malachi Faughnan told the Circuit Criminal Court it was in part due to slipshod work and in part 'to hide things'. He agreed that the accounts were inaccurate and the company didn't have enough money to operate effectively, although he denied specific knowledge of false information being entered in the books. He said he didn't go to Aer Lingus for help because ALH had been set up on the understanding that it would not borrow capital from the parent company. Judge Kieran O'Connor observed that ALH was run in a 'most appalling manner with false accounting to hide the fact that the company was, in effect, insolvent'.

As to the purpose of all this, Tom McCarthy, the Craig Gardner accountant who investigated ALH, told the court that the only effect of false accounting was to conceal the true position of ALH. The company would eventually have to find the money to clear out the false entries, though false accounting could benefit some individual trying to cover up. Apart from the false accounting there was also the matter of an unaccounted-for £715,000, which is why the Garda Fraud Squad was called in.

Eventually, in 1998, two men, Peter Keely and Desmond Flynn, were brought before the Central Criminal Court charged with conspiring, with Peter Noone, to defraud Aer Lingus Holidays by using company funds to buy property for themselves in Lanzarote. Peter Noone wasn't before the court because, as Judge O'Connor told the foreman of the jury: 'The short answer is I don't know. The real answer is that Mr Noone is missing.'

During the lengthy trial, former chairman Cathal Mullan and former chief executive Malachi Faughnan gave conflicting accounts about who knew what about the financial goings-on. Mr Faughnan, who was removed by the board in 1990, believed he had been treated harshly. The question of whether the ALH board or the parent company should have taken a closer look sooner was not resolved.

As to the fraud case against Peter Keely and Desmond Flynn, the court found them not guilty on 30 November. The judge ruled that purported evidence about movement of money in a London account was inadmissible. The 1992 Criminal Evidence Act would have allowed such evidence to be introduced. However, Judge O'Connor ruled that because the two accused were originally arrested and questioned in 1990, though not charged until 1994, the 1992 Act did not apply. The prosecution had no further evidence, so the judge directed the jury to find the accused not guilty. He said they were entitled to leave the courtroom with their reputations intact.

As for Peter Noone, he left Ireland before charges were brought. A warrant still stands for his arrest.

Ahern, Bertie: Domestic Violence

The rumours usually involved a supposed nurse from the Mater Private Hospital who told someone who told someone else that Bertie Ahern's partner, Celia Larkin, came into the hospital the other night, injured. And Bertie did it.

The 'other night' when Celia went into the Mater was months back. Or even years back. Or a week or two back. In various tellings of the rumour the timing was specific. This discrepancy regarding when the supposed visit to the Mater happened didn't undermine the rumour, it strengthened it. I heard she went into the Mater months ago; you heard she went in a week or two back. Put the two rumours together and breed a third: she was forever in and out of the Mater. To this rumour was added the rumour that Ahern's wife, from whom he was separated, had obtained a barring order.

For journalists, the Ahern rumours were tricky. They involved Ahern's private life, yet they were of legitimate public concern. If Ahern was in the habit of thumping people — whether or not they were women, whether or not they had a relationship with him — it was a matter of public significance. Domestic violence is a personal matter, true; but it is also a public matter, in that it involves lawbreaking. If the lawbreaker is also a lawmaker, the public significance is even more obvious.

At least two newspapers looked into the rumours and found not a sliver of evidence to back them up; no hospital record or witness, no barring order. In 1998 Ahern denied the rumours to two journalists writing a sympathetic biography of him. Serial rights to the book were bought by *Ireland on Sunday*, which launched a lurid radio advertising campaign that promised to tell 'the truth' about Ahern and his women. This created a row in which the allegations of domestic violence were finally aired in public. Presented with a story based on unsubstantiated rumour, the public paid little attention.

There were suggestions that the rumours originated with Ahern's enemies within Fianna Fáil, the Country and Western wing, those who had vowed revenge on the 'rat in an anorak'. Ahern found it impossible to scotch the rumours. It is very difficult to prove that you haven't done something.

Ahern, Bertie: The Right Question

Affable Bertie Ahern, seeking to keep his head above the stink of corruption still lingering from the Haughey era, contrived to give an impression of openness. The impression withered with his evasive responses to unfolding scandals. He backed Ray Burke, putting his credibility on the line by claiming to have conducted a thorough investigation of allegations made against Burke. The investigation was perfunctory. It was as though Ahern didn't want to know the truth. The extent of his involvement in the contacts between Fianna Fáil and developer Tom Gilmartin had to be dragged out of Ahern. He hid behind the Moriarty Tribunal when it was revealed that he co-signed a £25,000 cheque through which Charlie Haughey siphoned party money into his own account.

In the Sheedy affair, Ahern concealed the fact that he had intervened on Sheedy's behalf, and hid behind the formula which had rightly brought scorn on his Fine Gael opposite number, John Bruton. Ahern claimed that he would have told the full truth if he had been asked the right question.

See: Bruton, John: The Right Question.

AIB

No single institution within the state has been so involved in recent financial scandals as Allied Irish Banks. The bank blithely demanded and got state support, at a cost of millions to the taxpayer, when it made a mess of its ICI insurance subsidiary; it operated tens of thousands of bogus non-resident accounts for tax dodgers; it dodged tax it owed the exchequer, claiming to have come to a private amnesty arrangement with tax officials; it toadied to Charlie Haughey and Garret FitzGerald, while it dealt with ordinary customers with routine severity. When one aspect of the Haughey scandal was uncovered the bank lied to protect Haughey.

None of this has had any effect whatever on the bank's fortunes. In 1999 it clocked up record profits of £826 million and gave shareholders a total of 25 per cent in dividends. Questions about whether a bank with a consistent record of scandalous behaviour should be penalised or even whether it should continue to be licensed are taken seriously by no influential body, whether political or regulatory. The bank is successful in the only way that matters, making money, and only cranks and the terminally naive bother to question the behaviour underlying that success.

AIB: A Case Study

Richard Lonergan was a middle-aged farmer, businessman and one-time bookie from Rathard, Pallasgreen, in County Limerick. He banked with AIB. In August 1988 Lonergan owed AIB £14,000, in a term loan. At that stage he sold a premises in Limerick for £12,000. He brought £3,500 of that into the bank. According to an affidavit by an AIB official, Lonergan wanted 'for tax reasons' to keep this money away from his existing bank accounts. The money was put into AIB deposit account No. 18892014 under a false name, Richard Longton. The bank knew this was really Richard Lonergan, and the Longton account had the same address as Lonergan's other AIB account: Pallasgreen, County Limerick.

Lonergan's term loan debt gathered interest at a fierce rate. Eventually, in October 1990, AIB had a summary summons served on Lonergan, taking him to court to recover the sum of £19,721.90, plus £115 in costs. As these things do, the case dragged on, interest accumulated. Lonergan began a countersuit, claiming that the bank had bounced a £900 cheque and damaged his reputation as a bookie. He claimed that his business was grievously damaged.

In a letter dated three days before the case was due in court, in June 1998, the bank's solicitor said that, while prepared to enter into 'meaningful discussions', the bank's officials were 'quite happy that they will succeed in their claim'. On the day the case went to court the lawyers for both parties asked the judge to postpone the case for a short time. Two hours of negotiation followed. The bank offered Lonergan £10,000 to settle the case. His term loan debt — which had now risen to £36,000 — would be waived and the bank would pay all legal costs. Lonergan said no. The case would have to go into open court. All of it — the false-name account, the bank official's sworn affidavit that the bank was facilitating the opening of a false-name account for 'tax reasons' — would be opened to the judge, the media and the public.

Fifteen thousand, offered the AIB. Richard Lonergan thought about it, then asked for another £3,000, and finally settled for the £15,000. An hour later there was no one from the bank in court, nor was Richard

Lonergan present, when the lawyers told the court that a settlement had been reached. 'Oh good,' said Mr Justice Geoghegan, who had no knowledge of the detail of the case or negotiations. The lawyers asked him to strike out the AIB claim, and the countersuit. And to make no order as to costs. 'I'm delighted to hear it,' said the judge, pleased that the litigants reached a settlement and saved court time.

The most conservative possible estimation of legal costs would be £32,000. A more realistic estimate would be £80,000. Plus £15,000 for Lonergan; and the £36,000 debt write-off. So, AIB coughed up in the region of £130,000 to settle a case which, three days earlier, it was 'quite happy' it would win.

There wasn't a word about the case in the newspapers next day.

AIB: Bogus Accounts

Deposit Income Retention Tax (DIRT) was introduced in 1986. Before that time, it was up to taxpayers to declare whatever interest they earned from money in deposit accounts. The Department of Finance reckoned that vast numbers of people didn't bother and millions earned on deposit were not taxed. The introduction of DIRT meant that the financial institutions deducted a percentage of interest directly from accounts and passed it on to the Revenue Commissioners. As AIB's chief executive Tom Mulcahy later told the Dáil Committee on Public Accounts: 'What we are talking about is the banks acting as tax collectors on behalf of the state.' Not very effective tax collectors, as it turned out.

The only accounts not subject to DIRT were those of non-residents who had money in Irish banks but lived elsewhere. This regulation offered a ready loophole for tax evaders and they availed of it in their thousands, and the banks helped them.

By the late 1980s the Revenue Commissioners knew there was a problem with bogus non-resident accounts, particularly in the country's largest bank. AIB was told to clean up its act. In 1991 AIB investigated 87,000 non-resident accounts and found that 53,000 of them, holding some £600 million, were bogus, held by residents claiming to be non-residents. They were simply tax evasion scams.

The Department of Finance and the Central Bank were also well aware of the problem of tax evasion through bogus non-resident accounts. But they were paralysed by the fear that money would be moved out of the country. According to the July 1999 report of the

Comptroller and Auditor General into DIRT tax, tax evasion and 'the bogus non-resident accounts were seen as the lesser of two evils'. According to Maurice O'Connell, the governor of the Central Bank and formerly a senior official in the Department of Finance, it was a case of: 'For God's sake, whatever you do, don't rock the boat. The boat being the exchange rate . . . Anything sudden, anything drastic would probably have produced some very unwelcome consequences for the nation.'

So, it was softly, softly with the tax cheats.

An internal AIB memo from Mr J. O'Mahoney, group taxation manager, to the group internal auditor in February 1991 stated: 'We are being offered a way out of a very difficult situation which I believe will meet the needs of both the Revenue [Commissioners] and other Financial Institutions without it being published — this being very much in the interests of the bank.'

AIB thought it had secured a deal with the Revenue Commissioners. In effect, if the bank sorted out the bogus non-residents from 30 September 1991, then the pre-1991 tax evasion could be forgotten. It was to be a 'forward-looking' arrangement. Tom Mulcahy said a senior Revenue official told the bank: 'If AIB are prepared to be pragmatic the Revenue are prepared to look forward rather than back.'

However, the Revenue Commissioners flatly denied this version of events. There was no mini-amnesty for AIB's tax evaders. But there was also no attempt to follow up on DIRT arrears. In his statement to the Comptroller and Auditor General, D.A. MacCarthaigh, one of the tax officials dealing with AIB, blamed pressure of other work. He had been reassigned to a major inquiry into the drinks industry.

Whatever the arrangements between AIB and the Revenue Commissioners, overburdened PAYE taxpayers remained unaware of the bogus accounts scam until Liam Collins broke the story on 5 April 1998 in the *Sunday Independent*. Then, in October 1998, *Magill* magazine published AIB internal documents which revealed the extent of tax owed.

Anthony Spollen was the AIB's group internal auditor. In an internal memo dated 5 April 1991 he wrote: 'The Group Taxation Department has informed me that an Amnesty [with the Revenue Commissioners on the issue of DIRT due] can not be given without legislation going through the Dáil: the Group therefore has a contingent liability of c. £100m in respect of DIRT.'

The matter came before the Public Accounts Committee shortly after the *Magill* revelations. Tom Mulcahy said the £100 million figure of

DIRT owed, as estimated by the bank's own internal auditor, was a wild exaggeration. It was 'off the wall'. AIB later conceded that it owed between £25 and £35 million. Tom Mulcahy argued that the problem with bogus non-resident accounts was not an AIB problem, per se, it was 'industry-wide'. Everyone was at it.

The Comptroller and Auditor General's report confirmed Mr Mulcahy's contention, although the evidence suggested that AIB was still in a class of its own. (Indeed, in 1996, five years after the Revenue Commissioners thought they had tackled the AIB bogus accounts problem, £560,000 was collected in DIRT-related tax from hidden accounts in a branch of the bank in Mayo.) But even the state-owned ACC (the farmers' bank) was in on the act, at a cost to the exchequer of some £17 million in unpaid tax on bogus non-resident accounts.

See: Non-resident Bank Accounts.

AIB: *Evening Press*

On Friday, 28 January 1983 the *Evening Press* printed an article about Charlie Haughey's finances. It was written (under a Special Correspondent byline) by financial journalist Des Crowley and was based on what it called 'well-informed speculation'. Given the layers of deception surrounding Haughey's finances, the article was an accurate attempt to sketch some aspects of the subject.

The third paragraph of the article said: 'It has been rumoured in discreet financial circles for years that Mr Haughey owed £1 million to a major bank and that the bank had held its hand because of his elevated position.'

The next paragraph said: 'this correspondent can confirm that sources close to Allied Irish Banks insist that he owed them around this sum last year'.

This was almost entirely accurate. Haughey had owed AIB £1.14 million. The reference to 'last year' was wrong, as someone had paid the bank £750,000 against Haughey's debt at the beginning of 1980, and AIB had written off the rest.

AIB responded on 31 January with a statement which denounced the *Evening Press* for daring to write about the financial affairs of a 'well-known figure'. The statement disputed the article's claim that Haughey owed AIB around £1 million 'last year': 'This statement is so outlandishly inaccurate that Allied Irish Banks feel bound, as a special matter, to say so positively and authoritatively.'

It was not the newspaper article but the AIB statement which was 'outlandishly inaccurate'. The statement was one small brick in the protective wall which the likes of AIB built up around Haughey. At the time, Haughey still owed the bank a debt 'of honour' of £110,000. He, of course, never paid that.

The matter was raised at the Moriarty Tribunal, in March 1999, and a procession of AIB executives took the witness stand and swore that they hadn't a clue how the lying denial came to be released. It was suggested that some public relations chap, a man who had since died, had perhaps cooked up the denial. No one, it seemed, authorised him to do so, no one was even sure that he or anybody else had done so. It wasn't the first time that a tribunal would hear of questionable activity being ascribed to a person conveniently dead.

See: Dead Man Strategy.

AIB: ICI Bailout

The Insurance Corporation of Ireland (ICI) started off as a state-run insurance company providing cover for Irish Shipping. Later it developed as a general insurance company and was privatised. AIB bought into ICI in 1981, and in 1983 took over the whole company. The bank had invested a total of £86 million in acquiring ICI. It was a gamble undertaken by mature entrepreneurs who knew exactly what they were doing. If the gamble succeeded it would reap huge profits for AIB.

In March 1984, just a year after AIB took over the company, ICI came running back to the state after the big boys in the world outside had blackened its eye. Uncounted millions had been lost in ICI's London operation. Estimates put the figure at anything between £120 and £200 million. Not only ICI but AIB was in trouble. The directors of AIB, people fond of reminding us that there's no such thing as a free lunch, and who ostensibly regard The Market as the great regulator, went straight to Garret FitzGerald's coalition government, demanding help. If the bank was to meet its responsibilities it might go under. Suddenly, ICI wasn't a great profit opportunity for the private sector, it was a problem for the state.

The problem was dealt with — under the direction of Garret FitzGerald — by John Bruton and Alan Dukes, two stalwart defenders of The Market, who might have been expected to tell AIB to accept the swings and the roundabouts, that it is not the role of the state to prop up private enterprises which have got themselves into trouble. Instead, the Department of Industry and Commerce set up a company which acquired ICI. The state would take over the failed insurance company. AIB was very glad to hand over ICI, free of charge, writing off its £86 million investment but also saying goodbye to ICI's debts of at least £120 million.

The argument was that if the state didn't take over ICI and its liabilities the company would go down and take AIB with it, causing a crisis in the Irish banking system. The role of the state, it appears, is to use public money to protect the banking system when bad things happen to it, and otherwise to stay off the back of private enterprise. None of the usual voices who might be heard demanding that the state stay out of The Market let out so much as a peep.

So, AIB was propped up by the state, with loans and with levies extracted from other insurance companies and banks, all ultimately paid for by the customers and the taxpayers. There was no question of the state taking a stake in AIB in return for saving the bank. There was no suggestion that the bank seek a saviour in the private sector, where help would come at a price and the bank would have to concede equity, or even be taken over.

In the year of crisis, 1984, AIB's profits were £85 million. It maintained and improved on profits of that size in the years that followed. The bank itself could have paid for ICI's losses out of its profits, but it didn't see why it should. No sooner had AIB been assured that the taxpayers would bail out ICI than the bank announced that the debacle would not cost its shareholders a penny, dividends would be paid as usual. The bank behaved as though it were entitled to demand and receive taxpayers' money as and when required.

All of this was discussed in financial jargon, the public received little information. Even the politicians couldn't agree on the cost to the taxpayer. Garret FitzGerald, for instance, in his memoirs, claimed with pride that his government had arranged things so that the AIB-ICI bailout didn't cost the taxpayer a penny. Fianna Fáil TD Dick Roche, using Department of Finance figures, concluded:

> The net present value of the bailout of the AIB-owned Insurance Corporation by the government led by Dr Garret FitzGerald in present-day terms is £357 million. In the region of 9 per cent of the cost of the bailout has been carried by the taxpayers of the state. The state is still carrying the cost of an interest-free loan which Dr FitzGerald's government advanced to AIB in 1985. The cost of that loan to the Irish taxpayer is £2 million per year, approximately.

Journalist Vincent Browne calculated the net state handout to AIB at £18 million.

In 1999 AIB announced profits of £826 million, almost ten times its profits of 1984, but there was no suggestion that the bank might repay the state for the bailout.

See: FitzGerald, Garret.

AIB: This Great Little Nation

The following is the text of a letter sent to Charlie Haughey after he was elected leader of Fianna Fáil. It is from Michael Phelan, manager of the Dame Street branch of Allied Irish Banks. For years, Haughey had been rifling the bank's resources, drawing as much money as he felt he needed, treating with contempt a long series of requests that he make some effort to pay his debts. Mr Phelan was in the front line of this conflict and bore the brunt of Haughey's contempt for the bank.

11 December 1979
An Taoiseach
Mr Charles J. Haughey
Abbeville
Kinsealy
Co. Dublin

Dear Mr Haughey,

It gives me great pleasure to convey to you my warmest congratulations on your election to the high offices of Leader of Fianna Fáil and Taoiseach and to offer you my sincere good wishes for success in both.

To say the task you have taken on is daunting is an understatement but I have every faith in your ability to succeed in restoring confidence in this great little nation.

With renewed congratulations and kind regards,

Yours sincerely,

Michael Phelan
Manager

Alternative Ireland

I n a famous remark, Leona Helmsley, New York hotelier and crook, said that taxes are for the little people. Her sentiments were widely shared in Ireland.

While the scandals of the early 1990s shocked and enlightened us, by the end of the decade we were beginning to see more clearly the size and shape of what had been hidden. It amounted to more than the occasional rip-off by a greedy businessman or politician. It was nothing less than an Alternative Ireland, with its own banks and its own laws, its own tame Central Bank and compliant Revenue, its own planners, its own politicians, bought and paid for. And all operating free in an economy sustained by the work and the taxes of the little people, the mugs who take the law seriously and pick up the tab while Alternative Ireland is off getting its chin lifted in Paris or sunning itself in the Bahamas. There are movers and shakers, to whom the law does not apply, except the bits of it of which they approve. And there are the rest of us: drudges, consumers, workers, whose job it is to meet the demands of the market and to act as the mortar which holds the whole thing together.

By the late 1990s it had become clear that even the most extreme left-wing fantasies of the 1970s about how the system worked were somewhat on the conservative side.

Ansbacher Deposits

T hese were unearthed by the McCracken Tribunal in 1997. A Cayman Islands company, Ansbacher Cayman, was used to hold the vast resources of several dozen of Ireland's wealthiest people. The Ansbacher Deposits were one aspect of this operation, which carried on through the 1970s, 1980s and into the mid-1990s. Des Traynor, one of the country's most eminent business people, managed this massive fraud.

The money was held by Ansbacher Cayman, earning interest. Traynor opened a 'mirror' account in Guinness & Mahon private bank, of which he was de facto chief executive (he moved it to Irish Intercontinental Bank in 1992). This enabled his clients to have access to the money, although it remained technically 'offshore' and untaxable. Within this so-called Ansbacher account, memorandums kept track of the amounts coming in from Traynor's private clients, and going out. McCracken established that in 1989 there was £38 million in the account. Later probes would put the figure at a minimum of £50 million.

A computer software application, secret and separate from Guinness & Mahon's own computer software, kept track of the coded accounts. Accounts S8 and S9 belonged to Traynor's buddy, Charlie Haughey, the latter being his Deutschmark account.

Traynor's outfit worked other dodges for his clients, including the setting up of discretionary trusts and the arranging of 'back-to-back loans' secretly secured by deposits in Ansbacher Cayman, all designed to evade tax. The scandal, just the tip of which was uncovered by McCracken, was blown open in September 1999 following a dogged investigation by Gerard Ryan, an authorised officer assigned by Tánaiste Mary Harney to look into the Ansbacher Deposits. Harney's officials estimated that the overall Ansbacher operation serviced around 120 of Ireland's wealthiest and most respected business people and involved several hundred million pounds.

While the bogus non-resident scandal represented the wholesale criminality within the small business and professional classes, facilitated by the banks, the Ansbacher scandal was the top-of-the-range system of fraud operated for the benefit of the elite. Complex banking devices were put in place to eradicate what the conspirators referred to as the 'footprints' of the wealthy people.

In 1986 Traynor became chairman of Cement Roadstone Holdings, one of the largest building supply·companies in the world, and moved the operation of the fraud to his CRH office. Essentially he ran a private bank for twenty years, evading tax and laundering money for the benefit of the Irish elite. The evasion scheme was immensely complicated and detailed, and it would be argued that since technically the money was owned by Ansbacher Cayman, the beneficiaries in Ireland were not liable for tax, nor were they guilty of any offences. Individual clients of Traynor could argue that they believed the Ansbacher set-up to be a legitimate tax avoidance scheme and were unaware that Traynor was organising an illegal tax evasion operation.

The effect of the Ansbacher fraud, along with the non-resident fraud, was to massively shift the burden of funding the state infrastructure and administration to PAYE workers, primarily the working class. Pleas about the 'national interest' helped convince workers to keep wages down, and state services, in health and education, were cut to the bone. Those not paying tax could easily afford to privately buy such services.

Without the Ben Dunne drug scandal — sheer chance — and the fallout from that, which led to the revelation of the Lowry and Haughey scandals, the Ansbacher fraud would never have been discovered. How many similar schemes were operated by other crooked accountants remains unknown.

See: Furze, John; Guinness & Mahon (Ireland) Ltd; Non-resident Bank Accounts; Traynor, Des.

Áras Eight

President Mary Robinson was inaugurated on 3 December 1990. She wasn't moving into the living quarters of the presidential mansion, Áras an Uachtaráin, until after Christmas, but she went up and had a look around.

Mrs Robinson's victory had been widely welcomed, and in the course of her presidency her popularity would increase to levels undreamed of by other politicians. Fianna Fáil had at first assumed its candidate, Brian Lenihan, merely had to show up to win the election. Fine Gael had to struggle to find a candidate willing to become a certain loser. The party, however, felt assured of second place, and when its reluctant candidate, Austin Currie, was beaten by both Robinson and Lenihan the shock was so humiliating that the party kicked out its leader, Alan Dukes, and made John Bruton leader.

Mrs Robinson, unburdened by having to construct or try to implement policies, didn't have to alienate any section of society. She visited countless projects and groups and shook hands and showed her approval. She invited to Áras an Uachtaráin groups which were on the periphery of society. She encouraged, in the buzzword of the day, their inclusion. As a result of her widespread activities and undoubted popularity, Mary Robinson received media coverage which usually but not always stopped just short of adulation.

Even her behaviour in the case of the Áras Eight was glossed over by her media fans.

On that visit to Áras an Uachtaráin, on the day of her inauguration, the president carried out an inspection of various rooms. In one room she saw that a number of dead bluebottles had gathered on a window sill. She counted them. It is a strange image, the new president, solemnly counting dead bluebottles. It wasn't enough to note that she saw a 'lot' of dead bluebottles or even 'a couple of dozen' dead bluebottles. There were — and we might imagine her leaning over, pointing from one dead bluebottle to the next, twenty-six, twenty-seven, twenty-eight — yes — twenty-nine dead bluebottles on the window sill.

Eight people would lose their jobs following this.

It wasn't just the bluebottles that upset Mrs Robinson. In the days that followed, the new president decided that the household staff were too quiet. In fact, they tended to scurry away when the new president approached (one wonders why). They put out — and this was seriously advanced as a reason for the sackings — they put out too many pieces of cutlery on the table when the president wanted a light lunch for her guests.

The president saw herself as wielding 'a new broom'. Secretarial staff were inspected and were found, according to presidential handler Bride Rosney, to be 'vibrant'. So, they could stay.

The elderly people on the household staff apparently weren't 'vibrant' enough for the new broom. 'I wanted to have a happy Áras,' Mrs Robinson explained later. As for the housekeeper: 'I didn't like the housekeeper,' said Mrs Robinson. The housekeeper was sacked. Mrs Robinson brought in her former domestic help from her own home, Laura Donegan, and appointed her as her personal housekeeper.

This all happened within days of the inauguration. There were just two weeks to Christmas. Six of the eight elderly people who were being dismissed lived-in at the Áras. They would have to find new accommodation. The previous president, Paddy Hillery, had arranged to have the workers transferred into the staffing structure of the Office of Public Works. This gave them some security, and now that they were being pushed out of the Áras the OPW would have to find them new positions. But it was a shock, being swept aside by the 'new broom', just before Christmas. The icon of the new Ireland had arrived and they weren't good enough for her. And being given notice to quit their home added to the misery. Ex-President Hillery intervened and took one long-serving staff member, who had lost her home at the Áras, into his own house.

It is remarkable that these sackings took place so soon after the inauguration. The offences of the staff, as later outlined by Mrs Robinson and her supporters, seem incredibly trivial and easy to fix. There could have been any number of explanations for the bluebottles on the window sill. Mrs Robinson, who was in other respects a stiff and solemn president, found the place settings at lunch too formal. A word in an ear could have dealt with that. Instead, the dismissals were immediate, there were no second chances.

Mrs Robinson would make few missteps in her image-building throughout her presidency. She hired a personal/political manager, Bride Rosney, to guide and protect her from media Nosy Parkers and to shape her public mask. The media were slavish. Moulds were being broken, there was a new dawn, hope was in the air: these are just some of the meaningless clichés with which the Robinson media camp followers afflicted the populace. The

Áras Eight scandal caused a mere blip in the media beatification of Mary Robinson, the faultless icon of the New Ireland, a Mary Poppins for the 1990s. The Áras Eight were largely airbrushed from the record.

Arms Crisis

The 1970 Arms Crisis scandal, which brought ministerial sackings and a notorious trial in the South, was born in the ghettoes of Northern Ireland in 1969. Nationalists felt under siege as the RUC, 'B' Specials and unionist gangs sought to stamp out the unrest which had emerged from the civil rights protests. In July and August of 1969 the RUC killed seven of the eleven people who died, the 'B' Specials and unionists killed two more. RUC officers in armoured cars fired machine guns at homes. That's how nine-year-old Patrick Rooney died in his bed.

For decades, southern politicians had proclaimed their nationalism. Now, as nationalist representatives came down to Dublin in search of help, the southern establishment was being challenged to back up its alleged concern for the fourth green field. The northern groups, a mixture of citizens' defence committees, civil rights activists and IRA members, wanted practical help. They wanted political pressure put on the British: most of all, many of them wanted guns, for fear of a unionist pogrom.

Taoiseach Jack Lynch dithered. He feared that giving weapons to nationalists would incur the wrath of the British; he feared that such weapons would be used to revive the IRA, which was all but dormant. On the other hand, he feared the consequences of saying no. What if he said no and there was a pogrom and dozens or even hundreds of people were killed?

Others in the Lynch cabinet wanted the guns handed over to the citizens' defence committees. Donegal TD Neil Blaney organised deputations from the North to keep the pressure on Lynch. He and Charlie Haughey dominated a cabinet subcommittee which made the running on northern policy. As a result of the dithering, with widespread nodding and winking and cabinet ministers talking out of the corners of their mouths, government policy was whatever individual cabinet members thought it to be. Lynch didn't authorise the handing over of weapons, but neither did he explicitly rule that out. In September 1969 Jim Gibbons, Minister for Defence, authorised the acceptance into the FCA of fifteen civilians from over the border, for training in the use of weapons at Fort Dunree. If it was okay with the government to train northern people to use guns, some thought, then it must be government policy to see that they have guns.

The genesis of the attempt to bring in guns was a meeting in the town of Bailieboro, in Cavan, on 4 October 1969. Captain James Kelly, an Irish army intelligence officer, met with northern nationalists and the importation of arms was discussed. The previous day, Captain Kelly had gone to the home of cabinet minister Charlie Haughey, at Haughey's mansion in Kinsealy, and told him about the meeting that was about to take place in Bailieboro. Haughey gave Captain Kelly £500, to cover the expenses of the meeting.

The gardaí were aware of the meeting and on the day it took place a senior garda went to the secretary of the Department of Justice, Peter Berry, and told him that Captain Kelly was in touch with IRA members and was meeting subversives that day in Bailieboro. Berry tried, without success, to contact his minister, Mícheál Ó Móráin. He tried to contact the Taoiseach, with similar lack of success. He then got in touch with a cabinet minister who had once been his Minister for Justice, Charlie Haughey: an intelligence officer, an agent of the southern state, was meeting known members of the IRA. What was to be done? Haughey listened to the story of the meeting in Bailieboro and asked questions about the source of the information, without hinting that he knew all about the meeting before it took place.

Almost two weeks later Peter Berry was briefed by a senior garda on discussions about arms importation at the Bailieboro meeting. Berry claimed he told Taoiseach Jack Lynch about this the next day; Lynch denied he was told. It appears that blind eyes were turned. No one felt confident enough to intervene to stop the importation of arms.

Over the next few months money which had been allocated by the government for a Relief of Distress Fund for the North was siphoned off to be used in attempts to buy arms. In all, £76,000 out of £100,000 would be spent on one adventure or another. One potential source of weapons, an English arms dealer, turned out to be a British agent and £1,600 went down the tubes. A second attempt, involving a trip to the USA, also failed. Neil Blaney brought in a friend, Albert Luykx, an amiable Belgian businessman who seemed flattered at attention from Irish ministers. Luykx had contacts on the Continent.

A cooperative customs official helped let some arms come through. They were labelled as machine parts. The Special Branch knew about this from a senior IRA man who was informing. It didn't intervene for fear of compromising its informant.

On Valentine's Day 1970 Captain Kelly talked again to Charlie Haughey and 'put him fully in the picture'. Kelly and Luykx went to

Hamburg and on 2 April 1970 — as disturbances in the North escalated — made a deal with an arms seller, Otto Schleuter. This cost £28,000. The money again came from the government's Relief of Distress Fund. That day, with Belfast in violent turmoil, Minister for Defence Jim Gibbons authorised the sending of 500 army rifles to Dundalk, close to the border. These were for distribution to northern nationalists if the troubles became worse. The ambiguity of cabinet members, torn between fear of the consequences of letting weapons loose and fear of the consequences if such weapons were not available, can be seen in this kind of activity. The official/unofficial deal to import arms, made that very day in Hamburg, was another reflection of that ambiguity.

Peter Berry, secretary of the Department of Justice, would claim that on 13 April he told Taoiseach Jack Lynch about Captain Kelly's activities, and about 'police information about the participation of ministers in supplying arms to the IRA'. Lynch would deny he was told.

The affair staggered ineffectually on. It was now six months since the Bailieboro meeting where the arms importation was first discussed. Throughout April 1970 further efforts to import arms failed. Still, no one could be entirely sure if the intended importation was legal, if the involvement of ministers made it so. The police knew what was happening and were seeking to stop it, albeit treading very carefully among the governmental ambiguities. While there might be sympathy for what was happening to nationalists up North, arming the IRA was dangerous, and such guns could end up being used to kill policemen. And while the North remained tense, the apocalyptic mood of a few months earlier had eased.

Still, the plan to bring in the guns went ahead, with Haughey and Blaney making the running. When the guns were finally ready for importation through Dublin airport on 18 April 1970 Charlie Haughey, aware that the Special Branch was planning to seize the arms, rang Peter Berry. Could the cargo, he asked, 'be let through on a guarantee that it will go direct to the North?'

'No.'

'What will happen if it comes in?'

'It will be grabbed.'

'I better have it called off,' said Haughey. Haughey had a conversation with Jim Gibbons, Minister for Defence, in which he said he would have the importation postponed for a month. The scheme died right there.

Now there was a danger that information about what had happened might leak out. 'What will I do, what will I do?' moaned Jack Lynch to Peter Berry. Lynch was walking up and down, still dithering.

'Sack the lot of them,' said the secretary of the Department of Justice.

Lynch, as ever, compromised. He confronted Neil Blaney and warned him off, but he balked at tackling Haughey, who was recovering from injuries in hospital. On 30 April he told Peter Berry he had been assured there would be no repetition of the attempted arms importation.

Word was leaking out. On the very day that Lynch was telling Berry that it was all over, there would be no repetition, someone sent a note to Liam Cosgrave, leader of the Fine Gael opposition party. Although he would later paint himself as an implacable opponent of such carry-on, Cosgrave too dithered. He didn't want to be seen as the one who revealed what was going on. He tried to leak the information to the newspapers. When that failed he confronted Taoiseach Jack Lynch on 5 May. Knowing that the arms scandal was about to become public, Lynch decided to be seen to act decisively. He sacked Haughey and Blaney from the cabinet. Another minister, Kevin Boland, resigned in protest.

The official line now firmed up, the ambiguities of the previous months were denied: the attempted importation was completely unofficial, totally against government policy. Therefore, if it was illegal, someone had broken the law. Haughey and Blaney were arrested. The charge against Blaney was dropped at District Court level. Haughey would go on trial along with Captain Kelly, northern nationalist John Kelly and the Belgian businessman Albert Luykx.

Meanwhile, there was nervousness at government level, things were so unstable that anything seemed possible. At 3 p.m. on Sunday, 5 July Taoiseach Jack Lynch and six of his ministers, including new Minister for Justice Des O'Malley, gathered in the cabinet room for an emergency meeting. Peter Berry was called in, along with the garda commissioner and the army chief of staff. Berry had already had a phone call from President Eamon de Valera, asking for assurance that the police and army were dependable. Now, with the panic in the cabinet room palpable, Berry realised that the cabinet members wanted reassurance that there wasn't about to be a *coup d'état*.

When Haughey and his co-defendants went on trial the others put up the defence that the attempted importation had official sanction and they hadn't done anything illegal. Haughey set himself apart from Captain Kelly, John Kelly and Albert Luykx and simply denied everything. Jim Gibbons had played an ambiguous role in the events but now gave sworn evidence that there had been no government involvement in the attempted importation The judge concluded that either Haughey or Gibbons had committed perjury. Probably they both did.

Nothing was as clear-cut as some were claiming. The jury brought in not guilty verdicts.

The scandal increased northern unionists' belief that the IRA was an instrument of the southern government. It gave Haughey a sheen of republicanism which was in reality just one more mask that he thought for a time might be useful in boosting his career. The Arms Crisis happened when the green rhetoric so casually employed for decades by southern politicians came up against the realities of the northern conflict. Their bluff was called and they weren't sure how to react. They allowed the attempted importation of arms, then drew back, not in fear of unleashing violence but in fear of being caught playing footsie with a resurgent IRA.

It was a period of panic and confusion, of good intentions and poor judgment, of cowardice and uncertainty of principle, of inability to talk straight and mean what was said. It was a time out of which none of the participants emerged with glory.

Army Deafness Claims

More than 14,000 soldiers and former soldiers have, since the mid-1990s, claimed that their hearing was damaged by the work they did in the army and that they are entitled to compensation because the hearing loss could have been anticipated and prevented. The Minister for Defence, Michael Smith, called the rash of claims 'wrong and immoral'. They were, he said, 'the result of a cancer that is eating at the heart of our society'. That cancer was the 'compensation culture' and it was fuelled by 'a greedy minority of solicitors'. A judge hearing one of many deafness claims remarked that the minister was 'deliberately trying to interfere with the running of the court'.

The minister claimed that the compensation being paid to soldiers who the courts had decided had indeed suffered hearing loss would reach £1 billion by the end of 1999. After the Dáil Committee on Public Accounts investigated the matter its chairman, Jim Mitchell TD, estimated that the total army deafness claims could reach £5.55 billion. He thought that there should be new legislation and that the politicians should effectively decide what the courts could and could not do in the personal injuries cases such as these.

PDFORRA, representing the soldiers, pointed out that official documents show that since 1952 the army was well aware that loud noises could cause hearing loss and that soldiers' ears should be protected during, for instance, firearms practice. But they weren't. As late as 1986, the army refused to purchase the latest earplugs because they were too expensive. Some soldiers argued in court that they had asked for ear protection; others said they had got their own but were not allowed to use it.

By April 1999 a total payout of £57.193 million had been made in 2,977 cases. Another £16.07 million went in plaintiffs' legal costs; 2,671 cases were settled, with agreed payments made. Court awards were made in 159 cases; 111 cases were withdrawn. Just 36 were dismissed by the court.

Jim Mitchell concluded that 'either our compensation laws and practices, or the application thereof, are extraordinarily generous by international standards or the Irish Defence Forces have been massively negligent'.

Artane Industrial School

Among young boys growing up in working-class Dublin in the 1950s and later, Artane was a byword for fear. Behind the high walls and beyond the fields that separated it from the rest of the community, the Artane Industrial School was home to as many as 900 boys at any one time. Run by the Christian Brothers, it had a reputation for harsh discipline and terrifying corporal punishment. Today, like other institutions of its kind, it is a subject of criminal investigation.

Artane Industrial School was closed in 1969. At that time, there were 31 industrial schools in Ireland with more than 2,000 children. Ten years previously, there were 4,000 children in the industrial schools. And ten years previous to that again, there were more than 6,000 children in these institutions. Though a minority of children were committed to care by the courts because of truancy, begging, petty theft or other trivial offences, the vast majority — 70 per cent of boys and 95 per cent of girls — had committed no offence at all. Their families simply couldn't cope, or someone in a position of authority decided they couldn't cope. Maybe the father had died and the mother had no income, or the mother had died and the children were left alone while the father worked. Or the father had deserted, or the mother was unmarried. For fortunate children, the extended family gave the support needed to keep them at home, but many thousands were placed in institutions such as Artane. Keeping families together was not a priority for either church or state.

Bereaved children, neglected children, disturbed children alike were sent to the industrial schools, where they were segregated by sex, often

separated from their siblings, issued with regulation clothing and
footwear, and put under the care of people who had immense power, no
formal training in childcare and little supervision. The rules by which the
schools were run stipulated that each child should have a separate bed,
adequate nutrition, warm clothes and a basic education. The school
manager or his deputy was 'authorised to punish children detained in the
school in the case of misconduct'. There were no guidelines on what sort
of punishment was acceptable.

Patrick Touher has written two books about his years as an orphan in
Artane. He was taken, without explanation, from the protective
environment of a happy foster home and brought to this huge institution,
with its massive dormitories, 180 beds to a room. Looking back, he
believed that some of the men in charge were unsuitable, having been
forced by their families to join the Christian Brothers.

> Their frustration, born out of boredom and celibacy, was released
> in anger against the boys. To these men celibacy was like drip-
> feeding a caged tiger . . . I often lay awake in those dormitories of
> fear longing for love and affection from someone, anyone.
> Bedwetters were flogged naked and I found inexcusable the
> beatings and floggings for mere trivialities like whispering in the
> dormitories . . . the leathers used were 18" long and $1^1/2$" wide and
> had lead and iron slats inserted for added pain.

Occasions of corporal punishment and their severity were, he remembered, random and therefore all the more terrifying.

What was once viewed as a 'harsh regime' with 'a few bad apples' is
now a matter for gardaí who, in the course of investigating complaints of
physical and sexual abuse, have taken statements from about 200 men
who were in Artane School. In November 1998 the gardaí made the
unusual decision to issue a public appeal for contact from former residents
who were assaulted at Artane. One former resident recalled that, as an
adult, he required four operations on his hands to repair the damage done
by beatings in the school. He was also sexually assaulted.

And it's not just Artane and it wasn't just the Christian Brothers.
There are criminal abuse investigations in other industrial schools,
notably Letterfrack and Salthill, run by the Brothers. And two non-
clerical paedophiles who savagely abused young boys in St Joseph's,
Kilkenny were sent to jail. In 1997 David Murray was sentenced to ten
years for gross sexual abuse. Myles Brady, the man who succeeded Murray

when he left St Joseph's, was sentenced to four years for indecent assault the following year and died in prison.

The formative years for thousands of children who were reared in industrial schools were years of terror. Certainly, given the vulnerability of the children and the unchallenged authority of the people looking after them, there was nothing to stand between a paedophile or sadist and his worst behaviour. Yes, former inmates agree, there were kind people too, but the kind people stood back and did not stop the cruelty.

On 30 March 1998 the Christian Brothers took out advertisements in the national newspapers apologising to their victims. 'And we say to you who have experienced physical or sexual abuse by a Christian Brother, and to you who complained of abuse but were not listened to, we are deeply sorry.' In the same advertisement the order announced that it was setting up a free telephone helpline. 'As an initial step, we have already put in place a range of services to offer a practical response. Further services will be provided as needs become clearer.' The apology was not welcomed by all. One victim told the *Irish Independent*: 'They can burn their apology . . . we were like lambs to the slaughter when we were given over to them and this apology is an insult to us.'

But the Irish Society for the Prevention of Cruelty to Children welcomed the apology as a timely watershed. Other religious orders and the Catholic hierarchy were not so forthcoming.

Apart from the physical and sexual assaults, children in the industrial homes suffered other, more insidious forms of abuse and neglect. The 1970 Kennedy Report into the Reformatory and Industrial School Systems investigated the educational attainment level of the children in the schools and found it seriously inadequate. With virtually no aftercare system, institutionalised children were sent out into 'a world which requires an initiative and adaptability they do not possess'. Some children had so little contact with the outside world that 'they were unaware that food had to be paid for or that letters had to be stamped'.

More recent revelations, notably from the *States of Fear* documentary series on RTÉ, revealed that many of the thousands of children raised in industrial schools were not just abused, unloved and poorly educated, but even malnourished.

The problem of what to do about children who have no families, or have needs beyond the capacity of their families, is no more resolved now than it was when they were shut away in huge institutions where discipline was the primary concern. The large institutions are closed. Smaller ones like Madonna House closed after their own abuse scandals.

Today, there are about 3,500 children in care. About 3,000 of them are with foster families. About 500 are in residential homes. The Department of Health statistics don't mention how many are living rough or have appeared before frustrated judges who repeatedly have complained that for many disturbed children there is no suitable care arrangement available. In a two-year period to May 1997, 135 children in need of care spent an aggregate of more than 3,000 days in hospitals, not because they were sick, but simply because there was nowhere else to put them. A report commissioned by the Department of Health identified serious shortcomings in the childcare system. 'The conclusion to be drawn from this review of current policies and practices is that dysfunctional and inadequate families are being cared for by dysfunctional and inadequate services.'

See: Goldenbridge; Madonna House; Poor Clares; Trudder House.

B

Baltinglass, Battle of

James Everett was born in 1890, and became a trade union activist first among agricultural workers and then with the Irish Transport and General Workers' Union. He joined Sinn Féin after 1916 and acted as a judge in the Sinn Féin courts during the struggle for independence. He became a Wicklow county councillor in 1920, a Labour Party TD for Wicklow in 1922, and he ended up a solid fixture on the 'cute hoor' wing of politics. In the 1940s he joined a faction, National Labour, that briefly split from the Labour Party.

Everett assiduously watered his grass roots and stroked his con-stituents. If circumstances were different he would have lived and died an obscure and unremembered politician. In 1948, however, Fianna Fáil lost power and a coalition was formed. National Labour was a minor part of that coalition and Everett got his share of the spoils, being appointed Minister for Posts and Telegraphs. It was, it appeared, a position in which he could do little harm and from which he could dole out an amount of patronage and swank around Wicklow in his ministerial role. Then, in 1950, he appointed one of his supporters, Michael Farrell, to the sub-postmastership in the village of Baltinglass. Such positions were furiously sought after, providing not alone a good living but an amount of local prestige, and when you got such a position you protected it. For Farrell to get the position the sub-postmastership had to be taken away from the Cooke family, which had held it for generations. The woman who was in line for the job, Helen Cooke, protested to no avail. The job was in Everett's gift and the traditions of political patronage demanded that he should give it to one of his own.

The tradition of jobbery, the giving of positions to cronies and favoured ones, was a routine corruption in the Ireland of the time. Although Fianna Fáil, which had long been up to its neck in jobbery, made a big deal about the Baltinglass sub-post office issue, jobbery was regarded by most politicians as part of a way of life. Fianna Fáil had no problem with jobbery as long as it was in power. It was the blatancy of Everett's action, and the fact that aspects of the new coalition government had come to power promising to change the traditional way of doing things, that caused difficulties.

One of the bigger parties in the coalition, Clann na Poblachta, had made a name for itself by campaigning against jobbery. Now, the party dithered. Some of its best members were aghast at what Everett was being allowed get away with. One founder of the party, Noel Hartnett, resigned. Party leader Seán MacBride shrugged and remarked that 'unsavoury matters are inseparable from politics'.

The village was split in two and the Battle of Baltinglass was under way. The new sub-postmaster, Michael Farrell, owned a general shop in the village and this was boycotted. The Cooke family continued protesting. Incredibly, this took up the time of the government as it headed into the choppy waters of the Mother and Child crisis. Eventually, in 1951, unable to take the continuing boycott and the controversy into which his life had been plunged, Michael Farrell resigned as sub-postmaster.

James Everett continued to hold his Dáil seat for another sixteen years, until he died in 1967. He had been a TD for forty-five years, and was a minister from 1948 to 1951, and from 1954 to 1957, but if he is remembered at all it will be as the man whose cronyism tore a village apart and made jobbery a national issue.

See: Jobbery.

Ban, The

From the beginning, in the late nineteenth century, the Gaelic Athletic Association felt itself under siege, struggling to preserve and advance the traditional games of hurling and Gaelic football (it soon gave up on athletics). Inevitably, the GAA became caught up in the politics of the times, its chief adversary being the unionist-leaning Irish Amateur Athletics Association. These two bodies enforced boycotts of each other's games. Long after the IAAA had ceased to be a serious rival, long after the GAA had become established within the heart and soul of the new state that emerged in the 1920s, there remained The Ban.

You didn't have to play a 'foreign game' (soccer, rugby, hockey or cricket) to be thrown out of the GAA, you just had to attend one. Strictly speaking, even attending a dance run by a soccer club could be seen as promoting a foreign game and could get you kicked out of the GAA. Attending 'foreign dances' was ruled to be unIrish.

In 1938 two scandals erupted out of The Ban. The first began in February, when a popular Tipperary hurler, James Cooney, attended an international rugby game. Someone squealed on him to the Tipperary board of the GAA, he was hauled in and confessed his crime. The board had no choice: a three-month suspension from both the county team and his club, UCD, was automatic. This ruled Cooney out of playing for Tipperary in the upcoming Munster championship, against Clare.

Well, says Tipperary, if we can't have Cooney, we'll knock out one of Clare's players. And they complained that one of the Clare players had not only attended the same rugby match as Cooney, but had attended with Cooney. And Cooney gave a statement to that effect.

This was trumped by Clare. Since Cooney was suspended he was not a bona fide member of the GAA and therefore his statement that a Clare player attended the rugby game didn't count. Fair enough, said the central council.

This kind of small-minded bitterness burst onto the national stage a few months later and drew into its coils the president of Ireland, Douglas Hyde. The presidency had been established just the year before, under the 1937 constitution, and in a rush of conviviality the political parties had come together to choose Hyde for the role. Hyde was founder of the Gaelic League, with impeccable nationalist credentials. He was also Protestant, so despite that embarrassing Dunbar-Harrison affair no one could accuse the South of discrimination.

With his seat in the Áras hardly warm, Hyde attended a rugby international. It didn't seem to have occurred to him that he shouldn't attend foreign games, since such games were popular among substantial sections of the people.

At a meeting of the GAA central council in December 1938 it was noted that Hyde was and had been for many years a patron of the GAA. As such, he had no business attending a foreign game. A Galway delegate put down a motion to this effect and the delegates began discussing the matter. At which point the president of the GAA, Pádraig MacNamee, cut in. This discussion was academic, the rules were the rules and attendance at a foreign game incurred an automatic penalty, so he was ruling that Douglas Hyde, president of Ireland, was being removed as a patron of the association.

There was a backlash. In Mayo and Kerry and Roscommon and Kildare, members came out in defence of Hyde. There was a backlash against the backlash and by the time of the GAA annual congress, at Easter 1939, only Kildare put up a motion in support of the president. It was defeated by 120 votes to 11 and Hyde was thrown out of the GAA.

The Ban survived through the decades until it came under sustained attack in the 1960s, as parochialism was beginning to give way to a more confident, open attitude. Television had arrived, making a mockery of the rules. You couldn't attend a soccer match but there was nothing to stop you watching one on TV. What had started in the nineteenth century as a defensive measure by a fledgling institution was now seen as an outdated, bullying rule. As more and more GAA members demonstrated that a wider interest in sport did not dilute their love of the native game, The Ban became a subject of derision and it was formally dropped in 1971.

Beef Tribunal

I t was lengthy, costly and complex, but it need not detain us for long. The Beef Tribunal was set up by authorisation of the Oireachtas on 31 May 1991 and reported on 29 July 1994. The full cost has yet to be worked out but legal fees were estimated at around £30 million.

For a long time there had been allegations about corruption in the beef industry but nothing was done. On 13 May 1991 ITV's *World in Action* programme made a series of allegations about beef baron Larry Goodman's empire. Shamed into a response, the Haughey/PD government of the day set up the tribunal, headed by Judge Liam Hamilton. The terms of reference were impossibly wide, guaranteeing a long, complex hearing. There were a number of court actions aimed at limiting the tribunal's activities.

Some of the allegations made against the Goodman organisation were proved baseless. Others were shown to be true. Various scams — forging meat stamps and so on — were uncovered. There was a sophisticated multimillion-pound tax evasion scheme. No one went to jail for the scams; only low-level employees were convicted, and there was no identification of the 'persons unknown' with whom they conspired. The tax laws, and the culture of settlement within the Revenue, were such that no one was charged with fraud and a settlement was agreed.

The tribunal found no personal connections between various parties against whom allegations were made. Silly charges had been thrown around that various political decisions were based on friendship between Larry Goodman and certain politicians. This was nonsense. Judge Hamilton did not explore the financial relationship between beef barons and politicians, ruling that donations of tens of thousands of pounds were 'normal' political contributions. The issue of payments to politicians would dominate three subsequent tribunals: McCracken, Moriarty and Flood.

A personal antagonism between Taoiseach Albert Reynolds and PD founder Des O'Malley, then in coalition government, emerged at the tribunal. Reynolds used the privilege of the witness stand to accuse O'Malley of perjury and the government collapsed. When the tribunal report came out, Reynolds was in government with the Labour Party. Fianna Fáil broke an agreement with Labour and hijacked the report, giving Reynolds a head-start to announce that the report 'vindicated' him. The resulting distrust eventually brought about the collapse of that government, too, not to mention Reynolds's exit from government and his loss of the Fianna Fáil leadership.

The reporter whose work on *World in Action* started the controversy, Susan O'Keeffe, refused to give the tribunal the names of her confidential sources and was pursued by the state and charged with contempt. Only a technical hitch in the case saved her from a jail term.

See: Danaher, Gerry.

Best, Kenneth

As unequal fights go, this was in the David and Goliath category. In one corner: Margaret Best, a mother of three, with a primary education, living on a low income in rural Cork without even a telephone. In the other: the international drugs giant Wellcome, supported by thousands of research staff, a full legal department and some £200 million in annual profits.

Margaret Best is the mother of Kenneth, born in 1969, a happy, healthy baby. In September of that year he had his first 'three-in-one' injection, which included the whooping cough vaccine. That month he also suffered the first of many seizures which, although Margaret Best didn't realise it at the time, marked the onset of profound and permanent brain damage.

After years of consulting various medical specialists, Margaret Best became convinced that Kenneth's brain damage had been caused by the whooping cough vaccine which was produced by the Wellcome Foundation and distributed to GPs by the health boards. She first consulted a lawyer in 1973 and heard her chances of proving anything were slim.

In 1978 the government established a group of experts to look into several cases where parents believed that their children had been damaged by the vaccine. Time passed, nothing happened and the parents, including Margaret Best, got angry and protested at a sit-in at Leinster House. In 1982 the government's group concluded that fourteen children — including Kenneth — had probably been damaged by the vaccine. The parents were offered an ex gratia payment of £10,000 for each child, on condition they make no legal claims. Margaret Best didn't accept the money. Instead, she sued Wellcome.

In 1984 the High Court gave her access to Wellcome's and the health board's records. She got busy: photocopying, reading, looking for the evidence that she needed to build her case. She networked relentlessly with medical journalists, other parents of damaged children, sympathetic lawyers. By 1988 she had a legal team including senior counsel Dermot Gleeson who agreed to waive all fees unless and until the case was won.

One sympathetic lawyer gave her access to Wellcome documents amassed for an unsuccessful negligence case in the UK. Here she read about a particular batch of the pertussis (whooping cough) vaccine that failed routine tests and was unusually potent and toxic. It was identified as batch BA3741. It was the same batch that was used on her son.

The Kenneth Best case was heard in the High Court over eight weeks in 1989. The outcome was not what his mother had hoped for. Justice Liam Hamilton found that: yes, the vaccine could damage children and yes, Wellcome knew this, but Mrs Best hadn't proven that Kenneth's seizures followed directly on from the vaccine. The case was dismissed.

It was what Margaret Best described as her 'lowest point', but she didn't give up. She took her case to the Supreme Court, which in 1992 unanimously overturned the High Court decision. Twenty-three-year-old Kenneth Best — a fully grown man with the mind of a baby — was awarded £2.75 million.

Betting Tax Evasion

In presenting his first budget, in December 1997, Minister for Finance Charlie McCreevy told the Dáil: 'tax evasion in any form is totally unacceptable'.

Back in April 1984 McCreevy wasn't so uncompromising. He boasted that he had evaded betting tax. He and Fine Gael TD Brendan McGahon appeared on an RTÉ television programme called *Current Account*. They claimed that the 'penal' 20 per cent tax on off-course betting was 'immoral', and that they had made arrangements to evade paying it. McCreevy was then seven years a TD. He was well known as a gambler.

McCreevy's comments were discussed at a subsequent Fianna Fáil parliamentary party meeting, but no action was taken against him.

The then Minister for Finance, Fine Gael's Alan Dukes, said at the time that it was 'particularly inappropriate for Dáil deputies to show disregard for the laws passed by the Oireachtas'. McCreevy and McGahon were not open to prosecution, as it was the bookmaker and not the person making the bet who was legally responsible for ensuring the tax was paid. Neither suffered any setbacks as a result of his admission.

It was reported at the time that McCreevy and McGahon were questioned by the Revenue authorities but the tax officials were unable to ascertain which bookies were breaking the law. McCreevy was quoted as saying that Revenue Commissioners' questions about his betting were an invasion of his privacy.

In 1997 Charlie McCreevy was appointed Minister for Finance. It is believed that this was the first time in the history of the state — this state and perhaps any other — in which a politician who encouraged the evasion of taxes which a citizen considered to be immoral was appointed Minister for Finance. In his 1999 budget, McCreevy halved betting tax.

Bishop and the Nightie, The

There were many controversies surrounding RTÉ's *Late Late Show* from the 1960s into recent years. Peter Brooke sang about Clementine and lost his job as Secretary of State for Northern Ireland; there was uproar over lesbian nuns and Playboy Bunnies; in 1966 Brian Trevaskis broke through the deference and ferociously laid into the bishops; in 1999 the *Late Late* saw Pádraig Flynn self-destruct in full view of the nation and Terry Keane crush what was left of Charlie Haughey's reputation.

The scandal which remains symbolic of the programme's relationship with its audience, and that audience's increasing distance from the fading authority of the Ireland of traditional certainties, was the one that became known as the Bishop and the Nightie.

It was a dull show, on 12 February 1966, with no significant discussions, no stars, little entertainment value (except singer Joe Lynch and a chap who demonstrated a rare ability to sing out of key at will). Presenter Gay Byrne hadn't the slightest intention of challenging the authority of the Catholic church or flouting the prevailing morals of the day. Byrne, although having taken on a role which involved encouraging national debate in a time of change, was first and foremost an entertainer. From the beginning he delighted in, and knew that any broadcaster's strength lay in, keeping his audience interested and entertained. In an effort to liven up the show he decided to stage a light-hearted quiz, featuring a husband and wife. The format is well known in television light entertainment. Out of hearing of the other, one partner is asked a series of questions about life with the spouse. The spouses then switch places and the same questions are asked again, the fun being in the discrepancies between the answers given. Byrne himself wrote the questions: 'What sort of books does your wife normally read?', that sort of thing.

Two members of the audience, Patrick and Eileen Fox, volunteered and the whole thing got the studio audience joining in and laughing.

Down in Loughrea, County Galway, however, one man didn't find the proceedings at all funny. Most Reverend Thomas Ryan, Bishop of Clonfert, was watching the show and he was outraged. As part of the quiz, the Foxes had separately been asked what was the colour of Eileen's nightdress on her honeymoon. She couldn't remember. Joking, she finally said, to lots of studio audience laughter, 'None!'

Shortly thereafter the quiz ended, the somewhat routine show shuffled to its conclusion. At this distance, and given the sometimes provocative role of the media, one might suppose that the controversy was generated by a newspaper ringing the bishop and asking him for a comment on the show, and then stoking the scandal in order to generate headlines. In this case it was the bishop who made the running, deliberately setting out to cause trouble for *The Late Late Show*, which was then just four years old and not as secure on the Irish social landscape as it would subsequently become.

The Bishop of Clonfert summoned his secretary, the Very Reverend M.H. O'Callaghan, and dictated a statement. Fr O'Callaghan was then instructed to ring RTÉ and complain about this 'disgraceful performance' and to send a telegram to the station to the same effect. The hardworking Fr O'Callaghan then had to read the bishop's outraged statement over the telephone to the Sunday newspapers, who obligingly ran it on the front pages.

Gay Byrne got a phone call from the *Sunday Press*, asking for a response to the bishop's attack. Byrne was taken aback and couldn't imagine what part of the show had enraged the bishop. He had to ask and was told it was the reference to the nightie.

'I am absolutely furious about this,' said the absolutely furious bishop. 'This protest has to be made in fairness to Christian morality.'

The bishop announced that his sermon at Loughrea Cathedral next morning would feature a denunciation of *The Late Late Show*. He would ask his parishioners not to watch the show again.

'I thought it was all in good fun,' said the bemused Mrs Fox.

RTÉ had received just three phone calls about the quiz. Two of them complained that the format of the quiz had been lifted from a British TV show. One caller complained about the nightdress question.

The bishop's attack on the show brought a chorus of laments from assorted gentlefolk who now realised how outrageous the show had been. The Loughrea Town Commissioners called for *The Late Late Show* ('a dirty programme') to be taken off the air. The Mayo GAA Board and the Meath Vocational Education Committee passed resolutions condemning the show, and the *Irish Catholic* newspaper denounced what it had seen as 'a public discussion of bedroom relations'.

The scandal damaged the hierarchy. People found it hard to believe that a bishop could get upset over a harmless game; and harder to believe that His Lordship believed that his public intervention would be taken seriously by any but the most slavish elements. What hurt more than any intellectual argument about the relationship between the bishops and their flocks was the laughter. The incident made the hierarchy a laughing stock.

Some months after the incident the Bishop of Clonfert arranged a meeting between one of his clerics and a brother-in-law of Gay Byrne. The bishop asked that his regrets be sent to the broadcaster. In his autobiography, Byrne suggested that the bishop was the worse for drink on that Saturday night.

See: Mansfield, Jayne.

Bright, Honor

I t seemed as though she may have taken off her shoe to use as a weapon, but she had no chance. She was shot through the heart and died immediately. Her body was found by a workman three or four hours later, at 7.30 on the morning of 9 June 1925, at Ticknock in the Dublin mountains, near Lamb Doyle's pub. Honor Bright was a prostitute, and the scandalous events surrounding her murder threw a light on the realities of life in the first few years of the new Irish state.

She was twenty-five, her real name was Elizabeth O'Neill. She came to Dublin from the country, became pregnant and despite the usual pressures she refused to give her son away. She paid a woman to mind the baby in the hours while she worked as a prostitute to earn a living.

Some days after the murder a taxi driver was arrested and held for the best part of a week. He had driven Honor away from her beat at Stephen's Green a few hours before her body was found. The taxi driver was released following the arrest and charging of two men for the murder. One of the accused was garda superintendent Leopold Dillon, the second was Dr Patrick Purcell.

Superintendent Dillon was from Cork; he joined the British army as a teenager, in 1917, and later served in the Free State army before becoming a policeman in the service of the new state. Dillon was stationed at Dunlavin, County Wicklow. There, he met the local doctor, Patrick Purcell, who was also a peace commissioner.

On 8 June 1925, the doctor and the senior garda set out for an evening in Dublin. Dillon would later claim that he needed to visit Dublin to talk to another garda; the doctor claimed he intended going to the theatre; but it's plain that the two were setting out on a drunken sexual spree. They started drinking before they left Wicklow and continued drinking on the way. They drove to Dublin in the doctor's two-seater car, arrived at 6.30 p.m. and had dinner in the Bailey Restaurant, in Duke Street. They drove out to Blackrock, then split up, arranging to meet later in the Shelbourne Hotel. The garda was 'meeting friends', he said; the doctor's evening was spent in activities involving women and drink. After a session in a Donnybrook pub Dr Purcell squeezed two women into his two-seater car and drove them home to Drumcondra. They stopped on the way and he and one of the women went off together for a time.

The superintendent arrived at the Shelbourne at 8.30 p.m. but the doctor wasn't there. The garda spoke to a lawyer friend and later fell asleep in a chair. The doctor arrived at the hotel to collect the super-intendent at about 1 a.m. Across the road, talking to some cabbies, was Honor Bright and a friend named Bridie. The doctor approached the two women, propositioned them, and went into the hotel and found the garda. The two talked with the women and made a deal. The doctor went down Hume Street with Bridie and the superintendent drove Honor away in the doctor's car. When the doctor returned to Stephen's Green, the car had not come back, so he went down Hume Street again with Bridie. The garda had parked the car somewhere and had sex with Honor.

Later, Honor was driven away in a taxi and the garda and doctor set off home, arriving around 4.30 a.m. The superintendent slept it off in the barracks; the doctor crept into his home and upstairs to lie beside his sleeping wife.

The prosecution case was that the taxi driver dropped Honor in Harold's Cross; she met the doctor and the garda again, on their way home, and they drove her up the Dublin mountains. They wouldn't pay her, she got angry, one of them — probably the doctor — shot her dead. There was evidence that the doctor had a bulge in his coat pocket. He swore it wasn't a gun; it was a stethoscope, he said. He always carried a stethoscope with him, even on a night on the town. Was he carrying a stethoscope when arrested? No.

Although it scandalised respectable Dublin, the story of the doctor and the garda's night of debauchery reflects relaxed attitudes to sex and drunkenness which we don't usually associate with the Ireland of those decades. Those attitudes would change, as the new state settled down, adopted the pose of a Catholic state for a Catholic people, passed laws about 'evil literature', banned titillating foreign newspapers and innocent Hollywood movies, and drove prostitution away from the lights of the Shelbourne Hotel and down towards the dark paths around the Grand Canal. There would, in the famous phrase, be no sex in Ireland until the advent of television.

The jury went out for three minutes, then came back and declared Superintendent Leopold Dillon and Dr Patrick Purcell not guilty.

Browne, Bishop Michael

Priests and nuns and Christian Brothers supervised the institutions into which thousands of Irish children were dumped throughout the first fifty years of the state's existence. They received money from the state for this. The money was supposed to be used for the benefit of the children.

In May 1999 a businessman told Brian McDonald of the *Irish Independent* a story which cast a cold light on how the Catholic church sought to use some of that money.

Over thirty years earlier, the Sisters of Mercy ran St Anne's Orphanage at Taylor's Hill, Galway. The state gave a grant of £40,000 to St Anne's. Someone contacted someone on the outside, and word was sent that the sisters were in some distress. No less than £20,000 of the grant had been siphoned off by the Bishop of Galway, Michael Browne. The bishop wanted to use the money to send priests abroad to convert the heathen. Bishop Browne supervised the nuns' finances. It was a simple matter for him to divert the money.

A number of businessmen, contacted through a third party, decided to face down the bishop. This was the late 1960s, and questions were being asked, things were beginning to change, but even so it took some courage for respectable Catholics to confront their bishop and challenge his authority. The bishop was as angry as might be expected; his parishioners held their ground and suggested that they might go to the media. The bishop backed down, the money was returned to the orphanage account.

Bruton, John: Fund-raising

When Fine Gael came third in the November 1990 presidential election, leader Alan Dukes was thrown out. The new leader, John Bruton, found that the party was £1.3 million in debt, despite Alan Dukes's fund-raising efforts. Throughout 1991 he set about putting the touch on wealthy interests.

Bruton wrote begging letters to hundreds of business people. He also personally spoke by telephone to over a hundred wealthy individuals, asking them for money. He was personally handed contributions and he was informed of other contributions sent to the party as a result of his efforts. For instance, in April 1991 his friend Michael Lowry arranged a meeting at Ben Dunne's home in which Dunne handed Bruton a cheque for fifty thousand pounds.

The following year, 1992, Bruton was among those called to give evidence at the Beef Tribunal. One matter which was of concern was the extent to which wealthy interests were financing the political parties. The parties claimed that the identities of the people behind such contributions must necessarily be kept strictly confidential, known only to the trustees, so that there would be no question of senior politicians being even subconsciously influenced.

John Bruton was asked if he was 'made aware of the particular contributions made by a company or person?'

Bruton replied, on oath: 'No.'

He went on to explain that 'that is not to say that one might not, on a random basis, become aware of contributions that are made by particular individuals'. He said there was 'no systematic informing of politicians of contributions' and that party trustee Sean Murray 'doesn't disclose the information to anybody, as a general rule, not even to the party leader at the time'. He did not tell the tribunal that he had for months been engaged in direct fund-raising in which he was of necessity aware of the identities of donors.

In April 1997 John Bruton appeared before the McCracken Tribunal. That tribunal uncovered the facts of Ben Dunne's generosity to Bruton. On the witness stand, Bruton acknowledged that he had been 'intensively involved' in the systematic solicitation of money from wealthy interests.

In the starkest terms: the evidence John Bruton gave on oath in 1997 appeared to be the opposite of the evidence John Bruton gave on oath in 1992. Asked about the discrepancy, Bruton replied: 'In normal circumstances the party leader would not be involved in fund-raising and would not be informed of contributions received.' But, he said, because of the large party debt in 1991 those were not normal circumstances.

Mr Bruton's failure to inform the Beef Tribunal that his reply did not cover the entire period of his leadership up to then, the only period in which he had first-hand experience of what the party leader knew about fund-raising, left many confused. Happily for Mr Bruton, no one in his own party questioned this discrepancy. Labour and Democratic Left, being in coalition with Mr Bruton at the time, also found these matters unworthy of comment. Fianna Fáil, floundering in the revelations about the money flowing into the pockets of its former leader, Mr Haughey, apparently did not think it wise to make a fuss about fund-raising.

Bruton, John: Peace Process

After the collapse of the Albert Reynolds/Dick Spring government in November 1994, and the failure of the attempt to cobble together a new coalition with Bertie Ahern as leader of Fianna Fáil, John Bruton became Taoiseach. Fine Gael linked up with Labour and Democratic Left and formed a government without going through the process of a general election. Without doubt the most important issue inherited by Bruton was the Northern Ireland peace process. By February 1996, when the IRA broke its first ceasefire and killed two London newsagents, the process was bogged down in political manoeuvring, because of the dependence of the British Tory government on unionist votes. Bruton would be criticised for a lack of determination in pushing the process.

There was a somewhat uneasy response when Bruton's private attitude to the peace process emerged. In the summer of 1995, while being interviewed by a provincial newspaper reporter, Bruton was asked about the peace process. He erupted and ranted that he was 'sick of answering questions about the fucking peace process'.

The ease with which Bruton flew off the handle, particularly on a sensitive issue, was disturbing. Later that year, in December, Bruton was visiting a company, Indigo, when he decided to make a joke. 'Is Charlie Bird in the bushes?' he asked the firm's managing director. There were no RTÉ reporters, he was told, the visit was private. 'Good,' said Bruton, 'that means I won't be asked about the fucking peace process.' Again, when word of this exchange got out, it did not increase public confidence in the solidity of the Taoiseach's commitment to the process.

Bruton, John: The Right Question

Having just been elected Taoiseach, the leader of the Rainbow Coalition rose to speak to the Dáil. It was 15 December 1994, a month after the acrimonious collapse of the Fianna Fáil–Labour coalition in the wake of the Fr Brendan Smyth controversy and the appointment of Attorney General Harry Whelehan as president of the High Court. John Bruton was promising a different sort of government. He was committed to restoring public trust in the political system. 'The government', he said, 'must go about its work without excess or extravagance and as transparently as if it were working behind a pane of glass.' As former government press secretary Seán Duignan recorded in his diary: 'John gives a hostage to fortune right away, saying the government must always be seen as operating behind a pane of glass. That'll be the day.'

Not long after, the new Taoiseach appointed Dermot Gleeson SC as his attorney general and promised a tightening-up of procedures in that office. Bruton told the Dáil there were no conflicts of interests precluding

Gleeson from taking up the position. Of course, he was a well-established barrister who had represented many clients. So, in future, if conflicts did arise other lawyers would be appointed for those cases. What the Taoiseach neglected to tell the Dáil was that Gleeson had been informally consulted in a professional capacity by the civil servant in the Attorney General's office who was at the centre of the extradition delay in the Fr Brendan Smyth case, Matt Russell.

In May 1995 TDs were once again discussing Fr Brendan Smyth. A solicitor, representing the priest's victims, had sent a letter to the Attorney General claiming compensation from the state for his clients. The letter was not answered. Another was written and that too remained unanswered in the Attorney General's office. Progressive Democrat TD Liz O'Donnell, in the Dáil, pursued the Taoiseach for an explanation. Who, she wanted to know, was responsible for this second delay? Was it Russell again? Bruton replied that because the matter was being investigated he could say no more. O'Donnell persisted but Bruton didn't budge. He would say nothing that would 'prejudice fair procedure in this matter'.

That night, *Irish Independent* journalist Brian Dowling came across the information that the new attorney general, Dermot Gleeson, had a previous professional relationship with Matt Russell. The *Independent* faxed a number of questions to the Taoiseach. In a breach of trust with Dowling, the Taoiseach's office issued a pre-emptive statement to all the media giving the information he had refused to give in the Dáil earlier. The next morning, on *Morning Ireland*, Bruton said the information had not been given to the Dáil because 'the right question' hadn't been asked. 'I was more than willing to give that information if I was asked about it.'

It was a near-perfect repetition of Ray Burke's explanation to the Beef Tribunal as to why parliamentary questions on alleged irregularities in the beef business had been answered so narrowly, giving away as little as possible, even when there was much more information available: 'If the other side don't ask the right questions', said Burke, 'they don't get the right answers. It's not for me to lead them as to where they figure they want to go.' Fine Gael deputy Jimmy Deenihan said at the time that the way questions on the beef industry were dodged or clouded 'was a corruption of parliamentary democracy'. Bruton himself, during the last days of the Fianna Fáil–Labour government, complained that 'We have had truth by instalments. The time for total honesty is now.'

Seán Duignan put it best: 'That'll be the day.'

It wasn't the only time that John Bruton was parsimonious with information. On the last day of September, 1998, in his weekly column in *The Irish Times*, Vincent Browne wrote about the financing of political parties and the potential for corruption in a system which allowed undisclosed donations. He wrote, among other things, about Fine Gael's financial difficulties in 1994 and efforts by the party to attract donations from 'high net worth individuals' or HNWIs. In other words, rich people. 'I understand that on the very night that he became Taoiseach, John Bruton presided at the formal first meeting of his new government at Áras an Uachtaráin and then hotfooted it to dine with a HNWI.'

John Bruton was less than pleased and demanded a correction ('This was untrue'), which was printed in the next day's paper. Fine Gael negotiated with the newspaper for some hours, insisting on a precisely worded correction, and finally causing the paper to publicly express its 'regrets to Mr Bruton for this lapse and for the publication of inaccurate information'. The correction said: 'No meeting such as the one described by Vincent Browne took place on this evening.'

But, as it happens, there's a plaque in the K Club, in County Kildare, to commemorate a dinner between An Taoiseach, John Bruton and Michael Smurfit on 17 December 1994. It was the day after he'd become Taoiseach. The *Irish Times* correction accurately said that no such meeting took place 'on this evening', but held back the information that the meeting took place the following day. Browne accepted he'd got it wrong: 'So instead of hotfooting it on his first night in office to dine with a HNWI, he hotfooted it on his second day in office to dine with a HNWI. It's a pity he didn't refer to this when he was demanding a "correction" from *The Irish Times*.'

See: Ahern, Bertie: The Right Question.

Burke, Ray

B usiness people seemed to be queuing up to give Ray Burke huge amounts of money. In order to support the democratic process, of course. The size of the donations suggests that business people saw Ray as an indispensable element in Irish democracy.

Ray inherited his dad's Dáil seat in Dublin North. The da, P.J. Burke, held the seat from 1944 to 1973. Ray was an auctioneer, and also a member of Dublin County Council. As a councillor he had a role in deciding what land should be rezoned; as an auctioneer he was selling houses for developers who profited from rezoning. Questions were asked. In 1974, press reports claimed that the accounts of one developer, Brennan and McGowan, showed a payment of £15,000 to Ray, under the heading of 'planning'. The Garda Fraud Squad questioned Ray but nothing came of it.

Ray prospered, financially and politically, sustaining a ministerial career into the 1990s, as one of Haughey's reliables. When Albert Reynolds took over Fianna Fáil in 1992 he sent Ray to the backbenches. While he was there, rumours began to circulate that back in 1989 Ray had received pucks of money from developers. When another of Haughey's old reliables, Bertie Ahern, was forming his first cabinet in 1997, he was a bit concerned about the rumours. He made what he claimed were comprehensive inquiries: 'We were up every tree in north Dublin.' In the event, these inquiries turned out to have been quite perfunctory. For instance, he asked Burke if there was anything worrying him.

Burke — despite an abrasive style which earned him the dislike of many — always performed efficiently as a minister and Ahern wanted him on board. Burke was given Foreign Affairs. One minute Burke was dealing with the delicate negotiations that would eventually lead to the Good Friday agreement, the next he was stonewalling very specific allegations that he had pocketed an envelope full of developers' money. The allegations from James Gogarty, the old crook whose bitterness led to the Flood Tribunal, drip-drip-dripped into the public domain, until eventually — inevitably — Burke was publicly named as the alleged recipient of the money.

On 8 August 1997 Burke issued a statement denouncing the 'vicious campaign of rumour and innuendo' which was aimed at him. He acknowledged that in June 1989 he had received 'a totally unsolicited political contribution' of £30,000, from James Gogarty, an executive of a large building company, JMSE. And he said he accepted the money 'in good faith'. No favours were done. That was the end of it as far as Ray was concerned, and if anyone made further allegations 'I will take all necessary steps to vindicate my good name and reputation'.

Ray seemed to think that this would kill the rumours. He seemed to think that once he revealed that he accepted the money 'in good faith' there was nothing more to be said about a politician taking £30,000 from a builder who just popped in and handed over a chunk of cash. In that statement, the gulf between the citizenry and the political elite was stark. To most of us, the notion that a businessman would hand over thirty grand, in cash, to one of the most influential politicians in the country, expecting nothing whatever in return, was astounding. In our world, people do not give away tens of thousands of pounds just for the hell of it. Or out of a love of democracy. Many people, including Ray Burke, and including most major politicians, would insist that this is indeed the way the world works.

Ray seemed to think that what was important was his insistence that James Gogarty was wrong — that Ray received only £30,000 and not £80,000.

Fianna Fáil sought to calm things. It revealed that Ray had given £10,000 of the £30,000 to the party, so he hadn't kept it all himself. As it happened, this was untrue. Burke had accepted two gifts of £30,000. One from JMSE and the other from a company called Rennicks, a subsidiary of Tony O'Reilly's Fitzwilton. So far, this gift remained secret. (As did another donation of £35,000. All this and more went into Ray's personal bank account — he didn't keep political gifts in a separate account because his personal and political lives were 'seamless'.)

On 10 September Ray made another attempt to kill the rumours. He made a Dáil statement and took questions for an hour. The nearest he came to admitting that there was anything wrong with taking bundles of cash from a builder he'd never met before was: 'In hindsight, it should not have happened as far as leaving yourself open is concerned.' This meant there was nothing wrong with taking the money — but he was wrong to accept it because unscrupulous opponents could use it to make trouble.

Ray was too clever by half. He said he had never received a larger contribution than the JMSE money, neatly concealing the fact that he had accepted exactly the same amount from Fitzwilton. He implied that the £10,000 he passed on to Fianna Fáil came out of the JMSE money. In fact it came from the Fitzwilton money. He had to do that, as he had to explain where the £10,000 given to Fianna Fáil had come from; and he wanted it known that he had passed on money to the party; but he didn't want to reveal the existence of the Fitzwilton gift.

Ray began mixing his metaphors. 'Whatever comes out of the woodwork now, a line is in the sand. From this day on, D-Day, I am going on to the peace process.'

In little over three weeks, on 7 October 1997, Ray resigned.

The truth about the Fitzwilton donation came out; and *Magill* magazine published a letter from builder Michael Bailey to James Gogarty, in which Bailey discussed how to go about getting land rezoned, and how to get planning permission. The letter was dated a few days before the two went out to Ray's house with £30,000 in two envelopes. On top of all this, Ray's role in signing the eleven passports in the Mahfouz case came under scrutiny. And his brother died.

A proud, ambitious man, Ray was sick of having to turn out his pockets in front of the rabble. There was no let-up in the pressure, not even as he buried his brother. On the day of the funeral, Burke resigned not alone from the cabinet but from his Dáil seat. He retreated to his lovely house in Swords — built by his business associates of twenty-five years earlier, Brennan and McGowan — and awaited the attentions of the Flood Tribunal.

See: Flood Tribunal; Gogarty, James; Passports for Sale: Legally.

C

Carysfort

The last teachers trained at Carysfort College of Education, Blackrock, County Dublin, graduated on 22 July 1988. The college was closed because pupil numbers were falling, the national teaching force was young and few were retiring and the exchequer was hard-pressed for the £2.5 million it cost to keep Carysfort open.

The closure of Carysfort was decided by Gemma Hussey, Minister for Education in 1986. Her opposition counterpart, Mary O'Rourke, got wind of the move before the minister announced it and made mincemeat of Minister Hussey in the Dáil. The teaching unions joined in and the Sisters of Mercy who ran Carysfort expressed their shock. 'There was no consultation at all,' they said.

Despite all the controversy, the decision was not overturned by Mary O'Rourke when she became minister in 1987. The Sisters of Mercy — who were sitting on a goldmine of Blackrock property — decided they would sell the site, which consisted of about ninety acres of land and the college buildings.

Now it was the government's turn to express outrage. After all, who but the taxpayer had kept the college going, who but the taxpayer had invested in capital building projects? The nuns had legal opinion that said it was all theirs, although it later transpired that they agreed to pay the state something in the region of £2.5 million.

Eventually, the Carysfort property was sold in two lots: a large residential site and a separate lot comprising the college buildings and some fifteen surrounding acres. The college buildings site was sold to Pino Harris, a north Dublin businessman who made his millions buying and selling trucks. He is, by all accounts, an extremely wealthy man, well able to come up with the £6.5 million needed to buy the site. He sold it again, some six months later, to UCD, for £8 million. £1.5 million profit in six months.

UCD was planning a new business college — the Smurfit business school. It was to be developed at nearby Roebuck Castle at a cost of £5 million. UCD told auctioneer Fintan Gunne it wasn't interested in the Carysfort site. The Public Accounts Committee later noted that UCD was raising the Roebuck Castle money itself and the project would 'probably have cost the state nothing'. But in the end the business school didn't go ahead at Roebuck Castle. The president of UCD was encouraged by the then Taoiseach, Charlie Haughey, to go for the Carysfort option. He was told it was 'a great opportunity'. No one told UCD that the state's own Valuation Office had valued the Carysfort property at £3.8 million. Pino Harris wanted £8 million for it.

UCD required money from the government to buy Carysfort. A cabinet meeting in December 1990 duly approved funding for the transaction, though there was no formal memorandum for government presented to the meeting. A memorandum — explaining the reasoning behind the proposal — would be the more usual way to proceed with government business. Apparently, under cabinet procedure an issue can be raised orally by a minister if there is prior approval from the Taoiseach. According to the report of the Public Accounts Committee, this is how the Carysfort purchase received cabinet approval.

If there had been a government memorandum prepared for cabinet, the Department of Finance would have been involved, sorting out whether the deal was value for money. In the end, the purchase of Carysfort cost the state £9.7 million. The state provided the £8 million to buy the site, £3.7 million for equipment and adaptation costs. UCD came up with £2 million.

So, the site that cost Pino Harris £6.5 million earned him £8 million six months later. Charlie Haughey suggested the deal to UCD and Charlie Haughey made sure UCD had enough state money to do the deal.

Given what has happened to south Dublin property prices since the Carysfort deal, Pino Harris didn't do as well out of it as it seemed at the time. UCD, as it happened, made a very good deal indeed. The Public Accounts Committee concluded that although Carysfort provided a top-class graduate business school facility for UCD, it was not optimum value for the taxpayer.

Casey, Bishop Eamonn

The affair between Bishop Eamonn Casey and Annie Murphy lasted just a few months. In March 1973 Casey, then Bishop of Kerry, offered a refuge to Murphy, the daughter of an American friend. Her marriage had ended badly. Casey suggested she stay with him in Kerry. Within a short time Casey and Murphy were lovers. By October of that year she was pregnant. Their son Peter was born on 31 July 1974. Two months later Murphy left Ireland.

After initial attempts to push her to have the child adopted, Casey agreed to pay child support at a rate of $3,600 a year. He expressed no interest in his son and between 1975 and 1988 the child was raised in America by Murphy. Casey became Bishop of Galway in 1976. He maintained a high-profile role as a liberal bishop, comforting the poor at home and afflicting the oppressors on the world stage. He was a steadfast supporter of the Catholic church's political defence of its moral hegemony in Ireland.

In 1988 Casey's past came back to haunt him. Murphy's new partner, Arthur Pennell, arrived in Galway and that signalled the beginning of long-distance negotiation, mostly through lawyers, of a cash settlement with Murphy. In July 1990 Casey agreed to Murphy's terms: $100,000 for her, $25,000 for her lawyer. Casey financed this with £70,669 from a diocesan account. He made up the balance of $8,000 out of his own funds.

In the course of finalising the agreement, the bishop had a meeting with his son in the lawyer's office. It was a nervous, four-minute meeting and Casey's apparent coldness stunned sixteen-year-old Peter, who had known for years who his father was. The bishop told the boy he prayed for him twice a day.

The money was paid ten days later and the following month, Annie, Peter and Arthur Pennell moved to Kinsale, County Cork. They lived there for five months and Casey must have felt his fate closing in. It is reported that he began, around then, to study Spanish.

Murphy, Peter and Pennell then returned to the USA. Casey met Murphy at a New York hotel in August 1991, where they discussed money for Peter's education and spent the night together. Discussions about money continued, but Casey's apparent coldness was his undoing. He would ring Murphy, Peter would answer, Casey would treat him like a phone receptionist. In January 1992 Arthur Pennell approached *The Irish Times*. The newspaper put some of its best reporters on the story and quickly substantiated the allegations; then, uncertain, fearful that the paper's Protestant history would arouse suspicions about its motives, the paper sat on the story for three months.

Rumours leaked. On 5 May Casey went to Rome and resigned his bishopric. On 7 May, amid the stories reporting reaction to Casey's retirement, *The Irish Times* broke the bigger story by slipping in a small mention of payments to a woman in Connecticut. By now, Casey had come back to Ireland, said goodbye to some friends, arranged that wealthy patrons repay the £70,669 he had taken from diocesan funds, and fled to the USA and later to South America. On 8 May RTÉ's *Morning Ireland* carried an interview by phone with Annie Murphy, in which she freely spoke of her affair with the bishop, including the 'physical' aspect, and of how she had been carried away on 'gossamer wings'.

Initial shock gave way to public support for Casey. Then, as his treatment of his son and lover became clear, there was some pain and anger. When several days went by in which his fellow bishops seemed unsure of what to say, and it became clear that the hierarchy lacked a moral compass to guide it through this crisis, enormous damage was done to the institutional church's authority.

The sexual abuse scandals that followed, and evidence of the church's failure to confront the issue, made the Casey scandal seem relatively innocent. It was the hierarchy's befuddled response, as much as the scandal itself, which alienated many of the faithful. It was clear that the hierarchy wanted Casey kept far away through the 1990s. In 1998, after six years as a missionary in South America, he was allowed settle in England.

Cavan Rape Case

It took the jury ten minutes. On Wednesday, 27 May 1987 in the Dublin Circuit Criminal Court, nine men and three women concluded that a 21-year-old man charged with rape, buggery and indecent assault was not guilty. The man was duly acquitted.

As the then Minister for Justice, Gerard Collins, later told the Dáil, a particularly abhorrent and outrageous crime had been committed in Cavan town in the early hours of 3 December 1986. A man entered the home of a woman who was described in the court and in the media as a deserted wife. While her three young children slept upstairs the intruder raped, buggered and sexually assaulted her with a knife for two hours.

After the trial was over the woman said: 'They really hounded me on the fact that I was a deserted wife and they as much as said that I went out all the time, bringing home men every night and that I was a "scarlet woman" and that I was running some kind of an open house. I just felt I didn't have a chance.'

The gardaí felt they had a good case. The accused man had made a statement admitting the crime and there was supporting forensic evidence. But the jury, having been addressed at some length by Paddy McEntee SC, did not agree. Presiding Judge Frank Roe pointed out that the confession — later retracted — had been made the day after the accused had consumed several pints and a naggin bottle of vodka. Judge Roe also told the jury that 'the raped woman is a deserted wife . . . we must face the facts. It appears that it is not unusual for her boyfriend and perhaps other men to come to her home quite late at night, sometimes after the public houses have closed.' He added that this did not mean that the woman was 'keeping a house of ill fame'.

Paddy McEntee SC, an immensely experienced criminal lawyer, properly and skilfully defended his client. Controversy in what became known as the Cavan Rape Case centred on whether the prosecution case was less effective because the senior counsel assigned to it wasn't there for much of the time.

Paul Carney, now a judge of the High Court, then a senior counsel, opened the case for the prosecution. For each of the subsequent two days of the trial he was unable to attend the case for more than an hour because he had another legal engagement. He was appearing in a High Court case involving the constitutionality of part of the Fisheries Act. That meant that both the cross-examination of the accused and the summing-up to the jury were left to a respected but less experienced junior counsel.

The Minister for Justice told the Dáil that he shared public concern 'that a senior prosecuting counsel should be absent for any significant extent during the hearing of a serious criminal trial for which his services have been engaged'. The Bar Council held its own investigation and after seeing this report the minister said: 'in my view it does little to allay the public concern that has been widely expressed'. The chairman of the Bar Council told RTÉ's *This Week* programme that it was 'desirable' that counsel, having a brief, should be in court for the entire duration. However, he said, absence of one counsel did not contravene the Bar Council's code of practice.

Supporters of Paul Carney felt the controversy surrounding the Cavan Rape Case provoked unfair criticism of the barrister. But it didn't hurt his career. Indeed, he went on to become one of the more thoughtful judges on the bench, especially when dealing with sexual assault cases.

Celtic Helicopters

It must have been excruciating. Out at Kinsealy one morning, Joe Malone, businessman and former director of Bord Fáilte, was visiting Charlie Haughey. Malone had a friend with him. Charlie's son Ciaran came into the room and Charlie decided to play the proud father. 'Tell Joe and his friend all about Celtic Helicopters, your new company,' said Haughey. And then, as though genetically programmed to put the touch on wealthy people whenever the opportunity arose, Charlie said to the wealthy businessmen: 'Perhaps you'd like to invest in it?'

Malone had already declined an offer from Charlie Haughey to be chairman of Celtic. Now, not wanting to turn him down again, he agreed to invest £15,000.

Celtic Helicopters was set up in 1985 by Ciaran Haughey and John Barnicle. They were both directors of the company and both were pilots. To finance the start-up, they got help from Ciaran's daddy and Ciaran's daddy's crooked accountant, Des Traynor. Charlie and Des panhandled wealthy men of their acquaintance. Among those who coughed up were the aforesaid Joe Malone, hotelier P.V. Doyle, beef baron Seamus Purcell, John O'Connell TD and Cruse W. Moss, an American businessman. None of these people appears to have initiated the investment (and Celtic Helicopters was a lousy investment). They seem to have given money out of respect for Charlie Haughey, and it is not suggested that any of them hoped to take corrupt advantage of the investment.

The arrangements seem to have been somewhat loose. O'Connell, a former Labour TD who had recently joined Fianna Fáil, thought that contributing £5,000 was just the kind of thing a Fianna Fáil TD had to do if Haughey asked.

No record of the late P.V. Doyle's involvement was found in his accounts. (Doyle was a major donor to Charlie Haughey, arranging a £170,000 loan for him from Guinness & Mahon. Doyle paid the interest on the loan. When Doyle died, Des Traynor told his estate there wasn't a hope in hell that Haughey would pay back the loan. Doyle's widow had to pay it off.)

Joe Malone, while holding a £15,000 investment in Celtic Helicopters, was a member of the board of Aer Lingus, which had its own helicopter subsidiary, Irish Helicopters. Malone made the investment in his son's name. His son was a friend of Ciaran Haughey.

Des Traynor, who raised finance for Celtic, was also on the board of Aer Lingus, and chaired a subcommittee with responsibility for Irish Helicopters. The conflict of interest doesn't appear to have worried Traynor.

Cruse Moss was chairman of an American company, General Automotive, which made a fortune building fifth-rate buses for CIE in partnership with Bombardier at Shannon in the 1980s. Happy coincidence: Joe Malone was not only a fellow Celtic investor along with Moss, he was a senior executive with Moss's company, General Automotive, in the 1980s.

The first scandal to hit Celtic Helicopters came in 1991. A copy of a confidential report prepared for Irish Helicopters, the Aer Lingus subsidiary, by Dermot Desmond's stockbroking firm, NCB, was sent to Celtic Helicopters by someone or other. When this became known, Aer Lingus accepted that NCB didn't leak the information. And who was on the Aer Lingus subcommittee overseeing Irish Helicopters, who might have had access to the report? Des Traynor. But, of course, no one suspected Des of being involved.

Celtic got a lot of business from Ben Dunne, who was simultaneously tossing large chunks of money at Charlie Haughey at regular intervals. At one point, Dunne gave Ciaran a £10,000 tip, on top of the payments for his helicopter trips. Ciaran would claim at the McCracken Tribunal that this was a consultancy fee, but his claim was threadbare and McCracken didn't believe him.

Celtic made a living for Ciaran Haughey and John Barnicle but no more than that, and by 1992 the company was in trouble. An attempt to expand into helicopter maintenance, and the building of a hangar at Dublin airport, left Celtic needing about £600,000. Daddy's crooked accountant, Des Traynor, again put the touch on wealthy businessmen. He got a £47,532 investment from John Byrne, Charlie Haughey's old buddy, a property speculator with whom Haughey had been linked for decades.

A £100,000 investment was channelled through an insurance agent, Michael Murphy, who claimed the money came from a man named David Gresty, from Monaco. The money — for some reason — ended up in Charlie Haughey's S8 Ansbacher account. Michael Murphy was Larry Goodman's insurance agent, dealing with massive, complicated export credit insurance arrangements on behalf of Goodman. He was a tough businessman. Yet, when Celtic was unable to meet its insurance premiums, Murphy stepped in and paid them, at a cost of £92,000. He said it would be 'naive to suggest that if I were to pull the plug on that company I wouldn't suffer as a result of it'. People would talk. He might lose the business of big beef interests. To 'make an enemy of the son of the most powerful man in the state' would be bad for business. 'I don't know if you realise the power of Mr Haughey at the time.'

Pat Butler, who benefited from a passports-for-cash deal in which Charlie Haughey had a personal involvement, kicked in £25,000. Kerry hotelier Xavier McAuliffe, whose abortive marina plan beside his Skellig Hotel was supported by a Haughey government, invested £50,000. Guy Snowden, an American who installed and operated the National Lotto computer system, invested £67,000. Snowden was involved in alleged bribery controversies in lottery businesses in Texas and in England.

Charlie Haughey claimed to have nothing to do with Celtic Helicopters but that was clearly untrue. In March 1991 Des Traynor used Haughey's money in the Ansbacher Deposits to underwrite a £100,000 loan to Celtic from the bank he ran, Guinness & Mahon. Traynor arranged three similar transactions, including the paying off of a £150,000 loan to Celtic, using money from Charlie Haughey's S8 account in the Ansbacher Deposits. Ciaran Haughey said on oath at the McCracken Tribunal that he knew nothing of this. Judge McCracken didn't believe him.

Celtic Helicopters, in short, was a strange outfit from its creation in 1985, attracting investment from a variety of businessmen not noted for putting their money into dud companies. Without the Haughey name — and without Charlie Haughey's active involvement — it's doubtful if the company could ever have got off the ground, much less hovered unsteadily above us all for so many years.

Census Cancellation

It was traditional for governments to gerrymander constituency boundaries in order to give themselves an advantage at the next election. Despite strong arguments to leave the redrawing of constituencies' boundaries to an independent commission, the coalition government of 1973–7, under Liam Cosgrave, set about putting in the fix in the usual way.

The job was assigned to the Minister for Local Government, Jimmy Tully of the Labour Party. He was regarded as having done a great job, adjusting constituency boundaries and deciding on the numbers of seats per constituency, ensuring that the coalition parties, Fine Gael and Labour, would get a higher ratio of seats-to-votes than Fianna Fáil.

Fianna Fáil had carried out a similar exercise, designed to distort the electoral result, a few years earlier. Which didn't stop them moaning about what became known as the Tullymander.

In 1975 Minister for Finance Richie Ryan brought a proposal to cabinet which he believed to be loopy. It had been dreamed up by officials in his department and he wanted to show the cabinet the kind of off-the-wall money-saving ideas his civil servants were proposing. The idea was: cancel the census due to take place in 1976.

There would be a cost saving, but it would be false economy. Ireland's demographics were beginning to change, the emigration of the 1950s and 1960s had ebbed. If you don't know how many people you have, where they are grouped, the way the population is shifting, the numbers in each age group, it's hard to plan for the future. On such figures depend plans for schools and hospitals, roads and house-building, economic and employment policies.

As it happened, the population was indeed increasing at a fast rate, but without a census no one could tell for sure.

Richie Ryan was out of the country at the next cabinet meeting and the cabinet approved the Department of Finance proposal and cancelled the census. It was a stupid decision and Ryan was furious, but it was more than stupid. The scandal at the heart of a decision that promoted ignorance as a base for political and economic planning wasn't just about saving money.

In his memoirs, *All in a Life*, then foreign minister Garret FitzGerald revealed that 'for some members of the government part at least of the motivation for this decision was a concern lest publication of data from such a census should raise the question of a further constituency revision that might undo the Tullymander'. Better that the state remain in ignorance than that the opposition get an excuse to challenge the rigged constituency boundaries. It was a choice of party interest over public interest.

As it happened, the Tullymander was a disaster for the coalition. A slight swing to them would have given them an increase in seats. A swing against them, as happened in 1977, brought a Fianna Fáil landslide. An independent electoral boundaries commission was set up to end the gerrymandering.

A belated census was held in 1979, which indeed showed that there were major demographic changes under way. In Garret FitzGerald's words: 'There could scarcely have been a worse moment to cancel a census.'

There was an upside for the politicians: the population increase revealed by the 1979 census could be used to justify the expansion of Dáil representation, leading to the creation of an extra eighteen Dáil seats for the politicians to share.

Churning

This is a fraud which is recognised internationally to be practised by stockbrokers, insurance agents and others in need of a short cut to a few easy bucks. Churning is the creation of excessive transactions for the purpose of generating commission, rather than in the best interests of the client.

For instance, a stockbroker might notice towards the end of the year that income is going to be down on the previous year. He merely indulges in a little unnecessary buying and selling on behalf of a number of clients and racks up extra commission. As long as it's done carefully, the client need never know in whose interest the transactions were carried out.

In June 1998 *Magill* magazine exposed a wholesale churning culture within the Irish Life insurance company. Irish Life is one of the country's largest companies, with 300,000 customers. The practice was to convince customers that existing policies were no longer in their best interests and that new policies should be taken out. This did not benefit the customer at all, but generated commission for the insurance company employee.

The churning had been going on since 1983. *Magill* published memos showing that management uncovered churning practices in 1992, yet the scam continued until 1994, and even then, policies which were in the process of being churned were allowed to proceed.

The true extent of the churning, and the amounts — believed to be in millions of pounds — of which customers were defrauded, have never been established independently. Some claims were brushed off. If, for instance, an insurance broker churned your Irish Life policy you had no comeback. You were told the broker was your agent, not the insurance company's. Irish Life announced that over the previous five years it had sacked twenty-one employees for 'gross misconduct'. It condemned the *Magill* allegations as 'simply not true'. The company carried out a limited review-and-compensation exercise, and the Oireachtas Committee on Enterprise and Small Business made an ineffective intervention, but everyone soon entered a 'forward-looking' mode.

See: Forward-looking.

Cleary, Fr Michael

It wasn't a good year for the Catholic hierarchy, 1995. The paedophile Fr Brendan Smyth was finally behind bars and Bishop Eamonn Casey was well out of the public view in Ecuador, but that wasn't the end of the controversies. Bishop Brendan Comiskey made dissenting noises about the need for debate on priestly celibacy and got his knuckles rapped from on high. A short time later he made a hasty retreat to the United States to be treated for alcoholism. And Archbishop Desmond Connell was caught contradicting himself about whether church funds had been used to compensate victims of priestly abuse. And then there were reports that the late Fr Michael Cleary had fathered two children.

On its own merits a report that another priest had slipped up on the vow of celibacy mightn't have been big news. But Fr Michael Cleary, after career sidelines as the 'singing priest' and various excursions into media work, was probably the best-known rank-and-file cleric in the country. And few were as vehement in defending the traditional Catholic point of view whenever divorce, contraception and abortion were being discussed. If anyone knew how to take the gloves off in public debate, it was Fr Cleary. Even when the hierarchy was conceding that Catholics had a right to look to their consciences when considering how to vote in the abortion referendum, Fr Cleary, writing in the *Sunday Independent*, told priests to 'start this Sunday by telling your people about life and its origins . . . Tell them to vote Yes and make no apology about it.' He was no less vociferous during the divorce debate and complained that the 'bishops were very soft' on the issue and it was left to 'individual priests like myself' to make all the running. During what became known as the X case, Fr Cleary suggested that the story of the pregnant child at the centre of the case had been stage-managed by those wishing to find constitutional flaws in the abortion legislation.

Fr Cleary was a sort of model for the modern church: orthodox and conservative on theological issues, yet pastorally committed to the vulnerable and the dispossessed. Added to that, he had a talent for communication and he used it to great effect in his newspaper columns and in the last several years of his life as presenter of a daily radio programme. Along with that other great communicator, Bishop Eamonn Casey, it was Fr Cleary who was chosen to do the warm-up act for Pope John Paul II, at his ceremonies at Ballybrit racecourse, during the papal visit in 1979.

At home he kept an open house policy. Unmarried mothers and many others in need stayed with him. So there were no suspicions raised when Phyllis Hamilton came to stay.

Aged seventeen when she first met Fr Cleary, she was a young woman emerging from a traumatic childhood, characterised by family breakdown, abuse and institutional care. She was working as an auxiliary in St Brendan's Hospital in Dublin, hoping one day to qualify as a nurse. She first set eyes on Michael Cleary at one of his concerts in 1967 during his 'singing priest' phase. It was a novelty act that was popular for a while, a handy fund-raiser, and good for the profile of the church among the young.

By 1970 Phyllis Hamilton was pregnant and she moved into Fr Cleary's home, ostensibly just one more unmarried mother being given shelter by a decent man. That first child was given up for adoption. Another son, Ross, was born in 1976 and Phyllis, Ross and Fr Cleary lived together at his house in Harold's Cross, Dublin, until his death from cancer on New Year's Eve 1993.

Rumours about Fr Cleary's personal life were nothing new. Shortly after his death, friends rallied to his defence when *Phoenix* magazine published those rumours, without substantiation. Phyllis Hamilton later said she decided to tell her side of the story because, following Fr Cleary's death, she and her son felt they had been rejected and ignored by those close to him who knew the truth.

The picture that Phyllis Hamilton painted was one of a man who — unlike his friend Bishop Eamonn Casey — had supported and loved both mother and child. But his friends and family said the story was not true and they were outraged that it was being told when Fr Cleary was not there to defend his reputation. If the radio phone-in shows are a barometer of anything, this reaction was widespread but so also was there a reaction of anger at the hypocrisy of this high-profile priest who was never shy about giving advice on how Catholics should run their personal lives.

When the barrage of abuse seemed to be undermining and discrediting Phyllis Hamilton and her son, Dr Ivor Browne, with her permission, took the controversial decision to talk publicly about his knowledge of Michael Cleary's private life. Dr Browne, a consultant psychiatrist, had treated Phyllis Hamilton for many years and had discussed Fr Cleary with her several times. It was a relationship he disapproved of, simply because he 'knew it would end in a mess'.

Dr Browne revealed that he didn't just talk to Phyllis, he also talked to Fr Cleary. The knowledge that Ross was his child and Phyllis his partner was 'quite out in the open but, of course, he knew it was in the realm of confidentiality'. Dr Browne later faced censure from the Medical Council, which ruled that he had gone beyond what was ethically permissible, although it also recognised that he'd made an honest judgment and acted in the best interest of his patient.

Ivor Browne's intervention brought Phyllis Hamilton the vindication she felt she needed. As for Fr Cleary, Ivor Browne said he thought the priest simply couldn't face bringing the two sides of his life together.

Interviewing Fr Cleary for the *Sunday Tribune* in September 1993, the late Michael Hand wrote: 'When he entered the priesthood more than thirty-five years ago he told family and friends he was giving up the two most important pursuits in his life up to then: football and girls. Recalling that, Fr Cleary laughed and mentioned that in the best showbusiness circles, he was bound to add: "One out of two is not bad, eh?"' Pity about the football.

In February 1999 any last shred of doubt was removed when it emerged that DNA test results proved that Ross Hamilton was Fr Cleary's son.

See: Casey, Bishop Eamonn; X Case.

Collins, Eddie

In 1983 Taoiseach Garret FitzGerald believed he had to ask for the resignation of a junior minister, Eddie Collins, when the latter 'through inadvertence and clearly without any improper intent' had 'attended some meetings of the board of a family company'. FitzGerald, in his memoirs, explained that 'if I were to uphold propriety in public life I must ensure not only that no impropriety occurred — which in my view was clearly the case — but that no suspicion of impropriety be allowed to exist'. FitzGerald said it was perhaps the most painful personal decision he had to take as Taoiseach.

Collins lost his seat at the next election and left politics.

See: Coveney, Hugh.

Comiskey, Bishop Brendan

Dr Brendan Comiskey is one of those bishops who is rarely out of the news. He became an Auxiliary Bishop of Dublin in 1980 and took up the Wexford appointment in 1984. As chairman of the Episcopal Commission on Communications he formed a love-hate relationship with the media, going to bat regularly against what he saw as their sneering, anti-Catholic bias. But he could usually be relied upon for a quote, a comment, an interview. In the mould of his friend Bishop Eamonn Casey, he was another man of the people, albeit much tougher and less jolly.

The seismic shift in the Bishop Comiskey story happened on 11 June 1995 when an interview with the bishop by Olivia O'Leary was published in the *Sunday Tribune*. In it he said that because of falling vocations the Catholic church must start 'seriously considering' married priests. He said: 'This is not a theological issue. Everything that is alive changes and these changes aren't all that radical.'

As he later remarked, about forty American bishops had made similar public statements questioning policy on celibacy, women priests, and marriage for divorced Catholics. No big deal in America, but this was Ireland and the shock waves went out in several directions. On the one hand, liberals in the church were thrilled because, at last, the hierarchy was facing up to the issue. Support came not just from delighted priests but from a handful of fellow bishops.

The conservative side of the church — both here and in Rome — was not pleased. Less than two weeks after the O'Leary article in the *Tribune*, Bishop Comiskey got his public rebuke from Cardinal Daly. He wasn't named, but he didn't need to be. In a speech at Knock, Cardinal Daly emphasised the need for bishops to speak with one voice. He said: 'Personal opinions which depart from communion with the worldwide college of bishops, or which are at variance with the teaching of the Holy Father, are just that, personal opinions. They can not be said to carry the special weight of episcopal office or be an episcopal exercise of episcopal authority in the proper sense.'

He might as well have called the bishop a heretic. A few days later, writing in *The Irish Times*, Dr Comiskey responded, expressing his 'puzzlement' at Dr Daly's remarks and defending his right to call for debate on celibacy. It was, for him, not a personal opinion, but a matter of great pastoral concern, 'a matter of conscience, really'.

The spectacle of bishops arguing in public was extraordinary; shocking to the faithful, entertaining to the rest. In the weeks that followed, Dr Comiskey became an unexpected hero to the liberals in the church. Prophetically, one unnamed priest was reported saying: 'Will he be silenced in the end? Yes, but not for the celibacy thing. They'll find something else to get him.' As it happened, Bishop Comiskey silenced himself.

On Thursday, 14 September 1995 he asked the Vatican for permission to take sabbatical leave from his duties. A speedy two hours later his request was granted. By the weekend the word was out: Bishop Comiskey had left the country. On Monday, 18 September he released a pastoral letter informing the diocese of his 'decision to take a three-month sabbatical in the USA'. It was, he said, the official policy of the diocese for a priest to take a three-month sabbatical every ten years. Suddenly, the bishop was gone and the vacuum he left behind quickly filled with enough rumours to keep journalists busy in the coming months.

It didn't take long for the bishop, through his spokesman, to own up and admit that his sabbatical was taking place in a clinic for treating alcoholism. As it turned out, many in the media already knew about Dr Comiskey's drink problem. They just hadn't written about it.

Anyway, there were better stories to chase, some real, some fanciful. Luxury holidays in Bangkok, and by the way, do you know what Bangkok's famous for? Then there was the incident at the airport there. Was a boozy bishop really detained with no passport? And what about the apartment in Donnybrook, bought by the Ferns diocese for £80,000 at the bishop's behest and then later sold on to the bishop in his personal capacity? More worrying were reports that Bishop Comiskey had failed to deal effectively with reports of sex abuse by priests of the diocese.

In the absence of the man himself, there were no satisfactory answers to these allegations. The full story would have to await his return, first promised on Christmas Eve 1995, finally realised at the end of February 1996.

Bishop Comiskey's homecoming press conference opened with a long statement and then a question and answer session with about 100 journalists. He rebutted much of what had been printed in his absence. He had three holidays at a perfectly respectable resort in Thailand, not six, and not in Bangkok. When he travelled first class it was because of a courtesy upgrade. He was never arrested in the airport, but yes he lost his passport. All the finances in the diocese were in order and the Donnybrook apartment was, in the first instance, bought by him, with his own money. His treatment in America did not cost the diocese a penny. As for the child abuse scandals: he'd followed the best advice at the time, although with hindsight he saw that he could have done better.

It was a good performance and deflated some of the wilder stories that had circulated in the previous few months. But the child abuse issue remained, most especially in relation to the allegations surrounding the Monageer priest Fr Jim Grennan and Fr Sean Fortune, the Wexford priest who later killed himself while awaiting trial on twenty-nine sex abuse charges.

In 1988 ten girls in a confirmation class complained to their principal that Fr Grennan had abused them while giving religious instruction to them on the altar. The allegations were investigated and confirmed by health board officials, who passed on their findings to the gardaí and to Bishop Comiskey, who was manager of the school and Fr Grennan's superior.

But Bishop Comiskey did not remove Fr Grennan from his position. He was sent away for just three weeks and was back in Monageer for the confirmation of the same children he had abused. When he officiated at the ceremony with Bishop Comiskey some of the girls' parents walked out.

The local gardaí thought the evidence was substantial but no charges were brought. At his press conference in February 1996 Bishop Comiskey said he was advised by his lawyers to await the outcome of the garda investigation before dealing with Fr Grennan. He said: 'I have no idea in the wide world, as God is my witness, why that investigation was stopped.' But stopped it was and Fr Grennan remained where he was until his death in 1994.

A subsequent garda inquiry in 1996 found that the original investigation was inadequate but it also found there was no evidence of any 'collusion between any organisation and the Garda Síochána to stifle, obstruct or abandon the investigation'. So, who was to blame for the inadequate investigation? The statement didn't say. But it wasn't the health board: 'the South Eastern Health Board complied fully with its obligations'. Neither was it the local gardaí: 'no fault lies with the local gardaí based at Ferns'. Some of the original files had apparently gone missing and with Fr Grennan now dead there was nothing more to be done.

The Monageer schoolgirls, now adults, had welcomed the 1996 garda inquiry, hoping it would find out why they were ignored in 1988. Of the final outcome one of them said: 'We are no better off now. It was bad enough when this happened, but it keeps coming back. How could the statements go missing like this? I am disgusted and appalled at the way it has been handled.'

In the case of Fr Sean Fortune, victims and their parents said they complained to the bishop as far back as 1984. In the late 1980s a family was told that Fr Fortune had been sent to the UK for treatment, but when he returned he was moved to another parish where he had access to children. In a statement issued after Fr Fortune's funeral, Bishop Comiskey said: 'It's quite true that I received such complaints. It is untrue, however, to say I did nothing about them.'

See: Fortune, Fr Sean.

Compensation Culture

What was described as a loophole in the 1963 Local Government (Planning and Development) Act made several people very rich. Here's how it worked. A developer bought a piece of land that was not earmarked for development by the local authority. He applied for planning permission, usually for a housing development. He was refused. He appealed to An Bord Pleanála. He was refused again. But, if he was lucky, An Bord Pleanála would fail to list any one of a number of specified reasons as to why planning permission was being refused. If, for instance, An Bord Pleanála said planning permission was refused because there were no sewage facilities, then the developer would retreat empty-handed. But if An Bord Pleanála failed to mention one of many such 'non-compensatable' reasons for refusal, then the developer could look for compensation for the profit he would have earned had the property been developed. A number of people made money this way in the 1980s.

There was big money in compensation. In 1987 Dublin County Council was facing twenty-two separate compensation claims from developers totalling some £15.25 million. To avoid some payouts the council did deals with developers by giving partial planning permission or giving them lands that could be developed.

There were several celebrated compensation cases in the 1980s. XJS Investments, owned by garage owners Tom Murphy and Charlie Gunn, bought a site at Roches Hill, Killiney for £40,000 in 1981 and applied for planning permission for eighteen flats and fourteen houses. Dún Laoghaire Corporation refused. Among the reasons stated, the corporation included a 'non-compensatable' factor: that the proposed development would interfere with the visual and recreational amenities of the area. The decision was appealed to An Bord Pleanála, which also refused planning permission. But the wording of this refusal did not mention any 'non-compensatable' reasons. Noel Smyth and partners, solicitors acting for XJS, lodged a claim for £2.375 million compensation for what XJS would have earned had the development gone ahead. The corporation fought all the way to the Supreme Court, where Mr Justice Niall McCarthy questioned the role of An Bord Pleanála, which had, by failing to cite non-compensatable reasons in its planning refusal, undermined Dún Laoghaire Corporation. Members of An Bord Pleanála were appointed by the Minister for the Environment. In 1982 incoming minister Dick Spring sacked the Fianna Fáil appointees and reconstituted the board with a new appointments process designed to distance it from politics.

In the end XJS didn't get its money. The arbitrator appointed by the High Court was swayed by Dún Laoghaire Corporation's argument that Roches Hill was so rocky that building houses was not feasible and therefore it had no development potential. The arbitrator awarded XJS just £150,000, in April 1987.

Grange Developments, controlled by the Brennan and McGowan construction group, was luckier. It was awarded £1.9 million in compensation two years later. The battle between Grange and the county council had begun in 1980 when the company was refused planning permission for a large housing development on seventy-one acres of agricultural land at Mountgorry, east of Swords. The council dragged its feet, the matter ended in the High Court, and assistant city and county manager George Redmond subsequently gave Grange Developments its cheque.

It was after the 1989 payout to Brennan and McGowan that the compensation loophole was closed by new legislation.

Constitutional Immunity

The police believed they had reason to arrest a man on suspicion of drunk driving. They had watched him leave a café in Rathmines, Dublin, and get into his car and as he started up and drove a short distance they decided to stop him.

'What's your name, sir?'

'Senator Sean McCarthy.'

'Where are you coming from, Senator McCarthy?'

'Work.'

It was five o'clock in the morning, 23 November 1989. The gardaí doubted that this guy was coming from work. Oh, yes, he said, he was indeed coming from work. He was a senator, and he was coming home from work in the Seanad. The gardaí arrested Senator McCarthy and took him to Rathmines garda station.

Sean McCarthy was born in Tipperary in 1937. He became a respected medical doctor, winning medical awards in his early twenties, then working as a GP. In 1981 he won a Dáil seat in Tipperary South, for Fianna Fáil. He was a fierce Charlie Haughey supporter. As a doctor, he was aware of the damage that alcohol does and in June 1983 he proposed in the Dáil that every bottle of beer and spirits should carry a warning label similar to that on packets of cigarettes.

Now, in Rathmines garda station, Dr McCarthy refused to give a sample of urine or blood. Why? Because it was unconstitutional.

Dr McCarthy, like every good public servant, minister and humble backbencher, maintained a strong loyalty to the Constitution. And Dr McCarthy was neither humble nor a backbencher. From 1983 to 1987 he was Fianna Fáil spokesman on Social Welfare. From 1987 to June 1989 he was Minister of State for Science and Technology. At the June 1989 general election he lost his Dáil seat. He was subsequently elected to the Seanad.

And why, the cops wanted to know, was it unconstitutional for them to arrest Senator McCarthy and ask him for a sample?

Because article 15 (13) of the Constitution states that except in a case of treason, felony or breach of the peace, no senator or TD may be arrested going to or coming from either house of the Oireachtas. Article 15 (13) was designed as a guard against attacks on parliamentary democracy, to protect the right of parliamentarians to gather and disperse.

The police charged Senator McCarthy with refusing to give a sample. The papers went to the Director of Public Prosecutions.

Senator McCarthy had addressed the Seanad the evening before. He had recently been in Eastern Europe and he was reporting to his colleagues on his findings there, a matter of fascination to all. The Seanad had closed at 8.30 p.m. and Senator McCarthy had been arrested over eight hours later, in Rathmines, two miles away.

After addressing the Seanad he had gone to his office, he said, and — presumably determined that his colleagues should as soon as possible have the benefit of his elaborated thoughts on Eastern Europe — worked on a report on Eastern Europe for 'some several hours'. Senator McCarthy then left the Seanad. He stopped to get the morning newspapers and to have breakfast in the Rathmines café. And that, at five o'clock in the morning, was where the police had arrested him.

Senator McCarthy made two appearances before the Dublin District Court. He got legal advice to the effect that article 15 (13) of the Constitution 'quite probably afforded a defence to the charge'.

Outrage was expressed at what opposition TDs labelled an abuse of Oireachtas privilege.

Senator McCarthy turned up at the District Court again on 29 March 1990. By then he had received word that the charge was to be dropped, but he wasn't taking any chances, being accompanied by Fianna Fáil-connected barrister Gerry Danaher. In court, a solicitor representing the DPP withdrew the charge.

Leaving the court, Senator McCarthy refused to comment, except to say, 'I'm going fishing.' The Committee on Procedure and Privileges requested Senator McCarthy to make a statement on the matter in the Seanad. This he did, on 5 April 1990, when he gave what was a less than profound apology: 'If an expression of regret for what occurred will serve the best interests of this House, I apologise.'

At the next Seanad election, in 1992, Senator McCarthy lost his seat.

Coveney, Hugh

There is a principle that politicians, when appointed to government office, remove themselves from private business dealings. Hugh Coveney, Cork South Central Fine Gael TD, was a wealthy businessman with a deep attachment to politics. He became Minister for Defence and the Marine in 1994. In that capacity he had to put a distance between himself and his business dealings.

In May 1995, as a spin-off from a nasty little row involving Fianna Fáil business interests, it was revealed that Coveney had been soliciting business for his consultancy. The soliciting was informal ('If there's something happening, will you get onto some of the lads?'), which is the way these things are done in business.

It was a minor transgression of the rules but resignation appeared inevitable. Not because of any improper benefit, not because of any improper pressure exerted, not because anything corrupt happened. Coveney either didn't understand or ignored a very simple principle that is a basic rule of the game. If a soccer player picks up the ball and runs for the goal he gets taken off the field.

The principle was enforced in the cases of Con Ward in 1946 and Eddie Collins in 1983. Twelve years after the Collins episode, Fine Gael leader and Taoiseach John Bruton didn't see the need for such a clear-cut attitude to these matters. Faced with the Coveney scandal, Bruton waited thirty-six hours to see how the wind was blowing. Finally, as the pressure mounted, Bruton announced he was 'reallocating' Coveney 'to another important position in the government'. Fine Gael deputy leader Peter Barry cheerfully declared Coveney's resignation to be 'a move sideways'.

Either Coveney had broken an important rule or he had not. If he had not, there was no need to move him. If he had, the consequence was inevitable — resignation. There was no third way. If a footballer commits a red-card foul there is only one result; he cannot be simply moved to another position on the pitch.

There were several reasons why Coveney was spared the fate of Eddie Collins. There was the Cork factor, the need to avoid annoying an electorate that wanted a minister in the constituency. Coveney was resisting being removed. If he was sent off he would have to spend a couple of years on the sidelines before he could be brought back onto the front bench and, pushing sixty, he resented that. Coveney was widely regarded as a decent man and was very much liked. Just three months earlier Phil Hogan had been sacrificed and Fine Gael was perhaps starting to feel too goody-goody. And back in October 1994 nothing happened to Brian Cowen when he was caught in an alleged conflict of interest. All this combined to cause Bruton to lower the standard applying in such matters. Coveney had to resign, but would be immediately appointed to another ministerial position.

In politics, when defending such a move, the tactic must be to assert that the opposite is true. Ivan Yates said, 'The difficulty is the Taoiseach has raised the whole standards.' Michael Lowry gave the same impression, that Bruton had created new 'exacting standards'. In fact, Bruton had lowered standards from those applied by FitzGerald.

In 1998, taking his dog for a walk along a cliffside near his home in County Cork, Hugh Coveney had a tragic accident. Apparently trying to rescue his dog, he fell and died at the age of sixty-two.

See: Collins, Eddie; Cowengate; Hogan, Phil; Ward, Dr Con.

Cowengate

As Minister for Energy in Albert Reynolds's government, Brian Cowen had responsibility for mining licences. He was in the process of granting a licence to a company when it was revealed that he had shares in that company. Fine Gaelers prepared to put the boot in.

Cowen made an inviting target. He was twenty-four when he took a seat for Fianna Fáil in Laois/Offaly in a by-election caused by the death of his father, who had held the seat on and off since 1969. Cowen sat on the backbenches through the Haughey era. He backed Albert Reynolds's leadership moves and in 1992 was rewarded with a cabinet post. Although he was intelligent and capable, his aggressive style earned him the nickname Biffo (Big Ignorant Fucker From Offaly).

In October 1994 Cowen was in the process of granting a licence to Arcon Resources for a lead and zinc mine at Galmoy, County Kilkenny.

He was approached by a reporter from the *Sunday Business Post* who wanted to know if the minister could confirm that he had shares in Arcon. Cowen is said to have replied: 'God, have I?'

Cowen had bought 1,000 shares in a company called Conroy Petroleum, in 1990, at a cost of £960 and appears to have forgotten about them. That company had since become Arcon. On being approached by the reporter Cowen immediately sold the shares for £430, desperate to get them off his hands. He then went to Albert Reynolds and told him all about it.

Ministers are not supposed to have a personal interest in matters covered by their portfolio. Reynolds accepted that Cowen had done nothing wrong. Cowen made a Dáil statement in which he made an apology of sorts: 'I am genuinely sorry that an oversight on my part in failing to link, however inadvertently, a nominal shareholding in the then Conroy Petroleum and Exploration Company, with a possible perception of a future conflict of interest in dealing with a mining application by Arcon, should be a source of some embarrassment to me or my colleagues.'

It's a classic politician's apology ('possible perception'). Note that Cowen doesn't apologise for — however inadvertently — creating a conflict of interest. He apologises for causing himself and his colleagues 'some embarrassment'.

Technically, Cowen was in breach of cabinet guidelines and tradition suggests he should have paid the price. It happened to Eddie Collins of Fine Gael eleven years earlier. Rules are rules, but some people are more relaxed about these things than others. Everyone concluded that Cowen hadn't intended to do anything wrong so Fianna Fáil backed him and Fine Gael made a mess of attacking him.

There was some comment on the fact that a minister could simply forget where he had placed a thousand pounds, and there was an attempt to create a Cowengate scandal, but it soon died. The matter had one consequence, just four months later. No one had sought Cowen's scalp with more determination than Fine Gael's Phil Hogan. When Hogan got into trouble in February 1995 no one pursued his scalp with more determination than Brian Cowen.

See: Hogan, Phil.

D

Danaher, Gerry

Barrister Adrian Hardiman was representing Des O'Malley, leader of the Progressive Democrats, at the Beef Tribunal in 1992. Hardiman had been politically associated with the PDs. Among the many other barristers involved in the Beef Tribunal proceedings was Gerry Danaher, who was on the team representing the state. Danaher was close to Fianna Fáil, and its leader Albert Reynolds. One of the political factors dogging the tribunal was the enmity between O'Malley and Reynolds, who were then in coalition with one another, but bitter enemies on the issues before the tribunal.

Danaher and Hardiman had been friends since university days, and despite their separate political paths had maintained that friendship. In March 1992 Danaher urged Hardiman not to cross-examine Albert Reynolds personally when the latter came to give evidence at the Beef Tribunal. Leave it to one of the two junior counsel in the case, he said.

About three months later Danaher was speaking to Yvonne Murphy, in the Shelbourne Hotel. Murphy, another lawyer (and now a judge), is married to Hardiman. She too had been friends with Danaher since university. It wouldn't be in Adrian's interest to cross-examine Albert, said Danaher. Let him leave it to Gerard Hogan, one of the juniors. Adrian's future work and long-term interests could be affected if he did the cross-examination himself. Fianna Fáil would be in power for a long time, and the party had a long memory, he said. It was later found that this was designed to make Hardiman uneasy.

The Beef Tribunal dragged on.

In September 1992, two or three months after speaking to Yvonne Murphy, Danaher was in Doheny & Nesbitt's pub, in Lower Baggot Street. He was drinking with Paul O'Higgins, another barrister, another friend since university days, another friend of Hardiman's. There'll be trouble for Adrian if he cross-examines Albert, said Danaher. Let him leave it to one of the juniors. If Adrian does it there's people in Fianna Fáil, said Danaher, who have a lot of damaging information about his tax affairs, and it's on affidavit, and it will all be in the newspapers on the morning that Albert's cross-examination starts. Of course, Danaher himself didn't agree with this tactic, but there were those who did.

Again, it was later found that this was intended to cause Hardiman disquiet.

Hardiman became 'bewildered and distressed' by all this. In October his Beef Tribunal client, Des O'Malley, wanted something done about the threats. Hardiman, not wishing to harm his old friend Danaher, wanted to leave things be. He went to see Danaher, who entirely withdrew all perceived threats and said they weren't seriously made. He had drink taken, he said, and he apologised. Hardiman accepted this.

Someone told the Labour Party leader, Dick Spring, who approached O'Malley. Again Hardiman urged O'Malley that nothing should be done. Someone told the Bar Council, which contacted Hardiman. Again, pleading a close friendship with Danaher, fearing that publicity about the matter would cause his family distress, and perhaps distract from the Beef Tribunal proceedings, Hardiman urged the Bar Council to leave things be.

The Professional Practices Committee of the Bar Council wrote to Danaher on 5 November 1992, asking for an explanation of his comments to and about Hardiman. Two weeks later Danaher wrote back to the committee, stating that he had not made those comments to Adrian Hardiman.

About five weeks later, on 22 December, Danaher was in the bar of the Shelbourne Hotel, with drink taken, when he spoke to Diarmaid McGuinness, junior counsel to Hardiman at the Beef Tribunal. Danaher told McGuinness that when Des O'Malley had been cross-examined at the Beef Tribunal the state legal team had had access to confidential documents concerning O'Malley, and these had been used to prepare the cross-examination. They had been supplied by Fianna Fáil, he said.

McGuinness went to Hardiman; there was a meeting of the legal team, Des O'Malley became involved, and very quickly the whole thing exploded in front of the public.

On 6 January 1993, Attorney General Harry Whelehan exonerated Danaher, when he announced that he had investigated the alleged threats against Hardiman, and 'I am entirely satisfied that no attempt was made to influence the conduct of Mr O'Malley's representation at the Tribunal.'

Hardiman went ahead and cross-examined Albert Reynolds at the Beef Tribunal and did so expertly, aggressively and without any indication whatever that he was taking a soft line with the Taoiseach.

In February 1993 the Barristers' Professional Conduct Tribunal interviewed the various parties and in March it published its findings. Danaher, it concluded, had said what he was alleged to have said. The tribunal was satisfied that Danaher's comments were 'at the least . . . designed to cause some elements of unease and disquiet in Mr Hardiman's mind'. It decided that there was 'just sufficient doubt' preventing it concluding beyond a reasonable doubt that Danaher intended to intimidate Hardiman. The tribunal found that Danaher had made up the bit about the state legal team getting confidential documents concerning O'Malley, on which to base its cross-examination of him. It concluded that his November 1992 letter to the Professional Practices Committee, denying having made the comments to Hardiman, was a 'contrived and disingenuous' letter.

Danaher was ruled to have engaged in conduct unbecoming a barrister, and behaviour likely to bring the profession into disrepute; the report concluded that he acted in a grossly improper manner as a barrister, and that his conduct fell far short of the standards demanded of all barristers.

Danaher issued a statement welcoming the findings. The statement appeared to suggest that he had in some way been cleared. He welcomed the tribunal 'dismissing complaints of improper use of documentation and intimidation. The central allegations against me have been shown to be without credible foundation.'

Not quite. The complaint about improper use of documents fell because the tribunal concluded that Danaher invented the alleged use of such documents. The tribunal did not conclude that there was no credible foundation to the allegation that Danaher tried to intimidate Hardiman. The tribunal needed proof beyond a reasonable doubt before it could conclude that Danaher intended 'intimidation', rather than the creation of 'unease and disquiet' in Hardiman's mind. It concluded it didn't quite have that level of proof.

Danaher resigned from the state legal team at the Beef Tribunal. He appealed to the Barristers' Professional Conduct Appeals Board and in July that body confirmed that he had made the statements designed to cause Hardiman unease and disquiet, but it found him guilty only of 'breaching proper professional standards'.

In short, Danaher's conduct did not constitute conduct unbecoming a barrister. It is useful to know that such behaviour is not likely to bring the profession into disrepute; nor is it activity of a grossly improper manner; and such activity does not fall far short of the standards demanded of all barristers.

Dead Man Strategy

At the McCracken Tribunal in 1997, Charlie Haughey pursued his Dead Man Strategy. Haughey's accountant, Des Traynor, died in 1994. Haughey sought to evade responsibility for his acceptance of money from Ben Dunne by claiming that he knew nothing about it, it was all the fault of the dead man. Traynor was Haughey's close friend, as well as his accountant. The Dead Man Strategy meant dragging his loyal friend's reputation through the mud, but what the hell, even dead accountants have their uses.

Here's what Haughey said, in a prepared statement, when he took the stand at the McCracken Tribunal on 15 July 1997:

> Throughout my public life, the late Mr Des Traynor was my trusted friend and financial adviser . . . I never had to concern myself about my personal finances. He took over control of my financial affairs from about 1960 onwards. He sought, as his personal responsibility, to ensure that I would be free to devote my time and ability to public life and that I would not be distracted from my political work by financial concern. The late Mr Des Traynor had complete discretion to act on my behalf without reference back to me.

Later:

> My private finances were perhaps peripheral to my life. I left them to Mr Traynor to look after. I didn't have any problem in regard to them and I left the matter at that.

With Traynor dead, Haughey could simply deny knowledge of everything to do with his finances. He swore that if he knew what Traynor was up to, soliciting large amounts of money from Ben Dunne, he would have stopped him.

Unfortunately for Haughey, the strategy fell apart in February 1999, when the Moriarty Tribunal discovered Allied Irish Banks documents which proved he had been lying on the witness stand at the McCracken Tribunal.

The AIB documents listed meeting after meeting, phone call after phone call, between Haughey and AIB officials, to discuss his ever-expanding debt. At all but two meetings Haughey met AIB officials alone.

Des Traynor, who supposedly had taken complete control of Haughey's finances fifteen years earlier, is mentioned attending meetings twice. Each time, Haughey had to give explicit permission for the AIB officials to discuss his affairs with Traynor.

Once he started lying, Haughey had to continue. At the McCracken Tribunal, to protect his story of knowing nothing about his finances, Haughey had to pretend he didn't know where his income of hundreds of thousands of pounds was coming from. He never asked any questions of Traynor. He probably thought Traynor was borrowing it, he said. Counsel for the tribunal, Denis McCullough, suggested that there would have to be security for such loans, 'and the giving of that security would involve you in signing documents, executing mortgages, matters of that kind?'

Suddenly, it was important to Haughey to pretend that never, from 1960 to Traynor's death in 1994, was his Kinsealy mansion, Abbeville, mortgaged.

'No, not necessarily.'

'Not necessarily?'

'No.'

'It would require some sort of miracle to raise those sums of money, Mr Haughey, without some sort of security.'

'No, Mr Traynor would have the capacity to do that on his own on my behalf.'

However, the AIB documents uncovered by Moriarty were littered with details of the 'charges' on Abbeville held by AIB and the Northern Bank Finance Corporation. Here's a letter from Haughey, dated 25 March 1975, on 'Abbeville' notepaper, to AIB:

> I confirm having indicated that I am happy to let you have whatever security may be required including a second charge of all the properties mortgaged to the Northern Bank Finance Corporation . . . there will be no delay in letting you have a second mortgage.

At the McCracken Tribunal, Haughey had denied to counsel Denis McCullough that he had a mortgage, that he had any involvement in sourcing his money; it was all the dead man's work. This was so improbable that Judge McCracken intervened.

'To be clear, Mr Haughey, is it the case, then, that you never did mortgage Abbeville?'

'No,' lied Haughey, on oath.

'It was never mortgaged?' asked McCracken.

'No,' Haughey lied again, on oath.
See: Traynor, Des.

De Bruin, Michelle

Former Olympic swimmer Gary O'Toole was one of the few commentators not surprised by Michelle Smith's three gold medals at the Atlanta Olympics in 1996: 'From December 1993, I knew that's where she was headed.' The spectacular improvement, which would later cause so much comment and innuendo, occurred, he said, between August 1992 and December 1993. 'Her improvements were far from gradual and that was the time to question her performances.'

But outside the world of elite swimmers, no one questioned the Michelle Smith phenomenon until the Atlanta Olympics. There, the 26-year-old swimmer stunned just about everyone with four outstanding performances: three golds and a bronze. For Ireland, she was the first woman to win an Olympic medal, the first Irish person even to make it to an Olympic swimming final, the first Irish person to pick up so many medals. Time to rent the open-top bus and plan the homecoming.

Before the third medal was won, an American spoilsport started to rain on the Irish parade. Or so it seemed at the time. Janet Evans was the darling of the USA swim team and she was supposed to be the one with the medal hanging around her neck. Except she finished ninth in the qualifiers and was knocked out of the final of the 400 metres freestyle by Michelle Smith, who went on to take the gold. At a press conference later Evans remarked: 'Are you asking me if I should say she's on drugs? I think any time a person in any country has a dramatic improvement they ask that question. I have heard that question posed in the last few weeks about that particular swimmer . . . If you're asking me if the accusations are out there, I would say, yes, they are.'

The Irish Times described this careful and sincere response to a question as 'an outrageous and unsubstantiated attack on de Bruin'. Irish sports journalists divided into two increasingly antagonistic camps. One group defended Michelle. She had never failed a drugs test and she was one of the most tested athletes in the world. Give her a break and let the rest of us enjoy her success.

The others raised questions about her performance. Michelle's improvement had been dramatic. She knocked nineteen seconds off her personal best in fifteen months. There was no example to be found of any other swimmer making such spectacular progress. At twenty-six she was old for a swimmer. Most peaked at eighteen or nineteen. And then there was the Eric de Bruin factor. A former Olympic discus thrower, now Michelle's husband and coach, he and his training regime were what she credited for her success. But de Bruin was himself tainted by a failed drugs test. Worse still he was unapologetic. 'Who says doping is unethical? Who decides what is ethical? Is politics ethical? Is the world of sport ethical? Sport is by nature dishonest.' It was a quote taken from a 1993 interview with a Dutch publication and it came back repeatedly to haunt his wife.

None of this proved anything, but some sports journalists argued that it was enough to give them the right and responsibility to raise questions about how Michelle de Bruin's performance (she was now using her husband's name) was achieved. The problem was that raising the same questions over and over again began to look like begrudgery and harassment. De Bruin complained about a campaign of vilification. Some sports journalists were told by their papers to lay off Michelle.

Tom Humphries of *The Irish Times* was one who wrote most convincingly about the dilemma. 'Michelle Smith's performances have been astonishing. She herself has recognised that the questions that have been asked have to be asked. That is the horrible cleft of modern sport.' Urine testing couldn't detect some performance-enhancing substances and there was no will among sporting organisations to introduce the kind of blood testing that would. All that stuff about playing the game is strictly for the punters: sport is big business and drugs are part of it. So, the only thing left is trust. Athletes have to be taken on trust. Unfortunately for Michelle de Bruin, a significant number of journalists didn't trust her success and the questions didn't go away.

Writing in Atlanta, Tom Humphries predicted that for Michelle: 'A lifetime at the nation's bosom lies ahead. The choice of commercial endorsements are spread at her feet like rose petals . . . The rewards both material and spiritual will be immense. Answering a few questions as to how it all came to be was a small toll to pay.' It didn't turn out that way. There were small commercial deals but nothing like an Olympic triple gold winner might have expected. Even the homecoming was subdued. It didn't help that the weather was appalling, but despite the hype and the live television coverage there was no denying the truth: the crowds didn't turn out.

In the months and years that followed, the doubts about Michelle de Bruin grew. On the morning of 10 January 1998 Al and Kay Guy, FINA testing officers, called to Michelle and Eric de Bruin's home to carry out a drugs test. In April the swimmer stood accused of interfering with the sample. In August 1998, after further tests, FINA suspended Michelle de Bruin from competitive swimming for four years for tampering with the urine sample: specifically, contaminating it with alcohol. There was no mention of a banned substance, that came later.

At a press conference held after the FINA ruling, Michelle de Bruin vowed to fight on. 'I have always represented my country with pride. I have never cheated or lied. I have never taken a banned substance and I haven't lied in this case either.'

The Court of Arbitration for Sport heard the evidence and found otherwise. Michelle de Bruin was officially branded a cheat on Monday, 7 June 1999. The court accepted FINA's case that the swimmer was 'the only person who had the motive and the opportunity to manipulate the sample'. The motive was apparent when new technology was applied to urine samples taken from the swimmer between November 1997 and March 1998. These tests found evidence of the testosterone precursor androstenedione. Michelle de Bruin's swimming career was over.

Desmond, Dermot: An Apology

Johnston, Mooney & O'Brien owned a Ballsbridge site; it was bought by UPH, which sold it to Chestvale, which eventually (in a very complicated deal) sold it to Telecom Éireann. That's the background.

The following account of a small part of that story comes from the Interim Report of Inspector John Glackin.

On Friday, 16 February 1990, the *Irish Independent* published an article by Cliodhna O'Donoghue which claimed that businessmen Dermot Desmond and Michael Smurfit had an interest in a consortium which was selling the JMOB site to Telecom Éireann for a new head office. This was a serious allegation, as Smurfit was then chairman of Telecom. If it was true, he would be in the position of buying the site, on behalf of Telecom, from a company in which he had an interest.

This was also serious for Dermot Desmond, as he was in the process of advising and helping Smurfit buy the site.

Lawyers went to work on Smurfit's behalf, seeking a retraction from the *Independent*. Dermot Desmond rang up Vinnie Doyle, editor of the *Irish Independent*, directly. He also wrote to John Meagher, deputy chairman of Independent Newspapers, stating that he did not directly or indirectly hold a stake in the site, and 'I am not the beneficiary of any proposed sale of the site.'

The *Indo* talked to its reporter, Cliodhna O'Donoghue, who went back to her source, who wouldn't go public. The newspaper's lawyers immediately drew up a retraction. The wording was agreed with Dermot Desmond. The paper's lawyers couldn't make contact with Michael Smurfit's lawyers.

What to do? They had to publish the retraction the following day, Saturday, 17 February, to mollify Desmond. But if they didn't include Smurfit in the retraction someone might infer that the newspaper was saying that the bit about Desmond wasn't accurate but the bit about Smurfit was. This would compound any liability and get the paper into deeper trouble. It published a retraction on page 3 of the Saturday paper, stating that Dermot Desmond had no interest in the JMOB site and that the statement published the previous day that Smurfit had such an interest was 'totally false'.

Smurfit was unhappy with the retraction. He wanted a prominent apology and damages. He got in touch with John Meagher and expressed his unhappiness. A second retraction and apology was agreed. This was published on 23 February, a week after the offending piece. It said: 'Dr Smurfit does not have and never had an interest directly or indirectly in the site.'

And, just in case anyone might think that the paper was apologising only to Smurfit, and infer that Desmond had done something wrong, the apology included a statement that Desmond had no interest in the site. Smurfit asked for a significant sum to be paid to charity: the sum agreed was £1,500.

Seven months later it emerged that Dr Michael Smurfit had a stake in UPH, which bought the JMOB site and sold it to Chestvale. So, while it was true to say — as the *Indo* apology did — that Michael Smurfit had no interest in Chestvale, the outfit selling the site to Telecom Éireann, it was not true to say that he 'never had an interest directly or indirectly in the site'. Dr Smurfit was not aware, at the time of seeking an apology, that one of his many investments was in UPH. It was brought to his attention at a later stage.

And Dermot Desmond had an interest in UPH. And, after a long investigation, a government-appointed inspector, John Glackin, concluded that Dermot Desmond also had an interest in Chestvale, the outfit selling the site to Telecom. This was at the same time that Desmond was helpfully advising Smurfit in his bid to buy the site from

Chestvale. Desmond vigorously denied having such an interest and refused to accept the conclusions of the Glackin Report.

Inspector Glackin concluded 'that Mr Desmond induced the editor of the *Irish Independent* to publish an apology in February 1990 in relation to an article published by them on the previous day alleging his involvement in the JMOB site, when he knew that the original article was substantially correct and that he was not entitled to an apology'.

Desmond strongly rejected the conclusions of the Glackin report.
See: Desmond Letter; Telecom.

Desmond Letter

Thierry Jacquillat was managing director of the French drinks company Pernod Ricard. From June 1988 to November of that year Pernod Ricard and the British drinks company Grand Metropolitan were engaged in a tough struggle over who would take over Irish Distillers Group. It involved High Court and Supreme Court battles and negotiations with Revenue Commissioners. Dublin stockbroker Dermot Desmond, founder of the NCB stockbroking company and friend of Charlie Haughey, was pivotal in helping the French gain victory.

In the midst of the battles, when a plan for reducing tax liabilities was central to what was happening, one of those involved, Jim Flavin, said to Dermot Desmond, 'You know you should go off to Kinsealy and get the tax clearance.' Mr Desmond said he did not go to Mr Haughey's home and no one has seriously alleged he did. Mr Flavin later said his comment was made in a 'light-hearted' way.

On 23 November 1988 the Minister for Industry and Commerce, Albert Reynolds, gave the French victory his all-clear. On 16 December five members of the board of IDG resigned and Pernod announced the appointment of Thierry Jacquillat to the board. Subsequently, Jacquillat and Dermot Desmond had a meeting, followed by lunch, at which they discussed the fees NCB should be paid for Desmond's work. The meeting was inconclusive, with Jacquillat saying he needed further time to consider the matter. On 6 January 1989 Desmond wrote to Jacquillat, putting the arguments as to why NCB should be paid two million pounds.

Dear Thierry,

It was a great pleasure to see you again. As you wish to give some further consideration to NCB's fees, I thought it might be helpful if I summarised the factors which we reviewed both during our meeting and over a most enjoyable lunch. The first point I would reiterate is that our fee estimate of £2 million is put forward in the spirit of honesty and openness in which we acted for Pernod Ricard throughout the takeover battle. It was not conceived as an exaggerated opening position with a view to bargaining, but as a very basic and modest estimate of the value of our contribution to the success of Pernod Ricard's acquisition of IDG. I honestly expected you to accept it as such, giving you the opportunity to offer more.

Desmond then outlined some of NCB's activities on Pernod Ricard's behalf, including:

our interaction with the Irish media. We made sure that the Irish media started and finished as supporters of the Pernod Ricard bid and added greatly to its credibility as far as the media and the public were concerned.

. . . our passion for victory throughout the whole process, we bullied and policed every other party involved, from lawyers to tax experts and ensured that we either got a high-quality service from them, or else effectively supplied it ourselves.

. . . But for our intervention at the highest levels in connection with the Monopolies and Mergers decision, it is certain that Pernod Ricard would have been constrained to dispose of one or more brands and that GC&C would have been allowed to acquire in excess of 30 per cent.

We orchestrated entirely the successful campaign to get a positive tax opinion from the Revenue Commissioners, which involved using personal contacts at the highest level, including the Minister for Finance and the Secretaries of the Department of the Taoiseach and the Department of Industry and Commerce. Our success had a major impact undermining FII's credibility in court.

. . . We used up a large proportion of the favours we can call upon from our political contacts — and no doubt we will pay a price on the other side . . .

With kindest personal regards
Yours sincerely
Dermot F. Desmond

The letter was made public in October 1989, by Proinsias De Rossa, then leader of the Workers' Party. Dermot Desmond questioned the means by which De Rossa came by 'a private business letter' and accused De Rossa of 'KGB-style tactics'. He said he and NCB had acted with the 'highest integrity'.

Albert Reynolds, who had been Minister for Industry and Commerce at the time, said: 'I carried out my duties in a totally impartial manner as I did in every department in which I served.'

See: Celtic Helicopters; Desmond, Dermot: An Apology; Telecom.

Dessie O'Malley and Larry Goodman

It is unusual for us to get a close-up on the manner in which politicians and their financial backers treat each other. One such opportunity arose during the Beef Tribunal, when a letter from beef baron Larry Goodman to Des O'Malley, leader of the Progressive Democrats, was made public. The letter was dated 21 January 1987. O'Malley had for some months been trying to raise funds for his new party. In March 1986 he wrote to Goodman, soliciting money. Goodman liked to spread his money around the political parties, in support of the democratic process. He didn't give the PDs any money in 1986. First, he wanted to have a face-to-face meeting with O'Malley. In the words of his counsel at the Beef Tribunal: 'Essentially he put the question of a contribution on hold until he could meet' O'Malley personally.

On 20 January 1987 the two men met. We don't know the details of the meeting, but we do know that both men enjoyed it. Next day, Goodman wrote the following letter, and enclosed with it a cheque for £20,000:

Dear Dessie,

I was pleased that we eventually got round to meeting last evening. I apologise for taking so long to get back to you and had I known the present situation was going to break so soon [a general election campaign was under way], I would have asked Larry Power to cancel the meeting, knowing the organisational pressure that you would have immediately been put under. There are many issues we had planned to discuss and debate with you in a relaxed manner had we met sooner. However, that is totally down to me.

And here Goodman waxes lyrical, using words echoing those of the AIB manager who wrote a congratulatory letter to Charlie Haughey about his leadership of this great little nation.

> We all know the current state of the nation. The challenge is great but so is the potential. I have every confidence in your ability to recognise what needs to be done and to get on with it. I enclose my personal cheque, which I hope will be of some assistance to party funds. I would like to take this opportunity of wishing you personally and your colleagues every success.
>
> Best personal regards
> Yours sincerely

O'Malley immediately replied.

> Dear Larry,
>
> I am extremely grateful for your letter of the 21st of January and your exceptionally generous enclosure. I need hardly say that we are enormously grateful for such huge support. It is of inestimable value to us in financing the campaign and tremendously appreciated. I was delighted to meet you on the other evening but I am sorry that through nobody's fault things were rather rushed. I hope that you will have dinner with me in Dublin some evening after the election, when we can discuss matters in more detail, in a relaxed atmosphere.
>
> With renewed thanks for your exceptionally generous support.

O'Malley would later become one of the most relentless critics of Goodman and his beef operations. That makes all the more embarrassing the mutual fawning demonstrated by these letters. Give a politician twenty thousand pounds and access is assured, he'll even ask you round to dinner, where the man with the money and the man who may be in a position of power come to a meeting of minds on 'issues' and 'matters'.

See: PD Fund-raising.

De Valera and Hitler

Adolf Hitler was dead, the Allied forces were taking Berlin. The war in Europe was ending. Over the next few days there would be worldwide celebration of the defeat of fascism. On 2 May 1945 Taoiseach Eamon de Valera chose to visit the German Minister to Ireland, Eduard Hempel, to express his condolences on the death of Hitler.

It was argued that de Valera was merely maintaining, to the end, the strict protocol which had helped him steer a neutral course through the Second World War. When US president Franklin Roosevelt died three weeks before Hitler the Dáil adjourned as a mark of respect. De Valera was, from his point of view, merely fulfilling a diplomatic requirement.

'So long as we retained our diplomatic relations with Germany, to have failed to call upon the German representative would have been an act of unpardonable discourtesy to the German nation and to Dr Hempel himself . . . I certainly was not going to add to his humiliation in the hour of defeat.'

His assistant secretary of External Affairs, Frederick Boland, who would later represent Ireland at the United Nations, pleaded with de Valera in vain. De Valera made the visit, and the following day a representative of President Seán T. O'Kelly, Michael McDunphy, visited Herr Hempel to express condolences.

Allied troops had recently come across the death camps and revealed to the world the horror of what had gone on. De Valera's expression of condolence on the death of the architect of the holocaust spared Herr Hempel a diplomatic insult, but at the price of insulting the victims of the regime Hempel represented. That insult brought down on de Valera's head a wave of national and international condemnation. His enemies gloated, his friends shook their heads in incomprehension.

De Valera had chosen, with a typical mixture of naivety, stubbornness and arrogance, to use the death of Hitler to assert his independence. It wasn't about diplomatic niceties, it was a clumsy assertion of an independent stance on international affairs. Ireland — and he saw himself as the incarnation of the nation — would make its own way in the world, would take its own decisions, even at the cost of unpopularity, independently of the major power blocs. The policy might be laudable, but the manner in which it was asserted was repellent and regrettable.

The policy would last a decade or two.

See: Foreign Policy.

Doherty, Seán

Rumours and allegations about behind-the-scenes activities of Charlie Haughey's government had been widespread in 1982. Now, on Thursday, 20 January 1983, some substance was being put on the rumours. The new Fine Gael Minister for Justice, Michael Noonan, announced that outgoing Fianna Fáil Minister for Justice Seán Doherty had ordered the tapping of the phones of two journalists, Bruce Arnold and Geraldine Kennedy.

The following day Doherty issued a statement, claiming that he ordered the taps because 'national security was endangered through leaks of highly confidential papers and memoranda'.

The two journalists, on the other hand, believed Doherty ordered the taps to find out who from the Fianna Fáil party was feeding them information about the efforts to shaft Haughey.

Doherty's statement went on: 'My actions as referred to were motivated solely by my concern for the security of my country and were not at any stage discussed by the Government or with the Taoiseach.'

That Sunday, 23 January, on RTÉ, Doherty was asked if he had told the cabinet about the phone taps. 'No,' he replied. 'As far as I was concerned the government was not informed of what I was doing.'

Question: 'Mr Haughey did not know that you were tapping those journalists' phones?'

Doherty: 'No, Mr Haughey did not know that I was tapping those journalists' phones.'

That Sunday in 1983 the Fianna Fáil parliamentary party discussed the issue. Pearse Wyse asked why Doherty had tapped the phones. 'National security,' replied Haughey. 'There had been cabinet leaks.'

'What leaks?' asked Wyse.

To general laughter, Haughey replied, 'The Fianna Fáil farm plan had appeared, for instance, in the *Farmers' Journal*.' The excuse of cabinet leaks wasn't taken seriously even within Fianna Fáil.

Doherty resigned from the front bench under threat of dismissal. He went back to his home ground on 11 February and, addressing a huge crowd at the Forest Park Hotel in Boyle that Friday night, he thundered: 'Let it be two journalists or anyone else, if I think they're entitled to be tapped I'll tap them! Because they associate with people who are a threat in one form or another to this state. I would do it again, if necessary!'

Doherty's ministerial career was nasty, brutish and short. He lasted less than a year as Minister for Justice, and it was a rough year. The phone tapping was one controversial incident, another was the Dowra case. Despite the fact that his ministerial career did not bring gasps of admiration, Doherty seemed to believe he had a right to a place at the top table. Two years later he was moaning, 'I've carried the can long enough.' And always there was the hint that Doherty knew more than was good for some people and mightn't keep his mouth shut indefinitely.

Eventually, in January 1992, Doherty went on *Nighthawks*, the RTÉ late-night show, and hinted that others knew he had tapped journalists' phones. With a fixed grin, he lambasted the supposed Dublin 4 set. 'They've left their wives, most of them,' he sneered. 'They don't practise their religion and they don't want the rest of us to practise it either. They have no interest in most of the traditional values of Irish people.'

Despite the fixed grin, there was no humour in Doherty's outburst. He was taking a stand against those nasty, atheistic urban wife-swappers who are not real Irish people. And when he said of his enemies, 'I care for them — in a special way,' you didn't have to be Bruce Arnold or Geraldine Kennedy to be grateful that Doherty would never again have the power he once had.

A week later, on 21 January, Doherty went for the kill, claiming that he had in 1982 given Charlie Haughey transcripts made from the taps on the journalists' phones.

Given that Doherty's claim contradicted his 1983 assertion that Haughey didn't know about the phone taps, given Haughey's denial now of Doherty's claim, Haughey might have survived. It was his word, as Taoiseach, against Doherty, who had been consigned to the backbenches in controversial circumstances. However, Haughey was by that stage weakened by years of scandal and controversy and Doherty's claim was enough to drive him from public life.

See: Dowra; Kerry Car Crash; MacSharry Bugging.

Donations

Also known as gifts or contributions. Politicians solicit money from wealthy interests. They have always insisted that such donations, although made in secrecy, are laudable expressions of support for democracy. No favours are sought or given. And such donations are quite different from a politician — such as Charlie Haughey — accepting money for personal use.

If a politician accepts twenty grand and uses it to build an extension out the back of his house, that would be corruption. If he accepts twenty grand and uses it to get himself re-elected to a £40,000 job, or a £90,000 ministerial position, that is not corruption, it is democracy.

See: Favours: None Sought or Given; Taca.

Donnellan, John

You can criticise Irish politicians, but don't make jokes about them. Fine Gael TD John Donnellan, from Galway, was widely considered to be annoyed not to have been given a frontbench appointment in the early 1980s. Eventually, he became a Minister of State (or junior minister) in the Garret FitzGerald-led coalition of the mid-1980s. When FitzGerald gave up the party leadership after losing the February 1987 general election he was replaced by Alan Dukes. Donnellan was perceived to be upset when Dukes ignored him in the assignment of opposition portfolios.

At the 1987 Fine Gael ard-fheis, in October, Donnellan — who was chairman of the party's national executive — declined to preside over a session which would have involved him introducing Dukes.

In February 1988 Donnellan missed an important Dáil vote on the proposed closure of Barrington's Hospital in Limerick. The following month he gave an interview to the *Connacht Tribune* in which he criticised Dukes. Donnellan complained about Fine Gael's support for fishing rod licences. 'We as a party have taken an awful lot of wrong options and this was another one of them,' he said. 'The political ground is very fertile for us and has been for the past twelve months, but we are making very little use of it.'

It was what he said next that sealed Donnellan's fate: 'As a matter of fact, if it was raining soup Alan Dukes would have a fork in his hand.'

Within a month Donnellan was expelled from the Fine Gael parliamentary party.

At first, the Fine Gael establishment brushed the remarks aside. They were 'unimportant' and 'motivated by personal spleen', it was said. Then, Dukes struck. At a parliamentary party meeting on 20 April 1988 Dukes proposed that the whip be removed from Donnellan; Seán Barrett TD seconded the motion. It was seen as asserting the leader's authority within the party.

Some seemed aware of how all this might look. It was like a parody of one of those grimly satirical books that came out of Eastern Europe, in which someone makes a joke about the party leader and is instantly dispatched to the salt mines. TDs Paddy Cooney, John Kelly, Michael Begley and Brendan McGahon appealed for a lesser sanction, Donnellan apologised for the remarks on the basis that they lacked good taste and he regretted if Mr Dukes found them offensive. The parliamentary party voted by fifty votes to eleven, with several abstentions, to kick Donnellan out.

Donnellan, who had held a seat in Galway since 1964, left politics at the next election. Two years later, after the dismal performance of Fine Gael in the 1990 presidential election, Alan Dukes was deposed and replaced by John Bruton.

Dowra

I t was closing time, ten days before Christmas 1981, and Garda Tom Nangle wanted a take-out. He was at the bar of the Black Bush pub, in the village of Blacklion, County Cavan. He was being refused. A man who lived across the border in County Fermanagh, Jimmy McGovern, had been drinking in the pub, had left and now came back looking for change of a pound. He saw what was happening and passed a remark. Something like, 'Fuck the guards, they should all be in H Block,' according to evidence given at the subsequent court case. Shortly after this Mr McGovern ended up lying on the floor. Garda Nangle explained how Mr McGovern got into that position. He said that he believed Mr McGovern was about to hit him and 'in self-defence I put up my hand and it connected with him and he fell down'. Mr McGovern, a single man in his thirties, was taken to hospital in Enniskillen to be treated for a cut on his head and he later made a complaint to the gardaí.

Garda Tom Nangle, as it happened, was a brother-in-law of Fianna Fáil TD Seán Doherty. And two months after the incident at the Black Bush the new Taoiseach, Charlie Haughey, appointed Seán Doherty Minister for Justice.

Appeals were made to McGovern to withdraw his complaint. There was talk of £400 being offered in compensation. McGovern withdrew his complaint, then said he didn't get the £400. It didn't matter. Other witnesses had made statements to the gardaí and a charge of assault was laid against Garda Nangle. The case was due to come to the District Court at Dowra on Monday, 27 September 1982.

Some time in mid-September someone in the Department of Justice contacted a detective chief superintendent of the Garda Síochána with a query about a McGovern from Fermanagh. Ten days before the Nangle case was due in court, the detective chief superintendent rang RUC headquarters to pass on this query.

Several days after that the RUC became interested in Jimmy McGovern. He had had some involvement with H Blocks protests and the RUC wanted to know if he was a Provo activist. According to the autobiography of then RUC chief constable Jack Hermon, 'Careful local inquiries and limited surveillance were carried out in the area' and plans were made to arrest Jimmy McGovern on the morning of Monday, 27 September. McGovern was allegedly one of four Fermanagh men scheduled for arrest that morning.

This was the day McGovern was due to give evidence in court at Dowra, where Garda Tom Nangle was up on the assault charge.

On the evening of Sunday, 26 September, with no idea that he had become the focus of 'careful local inquiries and limited surveillance' by the RUC, Jimmy McGovern crossed into the Republic and went drinking in Blacklion. He then went dancing, and in the small hours of Monday morning he went back across the border and stayed with a cousin in the village of Belcoo. At about six o'clock that morning the RUC raided McGovern's home in the village of Markbank. When they found he wasn't there they raided the home of McGovern's cousin, in Belcoo, found McGovern and arrested him.

McGovern was taken to the RUC's Gough Holding Centre in Armagh, where he was searched, fingerprinted and seen by a doctor. Immediately after his arrest, and again after arriving at the holding centre, McGovern told the RUC he had to be in Dowra that day to appear in a court case.

The official explanation for what happened next goes like this:

An RUC sergeant in Armagh phoned a garda sergeant in Cavan. The garda sergeant in Cavan phoned a garda in Dowra. The garda in Dowra went into the courtroom and passed the message on to a superintendent. The superintendent then gave the message to the state solicitor who was prosecuting Garda Tom Nangle.

The message started out as something like: Jimmy McGovern can't attend the court in Dowra because he has been arrested and is being questioned by the RUC. By the time it got to the superintendent it was something like: there's a message from the RUC in Armagh that Jimmy McGovern won't be attending the court today.

It didn't seem to occur to anyone to tell the judge what was happening; it didn't seem to occur to anyone to inquire as to how the RUC knew that McGovern wouldn't be coming to court.

Meanwhile, the RUC questioned McGovern about connections with the Provos, which he denied.

At Dowra District Court the case against Garda Tom Nangle went ahead. In the absence of the alleged victim and main prosecution witness, Jimmy McGovern, District Justice John Barry dismissed the assault charge and Garda Tom Nangle walked free. For some unknown reason, said the judge, Mr McGovern's evidence 'was not forthcoming'.

At 7.30 p.m. that evening, hours after the court case was aborted, McGovern was released by the RUC.

Fr Denis Faul from Dungannon took up the case and complained about the arrest of McGovern. This led to an official RUC investigation, which eventually concluded that nothing untoward had been done.

The Director of Public Prosecutions appealed the outcome of the Nangle case and in April 1983 the appeal was dismissed by the High Court.

By now the Haughey government had lost a general election and Doherty was no longer Minister for Justice. The affair caused strain between the Garda Síochána and the RUC.

In 1984 Jimmy McGovern sued for wrongful arrest and false imprisonment. Five years later, to the annoyance of RUC chief constable Jack Hermon, while he was out of the country, the case was settled out of court. McGovern received £3,000 in damages and costs.

See: Doherty, Seán; Kerry Car Crash; MacSharry Bugging.

DPP Allegation

After the 1998 bombing of Omagh, repressive legislation was rushed through the British parliament and the Irish Dáil. On Wednesday, 2 September, in the course of debate on that legislation, a scandalous, unsustainable, unsubstantiated and unfounded accusation was made against the Director of Public Prosecutions, Eamonn Barnes.

In addressing the Dáil, Fine Gael TD Brendan McGahon asked why the legislation wasn't brought in thirty years ago or after the Enniskillen bomb. He asked, 'Why was it not done after Warrenpoint?', referring to the two IRA bombs which killed eighteen British soldiers on the day in 1979 when Lord Mountbatten was murdered.

Why was the legislation not brought in, asked Mr McGahon, 'when eighteen young men were butchered? And the Irish government knew who did it. And the DPP refused to prefer charges probably — probably — for political reasons.'

This allegation was made calmly, deliberately. No evidence was cited in support of the allegation.

The DPP is obliged to make his decisions on the grounds of the evidence presented to him by gardaí, using his professional judgment as to whether a winnable case can be brought to court. For the DPP to make a decision not to prosecute murderers on political grounds would be a major scandal and would bring his office into irredeemable disrepute. It is without doubt the most serious charge ever made against a public official: the protection, for political reasons, of people known to have committed multiple murder.

Anyone with an even casual familiarity with the DPP's record over a quarter of a century, during which time Barnes had repeatedly defended the independence of his office and resolutely steered clear of political controversy, would find such an allegation incredible.

The charge was made under parliamentary privilege, by a veteran Fine Gael TD. No public effort was made by Fine Gael to have the charge withdrawn or to protect in any way Mr Barnes's reputation or that of his office. The Ceann Comhairle didn't intervene, though attacks on people outside the house are usually frowned upon, as they cannot defend themselves. No colleague of Mr McGahon's objected to the charge being made. No former member of the Lynch government came forward to repudiate the allegation that that government had in some way protected IRA killers.

If such an unfounded allegation were made in print it would attract a libel suit. In the Dáil, anything can be said under privilege.

Dromad

Patrick McParland was well liked at Dromad garda station. He owned Dromad's Carrickdale Hotel. When he was arrested on suspicion of drink driving in the early hours of 13 September 1997 and taken to Dundalk garda station he asked that the gardaí at Dromad be informed.

It was 1.15 a.m. and Sergeant James Cunningham was on duty at Dromad. When he heard about the arrest of Mr McParland he drove to Dundalk garda station. You don't realise who you've arrested, Sergeant Cunningham said to Garda Eric McGovern, who had arrested Mr McParland and brought him to the station. Mr McParland was very good to the gardaí at Dromad.

Just doing my job, said Garda McGovern.

Continuing to do his job, Garda McGovern set about getting a doctor to take a sample from Mr McParland. He rang Dr Harpel Gujral, in Slane, who was the designated doctor on duty for police purposes that night, and asked him to come to Dundalk garda station to take a blood or urine sample from a prisoner.

Sergeant Cunningham went to see Superintendent Michael Staunton. The superintendent was in his office, working late because of a fatal stabbing that night in Dundalk. Sergeant Cunningham explained that a good friend of the gardaí, Mr McParland, was in custody and there was a doctor on his way from Slane to take a sample. There is a divergence of evidence about what was said next. Superintendent Staunton says he said there was nothing he could do. Sergeant Cunningham says that he proposed mounting a roadblock to intercept the doctor on his way to Dundalk and the superintendent said, 'That's the thing to do.'

It was now sometime between 1.30 a.m. and 2 a.m. In Slane Dr Gujral got up and drove off towards Dundalk. A couple of miles south of the town he came upon a garda roadblock and stopped. Sergeant Cunningham identified himself to the doctor and said that what he had to say was somewhat embarrassing, but the doctor wasn't needed, he should turn back to Slane. The doctor said he was told just to turn off his mobile phone and go home. With his mobile phone turned off the doctor would be unable to take any calls which might inquire as to what was delaying him, or why he hadn't turned up at Dundalk garda station.

Everything had been taken care of, the sergeant told the doctor, it was a very sensitive matter and this had been given the okay at top level. Off you go. The doctor was told his fee for coming out and taking a sample would be paid.

The doctor turned and was driving back towards Slane when Sergeant Cunningham drove alongside, signalled him to stop and told him again to go home. At 4 a.m., he said, the doctor should ring Dundalk garda station and tell them that his car had broken down. (A sample must be taken from a suspected drunk driver within three hours of his arrest.)

By 4 a.m. there would be no point in looking for another doctor, as the three hours were almost up, and Mr McParland would have to be released.

Unhappy with the turn of events, Dr Gujral rang the gardaí at his local station when he got home to Slane. There, Sergeant John Clarke was having no part of whatever was going on. He collected the doctor and personally drove him to Dundalk, where the doctor took a urine sample from Mr McParland.

Sergeant Cunningham was subsequently charged with attempting to pervert the course of justice. He claimed on oath that he had Superintendent Staunton's authorisation to set up the roadblock. He was just following orders. The superintendent denied this on oath. The prosecution argued that even if the sergeant's story was accepted — and the prosecution rejected it — he was still guilty, as it was no defence that he acted in concert with a superior to break the law.

The sergeant denied he prevented Dr Gujral from entering Dundalk, he merely told him what was happening and let him make up his own mind.

After considering the evidence for about an hour, the jury found Sergeant Cunningham guilty. The judge sentenced him to nine months in jail. Sergeant Cunningham was forty-three, with four children. He had been on the force for twenty-five years and his career as a garda was now ruined. The judge believed he had suffered enough and suspended the sentence, which seemed fair enough.

Outside the court, a burly and unidentified man walked up to press photographer Tom Conaghy and slammed the photographer's camera into his face, breaking a tooth. The thug got away.

Hotel owner Patrick McParland was, meanwhile, found guilty of drink driving and was fined £150 and disqualified from driving for a year.

Dublin Theatre Festival

Although it is now a routine part of the nation's cultural life, the Dublin Theatre Festival was almost strangled at birth, with scandal piling upon scandal.

In May 1957, the director of a play in the first Dublin Theatre Festival was arrested and thrown in jail. Alan Simpson was staging Tennessee Williams's drama *The Rose Tattoo*, at the Pike Theatre. There is a scene in the play where a character pulls his hands from his pockets and doesn't notice that he has inadvertently pulled out a condom, which falls to the floor. A female character spots the condom and gives him hell for his immoral intentions.

Aware that the sight of a condom might drive Dublin playgoers wild with lustful thoughts, Simpson took the precaution of staging the scene tastefully — there was no condom, the actors reacted to an imaginary condom fallen to the floor.

Even the sight of an invisible condom was too much for the Catholic Ireland of 1957. The League of Decency let loose a howl of despair and the authorities reacted. After the first night, a deputy commissioner of the garda sent an inspector along to the Pike, where Simpson was told that the play would have to be taken off. Simpson thought not. The play went ahead. Some artistic folk stood by Simpson, some found other matters that required their urgent attention. After a couple of nights, four detectives went to the Pike and arrested Simpson, physically wrestling him into submission. He was charged with 'presenting for gain an indecent and profane performance'.

The play was scheduled to transfer to another theatre for a longer run, but the controversy killed that plan stone-dead. Simpson was bailed and the case hung over him for a year, before the charge was dismissed. By that time the 1958 Dublin Theatre Festival was embroiled in controversy. Among the plays lined up were Sean O'Casey's *The Drums of Father Ned*, a dramatisation of James Joyce's *Ulysses*, and three pieces by Samuel Beckett.

Archbishop John Charles McQuaid was outraged. He could live with the Beckett stuff (it was mimed, no words to upset His Grace), but the O'Casey play was unacceptable and as for *Ulysses* — enough said. A broad range of Dublin opinion fell in behind the bishop. And the Dublin Theatre Festival of 1958 was cancelled.

See: *Spike, The*.

Duffy, Paddy

Paddy Duffy was Bertie Ahern's special adviser, in opposition and then in the Taoiseach's office. In December 1998, less than eighteen months after Ahern became Taoiseach, Duffy moved to cash in on the knowledge he had gained of the public service. He agreed to become a director of Dillon Consultants, a public relations and lobbying firm.

Recruiting Duffy was a coup for Dillon's. Companies hire lobbying outfits to steer them towards the appropriate ear into which they should whisper. Someone with Paddy Duffy's inside knowledge of the public service would know what buttons to push. He would also be known to public servants, from departmental clerks to ministers. His phone calls would be returned, he would be taken seriously. His inside knowledge would be invaluable and could give the company that hired Dillon's an edge over one that didn't.

We live in a market economy, just about everything is for sale. As a lobbyist, Duffy could earn far more than his special adviser's pay of £52,000. Unfortunately for him, he made a mess of it.

Dillon's first came to appreciate Duffy's potential in May 1998, when it contacted him to organise a meeting between Ahern and NTL, a client of Dillon's. NTL, a US-based multinational, wanted to buy Cablelink. Duffy set up the meeting. The following month, Duffy and Dillon's talked about Duffy signing up to work for Dillon's as a lobbyist.

On 9 December 1998 Duffy agreed to become a director and was given 5 per cent of Dillon's shares. He signed the necessary documentation. Towards the end of the month, according to Duffy's later claims, he changed his mind. He would stay another year with Ahern before becoming a lobbyist. Duffy would later claim that he told the head of Dillon Consultants, Paul Dillon, that he wanted to withdraw as a director. Dillon would not recall this.

In January 1999 Duffy signed the annual declaration of interests, necessary under public service ethics laws. Although still a director of Dillon's, despite having postponed his move to the firm for a year, he saw no need to declare the connection with the lobbying firm.

In February, Duffy attended a meeting in London with Paul Dillon and executives of a firm called APCO, with which Dillon Consultants was linking up. Duffy discussed the role that he would play within the lobbying firm.

In March, Dillon's filed the documents, in Companies House, which showed Duffy to be a director. The firm advertised his services on its internet website: 'Paddy Duffy, Director — twenty-five years experience as a political adviser at the most senior levels of government'. The most senior level of government is, of course, the Taoiseach's office.

Dillon Consultants offered its clients 'Formal and informal communication channels to government'. Its advert explained: 'Our experience and involvement in both politics and mass media give us access and influence at the highest levels of decision-making and agenda-setting.'

Over the next three months, NTL bought Cablelink for £535 million. Duffy played no role in this.

In April 1999, just before the purchase of Cablelink, Fine Gael's Alan Dukes heard about Duffy's links to Dillon's. He went to Mary O'Rourke, Minister for Public Enterprise, who was responsible for the sale of Cablelink. She immediately asked Ahern if this was true; he immediately asked Duffy if this was true; Duffy said he had no connection with Dillon's.

It didn't occur to Duffy to say a) I'm a director of Dillon's; or b) Dillon's is keeping a directorship open for me when I quit Bertie's office in a few months time; I had discussions in London just two months ago about my role in the firm.

On Wednesday, 2 June, Mark Brennock of *The Irish Times* asked Duffy if he was a director of Dillon's. Duffy immediately responded by claiming that he had been made a director of Dillon's in December 1998, without his knowledge. He said the head of Dillon's, Paul Dillon, made him a director 'as a gesture to me before Christmas. He had intended it as a surprise for me.'

This was nonsense. Duffy had signed the documents making him a director. When Brennock pushed him on this, Duffy accepted that he had known he was being made a director. He now said he told Dillon he had changed his mind and 'through a series of misunderstandings on my own part', was still listed as a director.

The Irish Times published the story on Friday, 4 June, and Duffy resigned the next day. At the heart of the scandal was whether it is proper for public servants to become involved — either before or after leaving the public service — with outfits selling knowledge of and access to the public service.

Dunbar-Harrison, Letitia

The state was still settling down after the war of independence and the civil war, feelings were raw, bigotry was close to the surface. In 1930 Letitia Dunbar-Harrison was appointed to the position of librarian in County Mayo.

The appointment was made by the Local Appointments Commission (LAC), which had been set up by Taoiseach W.T. Cosgrave in an attempt to bring some fairness into local government appointments. Without such a body, every position of financial reward or prestige in a county would be filled with relatives and cronies of the local party mafia.

The Mayo Library Committee, a subcommittee of Mayo County Council, had no role in the matter of appointments other than to endorse the LAC decision. Despite this, a meeting of the committee decided not to endorse the appointment of Letitia Dunbar-Harrison as county librarian. They didn't pussyfoot when they made the decision. There were no spin doctors in those days who might have come up with some halfway credible and unsectarian reason why Dunbar-Harrison was turned down. The committee members were honest to the point of bigotry: they weren't having her as county librarian because she was a Protestant. They threw in an additional disqualification, that she didn't speak Irish.

It turned out that the Catholic applicant that the mafia favoured for the job had failed her Irish exam, but that didn't count. Dunbar-Harrison was a graduate of Trinity College Dublin. At that time, Catholics were forbidden from attending TCD, which was said by the Catholic hierarchy to be a place of perversity, on pain of eternal damnation in the fires of hell.

The committee's vote had no legal standing. Its job was to rubber-stamp the LAC appointment. The government, somewhat embarrassed by the naked sectarianism at work, required Mayo County Council to overrule the Library Committee. Mayo County Council stood by its committee and the government was obliged to dissolve the county council. A bit of local nastiness was quickly becoming a national issue. The minister responsible for dissolving the council was General Richard Mulcahy. He did so not because of the councillors' sectarianism but because it had acted against the law. Besides, 'there are people in this country responsible for dictating to us what safeguards ought to be taken in the matter of religion' and they — the Catholic bishops — had not called for the banishment of Protestants from Mayo library. Of course, given what was going on, the bishops didn't have to.

The forces of Catholic bigotry gathered and surged. The Gaelic League announced that Dunbar-Harrison's appointment was 'one of the worst things done since Cromwell's day'. The Dean of Tuam, Monsignor E.A. D'Alton, had a few words to say: 'We are not appointing a washer-woman or a mechanic, but an educated girl who ought to know what books to put into the hands of the Catholic boys and girls of this county.' It wasn't that the dean wanted Catholic control of reading matter just for its own sake. The control of books had to be held in Catholic hands for fear that the ignorant flock might become exposed to dangerous unCatholic ideas. Suppose there were to come into print books which discussed birth control: 'Is it safe to entrust a girl who is not a Catholic, and is not in sympathy with Catholic views, with their handling?'

The opposition party, Fianna Fáil, in a Dáil debate on the matter, had no doubt about its loyalties. Its leader, Eamon de Valera, echoed the words of the Dean of Tuam: 'If it is a mere passive position of handing down books that are asked for, then the librarian has no particular duty for which religion should be regarded as a qualification,' he said. 'But if the librarian goes round to the homes of the people trying to interest them in books, sees the children in the schools and asks these children to bring home certain books, or asks what their parents would like to read; if it is active work of a propagandist educational character . . . then I say the people of Mayo, where . . . over 98 per cent of the population is Catholic, are justified in insisting upon a Catholic librarian.'

And de Valera, while making noises about the rights of minorities, was looking into his own heart and accurately reflecting the sectarianism of his people. That sectarianism thrived in the period that followed. The commissioner who had been appointed to administrate the county in place of the dissolved council went ahead and appointed Dunbar-Harrison to the library job. This brought about a boycott of the library services and most libraries in the county closed down. The solid united front of Catholic clerics and county councillors and national politicians, supported by their people, held firm and forced the government to bow to the sectarian mood of the day.

Dunbar-Harrison was removed from her post and transferred to the Military Library in Dublin. The next issue of the *Catholic Bulletin* carried the front-page headline, 'Well Done, Mayo'. A year later Fianna Fáil returned to government and the dissolved county council was restored to power.

Duncan, Anthony

It had just turned midnight, into Saturday, 13 April 1996, when departmental officials arrived at the home of Minister for Justice Nora Owen. Less than ninety minutes earlier a detective superintendent from Scotland Yard had arrived in Dublin with an extradition warrant for one Anthony Duncan, aged twenty-six, from Finglas. Part of the procedure involved was that the minister had to look over the case, ensure Duncan wasn't wanted on a political or revenue offence. The minister may intervene to stop the extradition process if either is involved.

As soon as the Scotland Yard officer gave the warrant and its accompanying documentation to the gardaí it was photocopied. Various people would need copies of the documents. One set was given to the Department of Justice officials to include in the file on the case being brought out to the minister's home. The warrant was brought to an assistant garda commissioner, who endorsed it.

At her home, Owen checked the documents: Duncan was wanted in connection with the planting of IRA bombs in Brighton and Bognor Regis two years earlier. Small bombs had been left attached to bicycles. Owen decided she was not obliged to intervene and her officials passed the word immediately to the gardaí that Duncan was to be arrested. At nine o'clock that morning gardaí raided Duncan's house, arrested him and took him to Lucan garda station. He was shown the extradition warrant and at 10.55 on Saturday morning he was brought before Judge Timothy Crowley at the Dublin District Court. There, solicitor Claire Loftus, representing the state, presented the warrant and the detective from Scotland Yard identified Anthony Duncan as the wanted man.

It was at that stage that Judge Crowley and Duncan's solicitor examined the warrant and found there was something missing. The warrant was printed on just one side of a sheet of paper. There should have been certification on the reverse side, but this was missing. This wasn't an original warrant, it was a copy. The case was immediately adjourned.

For the next two hours or so there was frantic background activity in an attempt to save the case, all in vain. At 1.45 p.m. the court reassembled and solicitor Claire Loftus told the judge, 'I am instructed that it is now clear there is a fundamental flaw in the proceedings before the court and in the documentation that has been produced. In those circumstances, I am not in a position to make any application and we cannot proceed further.'

Duncan's solicitor, Michael Hanahoe, asked for the case to be discharged. The judge concurred. Hanahoe said: 'I think it should be said that the document which arrived from England was the document that contained the flaw. I think that should be said.'

The judge was not happy. 'It is not the first time, in my own experience, that documents arriving from England were flawed,' he said. 'I think it is an imposition on the Irish courts that it should happen, and I strongly object to it. I take very grave exception to the time of this court being taken up by flawed documentation.'

Duncan was released. The gardaí immediately decided to arrest him on a charge of membership of the IRA. His supporters waved placards, denounced extradition and threatened photographers. Duncan was brought back before Judge Crowley and remanded in custody to Portlaoise Prison.

The judge was wrong about the source of the fundamental flaw. What happened was this: when the warrant arrived at garda headquarters at around 10.45 p.m that Friday night it was photocopied several times, along with the accompanying documentation. Only the front of the warrant was copied, and the certifications on the back were not copied. Copies of all the documentation were allocated as needed and all the spare copies were shredded. Unfortunately for the police, during the processing of the documentation the original warrant was lost.

The certification on the reverse of the warrant was an essential element. It contained, for instance, the statement of a British police officer that he had seen the warrant being issued by a magistrate. Without such certification the document was worthless.

That Sunday evening, the day after the extradition case collapsed, the British sent a new set of documents to Dublin.

Over that weekend, the media sought to establish what had happened. The British Home Office wouldn't comment to reporters; Scotland Yard, too, said nothing. A source in the Conservative Party claimed that the original documents sent from London were without flaw, but the Irish had presented photocopies to the court. This was quite true, but few paid any attention. In Dublin, 'senior sources' assured the media that the British were to blame. They should have been aware that copies would not suffice, the anonymous sources insisted. Privately, the Minister for Justice asked the gardaí to report on what happened.

Ulster Unionist councillor Reg Empey bought the Dublin line and called on the British Attorney General, Nicholas Lyell, to resign.

On Monday, 15 April 'Garda sources' told *The Irish Times* that 'the failure of the extradition warrant last Saturday was due to mistakes in documentation supplied by the British'.

Nine days later, when the case was mentioned in the Dáil, Taoiseach John Bruton said that he had no reason to believe there was any omission on the Irish side. Nor had he.

When the matter was raised in the Dáil on 15 May, a month after the case collapsed, the Minister for Justice said that the gardaí had not yet established what happened. Six days later Liz O'Donnell TD put down a follow-up Dáil question. That very day, over five weeks after the affair began, the gardaí finally reported to the minister on the conclusion of the official inquiry.

The scandal was not in the simple human error that arose when the warrant was processed; it was in the rush to blame the British, the anonymous briefings which put the blame where it didn't belong.

Wisely, the British continued to keep their mouths shut. Scotland Yard was even yet refusing to comment and the Home Office said it 'could not possibly comment on the actions of another country's police force. There is nothing else to be said.' By refusing to publicly admonish the Irish, the British were building up credit with the Dublin government.

Inevitably, there was someone insisting the whole thing was a conspiracy. David Wilshire, Tory vice-chairman of the backbench Northern Ireland group, said: 'If you expect me to believe this is an accident, then you are expecting me to believe the moon is made of green cheese.'

See: Lynch, Judge Dominic.

Dunne, William

What mattered in the case of *William Dunne v. National Maternity Hospital* wasn't just what happened in court. It was what happened outside the court that was every bit as significant.

There was, for instance, no Nurse Tierney in court. 'I have to challenge you on this,' said Murray McGrath SC, counsel for the National Maternity Hospital: 'I suggest there was no Nurse Tierney involved with you or your wife on the twentieth of March.'

And so, the record would show that Kay and Willie Dunne were less than reliable witnesses. If they dreamed up a Nurse Tierney as being involved in the matter, who knew what else they were dreaming up. Kay might have dreamed up the green notebook in which she told her lawyers she saw Nurse Tierney making notes after William was born. No such notebook was made available by the hospital.

Kay and Willie Dunne sued the NMH on behalf of their son, William, born severely brain-damaged at the hospital on Saturday, 20 March 1982. William's twin died. The case opened at the High Court in Dublin on 5 July 1988.

After hearing detailed medical evidence, the jury was out for almost eight hours when it found in favour of William Dunne and awarded him over a million pounds.

The hospital appealed. The crunch issue had been the monitoring of foetal hearts. The hospital had monitored only one heart when Kay was in labour. The Dunnes' lawyers argued that the other twin was in distress, leading to its death and consequent brain damage to William. If the hospital had monitored both hearts, they argued, the tragedy would not have happened.

Hospital personnel disputed this and swore that it was hospital policy to monitor only one foetal heart in twin pregnancies and that this was sound medical practice. The jury found against the hospital and made its million-pound award.

The Supreme Court overturned the verdict. The trial judge, said the Supreme Court, had failed to spell out a legal principle for the jury: if monitoring only one heart in a twin pregnancy was a 'general and approved practice' the hospital could not be found negligent.

But it wasn't a 'general and approved practice'. The hospital hadn't brought a single doctor to court who could testify that this was the practice in any other hospital in the world. However, the Supreme Court defined 'general and approved practice' as meaning a practice 'adhered to by a substantial number of reputable practitioners'. And five doctors from the NMH who had given evidence that they adhered to that practice were enough to constitute a substantial number of medical practitioners.

The case was retried. The Dunnes had to sell their ex-council house to fund the case. On the fifth day of the retrial the lawyers had to leave the court in a hurry, as the judge prepared to hear another matter. The Dunnes' solicitor, in a rush, picked up the wrong bundle of documents, belonging to the hospital's solicitor. That night he found, in that bundle of documents, Nurse Tierney's notebook. Kay Dunne had been telling the truth.

There was nothing sinister in this, the court was assured, it was a mistake. The hospital's solicitor told the court she had received the notebook in the course of a five-minute conversation with the nurse during the first trial. She never opened the notebook and hadn't thought it to be of any significance to the case.

While the court was discussing this matter, the Dunnes noticed that Nurse Tierney had just walked into court. The nurse took the stand and told how during the first trial she had been interviewed by a barrister in wig and gown who had examined her notebook. He was not any of the barristers involved in the case (and she didn't remember who had introduced her). He said the notes on Kay Dunne in her notebook weren't significant. Nurse Tierney was later told her evidence would not be required. The Dunnes' lawyers had known nothing of this.

The appearance of the nurse who previously didn't exist was disturbing enough. What happened next was stranger still.

In the interval between the Supreme Court decision and the retrial, Kay and Willie Dunne turned detective and tracked down one woman after another who had given birth to twins in the NMH. Ten of them agreed to come to court. One by one they took the stand and swore that during their labour the hospital had monitored both foetal hearts.

The case went no further. There was a break to allow the judge attend some conference and before the case resumed the hospital offered

£400,000 in settlement. The Dunnes, fearful of another Supreme Court reversal even if they won the retrial, agreed to settle.

The mysterious barrister who had interviewed Nurse Tierney during the first trial was never identified. The Bar Council declined to take an interest in exploring how it was that one of its members — or someone impersonating a barrister — had intervened in the case.

See: Gallagher, Blaise.

Dunne Family Wars

Almost all of the dramatic scandals and revelations which rocked Irish political life from the 1990s can be traced to an anonymous fixer working for Stouffer's Resort Hotel, Orlando, Florida. It was he who provided Ben Dunne with over forty grammes of cocaine in February 1992. Dunne was on a golfing holiday, paying for his mates to accompany him. He rented female escorts and sniffed line after line of cocaine, almost like a parody of the respectable businessman away from home.

Surrounded by friends, yet obviously very lonely and more than a bit disturbed, Dunne moved to a more expensive hotel, the Grand Cypress, paid $300 to rent a woman — Denise Wojcik — from an agency called Escorts in a Flash, and eventually freaked out, after a bizarre night spent sniffing lines of cocaine like a berserk hoover. He stood screaming on a balcony, seventeen floors above the hotel lobby, until a bunch of cops grabbed him and dragged him off, struggling all the way, to hospital. A police officer searched the room and found a huge stash of cocaine and almost ten grand in cash. The cop screwed up the search procedure and the charges against Dunne were minimised, from trafficking to possession. He was sentenced to attend an expensive London clinic to discuss his drug habits and was fined $5,000.

The real punishment was that his beloved position as head of the Dunnes Stores empire was to be snatched away. The Dunne empire had been built by Ben Dunne Sr, who died in 1983. He locked his five children — Margaret, Ben, Frank, Elizabeth and Therese — into a trust. In 1992 the empire was worth about £600 million.

On his return from Florida, Ben adopted a media strategy devised by his friend, businessman and solicitor Noel Smyth. The Dunnes had always guarded their privacy, but Ben now made himself available to journalists and frankly owned up to his failings. It worked. I was a fool, said Ben, I must accept responsibility, I'm sorry, I'll never do it again. And, charmed by his frankness, the media portrayed Dunne as a sheepish little boy caught with his hand in the cookie jar. Ben discovered that if you feed journalists they end up licking your hand.

Ben's sister, Margaret Heffernan, was outraged at the Florida episode. War erupted within the family. In July 1993 one of the sisters — Elizabeth — died suddenly. A second, Therese, would die suddenly a couple of years later. The tragedies didn't seem to turn the family's thoughts to the fragility of life, the impermanence of empire and the primacy of love, warmth and familial affection. According to affidavits made as the family war deteriorated into litigation, an ally of Ben's was ordered from his office, the locks were changed; Ben ended up screaming down a phone line, calling a Dunnes executive a 'fucking bollocks'. Then, Ben stormed into a meeting Margaret was having with some Waterford Foods executives. He was 'incoherent' and stubbed out his cigarette in Margaret's glass of mineral water.

Ben was reportedly earning a million and a half pounds a year around then, he was bought out for over a hundred million and the litigation was settled out of court. But before that happened, Margaret had commissioned a report from Price Waterhouse which examined Ben's conduct of financial matters; Ben had compiled a document aimed at portraying the family trust as illusory. Among the items dealt with in these documents were the financing of an extension to Fine Gael minister Michael Lowry's house, and payments to a certain Mr Haughey.

It was the material generated as a result of the Dunne family wars which led to the exposure of the multiple scandals which would keep us outraged and entertained right into the new millennium.

Journalist Sam Smyth got hold of the Lowry information. That tugged at a thread; journalist Cliff Taylor found out about the payments to Haughey; pretty soon the whole thing was unravelling. The McCracken Tribunal looked into the Dunnes payments to politicians, and exposed enough dodgy goings-on to necessitate the Moriarty Tribunal, to take the investigation further.

Back in Orlando, Florida, that hotel employee who provided the nose candy for Ben Dunne probably hadn't a clue what he started.

See: Haughey, Charlie; Lowry, Michael.

E

Embezzlement: Russell Murphy

When Russell Murphy told Gay Byrne he was dying of cancer, the broadcaster broke down and cried. At the accountant's funeral, Byrne later wrote, his tears were uncontrollable: 'I did not cry like that for my mother or my father . . . I was weeping, I suppose, for the end of an era. Russell was more than a good friend to me, I thought. He was my guide.'

Gay Byrne first met Charles Russell Murphy in 1959. Byrne was an up-and-coming broadcaster. Murphy was a well-known accountant, the best in the business. He was a flamboyant character, particularly popular among theatre folk. He became a father figure to Gay Byrne, a godfather to one of his daughters, the sort of friend who featured in their family rituals.

Russell Murphy was to handle all Gay Byrne's financial affairs for twenty-five years. Byrne trusted him completely. Murphy's clients, wrote Byrne, 'were envied. If you were with Russell Murphy you were in good hands and you were obviously a person of substance.' Murphy was a founder member of Bank of Ireland Finance, a director of both Bank of Ireland and Bank of Ireland Finance. After his death, friends searching for a word to apply to Russell spoke of his 'gravitas', his depth of seriousness, his trustworthiness.

Gay Byrne signed cheques and documents as requested. 'Our friendship prospered and so, I thought, did my affairs.' Everything appeared to be documented. Annual accounts were duly inspected.

Not long after Russell Murphy's death in 1984, Conor Dignam, one of the accountants who worked in his office, phoned Gay Byrne on a Sunday, saying he had to see him urgently. He drove out to Howth and told the broadcaster: 'I'm sorry to have to tell you this, but it's all gone.' Russell Murphy had taken at least one and a half million pounds from several clients. From Gay Byrne he had taken everything.

Murphy had to have known that his crimes would one day be exposed. The lies could not go on for ever. It didn't seem to bother him, and he blithely and ruthlessly used his friendships to line his pockets. An early death spared him the shame of exposure, but he must have known that once he was gone the secrets would come out. He appears not to have felt the need to make his peace with his clients or his close friend, Gay

Byrne, in that final period. To the end, he kept up the mask of professionalism, the mask of friendship.

Murphy stole from others, too, notably playwright Hugh Leonard, who lost a quarter of a million pounds. But to Gay Byrne there was the double blow, the loss of money and the ruthless betrayal: 'He was one of my closest friends . . . yet he embezzled all my life's savings.' Worse still, he borrowed money for himself, using Gay Byrne's investments as collateral. The most famous man in Ireland found himself, aged fifty, betrayed, broke and in debt. Murphy had even mortgaged Byrne's home and the broadcaster found himself telephoning various banks trying to find out which one had the deeds to his home.

The effect on Byrne was deep and lasting. Hugh Leonard could laugh ruefully, chalk it up to experience and carry on; Byrne not only lost all his money but the betrayal of his friendship shattered him. For a time his handwriting deteriorated to the point where he could not write a coherent sentence, the pen slid off the page. He had a pop psychology explanation: having signed whatever Murphy put in front of him, his mind now recoiled and his hand failed when it came time to sign anything.

Prior to the exposure of Murphy's duplicity hardly any financial scandals erupted so publicly. Murphy's lack of scruple seemed unusual in the Ireland of the mid-1980s, where trust in professionals in the financial world was still the norm. In a way, the Russell Murphy scandal was a forerunner of the wave of greed, lawbreaking and treachery which would be exposed in business and banking within a few years.

F

Fairview Park Murder

Declan Flynn almost made it out of Fairview Park alive. He was running across the grass, along the hedge around the playground towards the lights and safety of the main road. Behind him a gang of five young men followed. About ten yards on the wrong side of the gate they caught him. They beat and kicked him — five against one — until he lay silent in his own blood. Panicked now, they turned him on his side and they ran from the park. Before they ran they took his watch and £4 from his pocket.

Declan Flynn, a 31-year-old Aer Rianta employee from Whitehall, Dublin, inhaled his own blood as he lay there unconscious and died from asphyxia.

It didn't take the gardaí long to track down the culprits. The gang couldn't keep quiet about what had happened and, besides, they often bragged about beating up people in Fairview Park. They called it 'queer-bashing', beating up men they thought might be homosexual. There was another layer of pain added to the agony of the dead man's family as the crime was reported as the work of a gang who thought beating up homosexuals was a bit of a lark.

In March 1983 the case against Robert Armstrong, eighteen, Anthony Maher, eighteen, Colm Donovan, seventeen, Patrick Kavanagh, eighteen, and a fifteen-year-old whose name could not be reported, was heard by Justice Sean Gannon in the Central Criminal Court. The five pleaded guilty to manslaughter. At least three of the five had carried out previous attacks in the park. Anthony Maher's statement explained: 'A few of us had been queer-bashing for about six weeks before and had battered twenty steamers. We used to grab them. If they hit back we gave it to them.' As Robert Armstrong told the court: 'We were all part of the team to get rid of queers from Fairview Park.' On the night in question, Anthony Maher said: 'We didn't mean to kill Mr Flynn. I thought he was gay and was in the park to meet other gay people.' Patrick Kavanagh told the court it was the first time he'd attacked anyone in the park. In retrospect, he said: 'I think we made a mistake about Mr Flynn.'

Justice Gannon sentenced Armstrong and Maher to five years, Donovan to four years, Kavanagh to two years, the juvenile to twelve months. All the sentences were suspended and the five young men walked free. The judge said he must demonstrate the abhorrence of the community by imposing sentences but he didn't think it necessary they be served immediately. If the men got into trouble again, they would have to serve their time.

Two days later TDs in the Dáil were calling for Justice Gannon's resignation. Proinsias De Rossa said the only reasonable interpretation of the sentence was that the life of a person of certain sexual tendencies appeared to be in some way less valuable than that of any other person. David Norris said the outcome 'could be interpreted as a licence to kill'.

The Fairview Park case happened at a time of considerable public disquiet about the apparent discrepancies in sentences handed down by the courts and there was much debate, in the Dáil and in various media, about mandatory sentences, sentencing guidelines or at least sentencing seminars for judges.

Declan Flynn's father, Christopher, who said his dead son was not a homosexual, was horrified at the outcome of the case. 'I had expected that justice would be done and would be seen to be done.' Even the culprits expected to go to prison. After all, they'd gone into the park with the express purpose of finding someone to beat up. In fact, Declan Flynn was their second victim that night. They just hadn't planned on him dying. Talking to Maggie O'Kane of *Magill* after the case, Robert Armstrong said even after the judge imposed the suspended sentence he thought that meant he was going to jail. He said to his mother: 'What's happening, what's he mean?' 'You're coming home,' she said.

That was 1983 and Robert Armstrong was eighteen. When he was twenty-three he was back in court pleading guilty to raping a woman who was seven months pregnant. He and another man had broken into the woman's flat in Ballymun in the middle of the night. She was alone with her two young children. They were intent on robbery but then, as Armstrong told the court: 'We noticed that she had a flimsy nightgown that could be seen through.' So, they both raped her. Armstrong gave the children sweets to keep them quiet.

Judge Michael Moriarty, in the Dublin Circuit Criminal Court, described Armstrong as 'a considerable danger to society'. He sentenced him to ten years in prison.

Favours: None Sought or Given

Throughout the mid-to-late-1990s period of financial scandals the mantra repeated by various parties was 'No favours were sought or given.' Whenever a politician was caught taking a chunk of money from wealthy interests we were assured that 'no favours were sought or given', so everything was okay.

The tribunals set up to inquire into various scandals were given the impossible task of matching a particular gift of money to a specified favour. A politician or his party might receive fistfuls of money 'for electoral purposes'; some of that politician's decisions might benefit the donor of money; but a definite link still had to be made between a particular gift and a specified favour. Short of uncovering a piece of paper on which the politician promises to make a certain decision on foot of receiving a bribe, the task of proving a link between donations and favours is next to impossible. Every decision made by a politician can be said to have been made for any number of legitimate reasons.

Failure to produce such absolute evidence leads to the politician claiming he has been investigated and vindicated.

The evidence suggests that only the stupid or desperate enter into straightforward money-for-favours deals. More often, the money is seen as an entrance fee into a Golden Circle, where people look out for one another. The more clever business interests spread their money around various political parties. Legislation would invariably be kept within the parameters acceptable to the circle. Things undone mattered every bit as much as things done. The beauty of the system was that you could be part of it and quite sincerely believe yourself to have nothing to do with even the slightest whiff of corruption.

Fethard Boycott

Sean Cloney and Sheila Kelly grew up together as neighbours, both from farming families near the County Wexford village of Fethard-on-Sea, on the Hook peninsula. They remained close and as young adults began to go out together. And there the local curate stepped in. This was in the 1940s and Sean was a Catholic, Sheila a Protestant. Sean was advised to break off the relationship.

But Sean and Sheila weren't easily influenced and they went off to England where they married in a registry office. Later they were married in both Catholic and Protestant churches. Sheila, as was the requirement at the time under the papal *Ne Temere* decree, signed a promise to raise any children they might have in the Catholic faith.

By 1957 Sean and Sheila were back in Fethard. They had two daughters and the elder, Eileen, was nearly six and would have to go to school. A priest came to call and told Sheila bluntly that the child would have to attend a Catholic school.

The months passed and the pressure increased. In Sean Cloney's words, his wife 'didn't fancy being ordered'. He knew she was thinking of leaving and one day at the end of April he came home to find Sheila and the two children gone. Her family had no idea where she'd gone. The gardaí discovered her car abandoned in Wexford town, but there were no other clues. A few days later, Belfast barrister and associate of Dr Ian Paisley Desmond Boal arrived from Belfast to tell Sean his wife would consider returning if Sean would become a Protestant. Sean said no to this, but contact was maintained through Boal. Eventually, Sean was reunited with his wife and daughters, who were by that time living in the Orkneys.

Back among Fethard-on-Sea Catholics, it was thought, wrongly and unfairly, that the local Protestant church was involved in whisking the children away. On 13 May 1957 Catholics, led by the local clergy, began boycotting and shunning their Protestant neighbours and friends. Sheila's father, a cattle dealer, was among the first victims, because he had dared to give his daughter £40 before she left. Two Protestant shopkeepers lost all their Catholic customers; a Protestant music teacher lost eleven of her twelve pupils; and the Catholic schoolteacher at the local Protestant primary school resigned.

A Catholic bishop described it as a 'peaceful and moderate protest', and said that 'there seems to be a concerted campaign to entice or kidnap Catholic children and deprive them of their faith'. Not all Catholics agreed and when the matter was raised in the Dáil the then Taoiseach, Eamon de Valera, said that he had hoped 'good sense and decent neighbourly feelings would, of themselves, bring this business to an end'. He described the boycott as ill-conceived, unjust and cruel.

Sean Cloney did what he could to fight the boycott, but to little effect. Speaking on *The Gay Byrne Show* in December 1998 he recalled: 'At that time there was great fear of the power of the clergy. That if they disobeyed the clergy some blight or curse would befall them.'

Eventually, after more than a year, the boycott ended. The local priest went into one of the Protestant shops to buy a pack of cigarettes. His flock knew it was okay by the clergy to end the bigotry. But the shadow cast remains even now. Sean Cloney said people still don't want to talk about it. 'The Catholics are ashamed and the Protestants have a certain fear about what happened then. They don't want to talk about it either. 'Tis a very unhappy memory for them.'

As for Sean and Sheila, they were reconciled and after living for a while in England returned home. The issue of their daughters' education was never resolved. Sean said: 'Whether they went to a Protestant school or a Catholic school would have been seen as a victory for one side or the other, so they never went to school and we educated them ourselves.' Never a man to bow to authority, Sean Cloney was one of those who later helped put a stop to the activities of child abuser Fr Sean Fortune.

In May 1998 the Fethard scandal was finally put to rest when Bishop Brendan Comiskey publicly apologised and asked for forgiveness on behalf of his diocese, expressing 'deep sorrow and my promise to do whatever I can to make amends'. Sean Cloney said, 'I am glad to have lived to see this day.' A movie based on the event, *A Love Divided*, was released in 1999.

See: Fortune, Fr Sean.

FitzGerald, Garret

When Garret FitzGerald left politics he was made a director of Guinness Peat Aviation. In the early 1990s, to be favoured by the entrepreneurial giants who ran GPA was to be smiled on by the gods. GPA was an aeroplane-leasing company headed by Tony Ryan which had been spectacularly successful. More important, it was about to be floated on the stock market; money was about to flood into GPA and anyone holding shares was going to become very wealthy indeed.

FitzGerald fitted in snugly onto the GPA board. Also there was Peter Sutherland. Garret had been good to Peter. He had made him Attorney General and EU commissioner, the latter position allowing Peter to show off his talents and make the connections which would later see his career blossom, culminating with Sutherland being lifted into a multimillion-pound position at Goldman Sachs.

FitzGerald had an opportunity to buy GPA shares at $22 — a rock-bottom price; they were bound to shoot up. After a lifetime in public service, FitzGerald was comfortable but had no pot of gold. This was his chance to make a killing. He would borrow big and make his fortune. He went to AIB, borrowed some hundreds of thousands of pounds and bought 22,655 shares in GPA.

The flotation bombed. GPA went into a nosedive. The value of the shares fell. FitzGerald had gambled and lost. This is the famous 'risk' which wealthy business people talk about, the 'risk' they take which justifies the enormous rewards they are handed by their fellow 'risk-takers'.

FitzGerald owed a lot of money. AIB was welcome to the shares, and FitzGerald downsized his living accommodation, as many retired people do. He sold his house on Palmerston Road to his auctioneer son, Mark, and moved into an apartment in the house. FitzGerald remained more than comfortable, with a state pension worth around £60,000 a year, other business interests and a lucrative journalism sideline. From the sale of his house, he paid off his mortgage and was still about £230,000 in debt to AIB. He paid around £50,000 and the bank wrote off the rest of the debt. (There was also a small amount written off by Ansbacher Bank.)

AIB also paid for the gambling of other GPA investors, some of them more clever than FitzGerald. While Garret had taken out a straight loan, others took out 'non-recourse' loans. This meant that the only asset the bank could claim against the loan was the shares themselves. It was like getting a loan from a bank because you knew of a sure thing in the 3.30

at Leopardstown. The horse breaks a leg, and you give the bank your betting docket and walk away, not owing a penny. This is the 'risk' engaged in by such entrepreneurs.

FitzGerald hadn't known about the 'non-recourse' trick, and had to pay back some of his loan, but the bank let him off the greater part of the debt, anyway. In those circles, people are not supposed to pay their way in such circumstances, someone else will do it for them. These unpleasant matters are placed in a 'bad debt' category and claimed against the bank's tax liabilities. The taxpayer picks up the tab.

Fixing Court Fines

In April 1995 a retired district justice, Patrick Brennan, took a High Court case in order to challenge a tradition of political fixing of court convictions. The scandal of political fixing had been bubbling along for years, but no one had bothered to do anything about it.

There is a procedure known as petitioning, in which people convicted of offences ask that their fines or jail sentences be reduced. In theory it adds a humanitarian element to the hard-nosed world of criminal justice. In practice it became a routine matter of political interference with the courts. It was for that reason that Patrick Brennan brought the case; as a judge, he had become fed up administering what he believed was justice, fining people who committed offences, and then watching as the political fix went in.

It worked like this: you are caught for a minor offence, you don't fancy paying the fine, so you visit your local TD. In a political culture in which politicians set themselves up as super social workers, getting — or pretending to get — grants and houses and street lights and public phone boxes for their constituents, it became normal for politicians to be asked to help fix a fine. The politician contacts the Minister for Justice, who considers the case and puts in the fix.

In theory petitions were supposed to come from people who had been fined but who had fallen on hard times; the petition could bring an element of human concern where the law was bound by rules and conventions. Now, however, there were civil servants employed full-time processing the petitions flooding in from politicians doing favours for constituents. (The politicians might have done the paperwork themselves but they were too busy making tough law and order speeches.) By 1995 there were about 5,000 petitions a year hitting the Department of Justice. Two-thirds of these resulted in the reduction or dropping of fines.

Irish Times reporter John Maher came across a 1992 case in which a man was convicted of dangerous driving and driving without insurance. He was sentenced to five months in jail. He appealed and lost. So he petitioned the Minister for Justice, Máire Geoghegan-Quinn. She turned it down. The government changed following the 1992 general election and the man used his local TD to petition the new Minister for Justice, Nora Owen. She wrote back that she was making 'further inquiries' and added: 'This acknowledgment may be produced to the gardaí as confirmation that the above sentence is under re-petition.'

The minister's letter was sent to the cops. They did nothing: the minister's letter had the effect of putting the case on hold. The minister did nothing. Four and a half years went by. Finally, the man couldn't stand the suspense any longer and he went to the police and asked if it was all right if he did his time in prison. At that stage the matter became public. The man went to jail.

Former judge Patrick Brennan wanted the system declared unconstitutional. The High Court would not go that far but on 28 April 1995 said that the manner in which the petition system was being worked was an abuse of the Minister for Justice's power of pardon, that the minister 'appeared to have exercised a kind of parallel system of justice', and that the minister should use the power to remit sentences only in the 'rarest of circumstances'. After the case, petitions dropped to about 1,600 a year.

Flanagan, Oliver J.

A smarmy, vicious man, Flanagan came to epitomise the cute hoor in Irish politics. In later life, claiming on *The Late Late Show* that 'there was no sex in Ireland before television', he became a figure of fun, a fundamentalist clown. In his younger days he was a convinced anti-Semite. In the Locke Tribunal Report of 1947 he was characterised as a liar by the three judges who conducted the tribunal. It didn't do him any harm.

Flanagan first stood for the Dáil, in Laois-Offaly, in 1943, at the age of twenty-three. He had been elected to Laois County Council the previous year. He stood on the Monetary Reform ticket. Monetary Reform was a respectable way of saying Blame the Jews. The myth that Jews had a stranglehold on the world's financial system was part of the fascist ideology of the day. In Germany it had already helped bring about the holocaust. In Ireland a Catholic priest named Fr Denis Fahey was one of a number of people who tried to stir up anti-Jewish feeling. Oliver J.

Flanagan saw himself as a Christian warrior. Here he is, in the middle of the 1943 general election campaign, writing to Fr Fahey:

> Just a line letting you know we are going ahead with the Election campaign in Laoighis-Offaly against the Jew-Masonic System which is imposed on us. The people are coming to us — but it's hard to get the people to understand how they are held down by the Jews and Masons who control their very lives. I did as you told me to — placed my trust in our Blessed Lady and I am sure I will get a good vote here. The cause is a great one — for God and Ireland, and I hope we will win.

Once elected to the Dáil, in June 1943, Flanagan stood up in the chamber and made his views plain:

> How is it that we do not see any of these [emergency orders] directed against the Jews who crucified Our Saviour 1,900 years ago and who are crucifying us every day of this week? . . . There is one thing that Germany did and that was to rout the Jews out of their country. Until we rout the Jews out of this country it does not matter a hair's breadth what orders you make. Where the bees are there is the honey, and where the Jews are there is the money.

Flanagan more than doubled his vote at the general election the following year, from 4,377 to 9,856. After his lying to the Locke Tribunal in 1947 was exposed his vote at the 1948 general election soared to 14,369. Two years later he joined Fine Gael and in 1954 was made a parliamentary secretary, or junior minister. He got a similar position in 1975, in Liam Cosgrave's coalition, and after Paddy Donegan's 'thundering disgrace' debacle Flanagan replaced him as Minister for Defence. He was secretly a Knight of Columbanus and in 1978 Pope John Paul I conferred on him a Knighthood of St Gregory the Great. He remained a TD until 1987.

See: Locke's Distillery; Thundering Disgrace.

Flood Tribunal

This might well have been called the June 1989 Tribunal, as it came to centre on transactions which allegedly occurred at that time.

It was in June 1989 that Michael Bailey of Bovale Developments, a property developer, wrote to James Gogarty of the building company JMSE, inquiring about plans for around 700 acres of land owned by JMSE in north Dublin. Bailey was a Fianna Fáil supporter, known to party stalwarts such as Ray Burke. In the letter to Gogarty he claimed to be able to get the rezoning and planning permission which would transform the value of the land. It would take two years to achieve this and if JMSE wanted to go ahead, Bailey would take half the land as a fee for his services.

And it was just a few days later, in June 1989, that Bailey drove James Gogarty to the home of Ray Burke. Gogarty was carrying £30,000. He would allege — and Bailey would deny — that he also had a cheque for £10,000 and that Bailey had another £40,000 for Burke. 'Will we get a receipt for this?' Gogarty allegedly asked as they drove out. 'Will we fuck!' allegedly replied Bailey.

Gogarty would allege that he was paying Ray Burke a bribe on behalf of JMSE. And JMSE would allege that Gogarty was off on 'a frolic of his own'.

The Flood Tribunal came to concern itself with whether Bailey brought £40,000 for Burke — which both Bailey and Burke denied; and whether Gogarty's employer, Joseph Murphy Jr, was along on the trip to Burke's house (which everyone except Gogarty denied). To the rest of us it hardly seemed worth mounting a tribunal to find out how many people went to Burke's house, or precisely how much they gave him. The central fact is agreed: people with an interest in developing land made a pilgrimage to the house of a leading politician and a large amount of money was passed over. The minister accepted the money.

It was also in June 1989 that developer Tom Gilmartin allegedly gave £50,000 to Fianna Fáil's Pádraig Flynn.

Gilmartin was an Irish developer who had made a fortune in London and who returned to Ireland with great plans for developments at Liffey Valley and in the centre of Dublin. He came up against various obstacles and was told by friends that what he really ought to do was make a big contribution to Fianna Fáil. He did that, he believed, by giving £50,000 to Pádraig Flynn. Fianna Fáil never got the money; the obstacles remained in Gilmartin's way and he went back to England, a bitter man.

The Flood Tribunal, chaired by Mr Justice Fergus Flood, set out in 1998 to inquire into these matters and was delayed by various legal manoeuvres, which is standard operating procedure. When it began hearing the evidence of James Gogarty, in January 1999, it ran into very muddy waters and its progress slowed almost to a stop. Gogarty's play-acting, his determination to use the witness stand to blackguard people he didn't like, caused ructions. Garret Cooney SC, counsel for JMSE, took an age to cross-examine Gogarty, with lots of argy-bargy between the two. Cooney claimed that Judge Flood was biased against JMSE and that counsel for the tribunal was attempting to 'sabotage' his cross-examination.

These extraordinary allegations almost led to a breakdown of the tribunal. Judge Flood was not best pleased. Counsel for Bovale, Colm Allen, announced that he was preparing a 'big, big ambush' for Gogarty. Since an ambush is a surprise attack, it seemed rather silly to announce it in advance. In the event, it was widely agreed that the big, big ambush was small beer. Gogarty, a cantankerous old crook, ran rings around the two learned friends.

When Joseph Finnegan SC, counsel for Ray Burke, came to cross-examine Gogarty, he was brief and to the point. In less than forty minutes of courteous cross-examination, he disarmed Gogarty's usual tactic of playing the old martyr under attack from high-paid and aggressive lawyers. Finnegan laid out Burke's case and through simple questioning ascertained where Burke's story differed from Gogarty's.

One figure hovering at the edge of the tribunal's hearings gradually began to shift towards centre stage. George Redmond, assistant city and county manager, a central figure in the development of Dublin over the past three decades, was the subject of allegations by James Gogarty. That didn't mean much. Allegations are easily denied and who was to say which of two old men (if either) was telling the truth?

Suddenly, the scandal was taken onto a whole new level. On the evening of Friday, 19 February 1999 word started spreading: George Redmond had been arrested at Dublin airport, on his way back from the Isle of Man, with about £300,000 on him. The Criminal Assets Bureau had been tipped off and was keeping an eye on Redmond. In the weeks that followed other allegations emerged: of Redmond's loan of around £100,000 to a Dublin amusement parlour owner; of Redmond calling to the amusement parlour each week, to pick up a bundle of money; of George Redmond doing his grocery shopping at a wholesaler's, year after year, and charging his purchases to a pub owned by the amusement parlour owner; of a £10,000 gift to Redmond from toll bridge builder Tom Roche.

CAB investigators were reported to have found around twenty accounts under the control of George Redmond, with evidence that about a million pounds had passed through those accounts over the previous twenty years. Redmond was hit with a half-million-pound tax assessment, with possibly another million and a half in interest and penalties, and in July 1999 was charged with tax offences.

Almost in spite of itself, the Flood Tribunal, slow and lumbering, ill-tempered and at times absurd, by its very existence was beating the undergrowth in the world of planning and developing and all sorts of interesting people were to be found popping their heads up to say that favours were neither sought nor given.

Flynn, Eileen

Eileen Flynn had a few options open to her when she found out she was pregnant in 1981. She could have an abortion; she could give the child up for adoption; she could struggle on her own as a single mother; or she, the baby's father and siblings could continue to live happily as a family. Not surprisingly, she decided the last option was the best for everyone concerned. However, the nuns who employed her as a teacher in the Holy Faith convent school in New Ross, County Wexford, didn't agree. Eileen Flynn, twenty-six, was sacked in August 1982, just two months after her baby boy was born.

The official record holds that Eileen Flynn was not fired because she was pregnant. That would automatically be deemed unfair under section 6 (2)(f) of the Unfair Dismissals Act. The Employment Appeals Tribunal, the Circuit Court and the High Court all held that the nuns were entitled to dismiss her because by her relationship with a married man she openly rejected the standards of behaviour the school existed to promote. The pregnancy was simply proof of the nature of that relationship. That she was a good teacher who was paid by the state didn't matter.

Eileen Flynn came to New Ross in 1978 to work as a substitute teacher in the Good Counsel College. When a permanent position came up in the Holy Faith school, she received a strong recommendation from the college. One day, in the town, she came across a young child who had fallen down, hurt herself and was crying. She picked her up, brushed her down and brought her home. Home was Richie Roche's pub, a place described at the time as bohemian by New Ross standards. Richie Roche himself was described as a tall, gangly man with a beard and thinning red hair. He was married but separated, and vice-chairman of the local Sinn Féin cumann.

Meanwhile, the nuns of the Holy Faith Convent said they were hearing complaints about Ms Flynn's timekeeping, reports that she was not correcting homework and concerns about her public activities. But there was no written record of these complaints.

When the autumn term began in 1981, the principal had heard rumours that Eileen Flynn was living with Richie Roche. She later said she told the teacher she was keeping a file on her. By November Eileen Flynn was pregnant. Like many a woman before her, she bought a corset and hoped to get through the coming months undetected.

On 28 April 1982 news of Eileen Flynn's pregnancy reached Sister Anna Power, the manager of Holy Faith Schools in Ireland. She arrived in New Ross the next day and, as she told the Employment Appeals Tribunal: 'I put it to her it would be in her best interest if she could find alternative employment.' She also suggested that her brother, a parish priest in England, would look after her. Eileen Flynn turned down the offer. As she told the tribunal: 'I explained that I could not stand back from the situation. I was living in the town. My responsibilities and my life were there. It was not that I was pregnant. I was a family unit in everything but name.'

It was a point of view Sister Anna couldn't accept: 'She just flaunted it and did not try to hide it or to redeem herself.'

After failing at the Employment Appeals Tribunal, Eileen Flynn appealed her case to the Circuit Court and the High Court and lost both times. The outrage of teaching unions, women's groups, civil liberties groups and some politicians had no impact. Giving judgment in the Circuit Court case, Judge Noel Ryan said: 'Times are changing and we must change with them, but they have not changed that much in this or the adjoining jurisdiction with regard to some things. In other places women are being condemned to death for this sort of offence. They are not Christians in the Far East. I do not agree with this, of course. Here people take a serious view of this and it is idle to shut one's eyes to it.'

See: Kerry Babies; Lovett, Ann.

Flynn, Pádraig: £50,000

Why would a grown man with a serious job allow himself to be given a nickname as silly as Pee? And why would he refer to himself, in the third person, by that same nickname? Inexplicable, really, but it says a lot about Pádraig Flynn. On the face of it, an overweening buffoon but, behind the bluster, an intelligent and effective politician. There was many a cringe across the country when Pádraig Flynn was sent to Brussels as EU commissioner in 1993. But, as it happened, the cute hoor from Castlebar proved himself more than able for the job. Over the top, maybe, but Commissioner Flynn won respect among EU officials and politicians.

He looked a certain bet for a third term until property developer Tom Gilmartin came along with his allegation about a £50,000 donation. Gilmartin said he gave the money to Pádraig Flynn in 1989 when the latter was Minister for the Environment and treasurer of Fianna Fáil. Gilmartin was trying to get the political backing he needed to proceed with a massive motorway shopping centre at Quarryvale, to the west of Dublin, and another development at Bachelor's Walk in the city centre. As he remembered it, he lobbied various politicians and their minders and he was asked repeatedly whether he had given a donation to the party. He said he gave Pádraig Flynn £50,000 to get Fianna Fáil 'off my back' on planning issues.

In September 1998, in response to a story in the *Sunday Independent*, Pádraig Flynn flatly denied ever having received the money. Later, he said the *Independent* had 'misrepresented' his reply. Later still, he said he would not comment further, that anything he had to say he would say if called to give evidence to the Flood Tribunal of Inquiry into Payments to Politicians. In an interview with RTÉ radio he reminded listeners: 'You must understand that political donations to political parties or individuals — there's nothing illegal about that. There never was.'

Meanwhile, Fianna Fáil let it be known it never got the £50,000, though Gilmartin was adamant it was intended as a party donation. He had been told that making political donations was widely thought to be a good idea for anyone in his line of business.

So did Pádraig Flynn get the money that was intended for Fianna Fáil? It was a story that might have faded into the background until Justice Flood finally got around to it. But, instead of keeping his head down, the commissioner agreed to appear on *The Late Late Show* of 15 January 1999 and triggered his own destruction.

Commissioner Flynn, the Brussels sophisticate, would have tread more carefully. But the man with Gay Byrne that night was our old friend Pee Flynn, the same fellow who, by his crassness, put Mary Robinson into the Park. He was in rare form, having a whale of a time, telling Gay Byrne and his viewers what a great job he was doing in Europe. He had been honoured by a British university so, proud as punch, he read out the memorised citation. Politicians, he remarked, were either 'front runners' or 'safe people' and he was a front runner. And sure, he earned about

£140,000 a year but 'out of that I have to run a house in Dublin, Castlebar and Brussels. I have to tell you, try it sometime . . . the cars and three houses, three homes and a few housekeepers.'

It was a vintage Pee Flynn performance: over-the-top, breathtakingly insensitive and self-satisfied. It was also vintage Gay Byrne, giving him more than enough rope. So, asked Gay, what's all this about Tom Gilmartin and the £50,000?

'I said my piece about that. In fact I've said too much about that because you can get yourself in the High Court for undermining the tribunal. I ain't saying no more about it.'

Now, if he had just left it at that. But he didn't even pause for breath. 'I've just one thing to say. I never asked or took money from anybody to do favours for anybody in my life.' Which is not the same thing as saying you didn't receive the £50,000.

A moment later Gay Byrne asked again: 'But you're saying you never took money from anybody at any time for any reason.' Mr Flynn replied: 'I never took money from anyone to do a political favour as far as planning is concerned.' Which is definitely not the same thing as saying you didn't receive the £50,000.

As for Tom Gilmartin: 'I haven't seen him now for some years. He's a Sligo man who went to England and made a lot of money. Came back. Wanted to do a lot of business in Ireland. Didn't work out for him. He's not well. His wife isn't well. And he's out of sorts.' Tom Gilmartin was furious. 'I considered it a scurrilous statement because it seemed to indicate to me that he was giving the impression on public television that I was not compos mentis and therefore I was incensed.' By his dismissive bluster, Pádraig Flynn had destroyed whatever hope he'd had of riding out this political storm.

Tom Gilmartin had been sending out contradictory signals about whether he intended to testify to the Flood Tribunal. But Flynn's *Late Late* performance decided him. Later he told RTÉ's Charlie Bird: 'I wrote out the cheque. I didn't know who the payee was, or who Fianna Fáil used, if they had a trust or whatever so I asked him who I made it payable to and he says "Leave it, leave it on the desk there and it'll be all right."'

After the *Late Late*, Tom Gilmartin added details to the original story. He claimed that Flynn had phoned and faxed him since the original story broke asking that he tell the tribunal that the £50,000 was a personal donation, not one for the party.

Later, Commissioner Flynn told RTÉ's Tommie Gorman that any explanations he had to give he would give to the tribunal. But, said

Gorman: 'You never denied that you got the money.' Flynn referred again to the tribunal but added that there was 'no charge against me in so far as the terms of reference of the tribunal are concerned'. Gorman tried again: 'You're not actually saying that you didn't get this money.' The commissioner said nothing, stepped into a lift and viewers watched Flynn taking cover behind the closing doors. The doors were closing just as relentlessly on Pee's Euro career.

Flynn, Pádraig: *Saturday View*

B rian Lenihan appeared to be recovering from the scandal which dogged his 1990 presidential campaign, in which he gave two contradictory accounts of a controversial incident in 1982. His slide in the polls had stopped and was even reversing. Then, Fianna Fáil decided that the best way of hurting his main rival, Mary Robinson, was to emphasise her alleged socialism. Full-page newspaper adverts asked, 'Is the Left Right for the Park?' Helping implement this strategy, Lenihan's colleague Pádraig Flynn, on Saturday, 3 November, went on RTÉ radio's *Saturday View*. Flynn, like everyone else, was conscious of candidate Mary Robinson's media-friendly make-over. Flynn's attempt to disparage Robinson backfired.

'She was pretty well constructed in this campaign by her handlers, the Labour Party and the Workers' Party. Of course, it doesn't always suit if you get labelled a socialist, because that's a very narrow focus in this country. So, she has to try and have it both ways. She has to have new clothes and her new look and her new hairdo . . .'

Up to here Flynn was doing fine. Then, he began to self-destruct.

'. . . and she has the new interest in her family, being a mother and all that kind of thing. But none of, you know, none of us who knew Mary Robinson very well in previous incarnations ever heard her claiming to be a great wife and mother.'

Those few words would effectively halt Lenihan's recovery. Everything else was legitimate political comment, and Flynn was raising a fair point about Robinson's calculated reconstruction of her image, but the questioning of the genuineness of Robinson's commitment to her family crossed a line. Though Flynn later apologised, and Lenihan disassociated himself from the remarks, the damage could not be undone.

Foreign Policy

I t is difficult, looking back from this distance, to comprehend that Ireland once had an independent policy on international affairs. Those dour, pompous, conservative old men — of whom de Valera was the most visible — sincerely saw themselves as founders of a state, as statesmen, as the equals of the leaders of the great powers. While aware of the realities of Ireland's economic dependence on British markets, they sought to take an independent line. As leaders of a former colony, they had particular sympathies with the Third World.

The trimming of that independence, and the gradual falling into line with the new world order, began in the early 1960s. The USA was taking over the role previously filled by Britain and the other European colonisers, now exhausted by the Second World War. The USA, confident, triumphant, had a young, assertive president, John Kennedy.

In 1962 India was taking a particular line in its long-running dispute with Pakistan over the former state of Kashmir. Ireland's representative at the United Nations, Frederick Boland, had discussed the matter with India's foreign minister, Krisna Menon, and had agreed to back the Indian position.

In June, John Kennedy phoned the Irish ambassador to the USA, Thomas Kiernan, and asked him to help change Ireland's position on Kashmir. He wanted Ireland to propose a UN resolution pushing the US line. 'We can't put it forward ourselves without it being knocked, and we want Ireland to put it forward,' Kennedy said, according to Kiernan. 'If we can get you to come along we'll get others.'

In the same phone call, Kennedy said that his friend and aide Kenny O'Donnell 'mentioned something to me. I'll look after that.'

Frederick Boland balked at proposing the US line. He already had a deal with Krisna Menon: 'He'll be wild,' he said. 'We have a certain friendship with India from the old days, and so on, and we can't do it.' Ambassador Kiernan went over Boland's head, to the Fianna Fáil Minister for External Affairs, Frank Aiken. And Aiken immediately directed that the US line be followed. When he heard the request came from Kennedy he 'agreed without demur, no difficulty whatever', Kiernan remembered. 'We introduced the resolution, it was put through.'

So far, no scandal. Just some top-level and effective lobbying by Kennedy, the kind of thing that happens every day in foreign affairs. But what was that something that Kenneth O'Donnell mentioned to John

Kennedy, about which the president told the Irish ambassador, 'I'll look after that'?

Ireland had for some time been trying to get into the US sugar market. To do that it needed to be included among a number of countries allowed to sell a sugar quota to the USA. Ambassador Kiernan lobbied the president's friend Kenny O'Donnell, and O'Donnell mentioned it to Kennedy. Nothing happened for quite some time, until Kennedy mentioned it obliquely in his phone call to Kiernan. In his book, *JFK and His Irish Heritage*, Arthur Mitchell reports that 'a new bill suddenly appeared, specifically including Ireland'. Ambassador Kiernan said, 'We, for the first time, got in on the sugar market. The *Wall Street Journal* said that it was hard to understand how it happened, but somebody with a large smile in Washington seemed to have been responsible.' We sold our independence for the price of a few tons of sugar.

The following year, Kennedy visited Ireland. The young master, taking over responsibility from the tired old colonialists of Europe, was touring his estate.

Four years later, when an RTÉ current affairs crew was about to leave Ireland to do a first-hand report on the Vietnam war, Frank Aiken intervened and the RTÉ authority was told to call off the trip, which it did. Independent reporting of the war would probably be critical; this would annoy the Americans; and that wasn't allowed. The cancellation, said the government, was 'in the best interests of the nation'. Not to mention the sugar business.

Forgery

The Fraud Squad got a warrant to search a premises at Green Street East, Hanover Quay, Dublin on 16 November 1983. Gardaí led by Detective Superintendent Ted Murphy raided the premises in the hour before midnight. Inside they found two printing machines and a photo processor. One hundred and ten reams of paper were stacked to one side. The search took several hours. It was apparently a site where forgers had been at work. There were lots of waste-paper sacks, inside which were used sheets of paper on which someone had been experimenting with printing various styles of five-pound notes. The police found the kind of white opaque ink used to make watermarks on currency.

Nine days later the police raided the premises of Repsol, a printing company at 30 Gardiner Place. That was the address of the Workers'

Party. Repsol had a premises behind the party headquarters and printed material for the party. There was a bookshop in the front of the building. Repsol owned the whole building and prominent Workers' Party members were directors of Repsol.

Inside the Repsol premises gardaí found cardboard boxes similar to boxes found at the Hanover Quay premises. On inspection, they discovered that the boxes at the two sites had the same serial numbers. Printing plates were found: one was for a customs and excise document used in the importation of cars; another printing plate contained details of cheques drawn on an Irish Life Assurance account at AIB in O'Connell Street. There was a printing plate containing an impression of a stamp used for stamping international driving licences.

At the bookshop in the front of the premises, gardaí bought a booklet about the building industry. They compared it with printing plates found at the Hanover Quay site and found them identical.

Gardaí made no further progress in investigating the apparent forgery operation at Hanover Quay and just what was going on is anyone's guess.

Fortune, Fr Sean

H is victims waited years for a day in court that never came. There had been complaints about the Wexford priest sexually abusing young boys since the 1980s. If the church did anything about it, it was not apparent to the victims. But the garda investigation which began in 1995 resulted in twenty-nine charges of sex abuse involving eight boys, now all young men. The failure of his church superiors to act quickly and decisively against Fr Sean Fortune left a controversy that still lingers.

It took two and a half years for the case to come to court. Fr Fortune used the law to drag things out. He finally appeared before Wexford Circuit Court on 1 March 1999. Usually, he was an imposing presence. Over six feet tall, overweight, always dressed in clerical garb, always wearing dark glasses. That day he moved slowly into the courtroom on crutches. He told the judge he was feeling weak and seemed to fall asleep as he laid his head on his arm.

The next day the judge discharged the jury. Fr Fortune clearly seemed to be unwell. He was confused and seemed to think he was appearing on a murder charge. He was remanded to the Central Mental Hospital, Dundrum, for treatment but, because of a strike there, was sent to Mountjoy Prison. He was granted bail in the High Court and a few days later he killed himself with drink and drugs. He left a suicide note, apologising to his family and blaming the media for his troubles.

Two of the priest's victims spoke to Alison O'Connor of *The Irish Times*. 'There were two different Fr Fortunes — the priest who would go up to the altar and give terrific sermons about the evils of drink, sex and sin and the other one who would talk to young boys about homosexuality, interview them one by one, and abuse them.' Like all paedophiles he relied on secrecy and some of his victims, though they lived in the same rural community, remained unaware of each other until the day they met in court.

But even if he hadn't been abusing children, Fr Sean Fortune's behaviour was bizarre enough to warrant attention. He was curate in Fethard-on-Sea from 1981 to 1987 where he managed to split the community and foster antagonisms that continue to this day. In one locally famous row, he attempted to take over the community hall. Dances were cancelled, accusations were made, locks were changed and later sawn off.

He sent a 'chancellor' around on a bicycle to collect dues from those who had not been paying. He put a lock on the gates of the local cemetery so visitors would have to call to him to get the key. This lock was also sawn off. There were reports that during the 1983 anti-abortion referendum he put a doll on the altar with the slogan 'Don't kill me' painted on its nappy. He had huge energy and was famous for making money, though he left Fethard-on-Sea with bills local people estimate amounted to £20,000.

Fr Fortune then reinvented himself as a media guru. In the late 1980s he was sent by Bishop Comiskey to a media training centre run by the Catholic church in England. He then got involved with religious programmes made for South East Radio and after that established his own training organisation — the Institute for Journalism and Theatre. He persuaded an RTÉ producer, an RTÉ newsreader and an *Irish Independent* journalist to give lectures for him and set about making a great deal of money from courses which most agree were less than professional. He rented lecture rooms and studios in places such as UCD and RTÉ, thus giving the courses a credibility by association they didn't deserve.

But the abuse allegations eventually caught up with him. And there were more looming. Fr Fortune had worked in the Nazareth Lodge orphanage in south Belfast in the late 1970s and the RUC wanted to extradite him to face charges of serious abuse in 1979. And there were reports that police on both sides of the border had reason to suspect cooperation between Fr Fortune and other known paedophiles.

As a layperson, Fortune would have been seen as a criminal adventurer, a conman; as a priest he used his position of trust to facilitate his adventures — and then, slaking his sexual appetites, he used his position to repeatedly indulge in the ultimate betrayal of that trust.

Forward-looking

The term became associated with scandal in 1998, when the AIB explained its settlement with the Revenue Commissioners over bogus non-resident accounts which the bank had facilitated. The Revenue, according to an internal AIB document, wrote off around £100 million in tax owing on the crooked accounts. It was said that the Revenue would not look back at the fraudulent activities, the agreement with AIB would be 'forward-looking'.

The term came to mean the concealment of past misdeeds. If the Revenue come after you for taxes not paid in previous years you might try asking them to accommodate you with a 'forward-looking' resolution of the problem, i.e. waive your debt. If you are not a politician, a bank executive or a very rich person, don't count on a positive outcome to this request.

Friends of Ben

This is, in chronological order, an account of the money which Ben Dunne is known to have given to politicians. At the McCracken Tribunal the impression was received that Dunne gave this money out of his own funds. His generosity was much remarked upon. At the Moriarty Tribunal, Dunne insisted that every penny came from Dunnes Stores accounts.

Charlie Haughey, FF: £32,000; January 1987.
Seán Barrett, FG: £1,000; February 1987.
Fianna Fáil Dublin South-West branch: £6,000; March 1987.
Charlie Haughey, FF: £309,220 (£282,500 sterling); May 1987.
Seán Haughey, FF: £1,000; 1987.
Charlie Haughey, FF: £205,000 (£182,630 sterling); December 1987.
Jim Mitchell, FG: £2,500. Dunne gave Mitchell a £5,000 cheque, to be
    split with party leader John Bruton; 14 June 1988.

John Bruton, FG: £2,500; conveyed via Jim Mitchell; 14 June 1988.

Charlie Haughey, FF: £471,000 sterling; July 1988.

Charlie Haughey, FF: £150,000 sterling; April 1989.

Charlie Haughey, FF: £20,000. Conveyed via Mrs Maureen Haughey, for election purposes; 14 June 1989.

Seán Haughey, FF: £1,000; 1989.

Fintan Coogan, FG: £5,000; 1989.

Alan Dukes, FG: £30,000 for party funds, with a promise of another £60,000 (which was never paid); October 1989.

Charlie Haughey, FF: £200,000 sterling; March 1990.

Mary Robinson, presidential candidate, £15,000. Conveyed via Ruairí Quinn, Labour; October 1990.

John Bruton, FG: £50,000 for party funds; April 1991.

Charlie Haughey, FF: £210,000 sterling; November 1991.

Michael Noonan, FG: £3,000; 1992.

Ivan Yates, FG: £5,000; November 1992.

Michael Lowry, FG: £5,000; 1992. Other monies given to Lowry were in his capacity as a Dunnes Stores contractor.

Charlie Haughey, FF: £180,000; November 1992. £100,000 was apparently destined for Celtic Helicopters.

Fine Gael Limerick East (Michael Noonan's constituency): £2,000; 1993.

Ivan Doherty, FG general secretary: £100,000; May 1993, after meeting with John Bruton.

Fine Gael Limerick East (Michael Noonan's constituency): £1,000; 1994.

Colm Hilliard, FF: £1,000, contribution to a party fund-raising event; November 1994.

Furze, John

John Furze was a Cayman Island banker and a close associate of Des Traynor, Charlie Haughey's crooked accountant. Furze, a man with a flair for amateur dramatics, operated the Cayman Island end of the Ansbacher Deposits, while Traynor took care of business in Ireland. Furze died in July 1997.

See: Ansbacher Deposits; Traynor, Des.

G

Gallagher, Blaise

The medical aspects of the case are simply stated. Avril Gallagher was twenty-nine weeks pregnant when she arrived at the National Maternity Hospital in April 1992. Her son Blaise was born two days later. Avril Gallagher's story of her experience at the hospital was horrific. When Blaise was born he had no heartbeat. He was revived, suffered dreadful brain damage, is blind, can't even sit up unaided. The tragedy left his family with a pain that will never end.

The Gallaghers sued, the hospital denied liability. Incredibly, the hospital fought the case through preliminary hearings, then fought for twenty-three days in the High Court, dragging the family through the pain, fear and uncertainty of litigation, and then settled for £2.15 million without presenting any evidence for the defence.

After the settlement, the master of the National Maternity Hospital, Dr Declan Keane, made a disturbing allegation against the Irish judiciary. He told *The Irish Times* that no Irish judge would award against a child born with cerebral palsy. 'With the current adversarial climate our feelings are that all CP cases will receive money from a judge who knows that the child needs to be looked after for the rest of their lives.' Therefore, the hospital settled the Gallagher case.

First: this was a grave allegation, that judges make decisions not on the merits of a case but on sentimental grounds. It is demonstrably untrue. Second: if the hospital believed that, why did it fight for twenty-three days in the High Court?

Behind hospitals and doctors, in these matters, there are insurance companies. Cold decisions are made on the basis of which course — or change of course — will be most cost-effective. Truth, responsibility, compassion are not primary concerns in such circumstances.

See: Dunne, William.

Gallagher, Patrick

He went to jail. That fact alone makes Patrick Gallagher a rarity among white-collar criminals. He went to jail not just because he was crooked but because he let his crooked empire spread across the border to Northern Ireland, where white-collar crime is taken seriously.

The Gallagher empire was built by Patrick's father, Matt Gallagher. He came from a farming background in Tobercurry, County Sligo and, with his brothers, emigrated to England in the 1930s, worked as a builder's labourer, returned to Ireland in 1949 and set up his own building company. He bought land and built houses and became a rich man. Patrick was a middle child in a family of seven. It was an affluent childhood. The family home was a large house and stud farm at Mulhuddart. Patrick was a Clongowes Wood boy. At the age of twelve he was made a company director. When he left school at seventeen he was heir apparent to a growing empire. Matt Gallagher died in 1974 and Patrick took over. He was twenty-two. Like his father he had an eye for profitable property. House-building had served the family well for many years, but Patrick Gallagher soon learned that the real money was in property speculation. It was the time of office block proliferation and Patrick Gallagher made it his speciality. Georgian and Victorian architecture wasn't allowed stand in the way of monolithic office blocks. And there was never any problem finding state and semi-state bodies to provide tenants for Gallagher buildings.

'Patrick Gallagher plays Monopoly with the streets of Dublin; and St Stephen's Green is where he likes to land.' That's how journalist Mary Raftery described the wheeling-dealing Gallagher in an article published in *In Dublin* shortly before the group collapsed on 29 April 1982. The Monopoly motif remained apt. Except there was no get-out-of-jail card.

The deal that confirmed Patrick Gallagher as the man with the Midas touch was the sale of a property on St Stephen's Green to the Irish Permanent Building Society. In November 1979 he bought Seán Lemass House on the Green for £5.4 million. He sold it the next week for £7.5 million. It was the sort of stroke that sent a frisson of excitement down the spines of would-be speculators and their bankers. Ironically, the buyer was Edmund Farrell Jr, boss at Irish Permanent, another rich young man who had taken over from his father and who would also become enmeshed in financial controversy, although not so spectacularly.

After the Irish Permanent deal, the banks fell over each other to lend the brash young Gallagher money. He bought property, demolished old buildings, built new ones, sold them on and just kept getting richer. Or so it seemed. He owned land all over the country: shopping centres, arcades, a bank, a couple of mansions, a racetrack and the horses to go with it. He lived in a large house on Ballymacarney stud farm in County

Meath and he bought and refurbished the mansion Straffan House, County Kildare, now transformed into the playground of the rich, the K Club. He went about his business in a chauffeur-driven Rolls-Royce. He was a man who enjoyed flaunting his wealth. In an interview with the *Sunday Press* he said that he 'once told a stuffy bank board meeting that the three most exciting things in life are sex for the second time (you never get it right the first time), the first winner at Royal Ascot and a flight on Concorde'. It was the kind of nonsense that the media lapped up, and there was little clear-eyed analysis of the brat.

In truth, the Gallagher empire was overstretched. There was no money behind the façade, but as long as the deals kept coming the Gallagher myth was secure. For when Patrick Gallagher bought a property for millions, he didn't usually hand over the millions straight away. He'd hand over a deposit and by the time the full amount became due, the property was ready to be sold on for a profit. He just needed a bit of bridging from the banks. And he had his own bank, just in case.

It's appropriate that the Gallagher legend came apart on St Stephen's Green. Gallagher bought what is now the site of the St Stephen's Green shopping centre from the Slazenger family for £10 million. He paid a deposit of £50,000. The full amount was due two and a half years later, supposedly to give him time to develop the site. The plan was to sell the site to Irish Life for £15.5 million. But Irish Life didn't buy. Gallagher's house of cards was beginning to collapse.

He had already committed the future profit on the Slazenger deal to another deal. He'd bought the site opposite the Concert Hall on Earlsfort Terrace — a long-standing city centre eyesore — from his uncles. The uncles had bought it ten years earlier for £1.5 million and did nothing with it. They had planning permission for an office block and just as that was about to run out they managed to convince the corporation that development (and the jobs that go with it) was about to start. Planning permission was extended and the site was promptly put up for sale. Patrick Gallagher bought it for £9.5 million. The uncles were delighted. As the *Irish Times* headline put it: '£8 million harvest for weed growers'. Patrick had paid only a relatively small deposit for the site — £450,000 — and tried to sell it on in two lots. But the prospective buyers didn't take the bait.

That left him badly exposed. There was a last desperate deal about to be struck. Gallagher was to buy the H Williams supermarket chain. A supermarket is a great vehicle for ready cash and cash is what the overextended speculator needed. But the banks, who so wantonly loaned money to Patrick Gallagher, were now poised to pull the plug. It's reckoned that in interest alone, Gallagher owed six major banks £100,000 a week.

A month before his empire collapsed, Patrick Gallagher valued his companies' assets at £60 million. After the fall the realisable value had plummeted to £26 million. The banks were owed £30 million. The receiver began selling the mansions, the racehorses, the properties.

After the receiver was called in Patrick Gallagher told RTÉ he would relaunch his career. 'Absolutely, there is no question about it. I'm thirty years of age and my brother [Paul, his joint managing director] is twenty-five. We know how to dig trenches and build houses and do things.' Patrick Gallagher, having lost everything he owned and a lot he didn't own, set off for London to start again.

The Gallaghers' own bank, Merchant Banking Limited (MBL), was brought down with the rest of the empire. Merchant Banking's depositors had unwittingly bankrolled various Gallagher enterprises. In the Republic, the bank folded with £4.5 million owed to depositors. Some 600 people found they had lost their life savings. These people weren't high rollers. One widow later interviewed by RTÉ's *Today Tonight* spoke of the £900 her husband had deposited, a few pounds at a time, whenever he had anything to spare. If she only had it now, she told reporter Gary Agnew, she would install central heating to keep her warm in her old age. It was one of many small nest eggs that had been squandered by Patrick Gallagher.

Gallagher had another bank, MBL's subsidiary in Belfast, Merbro Finance. That too had gone to the wall but because of more stringent regulations in the North the depositors were protected and received compensation. And, while Patrick Gallagher was off rebuilding his career in London, the police in the North investigated what went wrong at the bank.

In April 1988 Patrick Gallagher was arrested in London. In Belfast Crown Court he pleaded guilty to theft of £120,000 belonging to Merbro which he used to buy two paintings which were not listed in the bank's assets. He also pleaded guilty to three charges of providing false information. A charge of conspiracy to mislead the Bank of England and defraud depositors was not proceeded with. Because Gallagher pleaded guilty the evidence accumulated by the RUC was not presented in the court. If it had been it might have formed part of criminal proceedings brought in Dublin.

In October 1990 Patrick Gallagher was sent to jail. Mr Justice Carswell told the court that Gallagher had furnished false information to the Bank of England in order to obtain a licence to conduct a deposit-taking business and then had used this money to finance his own high-risk development business. The judge accepted that Patrick Gallagher did not set out to swindle depositors. 'But you told lies to the Bank of England to obtain the necessary licence. The law can not condone this and it is necessary to mark the gravity of your offence.'

But what about the law in the Republic? Did it condone the Gallagher fiasco?

The liquidator assigned to Merchant Banking Limited reported in 1984. That report, in several volumes, was sent from the High Court to the Director of Public Prosecutions and from there to the Garda Fraud Squad. And there it sat for five whole years. In the autumn of 1989, the *Today Tonight* programme investigated the Gallagher affair and obtained a copy of the liquidator's report. The DPP asked RTÉ not to broadcast the programme because it might prejudice future proceedings against Patrick Gallagher. RTÉ delayed transmission for three months but finally went ahead with the programme in February 1990.

The liquidator's report had found several possible offences. There was evidence of false records, false returns to the Central Bank, falsified books, an asset fraudulently obtained, and fraudulent statements. The books did not reflect the true position of the bank for a number of years. And there were a number of transactions that clearly benefited the Gallagher Group at the expense of the bank's depositors.

No less than 79 per cent of the assets of the bank had been siphoned into Gallagher Group companies. Money from depositors was used as loans to the Gallagher companies. County councils also lost out. Normally, they collect money in the form of so-called performance bonds from builders as security against a housing estate being completed. In the case of Gallagher companies, councils were given and accepted deposit receipts from MBL which turned out to be worthless.

Having reviewed the facts of the case, the DPP, in September 1991, decided not to proceed against Patrick Gallagher. There was much debate subsequently about the inadequacies of the law in the Republic. On 18 July 1996 the liquidator of Merchant Banking Ltd reached a High Court settlement with Gallagher. The court was told that Gallagher would have to pay a sum of money but it was not revealed how much. He also had to undertake not to become a director of any Irish company for a period of five years.

Patrick Gallagher was always generous to his friends. When MBL collapsed there were several 'forever' loans to friends and associates on the books. One entry was for a £15,000 loan to Charlie Haughey. Haughey's name and that of his family company Larchfield Securities featured in the liquidator's report. It also featured in the original version of the *Today Tonight* programme but was dropped from the final edit. The Labour leader Dick Spring tried to raise the matter with Mr Haughey in 1990. Haughey, then Taoiseach, wrote to him: 'I categorically reject your outrageous suggestions and find it deeply offensive that you would write to me in this tone.'

As it happened, the £15,000 loan was small change. Patrick Gallagher, now residing in Zimbabwe, was called to the Moriarty Tribunal on 21 May 1999. He explained how, in 1979, the Sunday after he became Taoiseach, Charlie Haughey summoned him to Kinsealy. He held Mr Haughey in high esteem and 'some awe'. When he took over the Gallagher Group he told Haughey he intended to support him the way his father had done over the years. He helped him with various political expenses and would have given him about £3,000 a year. In 1979 he gave a lot more.

The new Taoiseach told Gallagher he needed to clear a £750,000 debt pretty quickly. Bottom line: he needed £600,000. We're flush with funds, said Gallagher, we'll give you half but we'll need something tangible in return. 'Right, that's fair enough,' said Haughey.

The something in return was a promise on a complicated land deal that collapsed with the Gallagher Group a few years later. Haughey kept his £300,000.

Galway Blazers

I t was as though the farmers of Galway had suddenly been struck by a fierce loathing of blood sports. In November 1947 significant numbers of them decided that the Galway Blazers, a hunting club which enjoyed terrorising foxes, would henceforth not be allowed to cross the farmers' lands. It had nothing to do with compassion for animals. The Blazers had elected Mrs James Hanbury as joint master of the hunt. She was Protestant and she was divorced and she had remarried. And no group of horse-riders who would elect a divorced woman to a position of authority was welcome to cross the land of good Catholic farmers.

The farmers received the backing of their local Catholic bishops — Walsh, Dignan and Browne — who said that the farmers were defending 'the sanctity and permanence of the marriage bond'. To remarry when a former spouse was alive was against the Natural Law. To allow the associates of such a woman to hunt on Catholic land would be to undermine the sacrament of matrimony. 'A person who publicly acts counter to Catholic principles in this matter cannot expect to be received by a Catholic people with the same favour, and to be given the same honour and privileges as those who respect Catholic moral standards.'

The bishops' statement was read in all the churches of the area. 'In these days, when there is so much moral laxity,' said Their Graces, 'Catholics must take care that they are not found in the camp of the enemies.'

The hunt rode out in December and was greeted by a deputation of farmers who wished to inform the riders verbally that they were not allowed cross Catholic land. Two gardaí on bikes policed the affair. A note greeted the hunt at a farm boundary: 'On Catholic principles and in the interest of good morals, the right to hunt over these lands is now withdrawn from the Galway hunt.' Bishop Dignan (who was reckoned to be what in those days passed for a liberal bishop) attached a similar notice to the front gate of his lands.

'What comment is there to make?' said Mrs James Hanbury (that was the style of the time, and contemporary reports do not record the woman's own name). 'I am a Protestant, my husband is a Protestant, we were married in a Protestant church and I do not feel that I am breaking any rule according to my own church.'

Before Christmas 1947 Hanbury said she had no intention whatever of resigning. On Stephen's Day she resigned. The secretary of the hunt, a Mr Comyn, denied the resignation resulted from the farmers' ban. 'This has nothing at all to do with it,' he said. And the Galway Blazers were again welcome to terrorise foxes on Catholic land.

See: Dunbar-Harrison, Letitia; Fethard Boycott; Flynn, Eileen.

Garda Conduct: Cork

In April 1994, in Cork city, two men who knew each other, Cathal O'Brien and Alan Ball, disappeared. Ball was Welsh, aged forty-two. He might have drifted back to Britain. O'Brien was twenty-three, and he was from Wexford, and he too might have moved on. They had each lived in a cheap flat at a house at 9 Wellington Terrace, Grattan Hill, on the outskirts of Cork city. Ball had been married. He had a connection with the British New Age travellers. O'Brien had worked for the Simon Community in Cork. Both were living casual lives and their disappearances did not arouse any immediate suspicions. One thing, though: they both vanished without cashing social welfare cheques to which they were entitled.

Eight months later, in December 1994, Patrick O'Driscoll disappeared. He was due to arrive at a relative's house on Sunday, 18 December, for dinner, and didn't turn up. Patrick O'Driscoll was aged thirty-two. He too lived a casual life but he regularly kept in touch with his family. He had four sisters and three brothers. He had been in a car accident and had lost one eye and had a tin plate in his head. He wore an eyepatch.

When he didn't arrive for dinner or make contact, three family members, a brother, a sister and her husband, went looking for him late that night. The last time anyone from his family had seen him was the previous Wednesday, 14 December. They went to his flat, at 9 Wellington Terrace. He wasn't there. His belongings were there, nothing had been removed. His medication, which he needed to take regularly, was still there. They met another tenant, Fred Flannery, who lived upstairs. No, he said, he hadn't seen Patrick recently. Last time he saw him was last Thursday morning.

Patrick O'Driscoll stayed missing over Christmas. His family knew there was something wrong. True, he was due to go to Wales for medical treatment, but he wouldn't just vanish, not without telling them where he was going, and not at Christmas.

They made and then withdrew a missing person report. They just weren't sure what was happening. Patrick drank; he had fits; anything might have happened.

Three days after Christmas, 28 December, Fred Flannery came calling. He suggested to Patrick O'Driscoll's brother-in-law that they go looking for him. Flannery was riding a motorbike. They looked in pubs, along a disused railway line, in a building, a hut. Flannery went into the hut on his motorbike. There they found a box which was used to hold eyepatches, the kind of box Patrick had.

By 2 January 1995 the family members were seriously worried and reported Patrick's disappearance to the police. Something must have happened to him. Patrick had said that he knew 'a terrible secret'.

The gardaí now made a connection between O'Driscoll and the two men who had disappeared eight months earlier, O'Brien and Ball. The connection was 9 Wellington Terrace, where they had lived at different times. The following month the gardaí put out a press release in which they asked for information from anyone who had seen the three men. The media speculated about the existence of a serial killer.

In May gardaí began digging in the Lotabeg, Glanmire area. They suspected a body might have been buried there. They found nothing, gave up. It may be that they missed something, as someone came along and dug something up. Men were heard digging, gardaí were notified about the unusual noises. They came back and found evidence that human remains had been dug up.

The gardaí conducted interviews with anyone they could find who might be relevant. One of these was Michael Flannery, aged fifteen. He was a nephew of Fred Flannery, the tenant who lived upstairs from Patrick O'Driscoll's flat. The story he told led to the arrest of Fred Flannery and his charging with the murder of Patrick O'Driscoll.

The way the nephew told the story: he knew Patch O'Driscoll, he often went to his uncle's house. One night he went there and he and his uncle and another man had tea in O'Driscoll's flat. Patch wasn't there. The two men and the boy shared three or four joints. The two men produced some tools: a bow saw and a Stanley knife. They got a few blankets and the two men went upstairs to Fred Flannery's flat. Michael stayed in Patch O'Driscoll's flat, with the radio playing, the TV on but the sound turned down.

The man with Fred Flannery came down when someone came to the door. He let a woman in, she came into O'Driscoll's flat and after a while Fred came down to join them. Will you dump a bit of rubbish for me? he asked the woman. Then he told Michael to come upstairs.

This is still Michael's version of events: In Fred's own flat the uncle took a hand out of a cupboard. The wrist and about three inches of arm was attached. I'm after killing Patch O'Driscoll, the uncle said. He produced a foot. There was a black sock with diamonds on the foot. The uncle said he killed O'Driscoll two or three weeks ago. Hit him once or twice with a hammer. Then put a rope around his neck and choked him, pulled on the rope. It took ten or fifteen minutes for him to die.

Michael described how the dismembered body was shared out among several bags. The other man and the woman helped Fred move bags from the house. Michael carried a bag that weighed about the same as a half-stone of potatoes. It was round.

Fred Flannery was brought to trial at the Central Criminal Court in Dublin, on 17 June 1996. His nephew Michael took the stand and told his story. On the sixth day of the trial the case collapsed.

Gardaí had taken statements from a number of people with whom Michael Flannery had spoken. He had talked of being on drugs. There were statements from people to whom Michael Flannery had spoken of the dismemberment of Patrick O'Driscoll's body, and those accounts were significantly different from the account he gave in court. Some people made statements in which they said they saw Patrick O'Driscoll alive several days after Fred Flannery was supposed to have killed him. The police had withheld statements not only from the defence but from the Director of Public Prosecutions and the prosecuting barrister.

When this was discovered on Friday, 21 June, defence counsel Paddy McEntee said that documents had been suppressed in order to 'lend a phoney credibility to the evidence' of Michael Flannery.

Mr Justice Barr said it was 'outrageous that prosecuting gardaí should have to have documents literally dragged out of them'. He ordered that the investigating gardaí should have no further part in deciding which documents were relevant, and that every single document be made available to the barristers. The trial was adjourned until the following Tuesday. The prosecuting counsel, Kevin Haugh, said he had been assured that all documents had now been made available. On the following Monday he found out that wasn't true. Yet more documents were found.

The garda explanation was that some documents were left out because they weren't relevant — the people who said they saw Patrick O'Driscoll alive after mid-December 1994 were mistaken. The documents were filed and forgotten, recalled only when the defence pressed the matter.

Judge Barr discharged the jury and freed Fred Flannery. He said the gardaí had 'consistently and deliberately resorted to a policy, the objective of which was to deprive the accused of his constitutional right to a fair trial in accordance with the law'. He rejected the garda explanation for the withholding of the documents and said there was 'a conscious and deliberate policy', probably orchestrated by the superintendent in charge and 'at least one of his investigating officers, to subvert the course of justice in the trial'.

The judge put a permanent stay on the prosecution of Fred Flannery, meaning he could never again be tried for the murder of Patrick O'Driscoll. He said the case was 'so tainted by the appalling misbehaviour' of the investigating gardaí 'that it cannot be satisfactorily retrieved'. Flannery walked free.

The conduct of the gardaí created a public scandal. A senior garda was appointed to inquire into what had happened.

Just over three weeks after the collapse of the trial, in the late afternoon of Friday, 19 July 1996, a man was walking his dog in Lotabeg Woods. His dog took an interest in a shallow mound of earth. The dog got hold of something and pulled. It took almost three weeks of forensic examination before it was established that the body parts found in the mound were those of Patrick O'Driscoll. The metal plate in his skull helped the identification. They found his severed head, limbs and torso.

Gogarty, James

Some came to think of James Gogarty as a hero. In truth, he was a crook, a corrupt man who by his own evidence set out to bribe a government minister.

Gogarty was a senior executive with JMSE, a large building firm. He claimed that he set out to bribe Ray Burke in 1989 along with his boss's son, Joseph Murphy Jr, at the instigation of his boss, Joseph Murphy Sr. JMSE alleged that the intent to bribe Ray Burke was all Gogarty's idea and Murphy Jr wasn't on the bribing expedition and JMSE had nothing to do with it.

Gogarty was introduced to Burke by Michael Bailey of Bovale Developments. Gogarty claimed Bailey gave Burke £40,000, Bailey denied it.

Burke claimed that the £30,000 which he got from Gogarty was a political donation, accepted 'in good faith'. What that means, and how one might accept £30,000 from a stranger in the building trade in bad faith, is something on which we will not dwell.

Gogarty, a greedy man as well as a corrupt one, wasn't getting enough hundreds of thousands of pounds in his pension and fell out with JMSE. Apart from a self-admitted attempt to bribe a government minister Gogarty's criminality stretched to tax fraud. He hid his money in an offshore account on the Isle of Man. In 1993 he was one of the many crooks who used the Tax Amnesty to launder his hot money. In retirement, Gogarty's resentment of the Murphys festered. He was looking for a way to screw them.

Some conservationists put up a £10,000 reward for information on corruption in the planning process, through Donnelly Neary Donnelly, a solicitors' firm in Newry, and Gogarty approached the lawyers and began leaking. It was his allegations against Ray Burke that created controversy, and his attempts to blacken the Murphys became tiresome. Burke resigned and Gogarty took the stand at the Flood Tribunal, where he became a hero to people who were delighted to see a pensioner mocking highly paid lawyers.

See: Flood Tribunal.

Goldenbridge

Christine Buckley told her story to Gay Byrne on his morning radio programme in 1992. She was born in 1946. Her mother was a separated woman who had an affair with a young Nigerian man studying medicine at Trinity College. Christine was put into care as an infant and at four years of age was sent to the Goldenbridge Orphanage, an industrial school run by the Sisters of Mercy in Inchicore, Dublin, where she spent the rest of her childhood.

She described to Gay Byrne a childhood of misery, neglect and systematic cruelty and abuse within the walls of the orphanage. It was a time when a child who lacked the protection of a strong and loving family had no rights at all. The state happily abdicated responsibility to the religious orders and they were let run whatever sort of system they saw fit. There were kind individuals certainly in Goldenbridge and other orphanages. But cruel people were also allowed exercise unchecked power over children and the kind people let it happen. Even those who have defended the orphanage system agree that these were 'harsh' places. Harsh was the norm and harsh included beatings with instruments specially made for beating children. Harsh included humiliating punishments for bedwetting. Harsh included long hours of enforced labour.

One of the people listening to Christine Buckley's story on *The Gay Byrne Show* was the television programme maker Louis Lentin. In February 1996 his programme *Dear Daughter* was broadcast on RTÉ. The public reaction to the programme was overwhelming. The story hadn't changed since Christine Buckley first told it to Gay Byrne, but public opinion had. It was a time when towns throughout the country were busy organising convoys of supplies and toys for children languishing in orphanages in places such as Romania. No one could organise a convoy to rescue children from Ireland's past, but it was time for their voices to be heard.

Dear Daughter, through the memories of women who spent their childhoods in Goldenbridge, documented a litany of abuse. One of many beatings left Christine Buckley with a scar that runs the length of her thigh. Young children were left in charge of babies. Babies were strapped to chamber-pots. There was a furnace room — a dark dungeon of a place — where punished children were locked away. And, there were hours and hours of childhood years spent making rosary beads which were sold to make money for the orphanage.

In the months that followed the *Dear Daughter* broadcast, people who had been raised in orphanages and industrial schools told their stories in newspapers and on radio. A lot of journalists had heard personal histories like these before, but never so many. There were stories of kindness too and many acknowledgments that the religious orders gave a home and an education to children who were society's outcasts. In the specific case of Goldenbridge, the target of much of the blame was Sr Xavieria, Reverend Mother there for almost a decade. After the *Dear Daughter* programme, some Goldenbridge women rushed to her defence. It became apparent that while some remembered Sr Xavieria with abject terror, to others she was strict but kind. The nun agreed to be interviewed some weeks after the programme. She was clearly devastated by the accusations against her. She denied the allegations of serious abuse and apologised for any pain caused. She agreed that children were hit with a 'slapper' but never so hard as to cause cuts or marks. A child had been put in the furnace room, but only for half an hour and not with her approval. In retrospect she knew the children 'should have been playing instead of working', making rosary beads. She knew some children were afraid of her and acknowledged 'at times I was too harsh'.

The difference between 'too harsh' and abuse is one of perception. In the case of the orphanages of the 1940s and 1950s, memory also comes into play. And while the truthful memory of an adult may be more accurate than that of a child, it's the child's memory that is more significant. If it felt like terror to a six-year-old, then it was terror. And the orphanages and industrial schools of Ireland were terrible places indeed.

There was no childcare training, no system of safeguards, no check on how individual children were getting on. Most of the children in these institutions were not abandoned. Their families had just fallen on hard times. Eleven-month-old Marion Howe was sent to Goldenbridge because her mother was ill and her father was working in the UK. Mrs Howe's other children went to neighbours during her convalescence but she was worried about finding a suitable arrangement for the baby. The almoner at the hospital arranged for the child to go to Goldenbridge. 'So, of course, I agreed to it, thinking I was doing the best,' said Mrs Howe, telling her story to Marian Finucane on *Liveline* forty-two years after the event. The baby died a few days later in Goldenbridge and the nuns sent a telegram to Mr Howe. He was told: 'Don't bother coming over. We will do the necessary arrangements.' But home he came, to find his daughter in the mortuary of St Ultan's Hospital, her legs so badly burned 'he could put two fingers right through both of them'. The nuns never sent for Mrs Howe at all. Neither did they offer an explanation of how the child died. When the Howes went to the orphanage they were left at the door. They got no post-mortem results. The gardaí refused to get involved.

That was 1955, when the Sisters of Mercy occupied a position of power and the Howes had none. The death of Marion Howe did not matter at all. In October 1997 the Sisters of Mercy agreed to pay £20,000 to Marion's elderly parents. The payment was made without any admission of liability and only after the order had been taken to court. They still could not give any explanation as to what happened to the child.

See: Artane Industrial School; Poor Clares.

Golden Circle

There are no membership cards for the Golden Circle. The term came into general use during various controversies in 1992 and has since been applied as a description of wealthy people allegedly involved in financial controversies.

There is no circle of conspirators. It's a bit more complex. There emerged — without anyone planning it — several circles, sometimes overlapping, of people who knew one another personally or by reputation as being likely to share a point of view about how things should be done, to share similar financial interests.

At one level are the very rich, who engage in multimillion-pound deals. They facilitate one another, provide backing which is reciprocated at another time; they sometimes share accountants and lawyers who create complex structures within which identities are concealed and tax liabilities reduced or eliminated. Through their professional, political and personal connections they are provided with short cuts and conceal-ments. In banking terminology they are KBIs and/or HNWIs.

There are other circles of lesser, though substantial, financial clout which operate along the same lines. Out beyond that, in what might be described as a kind of brass circle, embracing thousands of business people, tax-dodging facilities have been provided by the banks and tolerated by the Revenue.

No one designed this. It grew organically, as part of the maturing of the economy through the 1980s. People with shared financial and sometimes political interests formed alliances and looked after one another. Another level of society had its trade unions and tenants' organisations. The golden circles are looser, the connections are through social, banking, financial, political and professional networks. Common interests are recognised, backs are scratched. It is seldom that favours are sought or given: few have to stoop so low. Mostly, people in these circles know the right thing to do.

Wealthy interests connect with the political circles through donations; in return, the needs of the various circles are pandered to at a political level. This can be easily explained away, should anyone ask questions: these are go-ahead business people, what is good for them is good for the country. And the Revenue, and regulatory bodies such as the Central Bank, share the political establishment's view of these people.

The most important element in all this has been the lack of regulation. Politicians with intimate financial ties to the various wealthy circles have for decades been in charge of writing the laws governing their activities. This could lead, for instance, to a crook like Patrick Gallagher going to jail in the North, but escaping prosecution in the South because of the inadequate laws.

See: HNWI; KBI.

Great February Debacle

I t was a remarkable week. If ever there is a single week upon which we all look back and say — 'There, that was when our eyes were opened,' it was the week ending Friday, 19 February 1999.

At the Moriarty Tribunal in Dublin Castle, counsel for the tribunal, John Coughlan, patiently waded through a huge pile of documentation acquired from Allied Irish Banks, reading it aloud, stripping bare the pretences of Charlie Haughey, showing in excruciating detail Haughey's arrogance and the bank's timidity. And that was the week in which Garret FitzGerald's indebtedness to the banks was revealed. That week too, the polished image of supermarket baron Senator Feargal Quinn was tarnished by the revelations of certain business practices. And there were revelations about Fianna Fáil panhandling ten grand in political donations from wealthy people buying passports from the state; these people were making large donations to a political party the name of which they probably couldn't spell.

And then, late on the evening of that Friday, word began to spread around Dublin that George Redmond, Dublin city and county assistant manager, had been arrested at Dublin airport with hundreds of thousands of pounds on him.

For those who see the financial scandals of the 1990s as a great purging of the new Ireland, that was one week of revelation and truth, the memory of which is to be savoured.

Greencore

It is important mostly because it was the first of the financial scandals of the 1990s to become public. Very roughly, it went like this:

Siúicre Éireann, the Irish Sugar Company, owned 51 per cent of a sugar distribution company called SDH. In 1989 the four members of top management of SDH bought out the 49 per cent of their company that wasn't owned by Siúicre Éireann. It cost them £3.2 million.

To carry out this purchase, the Four Top Men borrowed a million pounds from a subsidiary of SDH, their own company. To do this they needed the okay of the majority shareholder, Siúicre Éireann. They got this with the help of Chris Comerford, the chief executive of Siúicre Éireann.

The following year, Siúicre Éireann was heading for privatisation. Before being floated on the market, Siúicre Éireann wanted to buy up the 49 per cent of SDH it didn't own, the 49 per cent bought by the Four Top Men at SDH. And in 1990 Siúicre Éireann paid £9.5 million for the 49 per cent which the Four Top Men had bought a year earlier for £3.2 million.

There was a profit of £6.3 million to be shared among the Four Top Men. Or were there five? Because Chris Comerford claimed that he had been offered a share in the buy-out of the 49 per cent of SDH.

Siúicre Éireann was privatised in April 1991, becoming Greencore. The Four Top Men and Comerford had a falling out, which led to litigation, which led to affidavits, which led to reporter Sam Smyth coming across the story. He published it in the *Sunday Independent* in September. Scandal erupted. Chris Comerford was forced out of Greencore, with a very generous compensation package. Several people sued one another and the whole thing was settled out of court in November 1995, with everyone involved getting large sums of money.

And they all lived happily ever after.

GUBU

An acronym, made up of the words Grotesque, Unprecedented, Bizarre and Unbelievable. Charlie Haughey used the words to describe the Malcolm Macarthur case, when the double murderer was arrested in the flat of Haughey's Attorney General, and Conor Cruise O'Brien made GUBU of them. GUBU became a kind of shorthand for Haughey's penchant for stumbling into controversy. Curiously, despite repeated use in the media and in political circles, the term never achieved popular usage.

Guinness & Mahon (Ireland) Ltd

A private bank, founded in Dublin in 1836 by Robert Guinness and John Mahon. Its London branch eventually became head office, and the Dublin bank became a subsidiary of the London bank.

Providing services to wealthy people, it offers 'relationship banking' which aims 'to relieve the administrative burden associated with managing your own finances, while providing peace of mind through our professional and discreet approach'. If you have in excess of £100,000 to invest, G&M will be glad to hear from you.

Between 1976 and 1986 the bank was run by crooked accountant Des Traynor, Charlie Haughey's friend. Traynor was deputy chairman and de facto chief executive of Guinness & Mahon. He used the bank to set up the infamous Ansbacher Deposits, through which people such as Charlie Haughey could have immediate access to their funds while those funds remained nominally 'offshore' in the Cayman Islands, clear of tax.

An audit of Guinness & Mahon in 1989 showed that no less than 35 per cent of the bank's liabilities was made up of the Ansbacher Deposits, then totalling £38 million. That figure was later estimated at a minimum of £50 million. This was merely one of the Rackets Traynor ran through Guinness & Mahon.

G&M has been owned by Irish Permanent since 1994.

Guns, Bags of

The Cosgrave coalition was just weeks in office in May 1973 when the security forces stopped a boat named the *Claudia* and captured five tons of arms intended for the IRA. There was some argy-bargy in the Dáil, with claim and counter-claim about the incident.

At this distance it is hard to appreciate the difference in atmosphere between then and now in terms of what people could get away with saying. Undiluted nationalism was taken as the norm, and there was little sensitivity to other views. Comments which today would be dismissed as rabid sectarianism were heard without causing any great upset.

The *Claudia* gun-running matter was discussed at Question Time in the Dáil. Fianna Fáil pressed Taoiseach Liam Cosgrave on how the affair was handled. A government supporter jeered at Fianna Fáil: 'Are you sorry the ship was caught?'

And Fianna Fáil TD for Cork North East Liam Aherne shouted: 'More guns we want, bags of guns!' He explained: 'That is my personal opinion and I make no apology for it.'

Many were scandalised, yet Aherne suffered no discipline. His colleague Bobby Molloy the next day claimed that Aherne had been feeling unwell and regretted his remark. Other than that, no one felt the need to apologise on his behalf or to kick him out of the parliamentary party or in any way chastise him. The previous year 472 people had been killed in the northern conflict, and in 1973 the figure would be 252, yet a Cork TD's call for more guns was not regarded as conduct unbecoming a member of either Fianna Fáil or the Oireachtas.

The following year, after the Dublin–Monaghan bombings killed thirty-three people, the dominant mood became one of fear of the northern conflict spilling over again into the South, and the tolerance of views such as those expressed by Liam Aherne virtually vanished. As did Mr Aherne, who didn't stand at the next election, and whose Dáil career consisted of one term.

H

Haughey, Charlie

The key to Charlie Haughey's character is in a few sentences he uttered in sworn evidence before the McCracken Tribunal. It was 15 July 1997, shortly after 10.30 a.m., and counsel for the tribunal, Denis McCullough, was questioning Haughey about the money he got from Ben Dunne. McCullough mentioned 'the lifestyle that you maintained', and Haughey took offence. Despite all the allegations he faced, this remark was the one that seemed to get under his skin.

'Because, I'd just like to make a point that I didn't have a lavish life-style. My work was my lifestyle. And I was — when I was in office — I worked every day, all day. There was no room for any sort of extravagant lifestyle. I'd just like to make that point.'

Haughey was a practised and unblushing liar, and his assertion that his big house, yacht, island, champagne and horsy lifestyle was less than lavish caused some merriment. In this case, however, he was telling what he sincerely believed to be the truth. This man rubbed shoulders with John Byrne, P.V. Doyle, Ben Dunne, Dermot Desmond, John Magnier, Michael Smurfit, Larry Goodman, Matt Gallagher, Patrick Gallagher. These were people with large fortunes, who lived the lives that suited them, free of money worries. Their homes were as luxurious as they wanted them to be. They never had to worry about affording anything they truly desired. They had access to as much art as they fancied, ate the best food and drank the finest wines, holidayed when and where they felt like it, dressed in the best threads. If they wanted to get somewhere quickly there was always a helicopter or a jet to hand. Dermot Desmond owned an airport. Their lives were embedded in the trappings of wealth.

And he helped make them rich. As Minister for Finance, as Taoiseach, Haughey's policies facilitated the development of Irish business — and without Haughey several fortunes might have been less than major. For instance, without Charlie Haughey the great John Magnier would not enjoy the fabulous wealth that comes from a business that is not only successful but tax-exempt. It was Haughey's decision — long before he knew Magnier — to make horse breeding a tax-exempt industry, and that made Magnier one of the richest men in the country.

Some of us might see Haughey's financial frolics as a crude rush to get his nose into the trough. To Haughey, from the 1950s on, he was merely taking sensible measures to ensure that he lived in a style befitting his position as one of the new elite. He, along with his brash contemporaries, was a mover and a shaker. He made things happen. In comparison with the wealthy business people with whom he mixed, Haughey could genuinely believe that his lifestyle — comfortable as it was — was not lavish, merely a reflection of his status.

The older generation had killed and had seen their friends die in the creation of an independent state; they hadn't gone through that to make a quick buck, and they reacted with distaste to suggestions of financial impropriety. Whether in the Locke scandal or the resignation of Con Ward, these people did not hide behind lawyers and legalisms, in these matters at least they had a sense of honour. It was a sense not shared by the new, thrusting generation, of which Haughey was the most self-regarding.

Although Haughey was well paid as a TD, minister and Taoiseach, it wasn't nearly enough. From the beginning, he sought ways of boosting his income to a level that was capable of sustaining a lifestyle that most of us would consider lavish. Initially, as an accountant, then in farming and horse breeding sidelines, his money-raising methods seemed fair enough. Except he wasn't a great success either at farming or (despite the tax exemptions he himself had created) at horse breeding. As time went on, Haughey sought easier ways to keep himself in the style to which he had become accustomed.

The grubby business of making easy money was buried under layers of accountancy tricks. In the 1960s there were suspicions about his involvement in land deals with Donogh O'Malley, who — along with Haughey — saw himself as one of the new princes of the bullish Ireland of that period. Nothing could be proven, suspicions were brushed aside.

Haughey engaged in a lucrative land deal in Dublin, buying a house and land at Grangemore in 1957, land which subsequently was rezoned. The land was in 1969 sold on to one of Haughey's friends, builder Matt Gallagher, after which Haughey bought his Gandon mansion and 250-acre estate at Kinsealy.

At this stage Haughey, country squire and occupant of the big house, believed he had it made financially. He went into debt, opening personal and business accounts with AIB. By September 1971 he was a quarter of a million in debt to the bank. Initially, under pressure, he made some attempts to pay off portions of his debt. By 1973 he was holding it down to around £300,000. By the middle of 1974 he had it down to around £170,000. Part of the debt arose from Haughey's stud business, more of it was a consequence of his carefree lifestyle. One way Haughey had of bringing down the AIB debt was borrowing from Northern Bank Finance Corporation. Borrowing from Peter to pay Paul.

As time went on and the bank behaved timidly, Haughey began to treat AIB as not so much a bank as a source of income. The AIB debt went up and up. Throughout the 1970s there was the cost of Haughey's lavish home life: his horses, his island, his paintings, his servants, his yacht. Although deep in debt, he spent £150,000 electrifying his house on Inishvickillane. Then there was his other life, as sugar daddy to Terry Keane, with whom he began a high-maintenance relationship in 1972, and with whom he would continue a twenty-seven-year affair featuring jewellery, wine, travel and the most expensive restaurants in Dublin and Paris.

In July 1974, at a meeting with AIB officials in Dame Street, Haughey said that he found any restraint on his accounts unnecessary and galling.

By June 1976 the AIB debt was £272,980. By the end of September 1976 the AIB debt was up to £304,964 and he owed Northern Bank Finance Corporation £220,000. Over half a million in total (plus a mere £25,000 or so to ACC).

The truly staggering point about the AIB debt at that stage was that the bank had not agreed to let Haughey draw this money. The limit, set in April 1975, was £173,776. Haughey just kept writing cheques. And the bank kept honouring the cheques.

And when his chequebook was empty it gave him another one. And another. By April 1977 the total debt to AIB alone was £401,929; by June 1978 it was £445,282. By June 1979 it was £876,405. The debt, including interest, had increased by an average of about £36,000 a month over the previous year. Nominally, Haughey had accounts into which he might be expected to put his income; in truth, AIB hadn't a clue what he was doing with his income. He didn't make deposits, just withdrawals.

As AIB officials timidly questioned Haughey about how he was going to put all this right, he assured them he would deal with the debt, and merrily continued writing cheques. When bank executives made nervous noises, Haughey threw any old story at them. He was about to sell bloodstock, he was about to sell land, he had an insurance policy somewhere. The bank didn't dare push him on any of this.

As early as September 1975, when Haughey was returning to the front bench after the years of exile that followed the Arms Crisis, an AIB memo noted 'the likelihood of Mr Haughey being a man of influence in the future'. He was, the bank decided, a KBI (Key Business Influencer), and as such should be handled with care, even if he insisted on withdrawing from the bank hundreds of thousands of pounds that didn't belong to him. AIB memo August 1979: 'Mr Haughey fails to see the precarious position he is in and obviously feels that his political influence will outweigh any other consideration by the bank.' And he was right.

Haughey was not shy of exploiting his position as a KBI. In September 1976, according to an AIB memo, he suggested he could be useful. He tut-tutted 'that the bank did not make use of his influential position and he indicated that he would be in a position to assist the bank in directing new business etc. He intends to devote a further 10 years to politics.' It was a barefaced offer to sell his influence as a senior public official.

In its trawl through AIB documentation on Haughey's frolics, the Moriarty Tribunal uncovered some fascinating hints about his hidden world. For years there had been denials that Haughey was in any way linked with his pal John Byrne's proposed Endcamp development at Baldoyle. This housing plan had huge financial potential until it came to nothing in the early 1980s under a Fine Gael/Labour regime. One AIB memo of February 1979 has this remark about Haughey: 'He told me that from a development in Baldoyle, which was now coming to fruition, there would be a sum of £200,000 coming to him.'

There was also a plan to work some kind of land deal with Patrick Gallagher, son of Matt, later convicted of fraud, whereby Gallagher would effectively fund Haughey and in return Kinsealy land would be 'parked' in some way with Gallagher. Although pushed by the bank to consider this, Haughey wanted to keep it in reserve. Most intriguingly, he spoke of the possibility of a £10 million deposit, through a Middle Eastern bank, into the AIB, at a lower interest rate than normal. AIB documents name the Rafidain Bank, a state-controlled Iraqi bank. The suggestion — which AIB didn't fancy at all — seems to have been that Rafidain would do AIB a favour as long as AIB kept funding Haughey. That Haughey appeared to have, as early as the 1970s, a connection with a bank controlled by Saddam Hussein was disturbing. Given the controversies involving the beef industry and Iraq, and Rafidain, that would erupt in the years that followed, the AIB documents' cryptic reference to Rafidain opened up endless avenues of speculation.

AIB finally dared, at a meeting with Haughey on 1 October 1976, to get uppity, and to demand he return his chequebooks. According to an AIB memo: 'At this point Mr Haughey became quite vicious.' He said he would not give up his chequebooks 'as he had to live'.

'You're dealing with an adult,' raged Haughey, 'and no banker will talk to me in this manner.' If the bank took drastic action, he said, he could be a 'very troublesome' adversary. This tantrum was enough to make the bankers back off and continue allowing Haughey to withdraw money that wasn't his.

By mid-1979, Haughey had hopes of succeeding Jack Lynch as leader of Fianna Fáil and Taoiseach. He wanted to clear the decks, and he began to make serious moves to get rid of the debt. Not by paying it off, of course. He offered £400,000 as a full and final settlement. The bank said no. By the middle of January 1980, with Haughey now Taoiseach, he authorised his crooked accountant Des Traynor to finalise a settlement. Despite what Haughey would later tell the McCracken Tribunal ('He took over control of my financial affairs from about 1960 onwards . . . The late Mr Des Traynor had complete discretion to act on my behalf without reference back to me'), Traynor was a sophisticated fetcher and carrier, acting on Haughey's instructions. It is clear from AIB documents that Traynor could take no action, nor enter any discussion on these matters, without Haughey's explicit direction.

The debt was now £1.143 million. AIB agreed to take £750,000 in settlement. Haughey was getting a £390,000 gift. The bank left a nominal £110,000 debt on the books, to which interest would not apply, which Haughey was to clear as 'a matter of honour'. This, of course, was never paid off. The bank, however, didn't bear the brunt of Haughey's welching. The £390,000 could be written off as a bad debt and claimed against tax liabilities. As ever, the taxpayer would pick up the tab.

The £750,000 to settle the debt was channelled through Guinness & Mahon, the private bank of which Haughey's crooked accountant friend Des Traynor was de facto chief executive and in which Haughey now opened an account. The land deal with Patrick Gallagher was put into effect; Haughey got £300,000 supposedly as a down payment for land at Kinsealy. The money was passed over but the land deal was never carried through. Haughey kept the down payment and kept the land. Gallagher was only too pleased to be of service to his hero.

It was within Guinness & Mahon that Traynor organised the Ansbacher Deposits, wherein Haughey's sterling and Deutschmark accounts were coded S8 and S9. And, with Haughey now Taoiseach, in complete control of Fianna Fáil, a Taoiseach promising hard-nosed national housekeeping policies which pleased his business admirers, he was widely praised by the wealthy. Between 1979 and 1987 no less than £1.5 million poured into his personal accounts at Guinness & Mahon.

During that period, Haughey eased out Fianna Fáil's money-man, Des Hanafin, whom he couldn't control, and got his own hands on the party's fund-raising mechanism. Party fund-raisers putting the touch on businessmen were told that the businessmen had already given money to the party through Haughey. No one had the guts to ask Haughey where the money went.

The possibilities involved in this became clear when it was revealed that in 1989 a £25,000 cheque from AIB's Baggot Street branch ended up in a Guinness & Mahon account controlled by Des Traynor. It was public funds, diverted from the FF 'leader's allowance', meant for party expenses. The cheque had been signed by Haughey and countersigned by Bertie Ahern, who appeared to have signed a blank cheque (in more senses than one) for his revered leader. Mr Haughey may yet provide an explanation. And £20,000 contributed to the fund for Brian Lenihan's liver transplant was diverted to Celtic Helicopters. That, more than anything else, sickened even hardened Haugheyites. Mr Haughey maintains that this diversion was inadvertent.

From 1987, Ben Dunne ladled hundreds of thousands of pounds into Haughey's grasping hands. Dunne was at the same time using his money to grease Michael Lowry's upward progress through the senior ranks of Fine Gael.

Repeatedly, Haughey fought back viciously when his political enemies, outside Fianna Fáil and within, threatened his position. Whatever vision he might once have had, in the years when he longed to be leader of Fianna Fáil, holding onto the leadership position was now a financial imperative. He needed the job, he needed the income, and he needed the prestige of the office, to maintain the loyalty of his backers.

He eventually was forced into retirement and might have ended his days with his reputation intact had not Ben Dunne become a cokehead, screaming his paranoia from the seventeenth-floor balcony of a Florida hotel. Haughey's efforts to deal with the consequent attentions of the McCracken Tribunal led to a criminal charge of obstruction. The revelations about him being on the take led to a £2 million tax demand. That demand was wiped out by an appeal commissioner who, controversially, happened to be Bertie Ahern's brother-in-law.

Haughey was central to the financial scandals revealed from the mid-1990s onward. As Minister for Justice, Minister for Finance and Taoiseach he presided over the threadbare laws, procedures and systems under which the state remained helpless in the face of widespread tax evasion and corruption. It was known for years that he was living beyond his means, yet none of his colleagues dared call him on it. The Revenue backed away, stayed away.

Although describing itself as 'the Republican Party', Fianna Fáil displayed towards Haughey the kind of deference and timidity more usually associated with royalty. Observers were often taken aback by the bowing and scraping which Haughey took as his due, and in which everyone from ministers to rank-and-filers seemed prepared to indulge. This crawling went way beyond the respect to which a party leader was entitled. It helped sustain Haughey's pose as a man of substance.

In the end, the man who craved wealth and demanded deference was broken on the wheel of his own greed. Measured against the disclosures of his status as a kept man, a poodle of the wealthy, his pretensions to grandeur appeared more laughable than ever.

See: Celtic Helicopters; Dead Man Strategy; Friends of Ben; Gallagher, Patrick; Passports for Sale: Legally.

Heavy Gang

No one paid too much attention at first, when allegations emerged that gardaí were beating up suspects. It sounded like Provo propaganda, which wanted us to believe that no republican was guilty of any crime, all confessions were beaten out of suspects, and every conviction was a frame-up.

The allegations in 1975 and 1976 were, however, remarkably consistent. Sleep deprivation, minor assaults, threats and beatings. There were more serious allegations: on at least one occasion the use of a gun to threaten a suspect; repeated punching in the stomach and the genitals. Sometimes, according to the allegations, care was taken that obvious bruising would be minimised.

It was a nervous period. The 1974 bombs in Dublin and Monaghan, and the collapse of the Sunningdale initiative, led the Cosgrave coalition into a containment policy. The northern conflict had to be kept on the far side of the border, republican activities in the South represented a threat to the state. Gardaí felt pressure to come up with results.

Confessions were obtained. Often, it seems, the confessions were true. Sometimes they weren't, and people alleged that they signed anything to get away from the interrogation. In one case a suspect jumped from a second-floor window after several hours of interrogation, suffering a fractured pelvis and broken nose. Gardaí denied allegations of ill-treatment.

The allegations remained consistent from area to area; the same names of gardaí cropped up again and again. One lawyer later said that some gardaí had a style all their own; he just had to look at the allegations of ill-treatment and he could guess the identity of the garda involved.

The Heavy Gang seems to have begun informally, with gardaí coming to know which of their colleagues in which sections of the force were prepared to take the gloves off when interrogating suspects. It developed from that into a still informal but recognisable group which saw itself as doing a distasteful but necessary job, in which occasional violence or the threat of violence was inevitable. There was no cohesive group answering to the Heavy Gang nickname; some gardaí drifted from one difficult case to another, and became hardened interrogators; others became involved in those practices very occasionally.

There was disquiet as the allegations circulated, eventually being exposed in *The Irish Times*. There was unease within the police force itself. In February 1977 two gardaí went to Garret FitzGerald, Minister for

Foreign Affairs in the Cosgrave coalition, and told him of their concerns. FitzGerald dithered, nothing was done. The story which other ministers held to — and most may even have believed — was that all the allegations were Provo propaganda, and the gardaí who confirmed the Heavy Gang allegations were pro-Fianna Fáilers seeking to discredit the government.

Eventually, as the political temperature lowered, as gardaí were promoted or by natural career progression moved into various areas of the force, the Heavy Gang seemed to fade away. There continued to emerge occasional and specific allegations of the extraction of confessions, sometimes involving gardaí who had been the subject of Heavy Gang allegations.

In opposition in early 1977, Fianna Fáil was vociferous in condemning alleged garda brutality. Gerry Collins, the FF spokesman on justice, demanded a public inquiry. Within months Fianna Fáil was in government and Collins was Minister for Justice. He dropped his belief that a public inquiry was necessary and some gardaí prominent in Heavy Gang allegations were promoted.

See: O'Brien, Conor Cruise.

Heffernan, Gary

Pseudonym for Charlie Haughey. It was used within Celtic Helicopters when booking flights for Haughey. A payment of £50,000 to Celtic Helicopters was alleged to be a 'prepayment' for helicopter use by 'Gary Heffernan'. There was a real Gary Heffernan, a friend of the Haughey family. He said he was 'flattered' that his name was used as code for the great man.

See: Celtic Helicopters.

Hello Money

For years the supermarkets extracted payments from suppliers in return for accepting their goods, or for placing the goods in prominent positions. This was known as 'hello money'. Suppliers could also be left waiting for six months to get paid, involuntarily providing the superstores with lengthy credit. The retailers came up with 'Long-term Agreements'

(LTAs), which ensured discounts of up to 5 per cent from suppliers. The president of the Irish Farmers' Association claimed in 1986 that in discounts from milk sales in the Dublin area alone, around £10 million a year was being siphoned off by the supermarkets.

The 1987 Groceries Order Act banned 'hello money' and some other practices.

Feargal Quinn, independent senator, head of the Superquinn chain, decided that this new law was 'illogical and crazy'. In 1988, a company called Retail Logistics was set up. It was owned by Brendan Rooney, a former director of Quinnsworth (and his wife, Carmel), and on the face of it Retail Logistics had nothing to do with Superquinn. However, suppliers who wanted to 'support' Superquinn could make payments to Retail Logistics.

How did the money get from Retail Logistics to Superquinn without breaking the law? Easy. Superquinn provided management services to Retail Logistics, which paid management fees to the supermarket chain.

The scandal erupted in February 1999, and the previously untarnished reputation of Feargal Quinn took a battering. Interviewed by RTÉ's Charlie Bird, Quinn appeared flustered and defensive. His company came under investigation by the Director of Consumer Affairs, Carmel Foley, and Superquinn announced that it would discontinue the practice.

Suppliers were extremely nervous about discussing the pressures on them to 'support' supermarkets, and claims that Superquinn was not the only chain requesting 'support' were nervously brushed aside.

Hepatitis C

The injection that eventually killed Brigid McCole was given on 5 November 1977. It would bring her a slow and painful death almost nineteen years later. The contaminated product that killed her had been made by the Blood Transfusion Service Board (BTSB) a year earlier. In that time, as we later learned from the Tribunal of Inquiry into the BTSB, there were several clear indications that the product was not safe, many reasons that should have prompted someone at the BTSB to say, wait, there's something wrong here, we're taking terrible chances.

But that didn't happen. Professional standards of care were ignored. Brigid McCole died and a further 1,600 people, mostly mothers, were infected with the virus that killed her: hepatitis C.

The product that caused so much grief was called Anti-D. It was given to women who had rhesus negative blood and who had given birth to babies with rhesus positive blood. When a rhesus negative woman carries a rhesus positive baby her body develops antibodies set on destroying rhesus positive blood. With each pregnancy, the number of antibodies multiplies and subsequent babies are at risk. This is called Rhesus Haemolytic Disease. Anti-D was given to such mothers, within forty-eight hours of birth, to prevent this fatal build-up of antibodies. It was, on the face of it, a wonderful medical development.

In 1976 a woman who came to be known as Patient X was eight weeks pregnant. She had Rhesus Haemolytic Disease, which meant the antibodies in her blood were attacking her developing baby. Her doctor recommended a course of blood transfusions, to remove her blood and replace it with compatible plasma. Up to nine litres of plasma a week for twenty-five weeks were taken from her. The replacement plasma was supplied by the BTSB. The treatment worked. Patient X gave birth to a healthy child.

Patient X's consultant, Dr McGuinness of the Coombe Hospital, remembers asking Dr Terry Walsh of the BTSB whether they should consider using some of that excess plasma for the manufacture of Anti-D. Dr Walsh said it probably wouldn't be suitable and Dr McGuinness thought no more of it.

But suitable plasma doesn't come easy and on 28 September 1976 the BTSB began making Anti-D from the plasma supplied by Patient X. Nobody asked Patient X for permission to use her blood. If they had, she would have told them no because she'd had TB years ago. It's as simple as that. If someone had asked permission, Brigid McCole and hundreds of other women would have been spared infection. Quite apart from that, medical guidelines published in 1972 said six months should elapse after a transfusion before a person can become a blood donor. This policy, designed specifically to protect against the transmission of hepatitis, would have excluded plasma from Patient X.

In November 1976, Patient X had a reaction to one of her transfusions, became jaundiced and was diagnosed as having hepatitis. The BTSB was informed and biochemist Cecily Cunningham was told to hold back Anti-D made from plasma from Patient X. In the next month several samples of Patient X's plasma were sent to the BTSB for testing. 'Infective hepatitis' was the conclusion each time.

Still, more Anti-D was made from Patient X's plasma in January 1977. There was a total of 16 batches, each containing between 250 and 400 doses. One of them was destined for Brigid McCole.

There was yet another opportunity to pull back from the brink in July 1977. The BTSB was told that three patients in the Rotunda Hospital had developed hepatitis after receiving Anti-D in May. The doses came from 'batch 238'. The source was Patient X.

On 25 July 1977, 103 days before Brigid McCole received her fatal injection, Cecily Cunningham, the BTSB biochemist who was in charge of the manufacture of Anti-D, was told not to use any more plasma from Patient X. There was no instruction about the Anti-D already made so Mrs Cunningham issued these batches as normal. Of course, there was no attempt to recall the doses of Anti-D that were already in the hospitals waiting for use.

On 11 August 1977 blood samples from the Rotunda women who were reported to have hepatitis, plasma from patient X, and samples of Anti-D made from her plasma were sent to Dr Dane of Middlesex Hospital Medical School for further testing. He could confirm that they were 'not dealing with hepatitis B' but could find nothing else. At this time hepatitis C could not be identified by any test, although doctors knew that a form of hepatitis existed that was neither the known A nor B variety. Dr Dane wrote that he would freeze the specimens in the hope that a future test would 'solve the mystery'. Among the frozen specimens was Anti-D from 'batch 250', the same batch that provided the lethal dose for Brigid McCole.

There were more reports of women receiving Anti-D in 1977 and developing jaundice, a symptom of hepatitis, but no one thought to recall the product. As the Report of the Tribunal of Inquiry into the Blood Transfusion Service Board later stated: 'It is a fundamental principle of blood transfusion and the preparation of blood products that should any question be raised of any substance concerning the safety of a product, even without convincing proof of infection, it should be totally recalled and supplies of it destroyed.'

Eight batches of Anti-D made with plasma from Patient X and each containing between 250 and 400 doses were later found to be infected with hepatitis C.

There appears to have been within the BTSB a startling unwillingness to confront what was happening. Despite the 'mystery', despite the suspicions of doctors whose patients developed hepatitis or jaundice, despite the knowledge that corners had been cut, people in the BTSB wanted to believe that the hepatitis had nothing to do with Anti-D, it was random infection.

The farce was repeated in 1991 when infected plasma from Donor Y was used to make Anti-D. Donor Y was another woman involved in a plasma exchange treatment. During one of her transfusions, she was infected with hepatitis C. In this case, there was inadequate testing of her before her plasma was released to make Anti-D. When, in 1992, plasma that had been taken from her in 1989 tested positive for hepatitis C, it was believed by Cecily Cunningham to be a false positive and in her own words she 'ploughed on' with the manufacture.

In December 1991, around the same time that Donor Y's infected plasma was being used to make Anti-D, the Middlesex hospital was able to report to chief medical consultant Dr Terry Walsh on the samples it had frozen in 1977. There was now a test for an identifiable strain of hepatitis called hepatitis C and the 1977 samples tested positive. So now we knew that the Anti-D from Patient X's plasma was infected with hepatitis C and that the infection had been passed on to the women who received it. Middlesex asked pertinent questions about what had happened in 1977. There was no response from Dr Walsh. The BTSB simply did nothing with this news.

It would be another two years before the scandal became public. In those two years more people became infected and those already carrying the disease in ignorance delayed vital medical treatment. Hepatitis C is an insidious disease. The symptoms can be vague: tiredness, lethargy, aches and pains, no energy. It can go undiagnosed for years while the virus works silently to destroy the liver. Women all over the country, Brigid McCole among them, knew there was something wrong with their health, but they didn't know what it was or what to do about it.

Dr Joan Power took up the position of regional director for the BTSB in Cork in 1989, and became the director for Munster in February 1991. After screening for hepatitis C was introduced in October 1991 she set about researching donors who had tested positive for hepatitis C. In January 1994 she identified a link between a blood donor who tested positive and the Anti-D she had received some sixteen years earlier. She discovered a disproportionate number of rhesus negative women among the donors who tested positive. She took this information to the medical consultants' meeting of the BTSB and was told by Dr Walsh that, yes, there had been a problem in the late 1970s. It was no longer possible to avoid the awful reality.

On Monday, 21 February 1994, the BTSB held a press conference stating the problem as minimally as was possible and asking women who had received Anti-D to come in to be tested. The problem was said to be most probably related to the late 1970s only. The numbers infected would likely be quite low.

Hospitals were telephoned and told not to use existing stocks of Anti-D. However, some hospitals didn't get the message and a further ten doses of the product were used.

In the days and weeks that followed, the lives of rhesus negative mothers all over the country were turned inside out. The medical establishment was ill-prepared for the crisis. GPs didn't have all the information their patients needed. Women, suddenly facing shortened lifespans, wanted to know what to do and if they had the virus, what about their husbands, what about their children.

The BTSB added insult to injury by the ham-fisted way in which it tested and counselled the victims. Women were made to stand in queues marked: 'Anti D/Hep screening please queue here'. They were asked if they ever used needles, if they had tattoos, and if they had many sexual partners. It was as if the first instinct of the BTSB was to find out if there was any other way in the wide world that the women could have contracted the virus.

By October 1994 some 55,000 women had been tested, over 1,000 were antibody-positive. Of those, some had symptoms, some had none, some had irreversible liver damage. They were told their medical expenses would be covered but at this stage there was no talk of compensation. The then Minister for Health, Brendan Howlin, would await the outcome of the Expert Group headed by Miriam Hederman O'Brien which had been established to find out how this had all come to pass.

With each week more information leaked out about the extent of the crisis and the ineptitude of the BTSB. Some women were infected in 1993, two years after screening for hepatitis C had been introduced. And the ripples had spread far beyond rhesus negative women. One hundred and three of those who had received contaminated Anti-D had in turn become blood donors themselves. They made 504 donations, resulting in 606 infectious blood components being prepared.

The Expert Group reported to the new Minister for Health, Michael Noonan TD, in January 1995, though the report wasn't published until April. The main finding was that Anti-D had been infected because it was made from the plasma of a patient who developed jaundice in 1976. By its own standards, even though there was no test for hepatitis C at the time, the BTSB shouldn't have used the plasma of anyone with jaundice, because it was a symptom of hepatitis. The 1991 information from Middlesex linking Anti-D and hepatitis was also revealed. And the Expert Group identified the 1991 source of infected plasma, Donor Y. But it wasn't the whole story. The Expert Group simply didn't have all the information. It would take the courage of a dying woman, Brigid McCole, to force out the truth.

From 1995 the hepatitis C story was really a story of women fighting back. 'Positive Action' was formed and began lobbying for compensation for victims. The Minister for Health, Michael Noonan, wanted a private, no-fault tribunal that would offer speedy payments. There would be no admission of liability and no apology. An applicant had one month to accept the award offered. If it was accepted, all right to further legal action was waived. Anyone infected by any blood product, not just Anti-D, could apply. The minister and the state were determined that the victims should opt for the compensation tribunal rather than the courts. If they chose the courts, they could expect a fight.

The minister was playing hardball. The victims were told they had a six-month period from January to June 1996 to apply for compensation. Positive Action was furious. As the deadline approached, many tried a twin-track approach and lodged claims both with the tribunal and in the High Court. Donegal woman Brigid McCole chose the High Court. By 1995 she was a very sick woman. Later her daughter would tell of endless nights when her mother screamed in pain, of the long journey of a suffering woman on the bus from Donegal for treatment in Dublin. Another woman infected by contaminated Anti-D spoke of watching her friend Brigid McCole decline: 'It was like looking into a mirror down the road for me. A piece of me died. It was just like that for everyone in Positive Action.'

The state did just about everything possible to stop Mrs McCole's legal action. One sick woman against one big bully. The sick woman died, but she won the battle against the bully.

In the first instance she tried to have her case against the BTSB, the state and the National Drugs Advisory Board heard under an assumed name 'Brigid Roe' to protect her privacy. This was challenged by the state and the application for anonymity was rejected by the High Court in February 1996. Mrs McCole had eight months left to live.

In 1996 Mrs McCole's lawyers got a High Court order for discovery of documents from the BTSB. They uncovered a previously unrevealed document which showed that the BTSB knew in 1976–7 that Patient X had infectious hepatitis, not just jaundice as the Expert Group had found. Further documents about hepatitis and a donor were found by the BTSB's new chief executive and revealed to the Dáil Public Accounts Committee. However, the BTSB pulled out of a subsequent Dáil committee meeting at the eleventh hour because of the pending McCole case. A statement said: 'the BTSB will be vigorously contesting at the trial (among other matters) the allegations of recent weeks relating to the implications of reports of a clinical diagnosis of infective hepatitis in November/December 1976'.

As the deadline for applications to the compensation tribunal approached in June 1996, the Minister for Health refused to budge on the issue of an extension. There was a rush of late applications but none from Mrs McCole. Her trial date was set for 6 October. Her lawyers tried to get it moved forward, citing their client's serious illness, but the application was opposed by the state and defeated.

In May lawyers for the BTSB made a cash lodgment in the court. This increased the pressure on Mrs McCole because it meant that when the case came to court, if she was awarded less than the amount lodged, she would be liable for costs from the time the lodgment was made.

Finally, the about-turn happened. On 20 September 1996, as Mrs McCole edged closer to death, the BTSB wrote to her admitting liability and negligence and apologising for infecting her. It offered her £175,000 to settle the case. Mrs McCole knew she was dying and accepted the deal for her family. She died on 2 October 1996 of liver failure. Brigid McCole was brought home to Donegal to be buried but her children were back in Dublin on 8 October to hear the BTSB apologise publicly in the High Court. After the hearing the McCole family issued a statement. In it they said their mother would have been happier to settle her affairs privately at the compensation tribunal, 'but she wanted a public acknowledgment that a wrong-doing had been done'.

It was a watershed. The BTSB apologised to all the victims and their families. The demand for a full public inquiry was unstoppable. Máire Geoghegan-Quinn wasn't just speaking for Fianna Fáil when she said that no other victim of the BTSB should 'be dragged through the courts by the state and no other person should have to go through such trauma and pressure to find out why they were infected'. The McCole family wrote to the Minister for Health outlining five questions they wanted answered. Four of these were incorporated into the terms of reference of the tribunal of inquiry that was announced on 15 October 1996.

But even still the Minister for Health, one of the most accomplished politicians in the Dáil, misjudged the depth of public anger and distress at what the BTSB had done to so many innocent people. During the debate on the establishment of the tribunal Mr Noonan questioned the motives of Brigid McCole's lawyers, as if the decision to take legal action were not legitimately Mrs McCole's own.

> Could her solicitors not, in seeking a test case from the hundreds of hepatitis C cases on their books, have selected a plaintiff in a better condition to sustain the stress of a High Court case? Was it

in the interest of their client to attempt to run her case, not only in the High Court but also in the media and in the Dáil simultaneously?

Members of Positive Action, viewing from the public gallery, walked out. Mr Noonan spent the next several days apologising.

One question the McCole family addressed to the Minister for Health was never answered. It concerned the state's legal strategy and strong-arm tactics in fighting the case brought by their mother. Question five in their letter to the minister asked:

> In their letter of 20 September 1996 the Blood Transfusion Service Board did two things, they admitted liability and they apologised but only in the context of a threat that were she to proceed with a case for aggravated/exemplary damages, and not to succeed, they would pursue her for costs. What was the justification for this threat?

The Tribunal of Inquiry into the Blood Transfusion Service Board reported to the minister in March 1997. It found that the main cause of infection was the plasma taken from Patient X and that a further cause was the infected plasma from Donor Y. There were many conclusions and recommendations but centrally, it found that, given what was known at the time and applying good medical standards, the Anti-D made from plasma of these patients should not have been used.

In the BTSB only one person was sacked, Cecily Cunningham. She took an unfair dismissal claim against her former employers. Two senior executives retired, one with a generous golden handshake on top of his pension. Following complaints from a number of victims a garda investigation began and was still continuing in 1999.

Hillery, President Paddy

On the Wednesday after the Pope left Ireland in October 1979 RTÉ's political correspondent, Seán Duignan, went on the nine o'clock news and told the nation that President Patrick J. Hillery was denying that he was having an affair. As much bemused as scandalised, the public hadn't a clue what was going on.

Throughout the Pope's visit the rumours had been flying. Hillery had an Italian girlfriend; a Spanish girlfriend; a Spanish boyfriend; the woman had had a baby in Brussels; or in Dublin; there were sexual shenanigans on a boat off the Isle of Man.

There wasn't a sliver of evidence for any of this, but the 2,000 foreign journalists following the Pope plagued their Irish colleagues for details. There were none. Another rumour went around — that the Belgian paper *Le Soir* was about to publish the rumours. It didn't. There was nothing to publish, just bar gossip.

Then Paddy Hillery shot himself in the foot. *Hibernia*, a current affairs fortnightly, planned a piece about the rumours. The story it proposed to publish didn't back up the rumours, it merely acknowledged the gossip phenomenon that had swept the papal press. *Hibernia* rang the Áras for comment.

Hillery immediately panicked and called in the editors of the three daily papers, plus the RTÉ head of news. The head of state believed himself to be in trouble and his instinct was to call in the lads. *Hibernia* was about to publish rumours of an impending divorce, said Hillery. What should he do?

Hillery wanted to merely deny unspecified rumours. Tim Pat Coogan of the *Irish Press* argued that that would just fan the gossip. People would be furiously curious about what the rumours were. Better to specifically acknowledge that the rumours concerned his personal life and to deny there was anything wrong with his marriage. Douglas Gageby of *The Irish Times* agreed. Then the editors passed the buck, suggesting to Hillery that what he really ought to do was call in their political correspondents and make a statement. Reluctantly, Hillery did so. When the hacks arrived a couple of hours later they were startled to be told that Hillery was not resigning, there was no 'other woman'. Why was he doing this? someone asked. Why not just keep his mouth shut?

Because of possible reaction to what *Hibernia* would publish tomorrow, Hillery said.

Seán Duignan excused himself. He had the nine o'clock news to do.

The other political correspondents went back to their offices and wrote fairly cautious stories. Coogan and Gageby talked by phone that night and agreed that Hillery's denials remained unhelpfully vague and the stories should be beefed up to contain specific denials of 'another woman'.

By then it didn't matter. Seán Duignan had driven across the city to RTÉ and an astonished nation watched Duignan, who was himself feeling that all this was somewhat unreal, tell them that the president didn't have any marital problems. The nation, which hadn't for a second had any notion of such problems, collectively blinked in amazement.

Hibernia came out next day with a bland story saying Hillery wasn't resigning.

There was a theory at the time that someone in the Haughey wing of Fianna Fáil spread the rumours. It's possible they did, for devilment. They never did like Hillery. There was a theory that the rumours came from the Garda Síochána. Again, no evidence. Probably it was just one of those things. Unfounded rumours of that type float around newspaper circles all the time. Had Hillery not panicked there would have been no scandal.

HNWI

A term used in banking and financial circles, indicating someone requiring special treatment. They are to be given easy loans and allowed 'non-recourse' facilities and if their investments falter their debts can be written off and claimed against tax, their activities subsidised by lower classes of people. HNWI means High Net Worth Individual.

See: Golden Circle; Non-recourse Loans.

Hogan, Phil

The Minister of State for Finance was expected to explain and stonewall, instead he resigned. Phil Hogan's resignation was a rare case of a politician taking responsibility when he might have blustered and bluffed and held onto his job.

Around midday on Wednesday, 8 February 1995, Budget Day, Hogan, having left a meeting and now due in the Dáil chamber, hurriedly examined two documents, okayed them and passed them to an adviser, Tim Wray. One was a press release, welcoming the budget; the other was a two-page document outlining the main provisions of the budget. Hogan intended using the latter to brief his Fine Gael colleagues later that day, once the budget speech had been delivered. There was a misunderstanding. Wray included the two-page briefing document with the press release and faxed the lot to the evening papers.

Over the previous few days there had been a major scandal, as people associated with coalition partners Fine Gael, Labour and Democratic Left leaked one budget secret after another. It was a breathtaking exercise in irresponsibility, as each party jostled to claim credit for various parts of the impending budget.

Phil Hogan's release of budget details was no leak; it was a mistake. The fax arrived at newspaper offices complete with Hogan's name and phone number on the top of each page. Yet, Fianna Fáil, annoyed at the budget leaks and unable to finger anyone for them, decided to unleash a barrage of condemnation, accusing Hogan of leaking the budget.

Hogan's boss, Ruairí Quinn, was lukewarm in his defence. 'He has to go,' said Fianna Fáil's Brian Cowen. 'Wrongdoing has been established.' The previous year, Phil Hogan had pursued Brian Cowen over the Arcon shares controversy. Now, Hogan was on the rack and Cowen was putting the boot in.

Next day, Hogan went into the Dáil and unreservedly apologised. He explained the mistakes in detail. He put the blame on his own lack of clarity rather than on his adviser, who actually sent the faxes. That lack of clarity, as he hurried to attend the Dáil chamber, caused confusion, he said. Then, as the opposition prepared to lash into him, he resigned.

It was so unusual to have a minister admit errors and resign that the Dáil was somewhat stunned. Some of those preparing to denounce Hogan found themselves feeling sorry for him. Something not unrelated to admiration was expressed in some quarters.

Those who had deliberately leaked confidential information in the days before the budget remained anonymous and paid no penalty. Opposition leader Bertie Ahern said that Hogan was an honourable man who had become a fall guy who took the rap for the leakers.

See: Cowengate.

Hospital Sweeps

B efore there was Charlie Bird or Sam Smyth or even Vincent Browne, there was Joe MacAnthony, investigative reporter. In 1973, in a three-page exposé in the *Sunday Independent*, he revealed the inner workings of the Irish Hospitals Sweepstakes. It was not a pretty sight. The number of wheelers, dealers and shady characters in the American distribution network who had allegedly pocketed money that should have been going to build hospitals was staggering. But if the public was outraged, it kept it to itself. The matter was raised once or twice in the Dáil but other than that nothing much happened. Other media did little to chase the story. One magazine tried to have another look under the lid that MacAnthony had lifted, but it was stopped. Publisher Hugh McLoughlin withdrew the July 1973 issue of *Profile* magazine. Its cover story on the Sweepstakes was, he said, 'a second-hand story. There's nothing illegal about the Sweep's activities in this country, it may be illegal abroad.'

If there was ever a licence to print money, it was the Irish Hospitals Sweepstakes, established in 1940 by former government minister Joseph McGrath, Richard Duggan and Spencer Freeman. It was the original Irish solution to an Irish problem. Get the emigrant community to foot the bill for public hospitals and make a packet of money for the promoters while you're at it.

This was all before state lotteries, when gambling was illegal in Canada and most parts of the United States. It was also illegal for one country to sell lottery tickets in another. Through the vast network of Irish emigrants and their descendants, Sweep's tickets were sold illegally. Some states in America turned a blind eye. When others didn't, the Sweep developed a complicated system of hoodwinking the police and postal authorities. As Joe MacAnthony revealed, the American distribution system involved bribes, backhanders or sweet deals for just about everybody involved. Canadian police reckoned that only one-third of the money raised ever found its way back to Ireland.

At home the deal was: 25 per cent of the proceeds to go to the hospitals, up to 30 for administration, and the rest for the prize fund. But the 25 per cent for the hospitals came only after certain expenses were deducted (including the aforementioned undisclosed bribes, backhanders and sweet deals). In the Grand National Draw of 1932, the tickets in the drum were worth £911,853 more than the published proceeds. But since the Sweep was reputed to have saved the hospitals from bankruptcy, no one much cared. And the people who ran the Sweep got very rich indeed. In 1973 MacAnthony estimated that the owners had amassed wealth of £100 million. They collected a fee for running the Sweep, many also got salaries and it's anybody's guess who made what on expenses. Then there were the sidelines. Richard Duggan, the former bookmaker who dreamed up the Sweep, realised there was extra money to be made buying shares in potentially winning tickets. When the tickets were drawn from the drum — and before the race was run — the names were phoned to an agent in New York and he'd contact the potential winners and offer a fixed sum for a half-share in the tickets. For the ticket-holder, it was a bird in the hand. For an experienced bookmaker it was a sure thing.

The Irish Hospitals Sweepstakes provided a launching pad for the wealth of the McGrath family. In an interview with the RTÉ programme 7 Days, Senator Paddy McGrath explained how the success of the

Sweepstakes enabled the family to build other businesses which made them very wealthy indeed. 'Business is a funny thing. First thing you have got to do is establish which is probably known as a track record. After that doors are open to you and everything else like that and you can go ahead from there . . . Credit is available to you. You can finance other businesses and so forth like that. That's where the Sweep came into the whole business . . . the success of the Sweep financed all our other industries, in other words enabled the finance for the other industries to be set up.' It was the other industries, such as Waterford Glass, he said, that really established the family as millionaires.

Even as Joe MacAnthony was writing his exposé, the fortunes of the Sweep were on the wane. Where once 55 per cent of capital expenditure on hospitals had come from the Sweep, now that figure was down to 2 per cent. In the United States, state lotteries were being established. At home, the Irish Hospitals Sweepstakes was on its last legs. Into the 1980s the only remote hope for survival was in securing the contract for Ireland's National Lottery, but that went to An Post. The Sweep closed in 1987 and 160 workers were sent packing with minimum redundancy payments. Those who had worked for the company for forty years got £3,300. There they were, in the recession-ridden 1980s, most of them in their mid-fifties, with no job prospects. The Labour Court agreed they'd been hard done by and said they should get another £10,000 but their employer, Hospitals' Trust Ltd, was in liquidation and couldn't pay.

The headquarters of the Irish Hospitals Sweepstakes, where the redundant employees had worked, was located in Ballsbridge in the heart of Dublin 4. The building and site were owned by the Hospitals Trust Board, a statutory body which distributed the funds gathered by Hospitals' Trust Ltd, the company which employed the workers. In July 1988 the site sold for £6.6 million. In its time it was a record price for property sold at auction. And it was an unusual auction. Admission was restricted to those who could produce bank drafts worth £250,000. That certainly kept out the riff-raff. And it kept out the redundant Sweep's workers — mostly middle-aged women — who were protesting outside.

Hume Street

I t didn't help that the people most identified with the campaign to preserve Dublin's architectural heritage were Lord this or Lady that. They made the property developers look like patriots as they knocked down the remnants of Georgian Dublin and slapped up office blocks. Old Ireland versus brash new Ireland. One government minister quoted by Frank McDonald in *The Destruction of Dublin* said of two demolished Georgian houses next to the National Museum: 'I was glad to see them go. They stood for everything I hate.'

In 1960 Busaras was the only office block in Dublin. Twenty years later there were about 300, most of them uninspired rectangles of glass and concrete. In the old phrase: half of them looked like the boxes the other half came in. The office block contagion did nothing for the city but it helped create and underwrite a new aristocracy of builders, developers and their political cronies.

There were punctuation marks along the way when conservationists tried to call a halt to it all. Hume Street was one such pause. It started on 15 December 1969 when a group of UCD architectural students noticed the scaffolding going up outside number 45 St Stephen's Green at the corner of Hume Street. A staircase had been ripped out, parts of the roof were gone. The students began an occupation that went on for six months.

Already, big chunks of Stephen's Green had been demolished. Georgian buildings were being knocked down like dominoes. The corner of Merrion Row was now dominated by an office block. The Green Property Company planned to do much the same with the corner of Hume Street. It had secured agreement from Donogh O'Malley, then parliamentary secretary of the OPW, to take over the state-owned adjacent buildings at 46 St Stephen's Green, and 1 Hume Street. The development had received outline permission and none of the conservation groups noticed. There were no objections and full planning permission was granted.

Architect Sam Stephenson, with many office blocks already to his name, was involved in the project. He said: 'Georgian Dublin is living on borrowed time.' Conservationists should stop 'bleating about preserving Georgian Dublin for posterity because they might not want it'.

In the early hours of Sunday morning of 7 June 1970 men armed with pickaxes and a battering ram smashed down the door of 45 St Stephen's Green. Protesters or no protesters, the demolition was under way. Four protesters — Duncan Stewart, Rosemary McCallion, George Hodnett and Marie McMahon — were inside. As word got around, they were joined by many others, including Garret FitzGerald and a large contingent of gardaí. Hundreds now joined the occupation and the demolition was stopped for the time being.

The government was otherwise occupied at the time. It was the middle of the Arms Crisis. Kevin Boland had resigned, Charles Haughey and Neil Blaney been fired. George Colley was now Minister for Finance and he came up with a compromise 'solution'. There would be no more demolition until Green Property Company secured planning permission for a scheme that would feature façades 'in a style that would maintain as far as possible the existing quality and character of the streetscape'.

Green Property developed the Hume Street site more or less as it wanted to behind a Georgian-ish façade. Over the next several years, crass office blocks gave way to phoney Georgian office blocks. It was an easy way out when a developer was faced with conservationist opposition and arguably led to even more office blocks receiving planning permission.

The Hume Street saga was replayed a few years later when architectural students tried to save St Ann's School and Molesworth Hall, two Victorian buildings, from property speculator Patrick Gallagher's plans to level them and build a large office block. He won an injunction in the High Court to stop the occupation and, in the dead of night, before the students could plan what to do next, the demolition workers moved in. Gallagher's office block was built and he earned more than £2 million by selling the building, complete with long-term tenants such as the EEC Commission, to the Aer Lingus Pension Fund.

Brats such as Gallagher determined the shape of Dublin.

I

Industry-wide

This innocuous term took on a certain meaning following the exposure in 1998 of AIB's involvement in bogus offshore accounts totalling in the region of £600 million. The bank defended its record in facilitating fraud by pointing out that this was an 'industry-wide' problem. Other banks were aiding the fraudsters and if AIB didn't provide this service it would lose market share.

Industry-wide, then, became a recognised excuse for disregard of the law. In non-banking language it roughly translates as 'Everyone is at it, so that's all right, then.'

Investment Fraud

M ark P. Synnott set up Mark Synnott (Life & Pensions) Brokers in the 1950s. His son, Mark A. Synnott, was a charmer who in the 1980s diverted the company into investments on behalf of clients. Mark A. appeared to know a lot about the stock market. Plausible, charming, crooked, he knew nothing about the stock market, or much else. Mostly, what he knew about was having a good time on someone else's money.

The scam was incredibly simple. Synnott convinced people to give him their money to invest. He promised returns of up to 25 per cent. People gave him their money. Generally, they were old people, vulnerable people seeking to stretch their savings. One man who had received compensation for the effects of thalidomide invested it all, £70,000, with Synnott.

As the 1980s turned into the 1990s, young Mark had taken in sums in the tens and hundreds of thousands. He enjoyed himself, lived a high life. He stole £40,000 from the firm to put as a down payment on the purchase of Cruicerath Stud, in Kildare. Trouble was, from about 1982 the firm had been insolvent. Synnott wasn't earning money from investments, either for himself or for his clients — he had merely banked the money. He withdrew money as he needed it to finance his every need. Synnott was living the fantasy of a successful broker, fascinated by his own charmed life.

Clients expected a dividend. Occasionally, some would withdraw their money. Synnott would simply pay them off from the money coming in from other clients. That kind of thing couldn't last and in 1991 the liquidator was called in. It was established that £2.3 million of clients' money was gone. Synnott was charged with fraudulent trading. Three charges involving funds of around £400,000 were pressed, and thirty-six other charges were dropped. His marriage broke up, he lost his home. The company was liquidated, the stud was sold, Synnott's home on Serpentine Avenue, Ballsbridge, was sold for £300,000, and when it all settled down there was a surplus of about a quarter of a million pounds, which was just enough to pay the liquidator's costs and fees. The clients who had trusted Synnott with their money in the hope of easing the circumstances of their old age ended up on social welfare. Synnott pleaded guilty and was sentenced to four years and three months in jail. He was the first company director in this country to be jailed for fraud.

Irish Permanent

As sweet deals go, it would be hard to imagine one much sweeter. Dr Edmund Farrell, executive chairman of the Irish Permanent Building Society, decided to sell his Foxrock, County Dublin home to the Irish Permanent. And it was agreed he could remain living in the house and could get it back whenever he liked — for the same price. In the meantime, the building society would pay for refurbishments. Here's how it happened.

In 1987 the ownership of Dr Farrell's Foxrock house was transferred to the Irish Permanent Building Society for £275,000. Later the Irish Permanent claimed that the price was £35,000 above its market value, but that's a detail we can leave aside for the moment. Dr Farrell had taken out three mortgages on the house over the years and he paid them all off three weeks after the ownership of the house was transferred. Presumably, that's what happened to a large chunk of the £275,000.

Then, Dr Farrell leased the house back from the Irish Permanent. The rent was £17,500 a year. Dr Farrell was now a tenant and the Irish Permanent was the landlord. Over the next four years the landlord spent £438,000 doing up the house. It was, as Dr Farrell explained, necessary because the house was used for corporate entertainment. Dr Farrell deducted some of his rent payments because of the disruption of the renovations.

One fascinating figure is that £89,000 was spent on 'soft furnishings'. That buys a lot of cushion covers and tea towels.

Four years after he sold the house, on 18 December 1991, the house was transferred back to Dr Farrell for the agreed price of £275,000. Indeed, the deal was that Dr Farrell could have bought it back for that price anytime until the year 2012. The soft furnishings bought for the house for £89,000 were sold to Dr Farrell for £34,000.

Around the same time that Dr Farrell needed £275,000 to buy back his house, a new clause was added to his contract of employment with the Irish Permanent. He received a special payment of £300,000 to agree that should he leave his job he would not work for another building society for a period of twelve months. It's what's known in the business world as 'golden handcuffs', to stop top executives going to work for rival companies. However, it was unusual in this instance because in 1991 Dr Farrell's contract with the IPBS had another five years to run and the board had an option to renew it for a further ten years after that.

In the early 1990s the world of building societies was changing. Members of the societies, particularly members of the IPBS, were complaining that they were not given enough information about how the company was run. For instance: how much money was paid in fees to individual directors? Was the £1.2 million in salaries and tax-free dividend payments given to five executive directors in 1992 not a tad excessive?

And, among the directors, moves to prepare the company for flotation on the Stock Exchange had already begun. These preparations resulted in Dr Edmund Farrell becoming front-page news. The society claimed that 'new information' about transactions involving Dr Farrell came to light as the society prepared for conversion to a public company.

On 10 March 1993 Dr Farrell, executive chairman, was suspended pending investigation. The next month, he was removed from the board 'without salary or perquisites'.

Edmund Farrell and his father before him, also Edmund, had run the Irish Permanent Building Society for almost forty years. Despite being in the ownership of its members it was effectively a family affair. Edmund Junior, who had qualified as a medical doctor, was brought into the IPBS at the age of twenty-eight. His father died three years later and it was said to be his dying wish that his son take over the reins of power. The board of directors agreed and in 1975 young Edmund became managing director. In 1975 he also bought the Foxrock house that was to cause so much trouble later.

In 1989 the Central Bank took over the supervision of the country's building societies. Before that the Registrar of Friendly Societies was the regulator but there was criticism that this was insufficient given the billions of pounds in shareholders' and depositors' money involved. But the Central Bank had failed, apparently, to spot anything unusual about Dr Farrell's transactions. In the middle of the Edmund Farrell controversy the Central Bank moved to improve the 1989 Building Societies Act and told societies that they must provide audited details of interests and transactions involving directors.

On 19 July 1993 the Irish Permanent Building Society issued proceedings against Dr Edmund Farrell for the recovery of money and property valued at £1.3 million. That sum included the Foxrock house, then valued at £600,000, a £100,000 property in Oughterard, County Galway, the £300,000 golden handcuff payment and payments to two companies set up by a personal financial adviser to Dr Farrell. In turn Dr Farrell sued the IPBS for £4.5 million for unfair dismissal.

The total sought from Dr Farrell was revealed in the Irish Permanent prospectus published for its £70 million bond issue. When the company was floated on the Stock Exchange in October 1994, its three executive directors got options to acquire shares at 180p per share. Chief executive Roy Douglas got options on 366,000 shares. The other executive directors, Peter Fitzpatrick and Peter Ledbetter, got options on 256,000 shares each. Edmund Farrell no doubt watched on with envy as the Irish Permanent share price rose steeply after flotation, guaranteeing huge profits for the directors. At the beginning of 1999 the price was about £8.80 per share.

In the years that followed, the Irish Permanent indicated there would be no settlement between the company and its former chairman. But the case was settled in November 1997. So, who won? The Irish Permanent got just £150,000 from Dr Farrell, to be paid over five years. And it released his pension fund worth £800,000. And it paid its own legal costs, and he kept the house. Dr Farrell, in turn, dropped his unfair dismissals case.

Had the case gone on, it was expected to last twelve weeks and cost each side £1.5 million. It was also expected that Dr Farrell would restate his original argument: whatever about the deal surrounding the Foxrock house, all the transactions were known to the Irish Permanent board at the time. There was the possibility that details revealed in court about how the building society had been managed in the past might undermine the stability of the new bank and its share price.

Reports in *The Irish Times* after the case suggested that the Irish Permanent considered it did well out of the settlement. This may well be true, despite the fact that the deal in no way reflected the seriousness of the allegations made against Dr Farrell four years previously.

J

James, David

As far as is known, Dr David James first began stealing in 1983. He was a distinguished art expert, one of the world's most eminent in his field, and his drift into crime seems to have been motivated by a mixture of greed and resentment.

Dr James worked for the Chester Beatty Library, at Shrewsbury Road in Dublin. The library was named after Alfred Chester Beatty, an

American mining engineer who had built a fortune in the early part of the century. Beatty travelled through the Far East buying anything that took his fancy. He bought Korans, goblets, helmets, manuscripts, swords, rugs, ancient maps, anything that wasn't nailed down. Beatty became a naturalised citizen of Britain in the 1930s and lived there into the late 1940s. For some reason he took a shine to the Ireland of that era and in 1950 he moved to Ireland and shipped his priceless collection of Oriental and Middle Eastern art, hundreds of tons of it, to Ireland, and the Chester Beatty Library was opened to the public in 1954. Two years later Beatty was given the freedom of Dublin, a year after that, at the age of eighty-three, he was given honorary Irish citizenship, and when he died in Monte Carlo in 1968 his remains were shipped to Ireland, where he was given a state funeral. He left his priceless collection to the Irish state.

Dr David James started work at the Chester Beatty Library in 1969 and in 1983 he had some expectations that he would be made director of the library. Not only did he not become director, but the man who did opted to reside in the house which the library had for several years provided free for Dr James and his family.

James had to move out and provide alternative accommodation for his family at his own expense. He began stealing.

David James was one of the leading world experts on Islamic art. He had written books and articles galore on his subject. So, when he began turning up in London art circles with pages from fifteenth- and sixteenth-century Korans for sale, this didn't seem unusual. It was understood that these were from his personal collection. It was easy crime. Most of the stuff that Dr James was stealing was uncatalogued. He was, as curator of the Islamic section, in a position of absolute trust. And the Chester Beatty Library had for years been in a state of chaos. There was a shortage of money, rows, resignations, artefacts remaining uncatalogued after decades, a strike of curators in 1986. One trustee of the library, resigning in frustration in 1988, told the Sunday Independent that the library was like 'something out of Fawlty Towers'.

When the issue was raised in the Dáil by Pat McCartan TD the Tánaiste, Brian Lenihan, said that reports of problems within the library, which was receiving large sums of public money, had 'no foundation whatever'. No problem.

Throughout this period David James continued stealing. Koran pages from the eighth and ninth centuries, paintings, ancient bookbindings, rugs, all disappeared from the library. Some of these were sold through friends, some through London art dealers, some through Sotheby's and

Christie's, the auctioneers, all unaware that the goods were stolen. Some stolen goods ended up in Bahrain, in Kuwait, in Berlin and Copenhagen.

James was disposing of the stuff as he needed extra money. He kept some rugs for his Sandford Road home, and some artefacts he kept as wall decorations.

Some of the items stolen are considered beyond price, but when the authorities finally attempted to put a figure on James's loot they settled on £455,340, a thoroughly conservative estimate. At the time he was arrested, James had received approximately £105,000 for items which he had managed to sell.

In 1989 James took a three-year career break and went to work for an Islamic art museum in London. His new employer provided him with a West Hampstead flat and James commuted back and forth between London and Dublin. He brought some of his loot to London and hung it on the walls of the flat. And he kept on selling the stolen goods he had accumulated.

Things started going wrong in April of 1991. Daniel Walker, James's equivalent at the New York Metropolitan Museum of Art, was in London. He visited an art dealer named Oliver Hoare (the man who was subjected to a barrage of strange phone calls from Diana, Princess of Wales) and was offered two pages from a ninth-century Koran. They would be worth in the region of £25,000 each. Walker was interested in buying and took back to New York transparencies of the pages.

He asked Estelle Whelan, an Islamic art expert in New York, what she thought of the pages. Estelle Whelan recognised them immediately. From 1983 to 1986 she had done research work at the Chester Beatty Library and had examined the pages she was now being told were for sale. She contacted Patricia Donlon, director of the National Library, who was on the board of the Chester Beatty, and the game was up.

Two months later, in June 1991, there was a break-in at the Chester Beatty. At first it was said that items worth a quarter of a million pounds were stolen. Then it was said that 'after a detailed check' the theft was found to be 'not as serious as first believed'. In truth, it can never be known precisely what has been stolen from the library. Many valuable items remained uncatalogued. There are stories of pieces being left aside and forgotten and then found years later. It is believed that among the items stolen during the break-in was a seventeenth-century jade book, embroidered with gold and of extraordinary value. But because of the uncatalogued nature of some of the library's items what else was taken remained a matter of speculation. It was that chaos which had made David James's thefts so easy to conceal.

In 1996 a 62-year-old man, Ronald Hartigan, was arrested in London and charged with possession of a thirteenth-century manuscript, the Suwar Al-Aqalim, worth £200,000. Such was the security of the Chester Beatty Library that it was being robbed from within and without, almost at will, by thieves with no connection with one another.

Meanwhile, the David James thefts were reported to the gardaí and James was picked up in September 1991 and charged. At his trial in February 1992 David James took the stand and said he stole because he needed the money. His salary, he said, wasn't as high as that of others of his rank in New York and London. He was under pressure. He deeply regretted what he had done.

Dr James promised to help in the recovery of the material he stole and the gardaí subsequently confirmed that he was cooperative. Some of the stolen material was believed destroyed in a fire in London, some was never found, some was believed to be in the hands of dealers as far apart as New York and Syria. Some materials were voluntarily returned by one Arab dealer when he realised the artefacts he had purchased were stolen. The value of these goods alone was £450,000. Obviously, the official estimation of the value of James's thefts, £455,000, was a woeful underestimate.

David James was highly respected in social circles and among his friends who took the stand to testify to his good character were Sheamus Smith, the film censor, and Seóirse Bodley, UCD professor of music. Written testimonials came from eminent people in Oxford and Tel Aviv and from the Irish ambassador to Egypt. Judge Michael Moriarty gave James a sentence of five years.

Jinks, John

He was the prototype gobdaw TD. John Jinks was elected to the Dáil in June 1927 for the National League, and survived as TD for Leitrim-Sligo for all of three months. The National League was an attempt to resuscitate the fortunes of the Irish Parliamentary Party, destroyed several years earlier by the upsurge of support for Sinn Féin. Jinks was one of eight TDs elected on the National League ticket. He was a little hustler of the type that would become widespread over the years to come: a politician who was also an auctioneer, as well as a publican, and a grocer into the bargain. Your granny might have referred to such a man as a grab-all.

The post-election period saw an effort to forge an alliance between the Labour Party, the National League and the newly formed and, in the words of Seán Lemass, 'slightly constitutional' Fianna Fáil, which was entering the Dáil for the first time. The three parties could just about outvote the Cumann na nGaedheal government.

On the day of the vote the combined parties topped the government by just one TD. A former Unionist MP, Major Bryan Cooper, having become a Cumann na nGaedheal TD, buttonholed Jinks. Ten years earlier Jinks had helped recruit young men for the British army, to be sent to the slaughter fields of the First World War, and much of his fairly slim support (he squeaked into the last seat with just 2,224 votes) came from ex-servicemen.

Major Cooper, and *Irish Times* editor Bertie Smyllie, argued with Jinks that his electorate wouldn't be happy if Jinks were to help put Fianna Fáil, the republican gunmen, into government. The extent to which drink played a role in the discussions is disputed, but Cooper eventually got Jinks onto the Sligo train. With Jinks out of the picture the Dáil vote was tied and the Ceann Comhairle's casting vote saved the government. Jinks lost his seat at the September 1927 election (he was bottom of the poll, with just 1,506 votes) and died seven years later. The scandal of the gobdaw TD with the small shopkeeper mentality, with the political commitment of a fieldmouse, helped create a certain kind of image for our parliamentarians and ensured a small place in history for Jinks.

Jobbery

The term is now out of fashion, although the practice is not. Jobbery is the implementation of the philosophy contained in the popular saying, 'It's not what you know, it's who you know.' Party supporters get a leg-up from the politicians whose careers they have worked to promote. There was a time when jobbery was practised shamelessly. Here's Fine Gael's Oliver J. Flanagan in 1965: he was, he said, 'a great believer in putting a friend into a good job', and his ambition was to attain a position from which he could fill 'every post I can, subject to qualifications and ability, with my own friends and political supporters'. And here's Fianna Fáil's Donogh O'Malley, the same year, saying the same thing: he had 'no hesitation, all things being equal, in supporting people who support me or us'.

This was the polite, public explanation. Once the party was in power, everything not nailed down was transferred to party supporters. Barristers, for instance, who supported the party in power got most of the prosecution and other state-side briefs. In 1974 the appointment of an independent Director of Public Prosecutions put a stop to that.

Public scepticism, boosted by open jobbery, and such affairs as the Baltinglass and Taca scandals, gradually led to a more subtle approach. The patronage became less blatant: obstacles which might have stood in the way of a party supporter's plans melted; obstacles unforeseen might appear in the path of someone unconnected, who hadn't graced the parties' election funds with something a damn sight more valuable than silver.

See: Baltinglass, Battle of; Taca.

Journalism

Down through the years, a number of journalists sought to uncover the financial scandals which would explode in all our faces in the late 1990s. On the whole, the media didn't do enough, were too trusting, too complacent, but there were serious attempts to get under the surface where the worms were wriggling.

In an atmosphere where legal vultures flap their wings at every sentence published, and seek to extract libellous intent from factual exposition, when there is always someone blaming the messenger, it is right for journalists to note — without vanity or complacency — not just the failures but the fact that journalism did its job as best it could, while others averted their eyes.

At *Magill* and later at the *Sunday Tribune*, Vincent Browne used to have a note, 'Haughey's finances', on virtually every editorial list he drew up. If the aspiration met with little success it is no wonder: even the tribunals — with power to examine bank accounts and company files — had trouble getting the whole truth. It is worth noting that the questions continued to be asked, and when the sleaze started flushing out from under the doors of Dublin Castle reporters made the connections that helped make sense of it all.

In the 1970s, Joe MacAnthony took on the Sweepstakes story and looked into the affairs of Ray Burke. In 1983 Des Crowley accurately revealed Charlie Haughey's debt to AIB and was branded a liar by the bank. Joe Joyce and Peter Murtagh dissected the Boss. Mary Raftery skewered Patrick Gallagher and documented the truth about the industrial schools. Susan O'Keeffe exposed the meat industry and Fintan O'Toole filleted the beef barons. Sam Smyth uncovered the Greencore and Michael Lowry scandals. Charlie Bird and George Lee of RTÉ caught NIB, Liam Collins of the *Sunday Independent* caught AIB, *Magill* caught Irish Life. Matt Cooper of the *Sunday Tribune*, Frank Connolly of the *Sunday Business Post* and Jody Corcoran of the *Sunday Independent* repeatedly threw light into dark corners, as did Cliff Taylor of *The Irish Times* and Brian Dowling of the *Irish Independent*. The relentless work of Colm Keena of *The Irish Times*, in putting the pieces together and presenting a comprehensible picture, was unmatched. Mary Caniffe, Carol Coulter, Siobhan Creaton, Ursula Halligan were among the many others who uncovered and analysed various parts of a variety of puzzles.

There was another journalist who in 1985 produced an extraordinary book which even today — especially today — makes fascinating reading. Frank McDonald wrote *The Destruction of Dublin* and had a hell of a time getting it past the lawyers. Even those who don't agree with all of McDonald's views about the aesthetics of Dublin architecture recognised a superb work of journalism. He introduced us to a world of characters who years later would strut and fret their hour upon the stage of one tribunal or another.

McDonald accurately described Des Traynor as 'Haughey's bagman'. No, said a lawyer who checked the manuscript for possible libel, you can't say that. So, it was taken out. And more with it. And the lawyer was right. Until the tribunals put certain matters on the public record, it was just too risky to tell the truth about Haughey and his like.

Even McDonald didn't grasp the extent of the sleaze and corruption underlying the pretensions of 'this great little nation', but his book accurately pinned down the patterns of behaviour — the property, the money, the connections, the deals — which were the foundations for much of the corruption that was going on.

And nothing was done about it. It was all lying there between the pages of a book, a dozen years before the McCracken Tribunal, and no one did anything. The Oireachtas turned blind eyes, the Revenue Commissioners made themselves busy putting small firms out of business, the Central Bank busied itself with cosy interpretations of prudential regulation, the state put its forces to work combating people who cleaned windows while claiming the dole.

See: Hume Street.

K

Kavanagh, Patrick

Poet Paddy Kavanagh, gruff and all as he was, was an unlikely source of scandal over thirty years after his death. The controversy that continues to swirl around his ghost is a sad echo of old feuds and deeply felt hurt. When Kavanagh died in 1967 he was buried at Inniskeen, County Monaghan. His grave was later marked by a teak cross, donated by his brother Peter, who had a zealous devotion to the poet's memory. After Patrick's widow, Kathleen, died a couple of decades later, she too was buried in the plot. The teak cross was removed, and a commemoration committee erected a headstone. Peter Kavanagh looked after the discarded cross.

Things simmered. In August 1998 the commemoration stone disappeared. It was replaced by the teak cross.

Peter Kavanagh, who lived in America, was home when this happened. He denied removing the stone. 'It seems to have been taken away by spirits in the night,' he said. He denounced the stone as a 'pagan monument', and said it was an insult to have it over the grave of 'the only great Catholic poet in Ireland'.

KBI

Banking jargon for member of the Golden Circle. It means Key Business Influencer. Translation: someone with connections, who may — if treated right — bring us business from another HNWI.

See: Golden Circle; HNWI.

Keane, Mr Justice Ronan

It is unclear if Terry Keane, in her *Sunday Times* memoir, set out to damage her husband, Mr Justice Ronan Keane, or whether the judge simply suffered what is known as collateral damage. Terry Keane's story, if true, disclosed personal details of her marriage which were the business of no one but a husband and wife.

One allegation by Terry Keane, of how Ronan Keane was appointed to the bench, was of public significance. Judge Keane was called to the Bar in 1954 and became a senior counsel sixteen years later. In 1979 he was appointed to the High Court and he was later appointed to the Supreme Court. In her memoir, Terry Keane claimed that in 1979 she 'said to Charlie that I thought our Ronan should become a judge'. Keane claimed that Haughey engaged in a political manoeuvre to have Ronan Keane appointed to the bench, as a way of testing his clout within Jack Lynch's cabinet. She claimed that two ministers, Michael O'Kennedy and Brian Lenihan, proposed Ronan Keane as a judge and 'carried the day' for Haughey.

O'Kennedy immediately denied that this happened. Brian Lenihan is dead. The judge remained silent. Despite the judge's excellent reputation, and the sleazy source of the allegation, a shadow had been cast on Ronan Keane's career.

Keane, Terry

According to Rory Godson and John Ryan of *The Sunday Times*, they were first approached in 1998 about the possibility of employing Terry Keane. For over ten years Keane had fronted a gossip column, The Keane Edge, in the *Sunday Independent*. Would *The Sunday Times* be interested in taking that column? The answer was no. There were discussions about Keane writing a 'memoir', but this came to nothing.

In the early 1980s, Keane wrote a fashion column for the *Sunday Press*. She was hired by the *Sunday Independent* and although much of the gossip column was written by others, The Keane Edge made her well known and was a great success with readers. The column had a strong line in puns; it exalted a café society that didn't exist, and promoted the social status of people with no accomplishment to their credit other than getting themselves mentioned in a gossip column. It was often nasty and intrusive.

Keane was long known within journalism and political circles to have been having an affair with Charlie Haughey. That connection was the basis for her prosperity as a gossip columnist; without it, she would have scraped a living writing low-profile fashion material. Her column was peppered with hints about her relationship with 'Sweetie'. This gave it a risqué touch. However, since it was also peppered with her claims to be Princess Diana's best friend, and similar fictions, the references to the Haughey affair could always be brushed off as a fantasy, a joke.

Had Keane sold her story when Haughey was Taoiseach she would have lost the goose that was gilding her golden egg. In May 1999, with Haughey under investigation by the Moriarty Tribunal, the high life he had shared with Keane for twenty-seven years wasn't so high any more. There was little social cachet in being the mistress of a disgraced ex-Taoiseach. Keane hadn't written anything for the column for two years. The column had run its course. There was word that journalist Kevin O'Connor had written a book in which the relationship with Haughey would be detailed. Keane's options were rapidly running out.

Had Keane gone to *The Sunday Times* with her memoir in 1998 she would have been in a stronger position. Now, after asking the *Sunday Independent* for a rise, and being rejected, she hurriedly agreed a deal with Godson and Ryan and quit the *Sunday Independent* just two days before *The Sunday Times* published the first of four instalments of her memoir. Keane didn't write the memoir. Having signed on with the paper, she merely answered questions on tape, the result was written up and she okayed it. The memoir was being put together just hours before the newspaper went on sale.

To boost the sales, Keane agreed to go on *The Late Late Show* of 14 May, the second last show presented by Gay Byrne. The revelation, and the brutality of the manner in which it was done, stunned many and generated some sympathy for Haughey, and a lot more for his wife, Maureen. Why so brutal? Perhaps, some speculated, it was a purely commercial matter; perhaps it was a last-ditch effort to so publicly humiliate Maureen Haughey as to drive her out of her marriage, leaving Charlie and Terry to pick up the pieces.

Keane claimed that she wanted to disown the *Sunday Indo* gossip column; and she was going public only because of the Kevin O'Connor book. How this fitted in with the previous year's talks with *The Sunday Times* about the possibility of moving the column to that paper, and about the possibility of writing a memoir, long before O'Connor's book was written, is anyone's guess.

Speculation put the payment to Keane at £400,000, but Keane admitted it was a mere £65,000, plus a two-year contract at £50,000 a year. She may have received more for the use of extraordinarily intimate photographs of herself and Haughey. Given that she had to give up a lucrative position at the *Sunday Independent*, her pay-off was rather on the low side. At that stage, however, Keane was in a buyer's market.

Kelly, Nicky

The gardaí got an anonymous tip. This gave them the legal right to round up over forty members of the Irish Republican Socialist Party on suspicion of holding up a mail train near Sallins, on 31 March 1976, and stealing over £200,000. The suspects were held at various garda stations around Dublin. Several emerged from forty-eight hours detention bearing bruises. Some signed statements incriminating themselves in the robbery. They later alleged they had been beaten by gardaí until they agreed to sign; the police denied this. Gardaí claimed in some cases that the suspects beat themselves up.

Six men were charged and the case was thrown out because the state took too long providing a book of evidence.

Of the six, only four were recharged and tried. Sixty-five days into the trial a judge, who had been sleeping on the bench, died, and the case had to be retried. Of the four accused, three were found guilty: Osgur Breatnach, Brian McNally and Nicky Kelly. Breatnach and McNally spent seventeen months in jail before being acquitted on appeal: it was found that their statements were taken in oppressive circumstances.

By this time Nicky Kelly had skipped bail and fled to the USA, convinced he was going to jail for a crime he didn't commit. He returned after Breatnach and McNally were released and was sent to jail for twelve years. Public disquiet resulted in a persistent campaign to get him released. After serving four years Kelly was released on 17 July 1984 on spurious 'humanitarian' grounds. Kelly continued to fight to clear his name and eventually received a state pardon and financial compensation.

See: Sleeping Judge.

Kennedy, Fr Michael

For a few short weeks in September 1995, the otherwise unremarkable town of Dungarvan, County Waterford became the AIDS capital of Ireland and the home of a modern morality tale that played to old-fashioned fears and prejudices.

At Sunday Mass on the morning of 10 September the handsome Fr Michael Kennedy (distant cousin and close friend of the more famous American Kennedys) told a gobsmacked congregation that at least five young men of the parish had been deliberately infected with the AIDS virus by an English woman. Angry at having contracted the disease herself, she was hitting back at men by having sex with as many as were willing. In six months, the priest told his startled congregation, she had slept with between sixty and eighty men in Munster. As well as the original five, the priest had tracked down a further twenty men who were now awaiting test results.

It was shocking stuff, but might have gone no further were it not for John Murphy, a *Cork Examiner* reporter who was in the congregation. The next day, Dungarvan's AIDS avenger was national news and before long international news. With every interview, Fr Kennedy revealed more details. The five infected men had all attended the same school. None was married but three were in steady relationships. The woman was a 25-year-old university graduate born of Irish parents but raised in England. She was 'petite, dark-skinned with a hint of red colouring in her auburn hair'. She was motivated by rage at the man, thought to be from Munster, who had infected her. Now in the final stage of her illness, disfigured by lesions on her face and racked by guilt, she had gone back to England to die.

The Southern Health Board stated that there had been no increase in HIV infection or inquiries in Munster. And, of course, it remained implausible that such a sexually active 25-year-old English redhead would go unnoticed in a town the size of Dungarvan. But Fr Kennedy stood by his story and there was no reason to doubt the priest's honesty or good intentions. In media reports, the number of men said to be infected rose from five to nine or a possible fourteen.

For any woman in the area who remotely fit the description, it was a trying time. However, despite hordes of journalists scouring Dungarvan, the woman and her victims were never found. As one local man was reported saying six months after the furore: 'Put it like this: it was a good sermon. After that I don't know. So far, the story is the only thing that has died here.'

The AIDS scare died away as the scare story lost credibility. Nothing more was heard from Fr Kennedy for a couple of years until he turned up in a photograph in *Hello!* magazine, at a wedding of one of the USA Kennedy clan. He was also with the Kennedys for the funeral ceremony of John F. Kennedy Jr in July 1999.

Kerry Babies

The scandal that puzzled the nation for months on end began with the finding of a newborn baby's body on the beach at Cahirciveen, County Kerry on the evening of Saturday, 14 April 1984. The baby had been stabbed several times. Experienced detectives stationed in Dublin, known colloquially as the 'murder squad', became involved in the investigation. Over two weeks later, on 1 May, gardaí arrested a young woman from the village of Abbeydorney, Joanne Hayes, along with her mother, aunt, sister and two brothers.

Joanne Hayes had had a baby the previous year by her married lover, Jeremiah Locke. She became pregnant again and in or around 12 April 1984 had the baby at home (either in a field or in her bedroom) and the baby died. Medical evidence couldn't spell out an exact cause of death, but there was no evidence of violence. Joanne wrapped the baby in a plastic bag and hid it in a hole a couple of fields away from the house. That two women should have babies around the same time, that one died at birth and the other was stabbed to death was a coincidence that would lead to much pain.

Joanne soon told gardaí that she had buried her baby on the farm. They didn't seem to believe her. Within hours, Joanne, her sister, mother and two brothers had signed statements. Joanne's statement said, and the others supported this, that she had stabbed her baby to death and she threw it into the sea at Dingle.

The case was open and shut until it fell apart, when blood testing revealed that Joanne Hayes and Jeremiah Locke could not have been the parents of the baby found stabbed at Cahirciveen. If Joanne did not stab the baby (and her baby was not stabbed), if she did not throw it into the sea (and the body of her baby was found on the farm, where she said it was), then how could she and her family freely have made detailed confessions describing that stabbing, describing the trip to Dingle, describing the baby thrown into the sea?

A tribunal of inquiry, headed by Mr Justice Kevin Lynch, was launched. It sat, first in Tralee and then in Dublin Castle, for a total of 77 days and heard 109 witnesses. The gardaí maintained an esoteric theory which explained the difference in blood group by claiming that Joanne had twins by two different fathers. There was also a theory that the dead baby's blood type changed, due to decomposition. The garda case was eventually shot down by a medical expert brought in by the gardaí themselves.

Judge Lynch never satisfactorily explained the confessions. He wrote a report which found that Joanne murdered her baby by choking it. The state pathologist, Dr John Harbison, had been unable to ascertain a cause of death. He could not say for certain that the baby achieved a separate existence. Judge Lynch found as a fact that the family intended bringing the dead baby to Dingle and throwing it into the sea, but changed their minds. Then, under garda questioning, they each — independently — invented such matters as Joanne stabbing the baby, and they remembered the trip to Dingle they intended making, told the gardaí they had in fact made that trip, embroidered their story, and thus freely confessed to a crime they didn't commit. Some found that a somewhat large leap of faith was required if one was to agree fully with the judge's findings.

The tribunal aroused strong feelings, not least about the manner in which witnesses were questioned by barristers. The controversy, following on the death of Ann Lovett and the Eileen Flynn controversy, created much debate about the position of pregnant women in Irish society.

See: Flynn, Eileen; Lovett, Ann.

Kerry Car Crash

In the hours before dawn of 22 September 1982 a Special Branch garda was driving a green Ford Granada near Ballybunion when it went off the road and into a field. The car ended up upside down, but although the driver was shocked and dazed he wasn't seriously hurt. From this unspectacular accident there arose a scandal in which the Minister for Justice was alleged to be driving around Kerry in the small hours of the morning with a blonde singer.

After a couple of weeks, word leaked out about the crash, and the name of Seán Doherty was attached to the affair. The media sniffed a Haughey-related scandal. An *Irish Times* photographer caught up with the crashed car in a Dublin garage. The garage owner rushed to pull the door shut, obligingly giving the photographer a shot of someone apparently attempting to conceal something. For almost a month, the Garda Press Office denied there had been any such accident. Then there were mutterings about the need to preserve confidentiality for security reasons.

Had everyone been open and frank from the beginning there would have been no scandal. But the ham-fisted attempt to cover up what happened created a series of bizarre rumours. It was said that Doherty was squiring a well-known blonde pop singer and they were on their way to or from an occasion of sin when Doherty's car went off the road, possibly blown off the road by the heat of the passion within.

The truth was much more humdrum. Doherty and some friends had been attending the races at Listowel. Being Minister for Justice, Doherty was accompanied by armed gardaí. On the evening of 21 September Doherty and his companions ended up at the Ambassador Hotel in Ballybunion. There they met others, including two women, who joined the four and before long there were ten people in Doherty's party. They moved on to a restaurant near Fenit. The partying, which was quite innocent, went on until four in the morning, at which point they all went back to the Brandon in Tralee, where some were staying.

The two women from the party needed a lift to Ballybunion, where they were staying at the Ambassador Hotel. An armed garda gave them a lift and on his way back his car went off the road. The driver was found by other gardaí and they took him to Tralee.

That should have been the end of the story. However, with sensitive politicians anxious to cover up what was little more than a night on the tiles, the deceit began. One of the party, Tom McEllistrim TD, claimed that they had all arrived at the hotel in Tralee at 2 a.m., instead of 4.30 a.m. This wasn't the brightest thing McEllistrim had ever done, as the party was seen entering the hotel at 4.30 a.m. He later explained that he feared embarrassment: 'You mustn't say to the press that you were inside a pub until four o'clock in the morning.'

Although there was nothing much to hide, in the atmosphere of the time the attempt to cover up what happened inevitably created a whiff of scandal which lingers to this day.

Throughout this period various journalists tried to dig up the truth. One senior journalist phoned Seán Doherty and told him he was about to run a story about the blonde singer, and he wanted to get Doherty's side of the story. Doherty swore that nothing improper had happened and pleaded that the story not be run. The story, which couldn't be stood up, was not run. Doherty had great difficulty during this phone conversation, speaking vaguely and in euphemisms, as he discussed his personal behaviour. He knew that the journalist's phone was tapped and that gardaí were listening to everything he said. Doherty knew because he had signed the warrant.

L

Lawlor, Liam

In a 1991 interview with the *Sunday Business Post* after he'd lost his seat on Dublin County Council, Dublin West TD Liam Lawlor mused that some day he'd like to be a government minister. 'I would like to bring my businesslike decision-making to a government department such as health, social welfare or education.'

Originally a refrigeration engineer, Lawlor is one whose name has cropped up from time to time over the years in various places where business and political interests merge. Property developer Tom Gilmartin paid the deputy £3,500 per month for a few months in the 1980s. The money was first reported as a consultancy fee. Lawlor later said it was a political donation. He would be consulting his accountant to make sure he had 'fully complied with the tax aspect' of the payments which he recalled getting over a period of three to four months.

Tom Gilmartin didn't explain much, except to say: 'I would not have that man consulting on a shithouse.'

In 1999 RTÉ's Charlie Bird uncovered a financial link between former assistant Dublin city and county manager George Redmond and the Dublin businessman and arcade owner Jimmy Kennedy. Bird's report stated that an unnamed politician met Kennedy and Redmond on Kennedy's premises. Lawlor issued a public statement identifying himself as that politician, but insisting that what was said about him was untrue. Lawlor said that while he knew Redmond and Kennedy he had never attended a meeting with both of them and had never met Redmond on Kennedy's premises.

Liam Lawlor was one of the politicians most identified with the rezoning extravaganza that took place in Dublin in the 1980s. The city planners — public servants — put together a county development plan designating which areas were suitable for which kinds of development. County councillors could get land rezoned in contravention of the plan by way of what is called a 'section 4' motion. During a term of office that lasted for six years, from 1985 to 1991, the Fianna Fáil-dominated council passed a total of 185 section 4 motions. Of these, 137 were vigorously opposed by the planners — usually because of inadequate sewerage, water or roads infrastructure.

Even Charlie Haughey later remarked that there had sometimes been an 'injudicious' use of section 4 motions. But the politicians who pushed them through argued they were necessary because the county development plan was too inflexible to meet social needs.

For property developers, each section 4 decision was a potential goldmine. If agricultural land could be rezoned for houses or a shopping centre, the developer stood to make a huge profit. For the developers the strategy was fairly simple. Buy agricultural land at a low price; lobby like crazy until the land is rezoned; collect profits. And because section 4 motions came first at council meetings, as per standing orders, other business simply fell off the agenda. During that time Liam Lawlor was one of the councillors who most often proposed or seconded section 4 motions.

Public reaction against such wanton rezoning probably cost Liam Lawlor his council seat in 1991, but he has always insisted there was nothing improper about rezoning. 'There was no abuse of section 4. The problem was that there was no other way we could grant permission to build houses in the area.'

Lawlor failed to regain his council seat in June 1999, when — ironically enough — he lost out to former party colleague Colm McGrath. McGrath had been deselected as a candidate by Fianna Fáil when he admitted accepting financial contributions from Owen O'Callaghan, the developer who took over the Quarryvale project from Tom Gilmartin. McGrath was re-elected as an independent.

Lawlor featured in another row in 1989 when he was chairman of the Oireachtas Committee on Commercial State-sponsored Bodies. He was also a non-executive director of Food Industries, a Larry Goodman company, and collected a salary of £6,000 a year to attend board meetings.

Irish Sugar came under the scrutiny of the committee because of plans to close its plant in Thurles. However, Fianna Fáil, in an election promise, had said it would keep the plant open. Thus, a consultants' report on the problems of the plant and its future was prepared for the committee. At the same time, Food Industries was proposing to buy the Thurles plant. The controversy involving Liam Lawlor revolved around whether he had seen the consultants' report prepared for the Oireachtas Committee, of which he was the chairman, and whether that information had been relayed to Food Industries, of which he was a director. A Dáil investigation exonerated him of any wrongdoing but he resigned his position on the committee. Subsequently, Liam Lawlor stated that he didn't believe there was anything wrong with politicians acting as non-executive directors as long as that interest is publicly declared.

Lawyers' Fees

The scandal of lawyers' fees erupted out of the Beef Tribunal, where some barristers were charging £2,000 and £3,000 a day, but there was nothing new about such a level of fees. In a 1989 case, appealed to the Supreme Court, the bill for just one side in the thirteen-day hearing made its way into the public domain. Senior counsel charged £10,000 brief fees, with an extra £5,000 claimed once the work got under way. A junior got two-thirds of those amounts. On top of this, the two seniors and one junior each charged £2,500 per day, amounting to £32,500 each for the thirteen days the court sat. That's a total of £97,500 in daily fees, plus a total of £40,000 in brief fees. And this, the appeal, was a small part of a much larger case that ran for weeks.

It is often pointed out that most barristers cannot charge such fees, and that is true. It is also true that some of the most experienced barristers in the country give their services at rock-bottom rates in criminal legal aid cases. But barristers run a closed shop, and this artificially inflates fees. You may hire a barrister at a reasonable fee, but if you lose you are liable for the other side's costs and those costs may be multiples of the fees agreed with your own lawyer.

It is not unknown for a winning side, knowing that the fees will come out of someone else's pocket, to agree to inflate fees to levels beyond those which would have applied had the decision gone the other way. It is known within the law business that in some such cases, letters agreeing inflated fees have been written at the end of a case and backdated.

There was no such chicanery at the Beef Tribunal, where money flowed like fine wine at a barrister's birthday party. One barrister got a brief fee of £175,000 and then charged £3,000 a day. Total: just short of a million pounds. Another got £2,100 a day on top of a £52,000 brief fee. Total: just under a quarter of a million.

Larry Goodman's legal fees were over £6 million. Mr Goodman also claimed and got £3,536 for his hotel accommodation. Taxpayers also forked out £33,900 for private catering for his lawyers (everyone else used the café downstairs). And Goodman had a PR man, Pat Heneghan, on the payroll, to help journalists understand what was going on. Mr Heneghan's bill went to the taxpayer: £162,361 (and 83p).

Our favourite fee at the Beef Tribunal was that paid to Seamus McKenna SC, appearing for Larry Goodman as a person (Goodman had another lawyer appearing for him as a business entity). McKenna, not only an amiable chap but one of the best lawyers in the business, was the subject of some puzzling remarks by the Taxing Master, who assessed the fees. Having carefully considered the documentation before him, the Taxing Master said that he 'could not glean what actual work Mr McKenna did'. The Taxing Master made it clear that he wasn't saying that Mr McKenna did no work, just that he couldn't see from the paperwork what work the barrister had done. The Taxing Master decided that Mr McKenna's work was worth every penny of £434,000. And who are we, reaching for our chequebooks, to disagree?

Legal Delays

There was admiration for Chief Justice Liam Hamilton's handling of the Sheedy affair, which cost two of his judicial colleagues their jobs. After his unimpressive Beef Tribunal Report, there was fear in political circles that he would produce another such effort. There was relief when he produced a clear, full account of the Sheedy matter. There was in some quarters, where supporters of the judges simmered, a bitter resentment of Hamilton. Shortly after the two judges resigned, information came out which raised questions about Hamilton's own performance as a judge.

Although Hamilton had a reputation as a superb administrator, when president of the High Court, delays in two isolated cases were drawn to public attention in the wake of the Sheedy case. In one instance, involving a dispute over a land sale, Hamilton heard the opening of the case in October 1993, then adjourned because he was very busy, heard the final two witnesses in October 1994, and didn't give a decision until September 1995. An appeal to the Supreme Court followed, and in October 1996 Hamilton was directed to prepare a report of the original trial for the Supreme Court. It took him another year to do that. A relatively minor case begun in 1993 was resolved in 1997.

Hamilton was a busy judge, and between 1991 and 1994 he had to chair the Beef Tribunal. However, delays can cause real damage to litigants. In January 1988 Liam Hamilton heard a short case involving about £50,000 in bankruptcy fees. He promised a judgment within two weeks. Right through 1988, 1989, into the 1990s, through the setting up of the Beef Tribunal, through the tribunal's report, the litigants awaited Hamilton's judgment. Governments rose and fell. Hamilton was made chief justice. Repeated efforts to get a judgment were to no avail. In May

1995 one of the litigants died of cancer; the following month, seven years after the case was heard, Hamilton delivered his judgment. In the words of *The Sunday Times*, which recounted the case: 'The long-awaited judgment ran to little over a page.'

The family involved took the state to the European Court, claiming £1 million in damages. The state settled, and insisted on a confidentiality clause, thereby keeping the details of the matter secret from the people picking up the tab, the taxpayer. The family in the other case set out on a similar course.

Hamilton, in reporting on the Sheedy affair, found that Judge Hugh O'Flaherty's actions were 'damaging to the administration of justice', and that the actions of Judge Cyril Kelly 'compromised the administration of justice'. It appears that some were disappointed that Hamilton did his job and was critical of fellow judges, instead of remaining loyal to the fellowship of the Bar. Hamilton in turn found himself the subject of questions about whether delays of several years, causing litigants much anguish, also reduced the citizenry's confidence in the administration of justice.

See: Sheedy Affair.

Lenihan Resignation Lies

When the 'mature recollection' fiasco seriously damaged Brian Lenihan's presidential campaign in 1990, the Fianna Fáil minister came under pressure to resign from the cabinet. Fianna Fáil's coalition partners, the PDs, needed to assert their disapproval of Lenihan, when he was caught telling two versions of a story. They let Taoiseach Charlie Haughey know that if Lenihan didn't go the PDs would be unhappy.

Haughey set about pushing out his 'old friend of thirty years'. He needed to do it without being seen to do it, as Lenihan was popular and if it was seen that he was pushed out rank-and-file Fianna Fáilers would be upset.

Monday, 29 October 1990: Haughey calls his Fianna Fáil ministers out to Kinsealy. Neither Lenihan nor Lenihan's sister, Mary O'Rourke, is invited. That evening, Haughey's media people begin spreading the word among journalists: Lenihan will resign tomorrow. The hope is that this will lead to speculation in the newspapers the following morning, creating the expectation that Lenihan is about to resign, resulting in a momentum that Lenihan will find hard to resist. Lenihan's people ring their media contacts, dampening the speculation.

Tuesday, 30 October: Lenihan arrives at Kinsealy that morning. Haughey presses him to resign. Lenihan says no. At 11 a.m. Haughey has to hurry off to meet Queen Beatrix of the Netherlands, who is arriving on a state visit. At the airport Haughey, fresh from putting pressure on Lenihan, tells reporters: 'I will not be asking for the Tánaiste's resignation from the cabinet. I will not be putting him under any pressure to resign, nor will his cabinet colleagues. It is entirely a matter for my old friend of thirty years.'

At Leinster House, a number of Lenihan's cabinet colleagues are at that moment putting pressure on him to resign.

Haughey arrives back from the airport and Lenihan goes to see him in his Leinster House office. Haughey resumes pressure on Lenihan to resign. He hands him a three-page resignation statement and asks him to sign it. The statement apologises for 'the embarrassment a carelessly inaccurate private interview seems to have caused the government' and announces Lenihan's resignation. Then — in order to preserve the lie that Haughey didn't push Lenihan — the statement says: 'This decision is mine and mine alone. I have not been subject to pressure from any quarter.'

Lenihan wouldn't resign. The next day, Haughey sacked him.

See: Mature Recollection.

Littlejohns, The

D on't worry, it's okay, Kenneth Littlejohn said when the London police arrested him. Everything was cool, he was one of the good guys. Ring the Special Branch, they'd know all about him. And they did.

Littlejohn was a thief, and not very good at it. He was bounced out of the Parachute Regiment back in 1959, suspected of theft, and he came to Ireland about ten years later when the British police wanted to talk to him about a £30,000 robbery. He became involved in the clothing business and adopted the name Kenneth Austen.

In November 1971 he returned to London. His time in Ireland had given him an idea for making his life of crime easier and safer. His younger brother Keith, another thief, was friendly with Lady Pamela Onslow. He had met her four years earlier, in prison. She was a prison visitor. He was behind bars for less worthy reasons.

Through Keith, Kenneth got in touch with Lady Onslow. He had information about the IRA, he could be useful in the conflict which had recently broken out in Northern Ireland.

Onslow contacted her friend Lord Carrington, defence minister in the Tory government of Edward Heath. A junior minister from Carrington's ministry, Geoffrey Johnson-Smith, was dispatched to meet Kenneth at Lady Onslow's Kensington house.

The meeting went well. The following day, Littlejohn met an MI6 agent. At that early stage of the northern conflict, British intelligence had skimpy resources in the South. Littlejohn impressed them with his tales of adventures among republicans.

Littlejohn was recruited. He would go back to Ireland with his brother Keith, they would engage in illegal activities along with republican contacts, they would send information back to their British contacts. The activities would provoke Irish government reaction, hopefully leading to pressure for the introduction of internment of the IRA. Kenneth referred to his armed gang as a 'special forces unit'. It was all very *Mission Impossible*: if you're caught by the Irish coppers we disown you.

How active the Littlejohns were over the following year is a matter of argument. Kenneth claimed a dozen bank robberies. He also claimed to have been urged by MI6 to kill a number of republican leaders. Kenneth's word cannot be taken as definitive and much of the brothers' claims are obvious fantasy. It is far more likely that they were given a nod and a wink, engaged in some robberies at the fringe of the republican movement, and agreed to be debriefed at a later stage, somewhat in the manner of a British businessman visiting Russia at the time and being told to keep his eyes open and report to British intelligence on his return. How useful the intelligence the Littlejohns sent back was is anyone's guess. Kenneth claimed to have collected information on arms dumps and on the disposition of the Irish army's forces near the border. This last was significant because there were at that stage genuine beliefs in the South and in Britain that an armed incursion by the Irish army was not out of the question.

Eventually, in October 1972, Kenneth and Keith and some republican friends raided the home of the manager of the AIB branch in Grafton Street, Dublin. His family was held hostage while he drove the Littlejohns into town. The brothers stole £67,000 from the bank and fled the country. It would have helped if Kenneth's ESB bill hadn't been left behind in the getaway car.

The gardaí were onto the Littlejohns. They contacted the London police, who raided the home of an associate and found Kenneth, who told them to ring the Special Branch.

The gardaí instituted extradition proceedings. The Littlejohns claimed they shouldn't be sent back to Ireland as they had been British spies on active duty against Irish terrorists. The British couldn't simply deny this, as the brothers could point to the Onslow/Carrington/ Johnson-Smith/MI6 connection. Neither could the British simply refuse to extradite a couple of bank robbers. An urgent meeting was arranged between British and Irish officials. Yes, the Littlejohns had meetings with one of our chaps from the ministry, but — good God, man — do you really suppose we'd authorise bank robberies?

Taoiseach Jack Lynch was informed that there was some basis to the Littlejohns' claims.

There was sensitivity about the presence of covert British agents in the South. The previous December, a month after the Littlejohns robbed the AIB in Grafton Street, bombs had gone off in Dublin, killing 2 and injuring 127. This happened on the evening the Dáil was to vote on severe anti-terrorist legislation. In opposition, Fine Gael was split. The party leader, Liam Cosgrave, was going to vote in favour of Fianna Fáil's bill; many of his frontbenchers were passionately opposed to the new laws. The bombs went off during the debate, opposition collapsed, the new laws went through. There was immediate and widespread suspicion of British intelligence involvement, perhaps using loyalists. This wasn't just republican paranoia. A month after that, a British agent was arrested in Dublin and charged with collaborating with a garda in an attempt to steal sensitive security information.

Now, just two months later, the Littlejohn extradition hearings in London were held in camera; the Littlejohns' story was not for publication in Britain. The two were sent back to Dublin in March 1973 and when they were tried five months later the Special Criminal Court refused to delve into their defence of being British government agents. They did the robbery, that was all the court was concerned with. Kenneth got twenty years, Keith got fifteen.

A scandal erupted, with allegations that the Irish authorities had been made aware of the brothers' connection with British intelligence. There were suggestions — unlikely, and with not a sliver of evidence — that the gardaí had been told to turn a blind eye. Jack Lynch, now out of office, vehemently denied being informed about the Littlejohns' MI6 connections. Documents proving that Lynch had in fact been briefed on the Littlejohns, after the meeting in January between British and Irish officials, were unearthed in the Department of Foreign Affairs. Lynch apologised and said that he had forgotten he had been told. Some found it difficult to believe that Lynch could have forgotten such a matter. His opponents within Fianna Fáil would ever after make jeering remarks

about his memory. Eight years later the Littlejohns were quietly released.
Humanitarian grounds.

Locke's Distillery

It may be that Seán T. O'Kelly, president of Ireland, was involved with
international gangsters, but probably not. The Locke's Distillery
scandal of 1947 led to a tribunal of inquiry.

Locke's Distillery had existed in Kilbeggan, County Westmeath since
1757. In 1947 business had declined to the point where it was up for sale
by the two remaining Lockes, Flo and Sweet. In the aftermath of the
Second World War, with Europe still traumatised by six years of conflict
and awash with adventurers seeking a quick buck, Locke's attracted the
attention of a group of international chancers.

They didn't seem so at the time. There was a man called Georges
Eindiguer, who was from Switzerland and who was said by *The Irish Times*
to be 'a well-known figure in international trade'. It was said of Eindiguer
that he arrived in Ireland in his own aeroplane, which was some trick in
1947. The Minister for Justice, Gerry Boland, would say in the Dáil that
Eindiguer arrived by commercial flight. Eindiguer had a secretary and
translator, a British chap by the name of Horace Henry Smith. They had
an associate named Hubert Saschell, an Austrian, who was then living in
Ireland, with a home in County Galway. The Swiss Eindiguer, the British
Smith and the Austrian Saschell made up an outfit called Trans-World
Trust, which was based in Lausanne, Switzerland. They very quickly got
the support of the Department of Industry and Commerce in their plan
to buy Locke's Distillery. The intention was, they claimed, that they
would manufacture whiskey for export, but they would also develop the
home market. They would revive the great and ancient little distillery.

Eindiguer and his translator, Horace Henry Smith, arrived in Ireland
on 3 September 1947. Two days later they retained an auctioneering firm,
Stokes and Quirke, and instructed it to purchase Locke's. Four days after
that Trans-World successfully tendered a bid of £305,000, to be paid in
US dollars, for the distillery (equivalent to £6.5 million today). The
contract required that the purchasers make a down payment of £75,000
within forty-eight hours.

At which point things began to fall apart.

There was a slight problem in getting the £75,000, nothing to worry
about, but Trans-World needed a little more time. And they were given it.

Over two weeks passed. On 25 September the three dodgy characters were entertained to tea at Áras an Uachtaráin, by President Seán T. O'Kelly.

The following day's newspapers mentioned the president's guests. It appears to have been this publicity which led to the exposure of the chancers. Gerry Boland got a phone call from a friend. There was something odd going on, he was told. One of those guys is not what he seems.

In fact, two of those guys were not what they seemed. Hubert Saschell, the Austrian with the home in Galway, had already come to the notice of the gardaí and a number of reports were compiled on his activities. Three months earlier he had been informed that he had a month to leave the country. And the British chap, Horace Henry Smith, wasn't Horace Henry Smith. Nor was he British. He was said to be Swiss, until the Swiss indignantly insisted he had nothing to do with them. He was, apparently, Russian. His real name was Alexander Maximoe, and he was wanted by the British police for obtaining a false passport.

Minister for Justice Boland immediately got onto his department and ordered an official from the aliens section and the head of the Garda Special Branch to come to his home, where he passed on the information he had been given.

Hubert Saschell, the Austrian, skedaddled to Paris. Georges Eindiguer, the Swiss, was questioned by police in Dún Laoghaire on 29 September, four days after having tea with the president. His passport was in order and he was released. Two days after that he fled the country. That same day, 1 October, Smith/Maximoe was arrested at Saschell's apartment in Hatch Street, Dublin, and the following day he was served with a deportation order and put on the mailboat to Holyhead. British police would be waiting for him there, to arrest him on the false passport charge. Midway across the Irish Sea, when the gardaí accompanying him had relaxed, Smith/Maximoe slipped away and jumped off the boat and was presumed drowned.

There were by-elections coming up and this all proved a treat for the opposition parties. William Quirke, of Stokes and Quirke, the auctioneers who acted for Trans-World, was a Fianna Fáil senator. He was also a family friend of President Seán T. O'Kelly. It was alleged that the president was up to something. It was alleged that a Dublin barrister, married to O'Kelly's niece, was acting for the chancers. It was alleged that Georges Eindiguer had smoothed his way towards the purchase of Locke's by presenting a gold watch to a son of the Taoiseach, Eamon de Valera (or had been advised to do so). One of the odder allegations was that the

Austrian, Hubert Saschell, had sold £25,000 worth of tweed in order to obtain dollars for the Minister for Justice, Gerry Boland.

This, among much other nonsense, came out of the mouth of Oliver J. Flanagan TD, in the Dáil on 22 October. 'He is an alien who sold £25,000 worth of Irish tweed to get dollars for you.'

'He's no friend of mine,' said Boland. 'I don't know who the man is but he is under notice to quit this country.'

'He got the dollars for you!' insisted Flanagan.

Flanagan was then an independent TD, elected in 1943 as a Monetary Reform candidate, at the age of twenty-three. He was one of the cutest of cute hoors in the history of the Dáil, making it his business to know every voter in every corner of his constituency, stroking unceasingly. At national level he goaded and poked at his opponents. In the Locke scandal, he hadn't a clue what was going on, but somebody had been up to something and Flanagan felt he had the right to lash out.

What seems to have been going on is that the Trans-World chancers didn't really want the distillery, they wanted its stock of whiskey. Locke's had in its storage some 60,000 gallons of matured and maturing whiskey. In the years after the war there was an international shortage of spirits and the whiskey stored at Locke's was estimated to be worth around £660,000 on the international market. In today's money that is the equivalent of over £14 million.

The expectation had been that Trans-World would maintain production, and meet its maximum export allowance of 8,000 gallons from that production, but the chancers had no intention of manufacturing anything. They were positioning themselves for a classic piece of asset-stripping. Political clout would have been necessary for them to break the quota and export the 60,000 gallons of matured whiskey.

The Dáil ordered a tribunal of inquiry, with three judges, and in its report the tribunal rejected the allegations made about political collaboration in Trans-World's scheme. There remained a suspicion that the tribunal's terms of reference were kept narrow for political reasons. The blushes of President O'Kelly would be spared, and he would not be pushed for an explanation of his involvement with the chancers. A minor official was criticised for a 'grave indiscretion' for allowing the chancers have tea with President O'Kelly without their having been fully checked out.

The tribunal's report was scathing about the allegations made by Oliver J. Flanagan TD. On the charge of a Fianna Fáil politician being involved: 'We are satisfied that it is wholly untrue, that it is entirely without foundation and that it was made with a degree of recklessness amounting to complete irresponsibility.' Flanagan was 'very uncandid and much disposed to answer unthinkingly and as if he were directing his replies elsewhere than to the tribunal'. In short, he was saying whatever he thought would boost his standing with his constituents, regardless of the truth. The report continued: 'In respect of two matters we are satisfied that he told us what he knew to be untrue.'

Flanagan suffered not at all from this. In the 1948 general election his vote increased by 45 per cent to over 14,000. Immediately after the publication of the tribunal report his performance was applauded by James Dillon TD, barrister and future leader of Fine Gael. He sent Flanagan a telegram which offered congratulations 'on the courage with which you discharged your public duty'. Flanagan at once adopted Dillon's wording and sent a telegram to Taoiseach Eamon de Valera. 'Proud of manner in which I discharged my public duty, and will do likewise again.'

The Locke Tribunal, it is interesting to note, was appointed on 7 November 1947, heard evidence from forty-nine witnesses, at eighteen sessions, and issued a final report on 18 December. Forty-one days, from appointment to report.

See: Flanagan, Oliver J.; Jobbery; Singer, Dr Paul; Thundering Disgrace.

Lovett, Ann

She was fifteen, pregnant and alone. Ann Lovett's secret had gone unnoticed by her school, by her community, by all of the many people who later said of course they'd have helped her if they'd only known. She was found dying on 31 January 1984, at the grotto of the Catholic church in Granard, County Longford. She went there to have her baby in secret, and she died after giving birth on the ground near the statue of the Virgin Mary. Her infant son died too.

For those who thought the position of women had improved beyond all recognition, the Ann Lovett tragedy was a dose of reality. Nuala Fennell, Minister of State for Women's Affairs, demanded a national inquiry 'regardless of whose sensibilities are hurt'. Mary Harney, then a Fianna Fáil TD, agreed: 'At a time when this country was engaged in the pro-life amendment debate, is it not sad and strange that a minor was going through what was obviously an agonising ordeal all on her own?'

The people of Granard, suddenly under unwelcome media scrutiny, insisted that this was a personal and private tragedy, not a public issue.

At the Mercy Convent where Ann was a pupil, the Superior, Sister Immaculata, said: 'If she was having any problems they had not come to my attention, or to the attention of the principal.'

The calls for an inquiry were, of course, ignored and died away. The Lovetts were an unfortunate family who, in the coming years, were to suffer more tragedy. Almost certainly, some responsible adults in Granard noticed Ann Lovett's pregnancy but none felt confident enough to intervene. Writing about the event in her *Cabinet Diaries*, the then Minister for Education Gemma Hussey revealed that department officials had, at her behest, investigated the details of the case and the level of pastoral care available at the Mercy Convent school. She concluded: 'what happened was the most appalling tragedy and it is hard to see how it could have been avoided'. She resolved that she would 'get some serious work done in widening the scope of sex education'.

It was an extraordinary period, during which the social realities for women in modern Ireland were exposed in the coincidental revelations of several stark, painful events. While Ann Lovett was dying, the unfolding Eileen Flynn case was hitting the headlines, and down in Kerry another unmarried mother from rural Ireland was doing her best to conceal a pregnancy, with not a thought in her mind that soon she too would be national news.

See: Flynn, Eileen; Kerry Babies.

Lowry, Michael

When the scandal first broke it looked as though the Minister for Transport, Energy and Communications, Michael Lowry, was on the take. The truth was somewhat more complex than that.

Reporter Sam Smyth revealed in the *Irish Independent* in November 1996 that Dunnes Stores had paid for a huge extension to Lowry's house in Tipperary. Taoiseach John Bruton tried to shrug off the allegation, making the extraordinary assertion that since this happened before Lowry became a minister it was no big deal. Lowry, however, had to resign. Five minutes later he posed for photographs with Bruton. 'Yes, indeed,' said Lowry, 'I'll pose with my friend. Best friend. Friend for life.'

Lowry had become a close political ally of Bruton's. There was talk of the minister one day becoming leader, Taoiseach. It is, looking back at it all, the political potential that Lowry represented that makes his story intriguing. What was Ben Dunne up to?

Lowry made a personal statement in the Dáil on 19 December 1996 saying that Ben Dunne paid for his extension in lieu of payments which Lowry was due for providing refrigeration services to Dunnes Stores. Lowry's Dáil statement was misleading, leaving out over a hundred thousand pounds in non-taxed payments from Dunne. Had he wanted to conceal money, said Lowry, surely he'd have opened an offshore account? This passage in his speech would subsequently sound like a private joke Lowry was playing on the public, when it was revealed that Lowry had in fact received non-taxed payments through an offshore account.

It emerged that Lowry's refrigeration company, Streamline Enterprises, was a virtual subsidiary of Dunnes Stores. Ben Dunne recruited Lowry in 1988 with the promise: 'You will be a wealthy man.' Dunne set the profit level of the company artificially and decided how much Lowry should get as a bonus. Financially, and in business terms, Lowry was in Dunne's pocket. Dunne and Lowry arranged matters so that Lowry could evade tax, with payments routed through offshore accounts and companies. The money spent on Lowry's house extension, £395,107, was put into Dunnes Stores' books as payment for work done on Dunnes' ILAC Centre premises. According to the McCracken Tribunal Report, Lowry 'operated his business on two levels, on one level through the company, which made a small profit and duly paid its taxes, and on a second level whereby large sums of money were paid to him personally in a clandestine manner'.

The year before Lowry became a minister he used the 1993 tax amnesty to launder his dodgy money. Lowry told Taoiseach John Bruton of this, after being appointed to the cabinet, and Bruton had to know that it necessarily involved Lowry in tax evasion, a criminal activity. Yet Bruton believed it right to retain Lowry as a minister.

Ben Dunne, like other businessmen, had spread money around the political parties. In 1989, for instance, he gave Fine Gael leader Alan Dukes £30,000, with a promise to make two other contributions of a similar size. Dukes lost the Fine Gael leadership and that promise wasn't kept. Instead, Ben Dunne began to use Michael Lowry as his point of contact with Fine Gael. From 1991 Dunne began to channel money into Fine Gael through Lowry, having already fed hundreds of thousands of pounds to Charlie Haughey.

In April 1991, Lowry arranged a meeting at which Dunne handed John Bruton a cheque for £50,000. The following year, Dunne gave Lowry £5,000 for his election expenses. And, unsolicited, he gave £3,000 to Michael Noonan and £5,000 to Ivan Yates, for election expenses, in each case using Lowry as the conduit. Dunne also gave £3,000 to

Noonan's constituency funds, in Limerick East. In May 1993, following another meeting between Dunne and Bruton arranged by Michael Lowry, Dunne gave Fine Gael £100,000.

Dunne had, in a systematic way, boosted Lowry's image as a man of substance. The £5,000 he channelled to Ivan Yates, for instance, was half of Yates's entire fund for the 1992 general election. In a Fine Gael not exactly bursting with organisational talent, Lowry's role as a fund-raiser put him into the front rank of the party. That same year, Lowry became chairman of the Fine Gael parliamentary party. So impressed was John Bruton with Lowry that when, in 1994, Bruton became Taoiseach he made Lowry a minister. Had Sam Smyth not spoiled the whole game, who knows how high Lowry might have risen, borne aloft on the financial wings of his friend Ben. Had Lowry become Taoiseach one day, he would have had even more for which to thank Ben Dunne.

As a minister, Lowry hired a PR outfit and began creating for himself the image of the cool, clean hero, taking on 'cosy cartels'. He was a man on the rise. The image was damaged by the Pat Tuffy episode and destroyed when the financial relationship with Ben Dunne became public, but up until this derailment, Michael Lowry was on the fast track to ever higher positions of power, and Ben Dunne was stoking the engine.

Dunne's political handouts were categorised as impulsive acts of generosity. There is little evidence that they were impulsive.

See: Dunne Family Wars; Friends of Ben; Tuffy, Pat.

Lynch, Judge Dominic

Some scandals erupt suddenly and there is little chance for anyone in a position of responsibility to react effectively. The Judge Lynch scandal ambled along for three months, with one opportunity to rectify matters followed by another and another, all ignored. Mr Justice Dominic Lynch asked twice to be relieved of the duty of sitting on the Special Criminal Court. The first time, July 1995, nothing was done. The second time he asked, a year later, Minister for Justice Nora Owen had her department prepare a memo; this was brought to a cabinet meeting on 1 August 1996 and it was decided to 'de-list' the judge from the court, as he requested, and to replace him with Mr Justice Kevin Haugh.

The Department of Justice was informed of the decision. Judge Haugh was informed, and a warrant of his appointment was sent to the Special

Criminal Court. A note of the government decision was sent to no fewer than six government offices on 2 August.

(The identities of those concerned were later cloaked in secrecy, and they were identified only as letters of the alphabet.)

The decision was first sent to Official G, private secretary to the minister. He was on leave. The decision was photocopied and sent to five other offices.

Officials A and M received the note 'for information'. It was filed and nothing was done about the information.

Officials B, C and F received the note and were supposed to do something with it. Official B was on leave until 15 August. When he returned he saw the note and saw that it had been copied to officials C and F. He was very busy, being an acting assistant secretary, with responsibility not only for courts but for immigration, finance and secretariat. He assumed that officials C and F were on the job, so he filed the note 'for reference'.

Official C was just a few weeks in the courts division and he just didn't know what to do with the note of the government decision. He might have asked his superior, Official E, but E was on leave. So Official C passed the government decision on to a junior official. When asked later, Official C couldn't remember which one it was. It had to be one of three, but each of them said: Not me.

So, there was one other copy of the government decision, and that went to Official F. She was very busy and had been drafted in to work on a specific matter. The government decision wasn't strictly her business, so she passed the note to someone else. Who? When asked later, she couldn't remember, but she thought it might have been a certain official in a certain section. Nope, not me, said that official.

The decision to de-list Judge Lynch had also been published in the official state noticeboard, *Iris Oifigiúil*, on 9 August, but no one seems to have noticed.

And there it rested, all through August and all through September. Judge Lynch, officially de-listed, no longer had the authority to sit on the Special Criminal Court, but no one told him. He continued his work, dealing with some of the most serious crimes of violence and subversion dealt with by any court, making decisions for which he no longer had legal authority.

At the beginning of October the Attorney General, Dermot Gleeson, was at some social function where he had a chat with Judge Harvey Kenny. Harvey Kenny mentioned the workload of the judges on the Circuit Court. Well, said Gleeson, you've got Dominic Lynch back from the Special

Criminal Court (or words to that effect). Oh, no, says Judge Harvey Kenny, sure isn't Dominic still sitting on the Special (or words to that effect).

The Attorney General was worried. On 2 October he wrote a letter to the Minister for Justice. Had anyone told Judge Lynch that he wasn't on the Special Criminal Court any more? Had anyone told the president of the Circuit Court?

Next day, 3 October, the letter arrived in the office of the minister's private secretary, Official G. But Official G didn't show it to the minister. He knew that the minister, Nora Owen, would ask him the answers to the Attorney General's questions, and he wouldn't know. First, he would have to get the answers to the questions, then he would show the letter to the minister.

So, Official G sent the letter to Official D, in the personnel division. It was 7 or 8 October before Official D got the letter. She decided it wasn't really personnel's business, so she sent it to the courts division. It arrived there, to Official C, on 9 October. Official C gave it to Official E next day.

Official E was busy, compiling responses to twelve Dáil questions which Minister Owen would have to answer five days later. He decided that this task had priority, so he put the Attorney General's letter aside.

Meanwhile, Judge Lynch was getting restless. It was July when he had asked for the second time to be removed from the Special Criminal Court, it was now October. Three months had passed and he hadn't even received an acknowledgment. On 10 October he wrote to the Minister for Justice, marking the letter 'Personal'. Any chance of being taken off the Special Criminal Court?

Because it was marked 'Personal', this letter was sent to the minister's constituency office, where it was opened by Official N. From there, it went to a file in the courts division of the Department of Justice, where it was carefully clipped to the letter the judge had sent back in July, filed and forgotten. Who filed it is anyone's guess.

Back in the courts division, on 15 October, Official E was finishing his work on the twelve Dáil questions. He now took up the Attorney General's letter (written thirteen days earlier) and passed it on to Official J, who had just returned from leave. Write to Judge Lynch, he told her, and ask him if he's been told that he was de-listed back in August, and if he wasn't, well, we're telling him now. Or words to that effect.

Official J wrote the letter that very day and showed the letter to Official E. Official E decided the letter had to be amended. The letter was passed back and forth between Officials E and J, through 16 October, 22 October, and into November.

A month had passed since the Attorney General wrote the letter, and it still hadn't reached the minister and wouldn't do so until Official J's letter of inquiry was sent to Judge Lynch and he replied. On 1 November, the Attorney General wrote a second letter to the Minister for Justice. He'd seen a mention in the newspapers that Judge Lynch was still on the Special Criminal Court, but he'd been de-listed by the cabinet back in August. This could cause legal difficulties.

This second letter was sent on Friday, 1 November. It didn't get to the minister's office until Tuesday, 5 November. When the minister saw it she rang Official C in the courts division. He thought the minister was talking about a different judge altogether and got back to her the next day, 6 November, to say that no, nobody was aware that this other judge had been de-listed (which, of course, he hadn't been).

No, he was told, we're talking about Judge Lynch. Has he been told he was de-listed three months ago?

Oh, Judge Lynch.

Official C rang Official E.

Judge Lynch? said Official E. Funny you should mention that. It was Official E who had received the Attorney General's first letter about all this, back on 10 October; and who had finished working on the twelve Dáil questions on 15 October, had got Official J to write a letter to Judge Lynch, had spent over three weeks revising the letter along with Official J, the letter which hadn't yet been sent, and now here was someone ringing up about Judge Lynch. Fancy that.

Suddenly, on 6 November, three months after the de-listing of Judge Lynch, it was all action. Everyone was ringing everyone else: the assistant secretary, the principal secretary, the Attorney General, the minister, the Director of Public Prosecutions, the department secretary, the deputy garda commissioner. It was after 7 p.m. that evening before the penny dropped. The Special Criminal Court had for three months been improperly constituted. It was feared that every accused person dealt with by Judge Lynch since August, and remanded or sentenced to jail, was being illegally held.

The minister was that evening attending the premiere of Neil Jordan's film *Michael Collins* when she got word. After consultations with officials, at 10.30 p.m., she ordered that sixteen high-security prisoners, dealt with by Judge Lynch during the three-month period, be released. Among them were Brixton Prison IRA escapee Nessan Quinlivan and Anthony Duncan, who had been involved in another Department of Justice scandal. The prisoners were released and immediately rearrested, then brought before a properly constituted court so that their detention could be made legal.

There were calls for the Minister for Justice to resign. She, of course, didn't. No one could understand why, at some point, someone hadn't just picked up a phone and rung someone else. 'Do ye talk at all?' asked Bertie Ahern in the Dáil.

An inquiry into the mess found it could not identify who was responsible at crucial points in the story, as people couldn't remember who they gave documents to, and others couldn't remember being given documents. The trail, the inquiry concluded, had 'run into the sand'.

In a test case, the Supreme Court subsequently ruled that there was 'no concerted plan on the part of the authorities constituting a conscious and deliberate violation of rights', and the rearrest of the sixteen high-security prisoners was lawful. The Lynch scandal, therefore, caused political embarrassment to the government but none of the high-security prisoners had to be released as a result.

See: Duncan, Anthony.

Lyons, Dean

He used a syringe as a threat, back in April 1997, when he and his mates stole £700 worth of video equipment at Crown Alley, in Dublin. A month later he used a syringe again, when he stole £30 from a man in Capel Street. Two months after that he was in custody, charged with one of the most horrific murders in the history of the state.

Dean Lyons was twenty-four, a junkie, homeless and hopeless. His family lived in Tallaght and tried to keep in touch with him, though he had left home three years earlier. He had one conviction for burglary, and he had been pulled in on a public order offence, allegedly seen taking heroin. He was arrested on suspicion of one of the syringe attacks.

In short, Dean Lyons was one of those lost, pale-faced, dead-eyed young men who can be seen around the city, nothing in mind but the next fix, their downward spiral towards an early death interrupted only by occasional prison terms when they're caught thieving for the money for their drugs.

Among the drifters around the north side of the Liffey, up towards Grangegorman, Lyons was known as a spoofer. He liked to put himself at the centre of things, to draw attention to himself. Despite his involvement in syringe attacks he was seen as a softie.

When he was arrested on the morning of 26 July 1997, it was like something out of *Miami Vice*. He was asleep in a Salvation Army hostel and outside cops were surrounding the place, dozens of them, some with guns. They came in mob-handed and took Dean Lyons to the Bridewell, where they started asking him about the two murders at Grangegorman.

The murders had shocked everyone, even gardaí who were used to this kind of thing. In the early hours of 7 March 1997 the killer had broken into a house in Grangegorman where three elderly psychiatric patients were living in sheltered accommodation. He got some knives from the kitchen and prepared to kill. He wasn't there to burgle or to rape, he was there to kill. He was full of rage and he did terrible things to two of the women in that house, Sylvia Shields and Mary Callinan. He went into the bedroom of the third, Anne Mernagh. She was still asleep, but perhaps his rage had been sated, as he walked away and left her to find the bodies of her two friends.

The murders happened close to the hostel where Dean Lyons sometimes stayed, and everyone was talking about what happened. Putting himself at the centre of attention, Dean Lyons told some other addicts he knew all about it, he had done it. As a known spoofer, he wasn't taken seriously. Through March and April, May, June and most of July, nothing happened. The gardaí, advised by a psychiatrist that whoever did the Grangegorman killings would almost certainly kill again, worked frantically to solve the case. Late in July an addict told the police about this guy Dean Lyons, who had talked about doing the murders. The police descended on the Salvation Army hostel. The story of what happened to Dean Lyons was unravelled by *Irish Times* reporter Jim Cusack, often in the face of official denial.

In the Bridewell, Lyons initially had nothing much to say. Later that evening, gardaí again questioned him, and this time a statement emerged. The statement had him admitting to one of the murders in the house at Grangegorman, that of Mary Callinan.

Lyons was remanded to Mountjoy. It was a relief for the gardaí to have the Grangegorman killer off the streets before he killed again. There were problems with the confession: he admitted just one of the murders, and close scrutiny of the statement showed discrepancies. But that's often the way; these kinds of things are never neat as in detective stories. Lyons didn't seem the type to kill at random; and he was a drained junkie who didn't appear to have the ferocious strength needed to do what was done in that house. But these things were, apparently, explainable.

In April 1997, a month after the Grangegorman killings, around the time that Dean Lyons was using a syringe to steal video equipment, around the time he was telling doubting friends that he was involved in the killings of the two women, a man named Mark Nash turned up at a

Dublin nightclub and met and became friendly with a girl named Sarah Doyle. Nash was a troubled man, born in Mayo, raised in Huddersfield, with a history of thumping his girlfriend, the mother of his one-year-old daughter. That relationship had foundered when he banged her head off the side of a sofa and tried to strangle her.

Nash was twenty-four, Sarah Doyle was eighteen. Three weeks earlier she had had a baby. Within weeks they moved into Nash's flat, at Prussia Street, not far from the Grangegorman house where the two women had been murdered. It wasn't long before he beat her.

Four months into the relationship, on 15 August, after a bad row, the two went down to Roscommon for a break. Mark took his baby daughter, Sarah took her baby son, and they stayed with Sarah's sister, Catherine Doyle. This was just three weeks after gardaí got a statement in which Dean Lyons admitted to the Grangegorman murders.

Catherine and her husband, Carl, had moved from Dublin to Roscommon to escape the pressures of the city. They had settled in with their four children, aged between one and seven. All six children were sleeping that night, when Mark Nash went to the kitchen and got some knives. The adults had been drinking, smoking joints. Nash stabbed Sarah Doyle and left her for dead. With ferocious energy he stabbed her sister Catherine and brother-in-law Carl to death. Sarah got out of the house and raised the alarm. Nash went on the run and was captured two days later.

Shortly after his capture, Mark Nash freely confessed the killings. He also told Roscommon gardaí about how he had killed two other women, at Grangegorman in Dublin, back in March. He made a confession which included details about the killings which had not been made public.

There now developed within the gardaí two opposing factions on the issue of who committed the Grangegorman murders. Those who had obtained a confession from Dean Lyons held to the belief that he was the killer; another faction was equally convinced that Nash was the killer. Nash was plainly a violent man, a strong man, whereas Lyons was a washed-out junkie. Lyons had no history of serious violence, whereas Nash had slaughtered two people with knives. The Roscommon murders, in their detail and in their ferocity, were akin to the Grangegorman murders. Each pair of killings seemed equally motiveless, powered by some kind of killing rage.

From late August 1997, just a month after Dean Lyons was arrested, Jim Cusack was writing in *The Irish Times* about the belief of some gardaí that Lyons was not the killer, and the expectation that he would be released.

Material appeared in other sections of the media rubbishing the *Irish Times* reports. Cusack stuck to his story and kept the issue in the public eye.

In October Mark Nash withdrew his confession to the Grangegorman murders. There was strong garda opposition to the release of Lyons, but there seemed little doubt of his innocence.

It was 29 April 1998 before the murder charge against Dean Lyons was dropped and he was released. He had been held for nine months, eight of those months after Mark Nash confessed to the murders.

A month after his release, Dean Lyons was back in court, charged with the two syringe robberies he carried out a year earlier. Judge Cyril Kelly sentenced Lyons to seven years in jail; the sentence would be reviewed if Lyons entered a drugs rehabilitation course. By now, after nine months in custody, Dean Lyons was off drugs and was living at home with his family. The prosecuting counsel told the court about Lyons being held for months on a charge of murder. She said the DPP had had no hesitation in withdrawing that charge, that the investigation of that case was continuing and Lyons was no longer a suspect.

How Dean Lyons's confession was made, a confession apparently solid enough to lead to a charge of murder, is still a matter of conjecture.

M

Macarthur, Malcolm

Patrick Connolly, Ireland's Attorney General, was looking forward to his holiday in the United States. It was Friday, 13 August 1982. He was due to fly out, via London, the following morning. When he arrived home to Pilot View, Dalkey, Dublin that Friday evening he was met by three detectives who wanted to talk to the man who was staying in his apartment as a guest.

That man was the double murderer Malcolm Macarthur. As he watched his friend being arrested the startled Attorney General remarked: 'I don't know what this is about, Malcolm, but whatever it is you're on your own.'

Even before he started killing people, Malcolm Macarthur was an odd man. He dressed in tweeds with silk hankies and bow ties. He affected a diffident but superior manner with an upper-class accent and an air of slight eccentricity. Acquaintances assumed him to be an academic. He was the only son of a well-to-do family, brought up on a 180-acre farm near Trim, County Meath.

At thirty-six, Malcolm Macarthur had never worked but always seemed to have money. He lived on an inheritance but by 1982 that was running out. He decided that armed robbery would be a good way to earn a living and he set about getting a weapon. In a disguise that featured a beard and phoney glasses he hung around clay pigeon shoots hoping to steal a rifle. When that didn't work out he scoured the papers looking for farmers selling shotguns. Donal Dunne, a farmer from Edenderry, County Offaly, had advertised a shotgun for sale. Macarthur decided to get that shotgun. First he had to get to Edenderry. He decided he needed a car. To get a car he armed himself with a hammer.

Bridie Gargan was a 29-year-old nurse who worked at St James's Hospital, Dublin. Thursday, 22 July 1982 was a particularly hot, sunny day and Bridie Gargan decided to stop for a bit of sunbathing as she drove home to her flat in Castleknock, through the Phoenix Park. Malcolm Macarthur, meanwhile, had wandered up the quays looking for a car to steal. Despite the weather, he was dressed in heavy clothes and a tweed hat and he carried a bag containing a lump hammer and an imitation pistol.

Macarthur came across Nurse Gargan sunning herself beside her car. He threatened her with the pistol, forcing her into the back seat. Once she was inside the car, he brought out the lump hammer. A gardener at the American ambassador's home nearby saw the two get into the car and then saw what looked like a struggle, the car shaking with the violence of what was going on inside. He tried to intervene, but Macarthur threatened him with the imitation gun before he drove away. The gardener raised the alarm, but by that time Malcolm Macarthur was racing through city traffic with an ambulance escort. A passing ambulance driver had spotted Nurse Gargan's silver Renault with the injured woman in the back and blood on the window. He noticed the St James's Hospital parking permit and assumed Macarthur was a doctor rushing an emergency patient to hospital.

Malcolm Macarthur drove into St James's Hospital, out again and abandoned the car with the dying woman in it. He took a bus across town to Finglas. There he went into a pub and shaved off his beard. He was no nearer to achieving his goal of becoming an armed robber.

Unfortunately for Donal Dunne, Malcolm Macarthur decided he didn't need a car, he'd hitchhike to Edenderry instead. There he met

Dunne, who drove him out to a local bog where he could try out the shotgun. At the first chance, he killed the farmer and took both shotgun and car.

Back in Dublin, Macarthur was fast running out of money and needed a place to stay. He looked up his old friend Paddy Connolly. The Attorney General was surprised to hear from Macarthur. He didn't realise he was in the country. Macarthur met Patrick Connolly through a mutual friend, Brenda Little. She had been a friend of Connolly's for some time. As her relationship with Macarthur grew, Connolly also got to know the man. Brenda Little and Malcolm Macarthur had a son in 1975 and for a short while they had lived in a flat in Donnybrook rented by Patrick Connolly. Before the killings, Brenda Little and Macarthur had been living in Tenerife.

Initially, the gardaí did not connect the murders of Bridie Gargan and Donal Dunne, but eventually the pieces of the jigsaw began to come together. They had the description from the gardener. Then there was the man who shaved off his beard in the Finglas pub and the man who was acting strangely at clay pigeon meets. Before he looked up Patrick Connolly, Malcolm Macarthur knocked on the door of Harry Bieling, an American living in Killiney. He purported to know him, said he'd been to a party in the house some years previously and mentioned mutual friends. Eventually, he took out the shotgun and asked for money. Bieling was lucky to escape with his life and the incident gave the gardaí more clues. An observant news-vendor gave further information and eventually Malcolm Macarthur was tracked down to 6 Carnsore, Pilot View, Dalkey, the home of the Attorney General of the Fianna Fáil government led by Charlie Haughey.

Haughey later described the events of July and August 1982 as 'grotesque, unbelievable, bizarre, unprecedented', from which Dr Conor Cruise O'Brien formed the acronym GUBU. The media used GUBU as shorthand to describe the plague of controversy that tended to follow Haughey.

As for the Attorney General, Patrick Connolly, he seemed to have underestimated the enormity of what happened in his apartment on 13 August. After the gardaí left with his house guest as their prisoner, he continued packing for his holiday. He telephoned the Taoiseach, who was at his holiday home on Inishvickillane, and told him what had happened. Either the Taoiseach, perhaps because of a bad line, didn't get the full gist of the story or, like Connolly, he didn't realise that the Attorney General's departure would cause public outrage. Whatever, Patrick Connolly left for his holidays the next morning, telling some very annoyed gardaí that they could question him upon his return. On a stopover in London, he was contacted by the Taoiseach, who asked him to return. Connolly said no, he'd continue on his way and phone when he got to New York. By the time Patrick Connolly landed in New York all hell had broken loose. The basic storyline was: double murder suspect hides out in Attorney General's apartment, Attorney General flees country after suspect's arrest. It didn't look good. Haughey's next conversation with Patrick Connolly was more decisive. He ordered him to come back and face the music.

Patrick Connolly drafted a public statement while travelling to London aboard Concorde. An Irish Air Corps plane brought him to Casement Aerodrome and from there he went to the Taoiseach's home at Kinsealy, County Dublin, where Haughey was waiting. Connolly offered his resignation and Haughey accepted.

In the Macarthur affair Patrick Connolly could be accused of naivety and foolishness, but nothing more. There was no way he could have known that Malcolm Macarthur was a murderer. But there was a significant amount of public cynicism and suspicion directed at the Haughey government and this generated a host of unpleasant and untrue rumours about Connolly's relationship with Macarthur.

As the trial approached, Malcolm Macarthur's lawyers did a deal with the Director of Public Prosecutions. He would plead guilty to the murder of Bridie Gargan, the state would enter a *nolle prosequi* in the case of the farmer Donal Dunne. From the DPP's point of view it was a good deal. There would be a guaranteed life sentence, no risk of a guilty-but-insane plea succeeding. From Macarthur's point of view, getting into prison with the minimum of public scrutiny was the best option. If he was ever to qualify for release, the sooner he faded from public memory the better.

So, on 12 January 1983, Malcolm Macarthur pleaded guilty to the murder of Bridie Gargan. Counsel for the prosecution said they did not anticipate proceeding with the second charge of murdering Donal Dunne. The prosecution had planned to call Chief Superintendent John Courtney to read a statement detailing the evidence. It was a gesture which might have satisfied public curiosity and allayed fears of a cover-up. But the presiding judge said that where there was a mandatory life sentence there was no need for evidence. The statement was never read and the trial was over in five minutes. For the family of Donal Dunne it was a particularly bitter pill to swallow.

The five-minute hearing fuelled public suspicion that the deal had been done to protect politicians and other influential people from details that might have emerged during an extensive trial. As it happened, there was no cover-up surrounding the Macarthur affair. It was truly as Charlie Haughey had stated: grotesque, unbelievable, bizarre, unprecedented.

McColgan Family

On 24 July 1979 Patsy McColgan arrived in the office of Sligo Social Services, a voluntary organisation run by the Catholic church. There she told Sr Áine that she wanted her children to be taken into care. Her husband was beating both her and the children, she said. They weren't safe. Sr Áine judged the situation to be serious and put her in touch with the social workers of the North Western Health Board. It was the first of many cries for help.

While her mother was talking to Sr Áine, Sophia McColgan, aged nine, was in Sligo General Hospital with a fractured nose. The doctor's note that accompanied her when she arrived at casualty said:

> Please see this battered child. Beaten by father this a.m. while in a raged state. He does not drink. Took child to sitting room, caught her neck with his hands, locked the door. The history has been related to me by wife's mother. Parents have been married ten years have four children. Lived in England . . . came home to Ballina-carrow, building a home there. The four kids have been beaten many times as has his wife. Observed and examined very frightened child, obvious injury to the nasal bone. Bruising under the upper lip . . . this family would need to be seen by a social worker.

That was 1979. In 1993 Joe McColgan was finally separated from the children he abused. Fourteen years after the alarm bell started ringing. Fourteen years during which the alarm bell never ceased ringing. The state finally intervened when one of the children, then twenty-one years old, told her story to the gardaí after a particularly horrific beating. Two years later, in the Central Criminal Court, Joe McColgan was sentenced to twelve years in prison for rape, buggery, indecent assault and assault of his children.

Back in 1979, a few weeks after young Sophia was hospitalised, her brother Gerry arrived at Sligo General Hospital after a savage attack. He had with him another letter from the same doctor (not the family's GP):

Please see again another child of the McColgan family. Case of child battering. Sophia, another child, was hospitalised a month ago with the same problem. Dr Heagney's office was notified and social worker has made contact. This child is a nervous wreck . . . Father grabbed child by the neck two nights ago over some trivial matter. Marks on neck noted. Father has an uncontrollable temper. Please advise.

Two years later Gerard's father broke his arm with a shovel. Gerard kept running away and told anyone who would listen that his father had caused his injuries. In 1982 Joe McColgan appeared before the District Court charged with assaulting his son. The case was adjourned and finally struck out.

Over the years, the evidence of abuse and the numbers of contacts with doctors, gardaí and social workers were nothing short of staggering.

There were, along the way, decent people who tried to help. Sister Colette, principal at Coláiste Mhuire in Ballymote, remembers a weeping Gerard waiting outside her office having been sent there for falling asleep in class. She asked did he want to be brought home. He said no, it would only cause more beatings. He spoke, convincingly, of the brutality of his father and his fears for his younger sister, Sophia. Armed with this information, Sister Colette attended a case conference on Gerard McColgan held at Markievicz House, the health board centre for community care in Sligo. Later she told the High Court: 'We were not listened to in the sense the allegations needed to be checked out and there was a crisis in the family.' The conference concluded that while Joe McColgan was certainly violent towards his family, they did not have sufficient grounds for legal proceedings.

Gerard was taken into care for a time in 1983 and there he began to talk about the sexual abuse. He said his father was abusing Sophia as well. The McColgans' family doctor, Dr Desmond Moran, examined Gerard and found no evidence of physical abuse. He also got Joe McColgan to swear on a Bible that he wasn't abusing his children.

In 1984 Val O'Kelly, a social worker reviewing the case, wrote:

It is my opinion that I am dealing with a very pathological family. The degree of abuse both physical and sexual is at an extraordinary level . . . Abuse is the norm . . . I have formed the opinion that he [Joe McColgan] is an extremely sick man . . . from the description that Gerard has given me about his sexual activities with Gerard and Sophia I consider him to be seriously perverted sexually . . .

So why did no one rescue the McColgan children? For starters, there was little coordination between the various officials who came in contact with the family. Many incidents were treated as isolated events when they were, in fact, part of a pattern. Then there was the sheer unpleasantness and threatening manner of Joe McColgan. Interfering in his family wasn't easy. But then, interfering with families never is. Later, Sophia told Susan McKay, author of *Sophia's Story*, 'There is so much secrecy and shame in families in this country. So many people know that there is a problem in their family about abuse, but they would rather ignore it and keep silent than face it and rescue the children.'

The truth, when it finally came out, was unbearable. The Central Criminal Court heard an unrelenting tale of terror, rape and violence. The miracle was that no one was killed. The monster at the centre of it all was described in court as a 'West of Ireland farmer', as the identity of the family was protected.

But the McColgan children had questions that weren't answered in the criminal case against their father. They wanted to know why, when the evidence was there for so many professionals to see, no one intervened. The four oldest children decided to take the North Western Health Board and the family GP, Dr Moran, to court.

They were no longer those anonymous children abused by the 'West of Ireland farmer'. They were four young adults, Sophia, Gerard, Keith and Michelle McColgan.

In the High Court, the health board adopted the traditional adversarial stance. First it argued that the statute of limitations applied. Sophia should have taken the case within three years of reaching majority. Never mind that her father was still abusing her for two of those three years.

Lawyers for the board also set about challenging the notion that the McColgans had been damaged by their father's crimes. Sophia was a competent functioning adult, so her childhood couldn't have been all that bad, surely.

The High Court case lasted thirteen days. The legal strategy of the health board — which was later credited to their insurers — ensured that the ordeal of telling the story was even more traumatic than it need be. The court heard how the sexual abuse started, how their father subjected them to mock drownings, how he tried to force Sophia and Gerard to have sex together, how he set up a room for the rapes, how he watched himself in a mirror, how he broke their bones, how he ran over Gerard with a tractor, how he ran over Michelle with a motorbike.

The case was eventually settled for an undisclosed sum reported to be around £1 million. There was no admission of liability. However, the evidence heard over those thirteen days and the report of a review group set up by the health board described a social service in Sligo that didn't provide even the most meagre of safety nets for vulnerable children. The report cited managerial flaws in the North Western Health Board. Information on the family was never collated. Reports were left in filing cabinets. Legal avenues that could have been pursued were not.

As for the family doctor, Desmond Moran, he said he never knew the children were being abused and there's no reason to disbelieve him. After the settlement he told the media that 'not a penny' had been paid by his side. It was a form of vindication, perhaps. The health board report on the case found: 'The health care professional most involved with the family was the GP. When [Gerard] disclosed sexual abuse, it caused shock, horror and disbelief, especially to the general practitioner and the social worker. [His] response was to perform a physical examination and feel relief when no signs were detected.' The report also criticised Dr Moran for turning to a chaplain for advice rather than an expert on child abuse. But Dr Moran's reaction was in keeping with the times. As he told the review group: 'I was trying to get him [Gerard] to get on with his father and mother and trying to keep the family together.'

In an interview with Carol Coulter of *The Irish Times* after it was all over, Sophia McColgan said she and three of her siblings decided to drop the anonymity that is normally afforded rape victims because sexual abuse thrived on silence. 'The silence is gone, there is no more silence now. We did it for all the victims.'

McCracken Tribunal

Formally known as Tribunal of Inquiry (Dunnes Payments), regarded as one of the more efficient tribunals. It was set up on 7 February 1997 on the order of Taoiseach John Bruton, as instructed by resolutions of the Oireachtas, following revelations about payments by supermarket chief Ben Dunne to Charlie Haughey and Michael Lowry. Efforts by retired judge Gerard Buchanan to inquire into these matters, without the power to call witnesses, got only so far, and it was deemed that a sworn inquiry was necessary.

McCracken submitted his report seven months after his appointment. Although rather over-respectful of some witnesses, and lacking what might have been considered a necessary aggression in public sittings, the tribunal did excellent investigative work in private, following the money trails from Dublin to London, the Cayman Islands and back again, and exposing the Ansbacher Deposits, the account wherein certain members of the Golden Circle kept their money. McCracken went to the limit of his remit, and it was necessary to set up the Moriarty Tribunal to take the investigation further.

McDaid, Jim

At around 8 p.m. on 2 February 1977 a group of six or eight people surrounded the home of UDR member Harold Harpur, near Castlederg, County Tyrone, and fired about sixty shots through the windows. Harpur escaped injury, but his brother-in-law was wounded.

That night, across the border in a bar in Letterkenny, a member of St Eunan's College football team, Jim Wilson, was having a stag party. The guests were mostly players from the team. One of them, Jim McDaid, then twenty-seven, was a local doctor. Another was James Clarke, then twenty-two. Although from the same area, McDaid and Clarke had little in common. McDaid had gone to UCG and become a doctor. Clarke got his Leaving Cert and left school, later working for the ESB. McDaid was unaware at the time that Clarke had become involved with the Provos.

Over a year later, Clarke was arrested by the RUC, interrogated, signed confessions, was tried and sentenced to eighteen years. He claimed he was beaten. Aspects of the confessions were questionable. After four years he took part in a mass escape from the Maze. He was later arrested in the South and ended up in Portlaoise prison. The RUC sought his extradition for charges related to the shooting at Harold Harpur's house.

Clarke protested his innocence and fought extradition. In 1989 the case went to the Supreme Court. That same year, Dr Jim McDaid was elected to the Dáil, for Fianna Fáil. Along with most Donegal politicians, McDaid believed that James Clarke was innocent of the charges of attempted murder in 1977. He had long remembered Clarke being at the stag party in Letterkenny on the night of the attempted murder. He had signed a statement to that effect before he became a TD.

In February 1990, as the Supreme Court was reaching judgment on the Clarke case, Jim McDaid was among a number of politicians who lobbied the Minister for Justice on the issue. Other TDs who expressed concern about the case at that time included Paddy Harte, Neil Blaney, Michael D. Higgins, Tom Kitt, Ivor Callely, David Andrews and Chris Flood. McDaid was in court when the Supreme Court ruled that Clarke should be freed. He left the court and congratulated Clarke, who was surrounded by jubilant supporters. A press photographer took a photo. McDaid went about his business.

Twenty-one months later Charlie Haughey appointed McDaid Minister for Defence. These were the last months of Haughey's reign. Haughey, in coalition with the PDs, was aware that he was in the final phase of his political career, there would be no more comebacks, and he intended hanging on as long as possible (he needed the salary). A few days before the reshuffle there had been a possibility that Fianna Fáil would dump Haughey, but this had come to nothing. The possibility had raised and then dashed Fine Gael hopes.

The McDaid appointment presented an opportunity to question Haughey's judgment. The press photo of McDaid in the company of James Clarke and his Provo supporters, outside the Four Courts, was produced. Proinsias De Rossa accused McDaid of 'chairing' Clarke from the Four Courts. Jim O'Keeffe asked: 'What had he been doing providing alibi evidence on behalf of a Provo?' Michael Noonan stuck the label 'Provo fellow-traveller' on McDaid.

Madeleine Taylor-Quinn spoke of McDaid, Charlie Haughey, Ray Burke and the new Attorney General, Harry Whelehan, as 'untrustworthy'. These four, she said, would comprise the cabinet security committee: 'It is an absolute disgrace that a combination of people of such irresponsibility and untrustworthy calibre can sit in such a responsible position.' She suggested that McDaid would leak information to the IRA: 'I wonder now, will the terrorist organisations of this country be privy to very secret security matters.'

These charges were endorsed by John Bruton and Peter Barry. In the Dáil, Fianna Fáil's Dr Rory O'Hanlon asked of Bruton: 'Does he stand over what was said here last night by Deputy Madeleine Taylor-Quinn?' Peter Barry, sitting on the Fine Gael benches, calmly nodded an affirmation. Crouched beside him, John Bruton nodded too. O'Hanlon asked: 'Does he stand over every word that she said?' The two most senior Fine Gaelers rejected the opportunity to in any way soften or qualify the charges laid against McDaid. Both of them nodded again.

Aware that the controversy was damaging the government, McDaid asked Haughey to withdraw his nomination. Haughey did so.

Within months, Haughey was gone. Peter Barry retired. Madeleine Taylor-Quinn lost her seat and ended up in the senate. John Bruton hung on to the Fine Gael leadership and became Taoiseach.

What could Jim McDaid have done to avoid being accused of being 'compromised' as a 'Provo fellow-traveller'? When he had reason to doubt Clarke's guilt he could have kept his mouth shut, perhaps even joined in the calls for Clarke's extradition. McDaid might have concealed his first-hand knowledge that Clarke was at a stag party when he was allegedly shooting someone. He might have stayed away from the Supreme Court. In those sensitive times, attending the Supreme Court could be viewed as a subversive act. Having attended the court, McDaid could have covered his face when he saw the cameras.

From the safety of Dáil privilege, Haughey's enemies savaged an innocent man's career and reputation. In 1997 McDaid was appointed Minister for Tourism, by Bertie Ahern. Not a whisper was raised against the appointment. The political mugging of Jim McDaid had served its purpose at the time and once Haughey was gone it never occurred to anyone to suggest that McDaid was unfit to sit in government.

McGahern, John

It didn't rate as a scandal back then, it was just a whisper. It was taken for granted, it was the way things were. Only in literary circles were there expressions of outrage. And in 1965 they didn't count.

John McGahern was a teacher at a national school in Clontarf, Dublin. He had aspirations to be a writer. In 1962 he received the AE Memorial Award for his novel *The Barracks*. Recognised for his powerful portrayal of provincial life, he had the makings of a serious novelist. In the summer of 1964 he took a year's leave of absence from the school to take up a Macaulay Fellowship.

The following year his second novel, *The Dark*, was published. It was a frank depiction of the realities of life for a young boy growing up in rural Ireland. The book was published in England and when it was shipped to Ireland in May 1965 it was stopped at customs. In June it was banned. In September McGahern returned from leave of absence. Although teachers' salaries were paid by the state, the Catholic church controlled the national schools and the parish priest in each parish was the manager of the local primary school. The parish priest at McGahern's school informed the teacher that he would not be allowed back into the school.

No reason was given. When the Irish National Teachers' Organisation raised its head on the issue the parish priest said that McGahern was aware of 'the valid reason' why he was getting the push. The parish priest denied that the sacking had anything to do with *The Dark*, but 'indecencies' in the novel were unofficially cited, as was the fact that McGahern had married in a registry office. The INTO backed off.

McGahern lost his principal livelihood. He went on to become a distinguished novelist. Oddly enough, although the ordinary editions of *The Dark* were banned, the Braille edition available to the blind was not banned.

See: Flynn, Eileen.

MacSharry Bugging

The assistant garda commissioner went to the minister's office, gave him the tape recorder, showed him how to use it and left. The minister set it up and waited for his cabinet colleague to come along.

It was 21 October 1982. Fianna Fáil had been in ferment for a couple of years, since Jack Lynch had been ditched as leader and Charlie Haughey took over. To some, Haughey was the Boss, taking his rightful place at the head of the party. To others he was an arrogant, devious man who was viewed with some suspicion and much distaste. Ranged against Haughey were the likes of George Colley, Des O'Malley and Martin O'Donoghue. Haughey's camp was bolstered by Minister for Justice Seán Doherty and Minister for Finance Ray MacSharry.

As one controversy after another hit Haughey's government, the efforts to shift him escalated. His opponents speculated that if Ray MacSharry, who had at one time been friendly with George Colley, could be convinced to change sides the Haughey camp could be torn apart. Rumours circulated that MacSharry had financial difficulties. Perhaps Haughey had bailed him out, some wondered, and now had some sort of hold over him. Hints began to reach MacSharry: there's a big chunk of money available, put up by wealthy supporters of the anti-Haugheyites, if MacSharry was financially compromised and needed help to cut his links with Haughey. A figure of £100,000 was mentioned.

MacSharry was furious. The suggestion seemed to him to be that he could be bought. He was told of a message conveyed through Albert

Reynolds that Martin O'Donoghue wanted to see him. O'Donoghue had been talking about money available to free anyone who might remain in the Haughey camp only because of some kind of financial compromise.

On 21 October MacSharry invited O'Donoghue to come to his office at 5.30 p.m., after the launch of the party's new economic policy, The Way Forward. MacSharry decided to tape the conversation with O'Donoghue. He asked around about the availability of tape recorders and Minister for Justice Seán Doherty that afternoon rang Assistant Garda Commissioner Joe Ainsworth, who was in charge of the security branch of the force, and asked him for the loan of a tape recorder. It seems not to have occurred to Doherty that garda equipment used to bug criminals and subversives really should not be available for use in internal political party squabbles.

'How are you, Martin?' asked MacSharry as O'Donoghue entered his office at 5.30 p.m. The greeting identified O'Donoghue for the tape.

O'Donoghue spoke of how Haughey might be removed and suggested that if 'yourself and a number of the other senior people in the cabinet would go [to Haughey], in effect, and say: Look, in the best interest of everybody, he just announces his resignation rather than have any form of contest.'

Then, if the four or five possible replacements for leader would go into a room 'and came out and said that we have a Pope, that would be it'.

MacSharry knew Haughey too well. 'You are talking about coming out of a room with a Pope: he is the Pope, in his mind. You see, this is the trouble.'

O'Donoghue argued against the traditional Fianna Fáil line of loyalty to the leader, right or wrong. 'I honestly believe there may be a different breed in the country. We are going to be hammered in Dublin if your man is still there, that's the long and the short of it.'

MacSharry sought to steer the conversation towards the hints of money, and O'Donoghue's conversation with Albert Reynolds. 'He was talking about money, and I really hit the roof when I heard my name mentioned in connection with money.'

O'Donoghue, who eight months earlier had pulled back from a clash with Haughey, said: 'I'm supposed to have been bought for fifty thousand pounds in February.'

MacSharry: 'I don't know whether it's true or not but what [Reynolds] was talking about was arising from a conversation with yourself . . . a conversation — I hate hearing bits and pieces and not being able to ask — and a hundred thousand pounds being offered.'

'I certainly didn't say that.'

'If I was to go around with the arse out of my trousers I would not take a brown penny from anyone.'

O'Donoghue: 'What was being said was if there is any suggestion of somebody being compromised financially that it would be sorted out.'

That was it. There was someone promising money, if money was needed, to pry Haughey's close supporters loose. To O'Donoghue it was money being used to counteract any financial pressure from the Haughey camp, but the morality of the thing was questionable. It is clear that the likes of MacSharry could read such a vague suggestion as an attempt at bribery.

O'Donoghue moved on to an issue that to MacSharry did not seem credible. O'Donoghue: 'But the money thing that I heard around town was that the Boss was in financial trouble and, certainly again, if that was one of the problems it would be better to organise some way of financing it.'

This seems to be a suggestion that, if necessary, Fianna Fáil supporters might organise a financial bail-out of Haughey. MacSharry didn't believe that the Boss could be in financial trouble.

'For Haughey to be in trouble, I mean, he has such — he couldn't be in trouble.'

'Is there not a persistent story around town, you know, that there's pressure on him to get — development from Baldoyle up because it's worth that much?'

MacSharry said that such rumours circulated about every Fianna Fáil leader. It was a media thing. 'Anything that hits Fianna Fáil.'

O'Donoghue: 'There's a lot of money around, all right, but not for CJ, not for him to stay.' Little did O'Donoghue know. Through the years, business interests were lining up to channel big money to Haughey through his crooked accountant, Des Traynor.

MacSharry: 'That kind of money, you could never have a situation develop where there would be money around to move a political party in any kind of situation.'

Immediately after the bugging, MacSharry gave the tape recorder back to Seán Doherty, who offered to have the tape transcribed. MacSharry said there should be only one copy. Doherty used gardaí to have the tape transcribed and three copies were made. One went to MacSharry, along with the original tape; one was kept by the gardaí; and Doherty kept the final copy.

News of the bugging became public knowledge just over three months later, after Haughey lost a general election. The incoming Fine Gael Minister for Justice, Michael Noonan, revealed that there had been taps on journalists' phones and that MacSharry bugged O'Donoghue.

Simultaneously, it was announced that the garda commissioner, Patrick McLaughlin, and the new deputy commissioner, Joe Ainsworth, were taking early retirement on full pension.

MacSharry explained that he had wanted evidence of any attempt to damage his character and integrity. O'Donoghue said, 'I think there's a very important distinction between setting out in the first instance to bribe people or intimidate them and — on the other hand — setting out, as I understand I was setting out, to see if that had happened and, if so, what we could do to overcome it.'

He later said that the money believed to be available to 'uncompromise' the likes of MacSharry was not a hundred thousand pounds but about half that. There was no indication of who had offered to put up the money.

See: Doherty, Seán; Haughey, Charlie.

Madonna House

Madonna House, in Blackrock, County Dublin, was an Eastern Health Board designated 'place of safety' for children who were taken into care, many because they were at risk of abuse or neglect in their family homes. Like other institutions that were designed to care for children in need, Madonna House was also a place of sexual abuse.

An investigation into allegations of abuse at Madonna House began in August 1993, after a child who had been resident there told her foster parent what was going on. Finally, about thirty children alleged abuse, some were under ten years of age when it occurred.

At any one time Madonna House could accommodate fifty children under the age of sixteen. Run by the Sisters of Charity, funded by the Eastern Health Board, it provided crucial emergency care. It was the place where gardaí would bring children found in dangerous situations.

The inquiry into what happened at Madonna House was commissioned by the Sisters of Charity and then submitted to the Minister for Health on 9 March 1995. A few weeks later, following legal advice by the Attorney General, an edited version of the report was published. Exactly who knew what and when they knew it was not clear from the published section of the report.

In May 1999 the *States of Fear* programme on RTÉ disclosed the part of the report that had been held back. It was seriously damning. Both staff and children reported concerns and allegations about abuse. They were not investigated. 'No report was made to the EHB or the gardaí. The children's social workers were not informed. No report was made to the Provincialate of the Sisters of Charity.'

The inquiry prompted the Sisters of Charity to close Madonna House. Not because of the abuse but — they claimed — because the kind of institutional care they could provide was out of step with modern needs.

In the inquiry report, twenty former residents, boys and girls, said they were abused by Madonna House maintenance man Frank Griffin. They were aged between seven and fifteen when the abuse occurred. Of nine former long-stay residents, who effectively grew up at Madonna House, all but one reported either physical or sexual abuse.

Frank Griffin had already been convicted by the time the report came out. At the age of sixty-five, he pleaded guilty to thirteen counts of indecent and sexual assault on five teenage girls. The abuse took place in his workshop when the children took their toys and bicycles to be repaired. He was sentenced to three years imprisonment in June 1994, with the last year suspended.

The unpublished section of the Madonna House report listed allegations against another man. He was dismissed, but no charges were ever brought against him. This man 'operated a regime of discipline which included episodes of physical violence'. Staff witnesses told the inquiry of hearing the sounds of violence against children through the door of a bedroom, of a screaming child left out in the grounds wearing only a bath towel, of children being systematically humiliated.

Quite apart from the sexual and physical abuse, the report listed other deficiencies in the care of children at Madonna House. There were allegations that children were deprived of food, that some were made pets of and given gifts while others got little personal attention. There was no aftercare service for children who had spent most of their lives in the home. The school attached to the home had underqualified teachers. The Department of Education disagreed with the children being taught in the home and would not provide teachers. Most noteworthy of all, the report found that the Eastern Health Board social workers least likely to refer children to Madonna House were those from the immediate area — best qualified to know what the place was like.

In 1999 the High Court heard a case in which a former resident at Madonna House sued the Eastern Health Board, as the body ultimately responsible for the well-being of the children. He said he was abused by a cleric who worked at Madonna House. Judgment in this case was reserved by Justice Cyril Kelly, who subsequently resigned over the Philip Sheedy controversy.

See: Trudder House.

Magdalen Homes

It wasn't all that long ago that the choice facing many single women who became pregnant was emigration, prostitution or incarceration. Throughout the country, there were buildings that specifically catered for the incarceration of such women. And it was widely accepted that these were charitable institutions. If they were different from prisons, it is only because prisons required that inmates first appear before a court of law.

Commonly called Magdalen homes, after the penitent prostitute of the Bible, they were run by various religious orders and provided the only refuge for a woman rejected by her family. Women were sent to Magdalen homes because they were pregnant, because they were worryingly headstrong, because they were mildly retarded, because they were orphaned, because they were thought to be in moral danger. Thousands of Irish women effectively disappeared when they entered these homes. For some there was no way out, although legally they were always free to go. Many stayed locked away as Magdalen women until they died. Some were put in these homes as recently as 1975.

The Magdalen homes operated under no law, received no public money, were subject to no external scrutiny. The Kennedy Report into reformatories and industrial schools, which focused on children in care, found that the two reformatories in the country catering for girls who came before the courts actually refused to accept 'certain types of girl offenders': specifically those thought to be involved in prostitution or those who were pregnant. These girls and others 'considered by parents, relatives, social workers, Welfare Officers, Clergy or Gardaí to be in moral danger or uncontrollable are also accepted in these [Magdalen] convents'. Published in November 1970, the Kennedy Report found 'at least 70 girls between the ages of 13 and 19 confined in this way'. So, just thirty years before the end of the twentieth century, one solution to child prostitution in Ireland was to institutionalise the children. There was no Magdalen home equivalent for men.

The Kennedy Report found the Magdalen system to be 'haphazard'. 'Its legal validity is doubtful and girls admitted in this irregular way and not being aware of their rights, may remain for long periods and become, in the process, unfit for re-emergence in society.' The Magdalen inmates received no education or training. To pay their way, the women worked in laundries.

Patricia Burke Brogan's 1992 play *Eclipsed* dealt with the impressions of a young nun who was sent to work in a convent laundry. It is an autobiographical work. In the 1960s, the playwright was Sister Perpetuo, a young novice. She was sent to work in one of the laundries. In an *Irish Times* interview she remembered:

> My job was to supervise the women. Most were very institutionalised but one or two who hadn't been there too long were rebellious . . . a number of them were single mothers whose children had been taken from them. Many of them stayed in the convent until they died. The most extraordinary aspect of it was that they were told that they were not allowed leave. They were locked in at night with double locks on the dormitory doors. Legally they could have walked out of the gate at any time but very few did. For many there was no place to go.

In 1993 the Sisters of Charity wanted to sell some land at their High Park convent in Drumcondra, Dublin. The land in question was a private cemetery where 133 women, who had spent their lives working in the convent laundry, were buried. The bodies had to be exhumed and so too were the stories of the unnamed women. Not the details, for if these exist they remain in the private possession of the convent, but the general brush strokes. The first body was buried in 1866, the last in 1983. Some were unmarried mothers, others were destitute. On many of the headstones appeared the name Magdalen: Magdalen of the Sorrows, Magdalen of St Anthony, Magdalen of the Sacred Heart.

Patricia McDonnell was one of several women who campaigned against the exhumation, arguing that it was the final insult to women who had been condemned to lives of suffering at the whim of family or priest. She had a relative who had been locked away when she was sixteen and was finally rescued by her family when she was thirty-five. Her only crime was to be an orphan, one girl in a family of brothers. The local priest thought she was in moral danger and she was sent away. That was in the 1940s, when a priest's decision had the force of law. Nearly twenty years later the woman was found in a convent laundry in Dún Laoghaire.

The laundry attached to the convent of the Sisters of our Lady of Charity in Sean MacDermott Street, Dublin closed in 1996. In its heyday, it had 150 women working in the laundry. When it closed, there were 40 women remaining, mostly elderly. As has happened when other convent laundries closed, those women remained under the care of religious orders. They are forgotten by the families who put them there and long past the point where they would have the wherewithal to live an independent life.

Patricia Burke Brogan says she wrote *Eclipsed* to give the Magdalen women a voice: 'I was one of the few who entered the laundry who came out and could speak up. Why did we do it? I don't know. It's a question I've been asking myself for a long time.'

Mallon Bugging

Wherever the truth lay — and we don't know — the Mallon bugging scandal was one of the more bizarre political scandals of the mid-1980s.

Seamus Mallon, deputy leader of the SDLP, regularly attended meetings of the Forum, in Dublin. The Forum was one way-station in the long trek in search of some kind of accommodation between the parties in the northern conflict. When in Dublin, Mallon stayed at the house of an SDLP supporter. In November of 1983 he reported the finding of a 'bugging' device, a microphone and transmitter, at his friend's home.

Officials from Posts and Telegraphs called to the house but Mallon's friend, suspicious that these officials were somehow involved in the bugging, wouldn't hand over the bugging equipment. The police looked into it and concluded that the device had been installed by gangsters who intended robbing the home.

The *Sunday Tribune* broke the story on 18 February 1984. Charlie Haughey blamed the British, alleging they were doing this to interfere with the running of the Forum. The *Sunday Tribune* suggested the gardaí might be behind it. Garret FitzGerald became convinced the bug was planted by the IRA in order to engineer a row between the SDLP and the Dublin government.

The microphone was from a telephone handset. It had been placed under a carpet, which would have muffled any voices in the room. The equipment seemed too elaborate to be a hoax and too primitive to be the work of professional buggers.

The mystery was never solved. However, the incident is notable in that it revealed the level of paranoia there was at that time. And that paranoia was probably justified. Whoever planted the bug, the truth was — and everyone knew it — that elements within the various bodies suspected of the bugging all had the motive, means, opportunity and willingness to do it. Whoever did it, the fact that the others didn't do it only means that they didn't think it worth while, or didn't think of it first.

Malocco, Elio

When the *Irish Press* newspaper had libel problems, Elio Malocco was there to sort them out. The young, confident, capable solicitor had a good record with the company. He had married into the de Valera family, which had from the beginning run the newspaper, and he had been made a director. Malocco was in partnership with another solicitor, Conor Kileen.

The company from time to time gave Malocco money to pay off litigants or to lodge money in court, in preparation for a libel fight. In September 1991 the newspaper's management was shocked to learn that the company had not been credited with amounts of money which had been paid over in one case. The company's financial controller and an accountant immediately headed for the firm of Malocco and Kileen. An angry meeting followed.

A court was later told that Malocco at once set about forging documents: Bank of Ireland receipts for £15,000, £21,600 and £17,500, and a notice of lodgment of £10,000. To show that a case had been settled, a Circuit Court notice of discontinuance was forged. It didn't work; the company pushed for an examination of Malocco's activities.

Malocco was charged and convicted of fraud and forging documents. He was sentenced to five years. There was no suggestion of restitution or remorse. No explanation was offered as to why a successful and apparently well-off professional would engage in such activities.

Malocco's partner, Conor Kileen, was convicted of helping Malocco cover up the fraud. The court was told he didn't benefit from the fraud, that he dissolved the partnership two weeks after he found out what was going on. Kileen was sentenced to twelve months in July 1996. He was released after six weeks.

Malocco bounced back in 1998, as publisher of a new men's magazine. The first issue immediately became embroiled in a legal tangle as a nightclub owner took action to prevent publication of an allegedly libellous article.

The Malocco scandal was one of the indicators in the early 1990s that behind the façade of professionalism in the new, confident, bullish Ireland, there was a frenetic greed at work.

Mansfield, Jayne

Protests by movie actress Jayne Mansfield that she was a good Catholic were of no avail. The scheduled opening of her cabaret act at the Mount Brandon Hotel in Tralee, County Kerry was abruptly cancelled just hours before she was to take the stage.

It was April 1967 and Mansfield's movie career was mostly behind her. She had over the previous dozen years acted in a number of movies, mostly bad ones, as a dumb blonde. She was neither. Her long blonde hair was a wig and her IQ was reported at 163. She was a downmarket Marilyn Monroe and although she had studied drama and longed to be taken seriously as an actress her movie career mostly featured her large breasts.

Now, her major source of income was a cabaret act, which she hustled from town to town. She was doing a tour of nightclubs in England and was signed up for the Tralee gig for a thousand-pound fee, by the ballroom manager of the Mount Brandon, representing the hotel's owner, John Byrne. (This was the John Byrne who would later achieve fame as a friend and alleged business associate of Charlie Haughey, backer of Celtic Helicopters, Ansbacher account holder and witness at the Moriarty Tribunal.)

Jayne Mansfield was, in the innocent terminology of the time, a sex symbol. Publicity for her Tralee show quoted a New York critic as saying that she sold sex better than any other performer. 'I am a sexy entertainer,' said Mansfield. That was enough for the Bishop of Kerry, Denis Moynihan. Crying scandal, he launched a campaign to stop her. A letter was read at all masses in St Mary's Cathedral, Killarney, and Monsignor John Lane appealed to the populace 'to dissociate themselves from this attempt to besmirch the name of our town'. He said that 'the very entrance of this woman to the town' was a slur on the Rose of Tralee festival.

On the afternoon of Sunday, 23 April, as a crowd at Dublin airport was cheering Mansfield's arrival, the hotel's directors met and a statement was issued saying the cabaret was being called off 'owing to the controversy'. Jayne Mansfield, on arriving in Tralee, denied that the show had been cancelled as a result of the bishop's campaign. Possibly to save face, she said the show had to be called off because her music sheets were lost. The manager of the hotel backed her up on this. The fact that the hotel had issued a statement saying the show was called off because of the controversy created by the bishop didn't count. 'I had the statement done up and it slipped out by mistake,' said the manager.

This was fourteen months after the *Late Late Show*'s Bishop and the Nightie episode, and people were beginning to laugh at the sexual preoccupations of bishops. That week's *Late Late* featured a sketch lampooning the Mansfield controversy. The show was denounced at the following week's meeting of the Tralee Vocational Education Committee, where it was described as 'suggestive and immoral'. Christian Brother Superior Kennedy said he never watched *The Late Late Show* but he was sure the committee was right. Of the committee members, only a Reverend McMorran, a Presbyterian minister, dissented from the attack on *The Late Late Show*.

Jayne Mansfield's public image was slightly but cheerfully vulgar. Her clothes, she joked, were 'tight-fitting but high-necked'. She had eloped at sixteen, been divorced twice and separated once, and her claim to a spiritual attachment to Catholicism didn't win much sympathy from the bishop. The fact that she wasn't merely a sex symbol, that she was someone with ambitions to rise above the brash side of show business, didn't matter; nor did it matter that she had five children, ranging in age from eighteen months to sixteen years, and that this was the only work she was getting. Her right to work, to earn a living, the right of a hotel to book her, the right of her fans to see her, were as nothing compared with the bishop's frown.

Two months later, hustling her act between cabaret gigs in Louisiana, USA, Jayne Mansfield died in a car crash.

See: Bishop and the Nightie, The.

Mature Recollection

The term was coined by Fianna Fáil candidate Brian Lenihan, on RTÉ's *Six-One News*, on Thursday, 25 October 1990, during the presidential election won by Mary Robinson.

Lenihan had gone on RTÉ's *Questions & Answers* the previous Monday, and in the course of the programme was asked about an incident back in January 1982, when a number of phone calls were made to Áras an Uachtaráin. The calls were instigated by Charlie Haughey in an effort to convince then president Paddy Hillery to exercise his right not to dissolve the Dáil, necessitating a general election, but instead to ask Haughey to form a government. Several phone calls were made, in one of which Haughey was alleged to have tried to intimidate an army officer. Haughey strongly denied this. On *Questions & Answers*, Lenihan denied making any of the phone calls.

Three days later, in a bizarre development, *The Irish Times* held a press conference at the Westbury Hotel at which a tape was played of an interview which Lenihan had given the previous May to an academic researcher, Jim Duffy. On the tape, Lenihan was asked: 'And did any of the calls get through to the president?'

'Oh, yeah,' said Lenihan, 'I mean, I got through to him. I remember talking to him and he wanted us to lay off. There was no doubt about it in his mind.'

A secondary scandal developed from claims that in revealing the contents of the tape Duffy was breaching the confidentiality of academic research. The role of *The Irish Times*, in hosting a press conference and giving the story to all media, instead of publishing it itself, led to accusations that the newspaper had become a player in the election.

Once the contents of the tape were revealed, Lenihan headed straight for RTÉ, and the *Six-One News*, in a desperate attempt at damage limitation. Instead of answering interviewer Seán Duignan directly he stared at the camera, looking somewhat frightened and pathetic as he insisted to viewers that while he said what he said on the tape, his 'mature recollection' was that he hadn't phoned Hillery that night.

Lenihan was on medication when he did the taped interview with Jim Duffy. It is possible it was the medication talking. However, Lenihan's biographer, James Downey, records that while sober and unmedicated, Lenihan told two journalists that he made the phone calls to the Áras.

The scandal seriously set back Lenihan's presidential campaign and led to his resignation from the cabinet, and the term 'mature recollection' went into the political lexicon. It is applied to politicians as a mock excuse when they change their story.

See: Flynn, Pádraig: *Saturday View*; Lenihan Resignation Lies.

Mespil Flats

An apartment for £28,000, in Dublin 4 near the Grand Canal, was a bargain, even in 1992. Offered such a deal, it's hardly surprising that investors decided not to look the gift horse in the mouth. It wasn't a deal advertised in the newspapers. It was a deal for people in a privileged position, whether they knew it or not.

Not privileged were the people who lived in the apartments that were about to be sold at bargain-basement prices. The Mespil flats were the property of the state-owned company Irish Life and their tenants had as much security of rent and tenure as could be found outside of local authority housing. But in July 1991 Irish Life was floated on the Stock Exchange and as a publicly quoted company, responsible to shareholders looking for dividends, the ethos began to change. It was time to get out of the benevolent landlord business.

Tenants who were coming up to twenty-year residency were shifted about within the complex lest they qualify for what little security was available under the 1980 Landlord and Tenant Act. One block of flats, Fir House, was put on the market with vacant possession. That generated offers for the entire complex. A company called New City Estates offered £8.15 million, an average of £28,000 per unit. It was more than an independent valuation had suggested and Irish Life decided to sell.

Irish Life did little at this stage to safeguard the future of the tenants. Most of them were elderly people living on modest pensions who'd assumed Mespil flats was where they'd end their days. Their homes were sold over their heads.

As the story was played out in the media, Irish Life insisted that 'the purchasers indicated that they didn't envisage any disruption to tenants and that they saw themselves as long-term investors'. However, New City Estates flatly stated that it had given Irish Life no assurances about continuity of tenure.

It was an unsettling time for the tenants. They were learning the identity of their new landlords. Some were being asked to move out. Some were told the rent was being put up. Some were left alone.

New City Estates had originally intended to bring in investors who would each buy a block of, say, sixteen flats. It would be a complex but manageable deal involving no more than twenty investors. But then interest rates soared and the bulk-buyers pulled out. New City Estates started selling in smaller numbers. Two days before the whole £8.15 million sale was to close, purchasers of two full blocks of flats pulled out. New City

Estates scurried about for more potential small investors. First National was already lined up with a mortgage package to speed along the process.

There was no time for advertising. New City Estates needed to find people who could buy at short notice and this did not include the tenants. Studio apartments went for less than £20,000. A two-bedroom apartment sold for £44,000.

Several well-known people were approached and invited to buy flats. Among those who did were publican Dessie Hynes, broadcaster Marian Finucane, former journalist James Morrissey, two of Albert Reynolds's daughters, the then Attorney General Harry Whelehan, tailor Louis Copeland, lawyer Paddy McEntee, Irish Nationwide boss Michael Fingleton. Some resold the flats later when they unwittingly found themselves in the middle of a public controversy.

Nearly a year after the sale, 196 former Irish Life tenants were still living in the complex, some of them paying an increased rent. About 58 tenants had left, 29 of the 299 flats were vacant. There were 30 new lettings.

One block of twelve flats with vacant possession was back on the market by May 1993. The auctioneer was seeking £52,000 for a one-bedroom apartment, £64,500 for two bedrooms, £74,500 for three. As the Sherry FitzGerald brochure pointed out: 'No sacrifice or compromise is necessary when you buy in the Mespil Estate. Everything a discerning purchaser could regard as being necessary for convenient living is to hand.'

Ministerial Pensions

Politicians arranged things so that former ministers got a pension after serving just three years in office. This meant that a serving TD who had been a minister got a healthy pension on top of a perfectly adequate TD's salary. It meant that politicians in their thirties and forties were receiving two incomes from the public purse.

The scandal was such that in February 1988 two former ministers, Des O'Malley and Bobby Molloy of the Progressive Democrats, voluntarily gave up their pensions rather than be associated with a system which had 'no moral justification'. This was no empty gesture. It cost O'Malley £9,000 a year and Molloy £8,500.

It wasn't easy for them to turn down the pensions. They found that even if they didn't accept the money they would have to pay tax on it. Eventually, after negotiations with the Paymaster General's office, it was arranged that the two would formally 'gift' their pensions to the state and wouldn't have to pay tax on the money they weren't getting.

The pension system was changed in 1992. Those already eligible for ministerial pensions could continue with the old system; those henceforth appointed to a ministerial position would be eligible for a ministerial pension from the age of fifty-five.

In November 1992 the FF/PD coalition fell. O'Malley and Molloy became eligible again for a ministerial pension on top of their Dáil salaries. Both in their fifties, they decided that the system had changed sufficiently — albeit while allowing former ministers to continue accepting a pension on top of a salary — to allow them to accept their pensions. What had in 1988 no moral justification was morally justified in 1993.

Des O'Malley said people had sneered when he gave up his pension: 'What thanks did I get for not accepting it over a two-and-a-half-year period?'

Moneylending Tribunal

W*orld in Action* exposed the activities of the Goodman Group and led to the setting up of the Beef Tribunal. Twenty years earlier, another tribunal of inquiry resulted from a TV programme. An RTÉ programme, made by the *7 Days* team and broadcast on 11 November 1969, examined the phenomenon of illegal moneylending in Dublin. It was produced under the control of editor Muiris Mac Conghail and reported by Bill O'Herlihy, better known today for his work in public relations and sports broadcasting.

The programme stated that illegal moneylending was rife in Dublin, that people feared violence if they didn't pay extortionate rates of interest, that the gardaí paid little attention to what was going on. The government outrage that followed this broadcast was directed not at the conditions in which illegal moneylending took place in Dublin but at the *7 Days* programme. A tribunal of inquiry was set up to investigate the programme's claims and to probe its working methods.

The tribunal found that there were serious flaws in the programme's research; that interviewees exaggerated the illegal moneylending problem; and that the gardaí were not turning a blind eye. There was truth in these findings. The programme exaggerated the problem, there was an amount of colourful hype which too often infects reporting ('Like giant tentacles, the moneylenders reach out to shadow every street and every housing estate in every part of Dublin').

The tribunal found that illegal moneylenders were concentrated in certain areas, that they numbered dozens and not hundreds, that many of the women borrowers were more afraid of their husbands finding out than of having their legs broken by moneylenders. The effect of the tribunal was to suggest that the police were on top of things, there was nothing much to worry about and RTÉ had lost the head.

In truth, violence by moneylenders was rare, mostly implied. Illegal moneylending was not a shadow on every street, it was the last resort of a substantial minority of people excluded from the regulated money-lending institutions, the banks and building societies. Both the RTÉ programme makers and the tribunal approached the Dublin working-class areas in which illegal moneylending existed as though they were examining an alien and somewhat dangerous subspecies, rather than an integral part of Irish society.

RTÉ's well-intentioned but flawed effort was seized on by the establishment. The programme became the issue, and the existence of dozens of illegal moneylenders in Dublin, not hundreds, was portrayed as evidence that there wasn't too much wrong with Irish society. The programme makers may have got some things wrong, but they were consciously concerned about and intent on examining one aspect of what today we call an excluded segment of society. The political establishment had no such social concern and were happy to put the whole affair down to excessive zeal on the part of the broadcasters.

The longest-lasting effect of the tribunal was to make any vigorous RTÉ current affairs examination of the status quo — let alone any challenge to it — feel like a dangerous adventure. Programme makers were aware that to go too far was to risk a tribunal coming down upon them from a height.

Moriarty Tribunal

The Moriarty Tribunal set up shop on 21 October 1997. But it was 28 January 1999 before counsel for the tribunal, John Coughlan, made his opening statement and the first witness was heard. In the meantime, Moriarty had been jumping through the various legal hoops which had become the norm, as parties under investigation sought to defend their constitutional rights.

Moriarty was set up after the McCracken Tribunal unearthed the relationship between Charlie Haughey and Ben Dunne. The Ansbacher Deposits, within which Haughey's coded accounts were supervised by his crooked accountant, Des Traynor, had processed tens of millions of pounds. Only some of it belonged to Haughey, and it was clear that not all the money Haughey was being drip-fed by the wealthy came from Ben Dunne. Therefore, the Moriarty Tribunal was necessary. Although Michael Lowry's business methods and tax fraud were largely established by the McCracken Tribunal, he was thrown into the Moriarty mix, a Fine Gael wrongdoer put under further scrutiny in order to give political balance to the tribunal, and to make the Fianna Fáilers feel less put upon.

Judge Michael Moriarty is a precise, pedantic figure who could be relied on to follow the evidence wherever it led. He and his counsel uncovered payments to Haughey which had not been revealed to McCracken. Ben Dunne declared himself to be 'astonished' to have forgotten about those payments.

Following the money trail, Moriarty uncovered the astonishing saga of Haughey's indebtedness to Allied Irish Banks throughout the 1970s, and AIB's toadying to the powerful. Moriarty, always courteous, only very occasionally impatient, engaged in no banter, made no quips, skilfully avoided confrontations with lawyers, methodically went about the business of investigating the relationship between Haughey, Lowry and their financial backers.

N

National Irish Bank

Like so many other scandals, the wonder of the National Irish Bank story is that it didn't break sooner. A respected bank — the fourth largest in the country — systematically and frequently steals money from its customers in order to boost profits. You'd think someone affected would notice or someone in on the scam would come to the conclusion that morally speaking this wasn't kosher.

But that wasn't the way it happened. The NIB story was a case of one controversy leading to another and that one leading to the whopper — that the bank's business was theft.

A trade union official told RTÉ's special correspondent Charlie Bird that National Irish Bank offered customers a deal whereby they could put their money in an offshore investment scheme, well away from the prying eyes of the Revenue Commissioners, but retain ready access to it in their local NIB branch. For a year, the trade unionist had held on to the information he gave to Bird; now that the Ansbacher controversy had focused public attention on systematic tax evasion and offshore accounts he thought it should be made public.

Charlie Bird joined forces with RTÉ's economics editor, George Lee, to track down sources and document the story. What they eventually found out was that National Irish Bank sold a product called Clerical Medical Insurance (CMI) to customers in Ireland. CMI was based in the Isle of Man. Money invested with CMI went into a numbered account. But it was routed back to NIB, which meant the bank got commission from CMI and held on to the deposit money and the customer could draw money out when required. CMI got substantial fees and the customer got far less, in the end, than they would have got had they left the money in a simple deposit account in the bank. So why do it? The only attraction was anonymity. People who invested with CMI needed to keep their money hidden, most usually from the Revenue.

On Friday, 23 January 1998, on the *Six-One News*, Charlie Bird reported that prior to 1994 NIB gathered information on customers who held non-resident accounts, accounts in false names, accounts with funds that had not been disclosed to the Revenue Commissioners. More than 150 customers agreed to invest in CMI in the Isle of Man. When they did, their money — less set-up charges and commission for NIB — was sent back to NIB. In August 1994 the amount invested in CMI was thought to have been £30 million.

The trade unionist who had originally told Charlie Bird about the CMI scheme said it was the poor man's Ansbacher. While the people who invested in CMI could not be described as poor, they weren't millionaires. As Derek McDowell TD said in the Dáil: 'We are talking about the local businessman, the local hotelier, the local garage owner: people involved in cash businesses who ultimately couldn't resist the temptation to hide their earnings from Revenue . . . they are the middle classes, respectable businessmen from all over Ireland.'

A public statement from NIB confirmed most of the information in the RTÉ report but denied any collusion in tax evasion. The reaction of the Minister for Finance, Charlie McCreevy, was relaxed.

> These things must be borne in context . . . the vast majority of taxpayers are compliant . . . the question of tax evasion is not a unique Irish problem . . . these things must be borne in mind rather than people going off half-cocked and making some ridiculous and outlandish allegations against the Revenue Commissioners and against other people as well . . . I'm trying to bring some reality to the situation with some of the outlandish allegations that have been made all round.

Asked what outlandish allegations, he said:

> National Irish Bank have pointed out themselves that the sums of money involved represent 0.1 per cent of their own total resources and that has put something in context.

For NIB the next step was to get an injunction preventing RTÉ using confidential bank documents Charlie Bird and George Lee had obtained. That was Friday, 30 January 1998. On Friday, 20 March, nearly two months after the gagging order was imposed, the Supreme Court gave its judgment. In a majority verdict it found in favour of RTÉ. Mr Justice Lynch delivered judgment: 'the allegation which they make is of serious tax evasion and this is a matter of genuine interest and importance to the general public . . . I am satisfied that it is in the public interest that the general public should be given this information.' As an *Irish Times* editorial stated, it was a 'significant tilt by the courts in favour of press freedom'.

The two reporters had been busy during the weeks of the injunction. One of Charlie Bird's sources was a banker. He was interviewed about the CMI scheme and the interview was broadcast with the banker's face obscured and his words read by an actor. But the same source also told Charlie Bird the much bigger story — that the bank systematically loaded interest and added fees to customer accounts in order to boost its own profits. It was taking money from its own customers.

This report had to wait until the injunction was lifted. When it was, NIB received a letter from RTÉ asking twelve questions about the increased interest charges deducted from customer accounts. NIB issued a fairly strong statement in response, perhaps trying to undermine the credibility of RTÉ's two reporters. It didn't matter. The story was ready to roll.

National Irish Bank's internal audits had revealed that some branches had been secretly overcharging customers to boost profits. When it was found out, the customers were not reimbursed. The documents were there to prove both increased interest and additional fees were charged without the customers' knowledge or consent.

Viewers were shocked. So was the government. An emergency cabinet meeting was convened after the story was broadcast. NIB issued a statement admitting the overcharging happened but said it went back many years and was no longer permitted. It stated: 'RTÉ has again allowed itself to be used by disaffected parties to promote out-of-date information . . . NIB is gravely concerned that RTÉ continues to present highly selective information leaked to it to undermine the bank.'

By the next day National Irish Bank was more contrite. An internal investigation was under way. Arthur Andersen consultants had been employed to carry it out. Two High Court inspectors, the Garda Fraud Squad, the Director of Consumer Affairs, an officer from the Department of Enterprise and Employment, and the Revenue Commissioners were also investigating. The Revenue Commissioners insisted National Irish Bank give them names and full details of all investors in the offshore CMI scheme. The anonymity the tax dodgers had paid for was gone.

Newspaper Shredding

There is in Ireland not only a laudable high regard for literary tradition but a strong fear of the written word. Censorship was for decades in the tight grip of those who feared the effects on the citizenry of what they called 'evil literature'. Evil literature included anything sexual and anything to do with birth control. For instance, a British Royal Commission Report on Population was banned here in 1948, for over a year, because it mentioned family planning. The fear of evil literature so permeated society that in April 1956 an entire consignment of the *Observer* newspaper delivered from Britain to Dublin airport was believed to have been confiscated by customs. The newspaper carried an article on family planning.

As the scandal of the confiscated newspapers created a public row it became clear that they had not, in fact, been confiscated by customs. The whole thing was smothered in secrecy, no one would come straight out and say why or how the newspapers disappeared. It appears that a customs official remarked to the distributor, when he arrived to pick up the newspapers, that he could be done under the 1929 Censorship of Publications Act if he distributed a newspaper with an article on family planning. And so could any shop that sold it. Such was the atmosphere pertaining in such matters that the distributor, not unreasonably, did a runner.

That incident occurred, appropriately enough, on 1 April 1956. And those were the bad old days, when our betters insisted on doing our thinking for us. However, in May 1992 a consignment of 2,000 copies of a British newspaper was shredded by distributors who were afraid to circulate the newspaper to shops because it carried an advertisement for the Marie Stopes Clinic in Britain, wherein abortions were performed. The X case had aroused fears of the power of the state to suppress any information about abortion, under the 1983 constitutional amendment guaranteeing the embryo a right to life equal with the mother's.

In the Dáil, Proinsias De Rossa TD read aloud the words of the advert. Radio station 98FM carried a report on this and was subsequently raided by gardaí, who believed they had a right to demand transcripts of the station's broadcast.

Another referendum had to be held to clear the legal air, so that everyone would know that it was okay to read the *Guardian*, and we could make up our own minds about anything advertised therein.

Non-recourse Loans

Certain people, usually in the HNWI and KBI class, are given premier facilities by banks, on the basis that they may in the long run generate big profit. One such facility is a 'non-recourse' loan. This, very roughly, means that if the project for which you borrow money comes up trumps we're all laughing. If it doesn't, you don't have to pay back the loan.

See: FitzGerald, Garret; HNWI; KBI.

Non-resident Bank Accounts

Throughout the 1980s and 1990s, large numbers of well-off people systematically looted the state coffers. They took what resources they needed from state expenditure and thought up criminal schemes to avoid paying their share of state taxes. The very wealthy had crooked accountants such as Des Traynor to organise their thefts. The merely well-off used their accountants and lawyers — and most of all their bankers — to facilitate their criminality. This resulted in the creation of thousands of bogus non-resident bank accounts.

Non-resident bank accounts should not be confused with non-resident companies, which present an entirely different opportunity for fraud.

Nor should bogus non-resident accounts be confused with bogus offshore accounts.

(Bogus offshore accounts, as operated by — for instance — Des Traynor, were accounts that were nominally in banks in, say, the Cayman Islands, while an equivalent account was maintained in an Irish bank. The owners of the accounts could draw the money from the local bank, yet the money — being technically outside the country — would not be liable for tax.)

Bogus non-resident bank accounts were opened in Irish banks, by people falsely claiming to be living abroad. These accounts were not liable for Deposit Interest Retention Tax (DIRT). Sometimes depositors used false names; sometimes they used the Irish language version of their names. Sometimes they used false addresses, sometimes addresses in the USA or Britain were supplied by helpful bank officials.

The money in the bogus non-resident accounts was almost certainly hot money, which had not been declared for income tax purposes. RTÉ's financial editor, George Lee, estimated that when everything was taken into account, the final liability to the state might be in the region of ten billion pounds.

AIB was the worst offender. Internally, at one stage there was a belief that it owed £100 million to the Revenue; this was scaled back to about £35 million, though the bank claimed to have acquired a private tax amnesty from the Revenue.

Bank of Ireland appears to have made genuine efforts to stamp out the fraud from an early stage. So large was the fraud that over £2 million was collected from the Miltown Malbay branch alone, after the Revenue stirred itself enough to act.

NIB customers stealing money from the state had been forced to pay back £11 million by July 1999, with several million more being discussed.

The state-owned ACC bank was up to its neck in the fraud, ending up with an estimated £17 million DIRT liability. Various other financial institutions had smaller involvements.

The effect of the massive fraud was a significant transfer of wealth from the working class to the middle class. As the state's finances were stretched in the 1980s, high rates of PAYE continued to be paid, state services were cut, people died on hospital waiting lists. Meanwhile, the state was defrauded of billions.

The Revenue and the Central Bank and the Department of Finance knew for years that this was going on and did little. The explanation offered later, when the July 1999 Comptroller and Auditor General's report revealed the extent of the fraud, was that the authorities were afraid that checking on such accounts might have frightened off 'genuine' non-resident account holders, who might have switched their money abroad. It was a threadbare excuse.

Though there were suggestions that a few token tax defrauders might be charged, there was no suggestion that the bankers, without whom much of the fraud could not have succeeded, would face charges.

Some who operated bogus non-resident accounts in the Bank of Ireland sued the bank, after the bank disclosed their bogus accounts to the Revenue in 1991. The tax dodgers had to pay up to the Revenue. In a lawsuit, they claimed that had the bank continued concealing the tax fraud from the state they could have taken advantage of the 1993 tax amnesty, and would have had to pay less than they had to pay when found out.

Claiming breach of confidentiality, they are suing the bank for the difference between what they paid the Revenue and what they would have had to pay under the tax amnesty.

See: AIB: A Case Study; AIB: Bogus Accounts; National Irish Bank.

Non-resident Companies

The amount of money laundered through Irish-registered non-resident companies is estimated at around £20 billion. This is just a guess, as these companies are covered in secrecy.

Non-resident companies should not be confused with non-resident bank accounts, which present an entirely different opportunity for fraud.

In 1989 the British changed their laws on such matters and Ireland was left as the last European country with fraud-friendly company laws. International conmen and crooks focused on this country. They could register companies here and those companies were free from taxation or scrutiny back home. Not trading in Ireland, they would be free from Irish taxation. Most importantly, the companies would not be subject to any regulation whatever, and so could be used to perform whatever tricks a clever lawyer or accountant could dream up.

For a fee, you could buy an off-the-shelf company, complete with 'directors', named people who acted as nominal directors of hundreds of companies. The names of the beneficial owners of the company were concealed and the company could be used to hide and launder countless millions.

Suddenly, Ireland had over 40,000 non-resident companies. Solicitors and accountants and various other professionals servicing this business were estimated to be making around £60 million a year. Some of the companies were legitimate, many were not. From the underworld of Moscow and various parts of Eastern Europe the criminals arranged to have companies opened in Dublin. US firms used such companies to evade taxation back home. Police from other countries began visiting here — in much the same way as tribunal lawyers from Ireland went sniffing around the Cayman Islands for information about Charlie Haughey's bent money.

The extent of the problem was revealed by Siobhan Creaton in *The Irish Times* in February 1998, and eventually the government moved on the issue. Law-abiding types in the Department of Enterprise wanted rid of such firms. The IDA and business representatives wanted them retained. Some of the non-resident firms were legitimate and might be a source of investment. Accountancy firms making a lot of money out of non-resident companies wanted things left as they were.

In February 1999, ten years after the problem began, new measures regulating the setting up of such companies, their duty to disclose beneficial ownership, and their liability for tax, were put in place. The motivation for tightening up the law had nothing to do with morality; the activities of the crooks had begun to get the International Financial Services Centre a bad name.

By the time the laws were changed, many a respected Irish professional had made a not-so-small fortune through servicing international gangsters.

O

O'Brien, Conor Cruise

When allegations of a garda Heavy Gang emerged in the mid-1970s the authorities dismissed them as Provo propaganda, and some no doubt were. When in 1977 gardaí themselves raised questions about a Heavy Gang in their midst they were dismissed as pro-Fianna Fáilers trying to create trouble for the Fine Gael/Labour coalition government. For years afterwards, those inquiring about the allegations were assured by Fine Gael and Labour politicians that nothing of the sort had happened.

Confirmation of the tolerance of a culture of violence within the force came belatedly and from an unlikely source. In his 1998 book, *Memoir: My Life and Themes*, Conor Cruise O'Brien, Minister for Posts and Telegraphs in the Cosgrave coalition, referred to the Herrema case. On 3 October 1975 republicans kidnapped a Dutch industrialist, Tiede Herrema, and demanded the release of three republican prisoners. On 21 October gardaí surrounded a house in Monasterevin, County Kildare, where Herrema was being held, and after an eighteen-day siege Herrema was released unharmed.

O'Brien, then a member of the government, tells in his book of how he spoke to garda contacts at that time and asked them how the police found out where Herrema was being held. He records that one of the detectives smiled and said:

> One of the gang had been arrested, and we felt sure he knew where Herrema was. So this man was transferred under Branch escort from a prison in the country to a prison in Dublin, and on the way the car stopped. Then the escort started asking him questions and when at first he refused to answer, they beat the shit out of him. Then he told them where Herrema was.

O'Brien adds, referring to his cabinet colleagues Garret FitzGerald and Justin Keating: 'I refrained from telling this story to Garret or Justin, because I thought it would worry them. It didn't worry me.'

So, we now know that in October 1975, sixteen months before *The Irish Times* made public the Heavy Gang allegations, at least one cabinet minister believed that the beating of suspects was acceptable within the police force. The culture of violence appears to have been so acceptable in certain quarters that detectives had no qualms about casually telling a government minister about a specific beating. The detectives must have felt confident that O'Brien would not report this conversation or make an official complaint.

It must also have been comforting to the detectives who discussed this with O'Brien that a cabinet minister saw nothing wrong with beating up a prisoner. This approval can only have encouraged those within the force who engaged in such violence.

What if the prisoner had been more stubborn? What if the prisoner didn't know where Herrema was? How far might the police have gone? How far can you go down that road before you find yourself wielding an electric cattle prod?

How many other people were lifted and beaten? The police 'felt sure' that the prisoner had information; the police felt sure of a lot of things around that time, some of which turned out to be right and some of which turned out to be wrong.

There is a lot that is implicit in O'Brien's acceptance of the right of the police to beat information out of a suspect. If the prisoner complains and an inquiry is held, the garda must lie or lose his job; if the case comes to court, the garda must commit perjury or go to jail. To tolerate police beating suspects is to tolerate the lying, the conspiracy and the perjury which may follow, and the subversion of the legal system which this entails.

Apart from all this, there is O'Brien's tone. He tells the anecdote with satisfaction. He mocks the worriers, FitzGerald and Keating, whom he plainly didn't like. He relishes keeping the violent secret to himself. They wouldn't have had the stomach for it. It takes a real man to understand that sometimes you have to turn a blind eye. The tone is uncannily like that of a mid-1970s armchair republican talking about 'legitimate targets' and explaining why you can't make an omelette without breaking eggs.

See: Heavy Gang.

O'Kennedy, Michael

As the Greencore scandal exploded in September 1991, and other scandals bubbled under the surface, politicians staggered and weaved like drunks in a minefield, unsure if the next step would bring yet another explosion. No minister looked so wary as Michael O'Kennedy, whose face seemed permanently to bear the expression of a startled kitten that has just heard a very loud and unexplained noise.

Greencore was within O'Kennedy's departmental area. As it happened, O'Kennedy would not become embroiled in any of the scandals which would stain other members of the Fianna Fáil regime of that period. No aspersions were cast on his honesty or competence. Such was the atmosphere of the time, however, that even the innocent were exceedingly nervous. At a routine function, RTÉ's Joe O'Brien cornered O'Kennedy and insisted on asking a simple question: was it a mistake not to put a civil servant on the Greencore board? O'Brien was not — no more than anyone else — suggesting any wrongdoing on O'Kennedy's part, merely querying whether it might have been a mistake not to ensure civil service supervision of a matter which subsequently erupted in scandal. O'Kennedy's reply is a classic example of the politician at bay as the scandals of the early 1990s exploded around him.

'It wasn't a mistake, when in fact the whole pattern, in the vast bulk of boards — I don't want to make any further comment on that — I don't want to say — had been, that there wasn't.'

It can be seen here that O'Kennedy started to answer the question, then decided he shouldn't comment ('I don't want to say'), but couldn't stop himself finishing the sentence in which he denied making a mistake ('that there wasn't'). Next, fearing that RTÉ (and most Fianna Fáil politicians have a massive and unwarranted fear of RTÉ) would edit the film to show him in a bad light, O'Kennedy felt he had to continue.

'So, please, and I know with, with the best will in the world and you ask a question like that, Joe, was it a mistake — I don't want to see a statement tomorrow on radio or television, me adopting a word that you've used.'

At which point O'Kennedy might have shut up. But he knew he had made a bags of it and finding himself in a hole he was unable to resist the temptation to continue digging.

'I mean, 'cos, that's why — the reason why I wanted — I've given you straight my position. Please report — I know you will because we — please report me for what I say, not by way of responding to what some, the question that's put to me. That's all.'

But it wasn't all. As Joe O'Brien persisted, O'Kennedy blundered on. 'I think that will all emerge in time. I have no reason at all — at all, at all — and the government made it very . . .'

And here something occurred to him, a flash of inspiration, an epiphany, and he didn't bother to finish his sentence about what the government did. You could almost see the weight physically lifting from his mind. It was as if O'Kennedy had just realised he personally had nothing to hide, so why not go for broke.

'I want full disclosure,' he blurted. And, having found a phrase which no one could misinterpret or disagree with, he repeated it like a mantra. 'Total and full disclosure, total and full disclosure. I can say this for myself and my department and my department is clearly . . . I am totally and utterly clear in my mind and conscience — totally — as to my role and my obligation. Totally and utterly clear in my mind and conscience.'

When Joe O'Brien asked if O'Kennedy believed he would escape unscathed from the controversy, the minister smiled a hopeful but wary smile and said: 'I said to you I am totally clear that there is no basis at all in anything I've said. There you are.'

A politician announcing on television that there is no basis at all to anything he has said is a rare and wonderful thing to behold.

P

Passports for Sale: Illegally

In the spring of 1987 London police started coming across Irish passports owned by foreign nationals in suspicious circumstances. A number of Moroccans admitted they had paid thousands of pounds for such passports. The police made inquiries and when they went looking for an Irish embassy official named Kevin McDonald he wasn't to be found. It was believed that McDonald had sold about sixty passports.

In August of that year McDonald was traced to Dublin and after prolonged extradition efforts (the usual defective warrant) he was finally extradited to Britain in May 1989. Four months after that, and over two years after his scam was uncovered and he fled London, he was found guilty of conspiracy and got two years in jail.

Passports for Sale: Legally

The legal selling of Irish citizenship started off as a reasonable measure back in 1956. The idea was that if someone wanted to live here and start a business they should be facilitated. Such people were granted residency and after a time they could apply for citizenship. They had to live here for at least four years within the eight years prior to applying for a passport. They also had to live in Ireland continuously for the year before they applied.

The intent was clear: if foreign entrepreneurial types wanted to create jobs here, and live here, the path to citizenship would be made easy for them. This seemed entirely reasonable.

The Garret FitzGerald government changed this in 1986. The state could waive the residency conditions if the business person was of Irish descent. Or — and this is where the scandal started — the business person had 'Irish associations'. There were plenty of foreign people who had settled in Ireland, who had Irish associations — jobs, businesses, friends, real connections with the country, making a real contribution — but this term had nothing to do with them.

'Irish associations' came to mean 'give us money'.

It was 1989 before the new interpretation was given life, and it is the period 1989–92 which gave rise to suspicions. Under Charlie Haughey, word went out that anyone with a million pounds to 'invest' would get a passport. There was no longer any need to start a business. You didn't — God forbid — have to live here. And invest didn't necessarily mean invest. A low-interest loan to be paid back in a few years would do. And it didn't have to be a million pounds. Half a million would do. And not only the 'investor' got the passport; passports could go to his seed, breed and generation.

The investing or loaning of a substantial sum of money to an Irish company became an 'Irish association'. Typically, a lawyer — or someone else representing a rich foreigner — would approach a minister. (On occasion, according to Bobby Molloy's experience, the minister would approach Charlie Haughey, who would 'vet' or question the applicant.) The lawyer or intermediary would identify a suitable Irish company; the money would be invested, and some time later the Department of Justice would naturalise the applicant and the passport or passports would be handed over.

Certain conditions were supposed to be met: you had to live in Ireland for a total of sixty days in the two years prior to the application; you had to swear fidelity to the state; you had to reside here after you got the passport; you had to be proven of good character. These conditions were not always enforced.

Very few people in Ireland knew about the passport-for-sale racket. PD member Bobby Molloy, Minister for Energy in Haughey's 1989 government, didn't know about it until told by Haughey that anyone approaching him to apply under the scheme must be brought to meet Haughey, for vetting. Molloy brought two such applicants to Haughey. One was an Arab, the other was from Hong Kong. Molloy said that he was initially approached by a representative of the foreign applicants, a Brian O'Carroll, a Roscommon architect. O'Carroll had strong Fianna Fáil connections. He will turn up again in this story.

In 1990 a Saudi Arabian billionaire, Sheikh Khalid bin Mahfouz, wanted a rake of Irish passports. Mahfouz would come under investigation in the multinational BCCI banking scandal and would eventually reach a settlement in which he paid hundreds of millions of dollars. He wanted no fewer than eleven Irish passports for Saudi Arabian and Pakistani nationals. He would, he said, invest £20 million in Irish companies.

It is known that Haughey recommended the Mahfouz deal, that Ray Burke, then Minister for Justice, personally signed the naturalisation papers, and that Haughey personally handed over the passports to Mahfouz. It is believed that the handover occurred at Kinsealy, though some reports say it happened at a Dublin hotel. Knowing what we know now about Haughey's tendency to acquire funding from rich men, is it possible that Haughey put the touch on the sheikh?

Mahfouz is known to have invested £3 million in Kerry airport, which was chaired by Denis Brosnan, chief executive of the Kerry Group. Mahfouz also put £4 million into Leisure Holdings, an outfit which invested in tennis clubs in Britain. Leisure Holdings was also chaired by Denis Brosnan, of Kerry airport. Prominent investors in Leisure Holdings were John Magnier, the wealthy horse breeder, and J.P. McManus, the bookie friend of Dermot Desmond. Whether this £4 million was part of the alleged £20 million pledged by Mahfouz in return for passports, or whether it was a separate investment, is anyone's guess. As is whatever happened to the rest of the £20 million.

The year after the Mahfouz deal, 1991, Brian O'Carroll made representations on behalf of a Palestinian family based in Jordan, the Masris. O'Carroll and a lawyer drew up a list of companies in which the Masris might invest. One of these was C&D Foods, the pet food company owned by the family of Albert Reynolds. O'Carroll approached government minister Michael Smith, who recommended the Masris for passports. The head of the family, Sabih Masri, met Haughey, to be 'vetted'. In March 1992 the Masris made what was in effect a soft loan of £1.1 million to C&D Foods, the pet food company, the family firm of Albert Reynolds. (Reynolds, who had now become Taoiseach, had removed himself from the running of the company when he became a minister in 1979.)

The Masris swore fidelity to Ireland on 25 November 1992, the day of the general election at which Albert Reynolds's government was expected to be kicked out. They got their passports three weeks later, before Reynolds and Dick Spring cobbled together another government.

The extent to which the residency requirements and the good character assessments were enforced can be seen in the farce surrounding the Masri case. In the processing of the application the state was told that the Masri family consisted of Sabih, his wife, Najwa, their adult children, Khaled and Sireen. It was Mrs Najwa Masri and her daughter, Sireen, who wanted the passports. Mrs Masri lived in Paris; Sireen, aged twenty, was studying art in Mount Vernon College, USA. The two liked to travel; it was a bummer, every time they wanted to make a trip, to have to return to Jordan to get a visa. Irish passports would make their lives easier. It was small change to the Masris to loan £1.1 million and to buy a residence in Ireland.

Although it was Najwa and her daughter Sireen who wanted the passports, confusion resulted in two passports going to Najwa and her son, Khaled. The Masris had to invest another half-million in a forestry project and daughter Sireen got her passport.

When the Masri case was dragged into the public arena in 1994, Dick Spring was in coalition with Albert Reynolds. Spring looked at the files; there was no evidence of illegality, no evidence of Reynolds intervening in the case, so Spring declared himself satisfied that everything was above board and that killed any possibility of further inquiry.

In the same year — 1991 — in which Brian O'Carroll was making representations on behalf of the Masri family, he also made representations on behalf of an American couple, the Lindzons. Gerry Lindzon opened two bank accounts with ICC, through which to channel the 'investment' money allocated to get a passport for Mrs Lindzon. He opened a third account, a deposit account in ICC, and made it a joint account with Brian O'Carroll so that the Fianna Fáil-connected architect had signing powers on the account. Ten thousand pounds was put into that account. In July 1993, the ten thousand, plus £524.59 in interest, was transferred by Brian O'Carroll to a Fianna Fáil fund-raising account.

Between 1989 and 1994 sixty-six people invested money in return for passports. In those sixty-six deals, ninety-five passports were handed out, including spouses and children of investors. In only ten cases had the applicants resided here for sixty days in the two years prior to application. In only seventeen cases were the 'good character' assessments carried out. In only seventeen cases did the new citizens reside in Ireland after they got their passports.

In 1994 Minister for Justice Máire Geoghegan-Quinn brought in guidelines which reduced the opportunity for corner-cutting. Another twenty-nine applicants, plus nine spouses and children, got passports. By 1998 the stink from the scheme was such as to force its close-down.

When Ray Burke's role in the Mahfouz passport deal of 1990 came under scrutiny in 1998 it added such pressure on Burke, already suffering allegations about receiving large chunks of cash in envelopes, that he resigned from public life.

About £90 million is alleged to have been brought in in return for citizenship. How much of that represented loans which were repaid is unknown. At best, the passports-for-sale scandal was a reckless scheme in which politicians sold citizenship as an easy way of boosting jobs. At worst, it was something a lot more questionable. If there is a single issue emblematic of the Haughey era this is it.

Payne, Fr Ivan

H is past came back to haunt him in 1993, when Fr Ivan Payne was confronted by former altar boy Andrew Madden. The young man was just one of many who had, as boys, been groped and sexually abused by the priest. Payne wasn't just any priest, he was a judge in the Dublin Archdiocese's Regional Catholic Marriage Tribunal. If you were looking for an annulment, you might well have found yourself explaining your intimate marriage details to Fr Payne.

Given his position, Payne found it handy to turn to the Archbishop of Dublin, Desmond Connell, when he found himself cornered by young Andrew Madden. The archbishop's involvement would change the nature of the Payne scandal.

Payne was ordained in 1967, and the following year was appointed chaplain to Our Lady's Hospital for Sick Children, in Crumlin. He was in that position for almost three years, and there he sexually abused sick children under his care. He later served in Canada and in Cabra in Dublin. He abused Andrew Madden in Cabra and when Madden made a complaint Payne was moved to Sutton, where he continued his abuse. The church got Payne a psychiatrist, who didn't object to the priest being placed again in positions of responsibility. Payne's abuse continued.

Andrew Madden confronted Payne in 1993 and announced his intention to sue the priest. Payne knew that this would lead to public exposure, perhaps with criminal charges to follow. He got a loan from diocesan funds, with the grace of Archbishop Connell, and paid Madden £27,500 to go away. The archbishop, told of an allegation of a serious crime, might have urged Fr Payne to fight it, if it was untrue; he might have urged the priest to turn himself over to the gardaí, if the allegation was true. He might himself have informed the gardaí. Instead, he helped facilitate Fr Payne to pay off his accuser, which kept the matter secret (if only for a couple of years).

In May of 1995, as revelations exploded about the extent of priestly sexual abuse of children, Archbishop Connell was interviewed by RTÉ's Joe Little. 'I have compensated nobody,' he said. 'I have paid out nothing whatever in compensation.' The archbishop went on to say: 'the finances of the diocese are not in any way used to make settlements of that kind'.

When, a few months later, the loan to Payne was revealed, the archbishop denied there was any contradiction. He had compensated nobody. 'The granting of a loan in 1993', said Fr John Dardis, the archbishop's press agent, 'does not reflect the archbishop's thinking in 1995.'

One could probe the semantics of the words loan and compensation; the difference between compensation by the archbishop, and the archbishop merely providing a loan to Fr Payne so he could compensate Madden. However the matter was parsed, it was shocking.

Andrew Madden went public with his complaint; Fr Payne was charged and in April 1998 pleaded guilty to thirteen sample charges of sexual abuse. Two months later, from the dock he made what appeared to be a genuine, remorseful apology to his victims. He was sentenced to eight terms of six years; two terms of five years; and three terms of four years. A total of seventy years. The sentences were to run concurrently, so the effective sentence was six years. Judge Cyril Kelly suspended the last four years, on condition that Fr Payne got treatment, so the effective sentence was two years. The DPP appealed the sentence and in July 1999 the Court of Criminal Appeal agreed that the sentence was unduly lenient and lifted the suspension, sentencing Payne to the full six years.

PD Fund-raising

At around 8 a.m. on Friday, 5 December 1997 a rubbish skip was left outside the head office of the Progressive Democrats, at South Frederick Street, Dublin. The party was having a 'clear-out' of its offices. Over the next ninety minutes the skip was filled with dispensable material. While this was happening, someone picked up a box of documents that was supposed to be taken off to the party archives, brought it outside and threw it into the rubbish skip.

Some passer-by had a look into the skip, perhaps a scavenger who happened along, perhaps someone who couldn't resist poking through PD rubbish, found the box and removed it. Some days later a courier delivered the contents of the box to the *Sunday Business Post*, addressed to reporter Frank Connolly. The reporter couldn't believe his luck. The files were packed with hundreds of documents detailing the PDs' relationships with the party's financial backers, covering the years 1987 to 1992. Confidential memos, letters and lists of donors, the kind of documents the political parties usually protect as though they were state secrets, had been dumped and were now available for publication.

The newspaper published the material that Sunday, causing two headaches for the PDs. First, both the party and the party's financial backers were embarrassed to find the donors' names in the public domain. Second, the material demonstrated very explicitly the relationship between political parties and business interests.

The names tumbled off the page: builders, insurance companies, motoring interests. A thousand pounds, five hundred, two hundred, three thousand; some contributors giving repeated donations. Ten thousand pounds from Waterford Glass Group, the same amount from Tara Mining. Five thousand from Don Tidey, executive at Power Supermarkets; four thousand from Tony Ryan of GPA; two thousand from an executive of the solicitors outfit Arthur Cox and Co.; four thousand from an executive in Stokes Kennedy Crowley, followed two years later by two and a half thousand; a thousand from someone in J&E Davy; five thousand from De Beers, the diamond company; fifteen hundred from Clayton Love Jr. A thousand from one meat company, five thousand from another. From Larry Goodman, twenty thousand.

A miserable five hundred pounds from Taylor Associates, the company headed by investment broker Tony Taylor, who would later go on the run.

Twelve thousand from Smurfit's in 1987 and the same again in 1989, drawn on an offshore account in Jersey. Then, in 1992, a cheque from Smurfit's for £30,000. Fund-raiser Paul Smithwick wrote to then party leader Des O'Malley, enclosing a copy of the cheque and suggesting that a thank-you note to Michael Smurfit might be appropriate. 'Michael will prove to be an extremely good supporter of the party and I cannot tell you how appreciative he was for our confidential meeting in January.'

All of this was quite legitimate, of course. O'Malley, as Minister for Industry and Commerce, was entitled to meet leading lights from the worlds of industry and commerce. And wealthy business interests are entitled to give their money to whomsoever they wish. But what was this 'confidential meeting' about?

Denis Lucey of Dairygold was frank, in a 1992 letter to O'Malley, about delaying a response to a request for funding as he was 'anxious' that the Beef Tribunal 'pressure for disclosure would have passed'. Now that that was out of the way, Dairygold would cough up £8,000 to aid the PDs' pro-Maastricht referendum campaign. Dairygold had given £3,000 the previous year. Lucey explained that the company very much appreciated 'your own and your party's efforts on behalf of the food industry and, in particular, the levelling of the pitch in one particular sector. If that had not happened Dairygold would not have become involved.'

We don't know what area of the pitch was being levelled or in what manner.

Among the treasure from the skip was a briefing note prepared by Paul Smithwick for a 1991 lunch in the members-only Kildare Street Club, at which Des O'Malley would meet business interests, including property developer Mark Kavanagh (who two years earlier had donated £2,500) as well as insurance company executives. 'They are very supportive of you personally, and appreciative of your endeavours,' wrote Smithwick.

And there was a letter from the party treasurer, Paul Mackey, responding to a request from O'Malley that he supply names of people who might be appointed to state boards: 'Attached find my list of names with details. All these people have been very loyal supporters since the formation of the party,' wrote Mackey. He followed this up with a note which read: 'I would appreciate it if some action were possible. It would make my job easier on the fund-raising side.'

One of the names was that of Paul Smithwick, who had worked hard to raise funds for the PDs, and who would eventually be appointed to the board of Coillte Teoranta. Mackey wrote alongside Smithwick's name: 'When on side he cannot do enough for you. Has performed in the past. Hungry for prestige and connections.'

The PDs appointed Senator John Dardis to investigate the scandal of the dumping of confidential files in a skip on a public street. Dardis didn't find out who threw the files away but concluded there was 'no suggestion of malicious intent' and he made recommendations for improving office procedures. Creating an image of a box of files deciding of its own accord that it should do a runner, Senator Dardis stated his belief: 'the box saw its way into the skip'.

Pick-Me-Ups

This is the term applied to one type of financial relationship, exposed in 1998, between political parties and their wealthy backers. Instead of (or as well as) financing the parties directly, by secret donations, the wealthy backers paid off specific party debts. For instance, a party might run up debts printing posters, or arranging transport, or perhaps providing catering facilities for a conference or ard-fheis. Arrangements would be made for the bill to be sent to the wealthy backer.

For some pick-me-up donors, there were advantages over making a straight donation. The payments could be hidden from auditors and shareholders. They could be passed off as legitimate business expenses. Such payments could then be written off against corporation tax. The company might even claim back VAT on the payment. If a company paid £30,000, and claimed back £6,000 in VAT, the taxpayer got to pay a fifth of the donation to the political party.

This was fraud. Representatives of all the main parties knew about this and they not alone didn't report it to the cops, they encouraged it.

Poor Clares

In Cullies Cemetery, Cavan, there's a headstone that reads: 'In Loving Memory of the Little Ones of St Clare. R.I.P. Children pray for us.' In the ground beneath lie the remains of thirty-five children and an old woman who died in a fire in St Joseph's Orphanage on the night of Tuesday, 23 February 1943. Their names have been added to the grave only recently. They weren't even buried in separate coffins. The thirty-six bodies taken out of the fire were put in eight coffins.

At the funeral Mass the Bishop of Kilmore said: 'Dear little angels, now before God in Heaven, they were taken away before the gold of their innocence had been tarnished by the soil of the world.'

None of the girls who survived the fire and later told their stories to Mavis Arnold and Heather Laskey for their book *Children of the Poor Clares* remembers life in St Joseph's Orphanage as a time of golden innocence. Life there was as harsh as it was in the other industrial schools. There were beatings, cruelties, inadequate schooling, poor nutrition.

If the Poor Clare orphanage was any different it was because it was even more isolated than the others. The Poor Clares were an enclosed order, probably even less equipped to look after eighty babies and girls than other religious. After the fire, the belief persisted, locally and further, that so many children died because the nuns had been reluctant to allow them be seen running out of the convent in their nightclothes.

The fire was discovered at about 2 a.m. Forty minutes later it was all over. The subsequent inquiry found there was no one to blame. There were doors locked, the local fire service was inadequate to the job, there was no evacuation plan. As men from the town broke down the orphanage doors in a rescue attempt, children were sent from one dormitory up the stairs to another, where they eventually became trapped. Local football hero Louis Blessing later said that all he could see, 'framed against a background of flames, was a sea of childish faces against the window'.

St Joseph's was one of several industrial schools run by religious orders. They were originally set up in 1868 to meet the needs of orphaned, abandoned or otherwise destitute children. The Department of Education took over the running of the schools after independence in 1921. In 1949 there were 6,378 children in these schools; in 1984 there were 796.

There were rules and standards set down about the running of industrial schools but there is little evidence that they were strictly enforced or closely monitored. The children, though the responsibility of the state, were effectively left to the mercy of the religious orders and the individuals in charge.

Some of the children never left institutional care, spending their adult lives working in the so-called Magdalen laundries. Those who did manage to live on their own were ill-equipped to do so. A 1968 Legion of Mary report on young prostitutes in Dublin noted:

> We find that the greater proportion of those involved are illegitimate orphans who have spent the greater portion of their childhood in orphanages and convents . . . They appear to have no training but only warnings about how to behave with boys and men. They appear to have received little or no training fit to earn them a living . . . In this state they are suddenly discharged into public life.

St Joseph's Orphanage closed in 1967.
See: Artane Industrial School; Goldenbridge; Magdalen Homes.

Q

Quinn, Ruairí

Eithne Fitzgerald wanted to raise money that could be used to promote her election campaign in Dublin South. So she wrote a letter and asked people to come to lunch.

Fitzgerald had been elected for Labour in 1992, in that general election's major revival of Labour's fortunes. She topped the poll with 17,256 first preferences, the highest vote in the country, and left hardened political hacks looking on in awe.

In the subsequent coalition government, Fitzgerald was appointed Minister of State in the office of the Tánaiste, Dick Spring. Her most notable task was creating and steering into law the Ethics in Public Office legislation.

The letter she sent out on 27 February 1996 was on notepaper headed with a harp and the address of her office in Government Buildings. The letter was to be sent out to 700 people. It was going to be a big lunch.

The letter invited people to pay a hundred pounds each to attend lunch in the Sylvan Suite of Jury's Hotel, Ballsbridge, Dublin. In return for the hundred pounds they would 'gain access' to the Labour Party Minister for Finance, Ruairí Quinn. The minister was then in the process of finalising his budget and had already published a preliminary outline of his financial plans for the coming year. Fitzgerald's letter pointed out that this legislation 'is of major interest and importance to key sectors in our economy', of which there is little doubt.

If you paid a hundred pounds you would get 'a rare opportunity to gain access to the minister in a semi-formal environment'.

So it cost a hundred pounds to chat up the Minister for Finance as he prepared legislation which might affect your business. The letter was shown to Quinn and it was okay by him.

After about 350 letters had been sent out word got back to the opposition and they saw a chance to embarrass the politician who had been derided as the 'Minister for Ethics'. Charlie McCreevy of Fianna Fáil and Bobby Molloy of the Progressive Democrats raised the matter in the Dáil. They condemned Fitzgerald for 'selling private briefings to selected business people to benefit her own constituency organisation'. Molloy's leader, Mary Harney, called on Fitzgerald to resign.

Quinn immediately saw the danger and apologised to the Dáil. 'That letter should not have gone out on official government notepaper,' he said. 'I apologise to all parties in the House. It will not happen again. I accept responsibility for it.'

Quinn had made a mistake, and in making that mistake, had shifted the ground on which the scandal would be discussed. The letter wasn't sent out on official government notepaper; it was sent out on notepaper which Fitzgerald used for constituency purposes, giving her Dáil office address. It could pass for official government notepaper but it wasn't departmental or government notepaper.

Later that day Fitzgerald also apologised to the Dáil. Her apology was 'for any impression that may have been created that this was an official, as against a Labour Party, function'.

The controversy had been diverted into a row about the heading on notepaper, rather than the principle of selling access to the Minister for Finance. No one could imagine that Ruairí Quinn would change his legislation in return for a donation of £100. But those with that kind of money to spend on lunch had the ear of the minister; their arguments for this or that adjustment might have validity. The minister might or might not see that validity. Money bought access, allowing lobbying to be done. Those without a hundred pounds to spend on lunch didn't get that access to the minister, 'in a semi-formal environment', at precisely the time he was finalising his legislation.

Government office does not belong to the politicians who pass through it. The fact that politicians feel free to charge money for access to the holder of that office suggests a particular attitude to democracy which no amount of ethics legislation can put right.

The fact that the scandal was so easily diverted into a question of whether the letterhead was appropriate suggests that the opposition weren't terribly upset by what had been done. Having embarrassed Fitzgerald and Quinn, and thereby scored some political points, the opposition didn't press too hard. They knew they might want to charge rather more than £100 per head when it came to their turn to occupy government office.

At the 1997 general election Eithne Fitzgerald got 6,147 first preferences and lost her seat.

R

Rezoning

Some will argue that there was too much rezoning of land in Dublin over a period of decades; some say there was too little. What is beyond doubt is that much of the rezoning was led by the demands of speculators and developers out to make a buck, rather than by the housing needs of the people. Rezoning happened in a chaotic, unplanned way. Allegations of corruption bubbled under for years, until they erupted all over the Flood Tribunal. There were times when it seemed that councillors had discovered that the Third Secret of Fatima was 'Thou shalt rezone', as they set about their tasks with relentless zeal.

Consider the events of 19 February 1993, when Councillor Trevor Sargent of the Green Party stood up at a meeting of Dublin County Council and took an envelope from his pocket. The Greens had received a letter from a developer asking that they support a rezoning proposal. In the envelope was a cheque for one hundred pounds. No favours sought or given. Just, 'Here's a little something', and if you feel you should vote to rezone the land, there's no connection; decide on the merits of the issue.

During a rezoning debate, Sargent held up the cheque and politely asked if anyone else present had received a similar cheque.

There was a violent reaction. Shouts of 'Withdraw, withdraw.' Sargent said he had merely asked a question. He was told to sit down and did so, whereupon numbers of Fianna Fáil and Fine Gael councillors gathered around him trying to get the cheque. One councillor grabbed him about the neck. The meeting was adjourned.

The developer who sent the cheque subsequently told *The Irish Times* that he included the money merely to make sure that the letter was read; they 'might at least read it before throwing it in the bin'. So some developers believed that sending £100 might get councillors' attention. What else they believed you had to do to get councillors to see things in a certain light is best left to the imagination.

S

Scrappage

As the 1999 local elections approached, the political parties had a problem. Too many old codgers were hanging onto their council seats. There were too few openings for young party hustlers seeking to create a political base from which to move into national politics.

The parties could have asked the old codgers to step aside. Or they could have moved against them politically, arguing and organising for the selection of fresh candidates. This, however, would have caused internal dissension. So the parties came up with a bright idea: use taxpayers' money to lever out the old codgers. It was formally called the Local Authority Members' Gratuity Scheme. Fianna Fáil's Minister for the Environment, Noel Dempsey, got the job of steering through this political scrappage plan.

For each year, up to twenty years, served on a county or borough council, the councillor was offered £750 to go away. For each year over twenty years the pay-off was £500. So a councillor with twenty-five years would get £17,500. Councillors who stood for election and lost their seats would get nothing.

There was no benefit to the taxpayer in this. It was purely of benefit to the political parties, as it helped them make space for their up-and-coming political hustlers. It gave councillors who would have been retiring anyway an unexpected golden handshake. A total of 481 of them took up the offer, at a cost to the taxpayer of £5.3 million.

Sex Abuse: Clerical

According to figures compiled by the Catholic church and released in March 1999, 35 priests, brothers and ex-clergy had by then been convicted on child sex abuse charges since 1991; 27 were in the Republic, 8 in Northern Ireland. Twelve further cases were pending, one against a priest and eleven against former Christian Brothers. There are 7,600 priests in Ireland and 1,000 Christian Brothers.

See: Artane Industrial School; Comiskey, Bishop Brendan; Fortune, Fr Sean; Payne, Fr Ivan.

Sex Abuse: Swimming

I t would be difficult to imagine an environment more suited to satisfying the appetite of a child abuser than that created by the Irish Amateur Swimming Association (IASA). All the ingredients were there but none of the safeguards. George Gibney was the best coach Irish swimming had ever known. He got results, and because of that became a man of immense power within the world of amateur swimming. He used that power to find, manipulate and silence his victims.

One of Ireland's most successful swimmers, double Olympian Gary O'Toole, formally made swimming officials aware of the allegations against George Gibney in December 1992. He, a fellow swimmer and another coach collected information from several victims and urged them to come forward. A garda investigation resulted in charges being brought but George Gibney won on a legal point and the case was dropped. However, his victims supplied sworn affidavits to the *Sunday Tribune* and the story was out.

The charitable view is that the Irish Amateur Swimming Association sat on the fence and did nothing throughout the Gibney affair. But it was worse than that. There was no restructuring, no new procedures, no soul-searching, no counselling for victims. Indeed, after the court battle was over, Gibney was able to hold swimming clinics in Northern Ireland, thereby sending a powerful message to his accusers.

The man who succeeded George Gibney as national coach was Derry O'Rourke. He too had been sexually abusing young swimmers for years. However, his time at the top was short-lived and he found himself facing sexual abuse charges in 1995. Unlike Gibney, he could find no point of law to save him and is now serving a twelve-year sentence for his crimes.

Another power-broker in the IASA during the Gibney years was former president of the Leinster branch Frank McCann, now serving a life sentence for murdering his wife and foster daughter. He killed them in a house fire, because he didn't want his wife, Ester, to know why the health board was blocking their adoption of baby Jessica. The social workers knew he had fathered a child by a seventeen-year-old swimmer. McCann was one of the officials who heard the first of the allegations against George Gibney. He told the accusers to 'back off'. In response to the looming scandal he said he hoped to fuck it wouldn't break while he was in office.

During all of this controversy the IASA defended itself, as if the child abuse problem was just an unfortunate bit of history. It wasn't until the

Minister for Tourism and Sport, Jim McDaid, announced in February 1998 that the organisation would get no more public funding until it sorted itself out that reality began to dawn.

An investigation set up by Dr McDaid under the chairmanship of Dr Roderick Murphy SC heard testimony from twenty abuse victims and twelve parents. The Murphy Report revealed horrific details of abuse going back to the mid-1970s. It also offered a devastating critique of the Irish Amateur Swimming Association as an organisation responsible for the welfare of children.

On 24 January 1999 the Irish Amateur Swimming Association was voted out of existence and a new organisation, Swim Ireland, was set up amid acrimonious debate. New structures and child protection officers were promised. But the victims of Gibney and O'Rourke refused to back the new organisation while former IASA officers held positions of responsibility. Swim Ireland was still living in the shadow cast by Frank McCann, Derry O'Rourke and George Gibney. The problems the swimming community had in demonstrating its readiness to rid itself of known child abusers can be seen in the fact that not until 1997 did George Gibney lose his status as a lifetime member of the IASA.

Olympic gold medallist Michelle Smith de Bruin was coached, but not abused, by Derry O'Rourke. After the court heard the details of his methods of abuse, she asked: 'Why did no one question if he should be allowed to take young girls on their own into the gym in the dark to hypnotise them or to the pool for special attention? Why did no one question when he made lewd comments about the young girls?'

Shaw Park

There were over 500 people on the local authority housing waiting list in Carlow in 1997, and the Shaw Park proposal would make just a tiny dent in that number. The county manager had come up with the plan the previous summer and now the urban district council was backing it and just about everybody thought was a good one. It was for sixteen council houses and ten private houses built by the Carlow Friendly and Cooperative Society. The council would sell the land to the Coop at a subsidised price. It was an 'infill' development and there would be a mix of private and council housing, which helped make it the kind of project that politicians like to boast about.

The site chosen for the project, Shaw Park, was 5.27 acres. It had started out as a green space, a public amenity, and over the years had fallen into disuse. Back in 1971 a swimming pool had been built there and had been formally opened by Fianna Fáil minister Bobby Molloy.

There were two other public parks in Carlow: Graigecullen Park, 12 acres, and Hanover Park, 13 acres, both of which were scheduled for renovation. In 1991 the 5.27-acre green space was formally dedicated and relaunched as George Bernard Shaw Park, with Senator David Norris doing the honours.

Within a short time Shaw Park had become a bit of a problem. A new swimming pool had been opened at Graigecullen Park, after a fund-raising campaign by a couple of local priests. It was an indoor pool and was very popular, being open from seven in the morning to eleven at night. The outdoor swimming pool at Shaw Park, not surprisingly, couldn't compete and was closed down. Shaw Park is thirty yards off the main road, and is somewhat secluded behind a row of houses. Unsupervised, it had become a gathering place for young people on the loose. There had been some vandalism at the derelict pool, with manhole covers removed, the dressing rooms trashed. The play equipment had been removed by the council.

Graigecullen and Hanover Parks were, by comparison, thriving. The county manager's view was that it was 'unlikely that the urban council will have sufficient financial resources to maintain three park areas in a town the size of Carlow'. Hanover was already being renovated, Graigecullen was next. Shaw Park was the smallest and the poor relation.

The plan was to build twenty-six houses on just under three acres of the 5.27-acre green area, and to landscape the rest. With houses in proximity, there would be what the county manager called 'visual social control', which should make the area less attractive to kids hanging out and indulging in petty vandalism.

Aware of disquiet among private house owners living along the Athy Road, the council proposed to build a two-metre-high wall between the private houses and the new project.

The house plans were prepared by the Coop, a draw was arranged to allocate the houses. People knew in which house they would be living, who their neighbours would be. Tenders were invited. In February 1997 the urban district council proposed house designs. In May it approved the selling of the sites for the Coop houses. In June the housing construction section of the Department of the Environment gave design approval and told the urban district council that as long as the costings remained below the estimated ceiling it could go ahead and accept the lowest valid tender without seeking the department's approval.

That same month, June 1997, there was a general election and a new government came into power, a coalition of Fianna Fáil and Progressive Democrats. Bobby Molloy was appointed Minister of State at the Department of the Environment, with responsibility for housing and urban renewal. Molloy had been a Fianna Fáil TD since 1965 and had joined the PDs on their formation in 1986. A month after the election Molloy met a colleague, Jim Gibbons, at a function. Gibbons was the son of the late Jim Gibbons, protagonist in the Arms Crisis. Jim Junior had recently unsuccessfully sought election to the Dáil, running in Carlow-Kilkenny. As a consolation prize, he had been made a senator, nominated by Taoiseach Bertie Ahern as part of the coalition deal with the PDs. Gibbons was made chairman of the PD parliamentary party.

Gibbons lived on Athy Road, Carlow, in one of a number of private houses adjacent to Shaw Park. When the Shaw Park project was made public in the summer of 1996 about forty people had signed a petition opposing it. Some had written to the council.

At the function, Gibbons drew Molloy's attention to the plans for Shaw Park. According to the minister, Molloy remembered opening the swimming pool at Shaw Park in 1971, twenty-six years earlier. He recollected a vision of 'vivid colour and beauty and a happy local community'. He asked his departmental officials for a report on Shaw Park and was 'surprised and horrified' to learn that the green space had deteriorated and was to be used to build houses. He decided that he had to preserve that open space. 'That is exactly what happened,' he would later tell the Dáil.

In July planning permission was granted for the Coop houses. In August Bobby Molloy wrote to the urban district council, withdrawing permission for the project. Another site would have to be found.

The county officials reconsidered the available options and insisted that Shaw Park was the only suitable site; another site suffered flooding, another option was too far out of town. Shaw Park was far from being an amenity, the space was not properly used and its location made it a magnet for antisocial activity. Putting houses on about half the space would at least help make the other half a supervised area. Also, as the county manager pointed out in a letter to the minister in October, the UDC had entered into a contract with the Coop. Pulling out now would have serious financial consequences.

On Tuesday, 2 December Minister Molloy formally overturned the council's decision. The project would not go ahead.

On Thursday, 4 December local Fine Gael TD John Browne raised the matter in the Dáil. Bobby Molloy insisted that he was opposed to the use of green spaces for building houses. He had arranged for some officials from his department to visit Carlow and meet with Coop and local authority members.

On Thursday, 11 December Fine Gael put down a Dáil motion condemning Molloy for allegedly undermining 'decisions properly and democratically taken by Carlow Urban District Council and approved by his department'. The motion demanded that Molloy outline 'his contacts in the matter with Senator Jim Gibbons'. It was to be discussed in five days time.

The following day, Friday, Molloy's officials met with Coop and Carlow UDC members and the arguments for going ahead with the proposal were reiterated. That evening, Molloy abandoned his opposition to the houses and gave the project the go-ahead.

When the Dáil came to debate the matter the following Tuesday, Molloy proposed an amendment to the motion. This deleted the condemnation of his actions and noted that he had now approved the project. His officials had discovered that the other possible sites were not suitable, he said.

'They knew that all the time,' called out Fine Gael TD John Browne.

Minister Molloy said he hoped 'that communities will see that in me they have a champion for the retention of the open spaces'. He said that up to the previous Friday evening he had been still considering the matter and had not definitely decided against it until his officials reported to him, therefore his approval of the project was not a U-turn.

The opposition claimed that had Fine Gael not put down the motion condemning Molloy, forcing a Dáil debate, he would not have changed his mind and allowed the houses be built. They wanted to know why he chose that project, above all others, in which to intervene personally. 'He might have looked out Jim's back window,' said one deputy. They accused Molloy of seeking to block the project in the interests of Senator Gibbons. They accused him of wanting to protect the owners of private houses from the encroachment of council house dwellers. 'Pathetic,' said Minister Molloy.

The government won the subsequent vote, by seventy-three votes to sixty-four, and the motion was passed, congratulating Minister Molloy on his conduct of the affair.

See: Tully Allegations.

Sheedy Affair

Handbag-snatching is a 'particularly heinous' crime, said the judge. He sentenced Sabrina Walsh to nine years in jail. She was twenty, a drug addict; she had picked up the bag from the floor of Cafe en Seine, a trendy bar in Dawson Street. It belonged to a tourist and it turned out there was a lot of jewellery in the bag. Nine years seemed a lot for the non-violent theft of a handbag. Sabrina Walsh appealed and in October 1998 the case went before Mr Justice Hugh O'Flaherty, who reduced it to six years.

The legal establishment defended the sentence. It would be reviewed in two years, it was said, and if Walsh kicked her drug habit she would be released. The sentence was a means of getting her off drugs, perhaps saving her life. If that was true it was a crude and risky way to handle an addict, a brutal form of social engineering. And if Walsh was unable to kick her addiction she would serve another four years for being an addict. Addiction is not a crime. And while the legal establishment came up with that humanitarian defence of the sentence, Judge O'Flaherty himself gave no such rationale. He said that bag-snatching was a 'cancer' in society that had to be stamped out and his court was sending out word that bag-snatchers would get long sentences.

The Walsh case was not the first in which doubt had been cast on sentencing policies among the Irish judiciary, but it — along with the Fairview Park murder case scandal — was one of the starkest. Judge O'Flaherty dealt with Walsh just days before he took a walk with his dog near his home and bumped into a neighbour's son, Ken Anderson.

Anderson introduced O'Flaherty to a woman, a sister of a Philip Sheedy, a 31-year-old Dublin architect who had been sentenced to four years for killing a woman by dangerous driving. On 15 March 1996, Sheedy had been drinking, got into his new sports car, sped off with such recklessness that he hit a roundabout and the car was launched into the air, landing on a car in which the Ryan family from Tallaght was returning from a trip to a swimming pool. John Ryan received serious head injuries, his two children had their wrists broken, Anne Ryan was killed instantly.

The case was brought before Judge Cyril Kelly, at the Circuit Court and on 11 June 1997. Had Philip Sheedy stolen a sports car and done what he did he would have got up to ten years in jail. Those who steal cars, drink, speed and kill are a danger to society. Those who buy cars, drink, speed and kill do not incur a similar sanction.

For reasons of his own, Judge Kelly passed the case to Judge Joseph Mathews for sentencing. According to Mathews, Kelly suggested a suspended sentence. The man was 'a graduate', he said, from a 'good family'.

Mathews read the papers in the case and was disturbed by the 'extraordinary degree of recklessness' shown by Sheedy. This wasn't a non-custodial case, he decided. He went to see Judge Kelly and told him so. Kelly, according to Mathews, didn't say a word, merely held up his arms in a gesture suggesting that Mathews should do what he thought fit. Disturbingly, Kelly later denied that this meeting happened, and denied suggesting a suspended sentence.

On 20 October 1997 Judge Mathews gave Sheedy four years in prison, to be reviewed in two years.

Sheedy had an easy time of it. A few months in the training unit in Mountjoy, then a move to Shelton Abbey, virtually an open prison. Meanwhile, there were some unusual developments on the legal side. Sheedy asked for and was granted the removal of the two-year review date. There was a decision not to appeal the sentence. The review date would have meant that Sheedy would have to serve at least two years. The removal of the review date meant that Sheedy might be released because of overcrowding within the prisons; or there could be an intervention by some authority.

In Ireland, it is understood that social and administrative structures dealing with housing, finance, health, sport, state grants and just about everything else — including the law — can be approached in all sorts of ways. Whatever the official route, it is always possible to have a word with someone who might have some clout. This understanding is expressed in the phrase: 'It's not what you know, it's who you know.'

Philip Sheedy's family and supporters pulled out all the stops. Before Sheedy was jailed, there was an approach to former Fianna Fáil TD Jim Tunney, through his wife. Tunney suggested that Sheedy get a letter of recommendation from his local TD. Sheedy approached Fianna Fáil TD Brian Lenihan Jr and was interviewed and given such a letter. Sheedy's lawyers got a psychological report on their client from Fianna Fáil senator and psychologist Dr Don Lydon.

In July 1998, when Sheedy had been nine months in jail, an approach was made to Taoiseach Bertie Ahern: could Philip please have day release from Shelton Abbey? Sheedy would work as an architect on some FÁS community project, and return to Shelton Abbey each night. That it might be inappropriate for a Taoiseach to make representations on behalf of a man who had recklessly killed a woman in front of her children didn't seem to occur to anyone, least of all Ahern. He passed the query through his private secretary, to the private secretary of the Minister for Justice, John O'Donoghue: 'What's the story?' he asked.

Here, a mistake was made: some bureaucrat thought that the two-year date for review of sentence was still in place, so Sheedy couldn't benefit from any form of early release. Had that mistake not been made, the voluntary lifting of the review date by Sheedy, combined with an expression of interest by the Taoiseach, would probably have got Sheedy out on day release.

One of Ahern's closest associates, Councillor Joe Burke, a builder, was a business associate of Sheedy. In October 1998 he visited Sheedy at Shelton Abbey.

That month, Judge Hugh O'Flaherty was approached in the street by Sheedy's friend, Ken Anderson. And Anderson introduced O'Flaherty to his companion, Philip Sheedy's sister. The meeting lasted just minutes. O'Flaherty was told that Sheedy's health was deteriorating. Could a review date, once removed, be reinstated? O'Flaherty thought it might. 'Leave it with me,' he said, according to Ken Anderson.

O'Flaherty had no business involving himself in such a case. Any deterioration in Sheedy's health should have been brought to the attention of, and would be monitored by, the governor of Shelton Abbey. It is not the business of a Supreme Court judge, who might well at some future date be called on to rule on some aspect of the case, to take on the role of social worker, or to act as a 'leave-it-with-me' TD, making representations for constituents.

O'Flaherty called Circuit Court registrar Michael Quinlan to his chambers and asked if the Sheedy case could be listed. O'Flaherty would claim that he was merely 'seeking confirmation of a feasibility'. The registrar, however, took 'could the case be relisted' as a request, suggestion or instruction from the Supreme Court judge. Quinlan had it relisted immediately and informed O'Flaherty.

Supposedly, O'Flaherty became involved merely to see if the two-year review date could be reinstated. But there was no attempt to reinstate the review date, which was October 1999. Instead, the case had been listed for review just thirteen months after Sheedy was convicted.

Sheedy had let go his original legal team; his new solicitor, Michael Staines, hadn't even formally come on record as representing Sheedy when he received a call from Registrar Quinlan, asking him if he was applying to have the case relisted. What was this about? Staines asked. 'You don't want to know,' said Quinlan.

On 12 November the case came before Judge Cyril Kelly. Kelly should not have heard the case, as it was Judge Joseph Mathews's case. Not alone did he hear it, he jumped it ten places on the list, from 19 to 9. Eileen

Creedon, a senior solicitor from the Chief State Solicitor's office, was as it happened out of the room, taking a phone call. The state was represented only by Stephen Browne, a law clerk who had no right of audience before the court.

Kelly didn't hear any argument against freeing Sheedy; he didn't even hear any argument for releasing him. He didn't ask for an application from Sheedy's barrister, Luigi Rea; he didn't ask to hear any of the character witnesses gathered by Rea. Judge Kelly immediately said: 'This is a case in which I have had the benefit of a psychology report and I have grave concerns in relation to his mental condition at the moment. Okay. So, I will suspend the balance of his sentence.' And that was that. It took less than a minute.

Sitting in front of Sheedy, court registrar Michael O'Donnell was puzzled. How could the judge have read a psychological report? How could he have read any of the report? O'Donnell had handed the case file to the judge before the hearing began.

The only reports on Sheedy's mental condition were reports prepared over a year earlier, by Fianna Fáil senator Don Lydon, for Sheedy's trial. There was no up-to-date report in the case file which would have given Judge Kelly reason to have 'grave concerns' about Sheedy's mental condition 'at the moment.'

Sheedy walked free, less than three weeks after Judge O'Flaherty intervened, and returned to his architectural work.

And the very next day, 13 November, Judge Kelly was back in Court 24, dealing with another sad case. Three teenagers read in the *News of the World* that there were treasures hidden in the centuries-old coffins in the burial vaults of St Michan's church, in Dublin. They made torches out of broomsticks and rags, just like Indiana Jones, and broke into the vault. They smashed 300-year-old coffins, one of them played football with the skull of an infant. The torches started a fire; coffins were destroyed; the fire brigade poured water on the fire, destroying more coffins. One of the boys, Anthony Dillon, thirteen at the time of the crime and now seventeen, came before Cyril Kelly, who sent him to jail for six years, no review. Several months later, the other two teenagers would come before Judge Michael White, who gave them three years probation each. Coincidentally, Dillon and Philip Sheedy had the same barrister, Luigi Rea. One client fared considerably better than the other. One might conclude from these sentences that destroying old bones was considered six times more serious than killing a woman in front of her children.

Judge Cyril Kelly, in conversation with barrister Luigi Rea, was told that there was no up-to-date psychiatric report in the Sheedy file. Kelly suggested that Rea get one and put it in the file. Rea conveyed this suggestion to Sheedy's solicitor, Michael Staines. Staines said he would not do that. Placing a report in a case file in such circumstances would have amounted to falsifying the case record.

Very quickly, the story of Philip Sheedy's unorthodox release swept through the Law Library. The fact that a Supreme Court judge was involved became known. The fact that the review of sentence had gone ahead in the absence of the sentencing judge, and in the absence of a representative of the DPP, was noted.

Sheedy was seen in the street and Anne Ryan's family complained to the gardaí, who made inquiries. Word got to the Attorney General, the DPP appealed the suspension of Sheedy's sentence and, rather than contest the issue in court, Sheedy voluntarily returned to prison.

The Chief Justice, Liam Hamilton, was given the task of investigating and writing a report on the affair. Because of Hamilton's fuzzy, wishy-washy Beef Tribunal Report there were fears in political circles that he might take a soft line. In the event, he was sharply critical of judges O'Flaherty and Kelly and both resigned, as did Registrar Michael Quinlan. Minister for Justice John O'Donoghue authorised increased pensions for the three, in Kelly's case, for instance, from £17,000 to £30,000 a year. Kelly and O'Flaherty declined when asked to cooperate with an Oireachtas committee inquiry into the affair.

Singer, Dr Paul

The visitor was Gerard O'Brien, an accountant from the firm of Craig Gardner and Company. Paul Singer was sitting behind his large mahogany desk when O'Brien came in. The desk had a row of variously coloured telephones; if Singer was on a call from New York on one phone he liked to be able to take a call from Zurich if it came in on another line. Singer was, as ever, showing off, eager to use his ebullient personality to impress, to gain an edge. He rose and greeted his guest and went into his usual charm offensive. Singer turned and found that O'Brien had moved behind Singer's desk and was sitting in the boss's chair. The game was up, it was all over, O'Brien wasn't the type to be taken in by the bonhomie. He was here to liquidate the company. It was, as of now, a voluntary liquidation, but Singer's days of calling the shots were over.

It was Monday, 25 May 1959, five years after Singer, a 42-year-old conman, arrived in Ireland with a plan to rook investors. He had worked on people's greed, the desire for easy money. Now, his con game was collapsing. At a meeting of directors the previous day he had chosen voluntary liquidation as a way of holding worried investors at bay. Within two days the cops would be trawling through the company's books; by the end of the week four directors of the company, including Singer, would be under arrest. Soon, accountant Gerry O'Brien would begin the process of winding up the company.

Singer was born in 1911 in a part of Europe which would later become Czechoslovakia. His family moved to Austria when he was fourteen and to London five years later. For over twenty years Singer worked with his father's finance firm, until it collapsed owing tens of thousands of pounds. Four months later, in February 1954, Singer moved to Ireland, in search of a business opportunity. He found a nation that was easily plucked. This was just seven years after the Locke's Distillery scandal, and perhaps word was circulating among international hard chaws that Ireland was an easy touch.

Singer soon settled on a Dún Laoghaire auctioneering firm, Shanahan's, as the vehicle for his con. He charmed the Shanahan family into joining him in a stamp auctioneering enterprise. Singer was merely an amateur philatelist but he was superb at public relations, at creating excitement. He was fat, folksy and full of enthusiasm. He produced a newsletter clumsily titled Green I.S.L.E. Philately, to promote the business. (It stood for Green Ireland Stamp Lovers' Edition Philately.)

Shanahan's was soon besieged by people who couldn't wait to hand over their money so that Dr Singer (he had a doctorate in political science from Lausanne university) could make them rich.

It was simple. Singer advertised for people who had 'small capital which you want to invest with absolute security, but with an unusually large return'. There is no such thing as an absolutely secure investment guaranteeing a large return. Singer's offer was: invest, wait four months, and you'll get a 20 or 25 per cent return. Successful cons play on the greed of the victim. The prospect of such easy money wiped away all doubt.

In the Ireland of the mid-1950s, where the economy had ground to a halt and people were emigrating by tens of thousands annually, the middle class, cautious and smug, largely rejected the role of the bourgeoisie — to fund and profit from the development of the economy. They hoarded their money and sat tight. Figuratively — and perhaps literally — they kept their money under the mattress. And along came a jolly, fat, cigar-puffing man with a plan to give them a big, fast profit, without risk. Rivers of money flowed into Shanahan's. In the third year of the con the suckers handed over £5,250,000. That is, in today's money, the equivalent of £77 million. And that was the investment in just one year.

On the surface, the business was uncomplicated. People gave Singer money and he went searching, in Ireland and abroad, for stamp collections. He brought the stamps back and auctioned them and the investors benefited from the enormous profits. It was Singer's genius at spotting a philatelic bargain that allowed him make a fortune for his clients. That was the theory.

The scam was based on the old Ponzi routine, known the world over and named at the beginning of the century after a notorious Boston conman. You think up any old scheme, invite people to invest, promise huge returns — and then pay dividends out of incoming investments. The fact that you keep your promise to pay big dividends convinces the gullible that they're onto a good thing, word spreads and ever-increasing numbers of fools want a part of the action. The money flows in. It works fine until something happens that makes people lose confidence. Then they start asking for their original investments back and the whole thing collapses.

Singer flew to Zurich, New York, Paris and Montreal in search of stamp collections to buy. By now Shanahan Stamp Auctions Ltd was employing over ninety people and sometimes when Singer returned to Dublin he had the staff meet him at the airport, singing 'For He's a Jolly Good Fellow'. Gullible journalists wrote up the master's latest adventures in the stamp trade, and business went ever upward.

To give the con an appearance of solidity, to fool auditors and to explain where the handsome dividends were coming from, Singer held regular stamp auctions. These were rigged. Singer simply invented the amounts supposedly earned at the auctions. In one year investors got £1.7 million in dividends. Yet the books showed that only £1 million had been made at auction. And of that, only £350,000 represented real sales. The rest had been invented by Singer. He simply put down made-up sales figures beside the names of known stamp buyers. Or he would make up names. A 'Mr Zombie' bought huge amounts of stamps, according to the books.

The auctions were to give the business an appearance of reality, but bore little relationship to anything. Singer plucked figures from the air, deciding the dividend due to each group of investors.

If the company 'sold' £1 million worth of stamps, Singer would take 10 per cent of that as the firm's commission. He would take that money out of the ever-flowing inward investments. How much he squirrelled away in foreign bank accounts was never revealed. He bought a large mansion in Foxrock, on thirteen acres, and employed a butler; he hired a chauffeur to drive him around in a limo.

On average, only two requests per day came in from investors looking for their original investment back. Most were happy to leave their money with Singer as long as the huge interest kept coming.

The con could continue only as long as investors had confidence in Singer. On 9 May 1959 someone — perhaps a former employee of Shanahan's — broke into the premises and stole a recently bought collection of stamps. The collection was worth in the region of half a million pounds and it was uninsured. Media reports created public unease. Singer's charm wasn't enough to set people's fears at rest and they came in hordes, looking for their money back. Eventually, about 9,000 fools came looking in vain for the £1.8 million he owed them.

Singer was charged with thirty-nine counts of fraud. Over a four-year period he was convicted and sentenced to fourteen years in jail, appealed and won, was retried and acquitted. He quickly left the country. His wife, Irma, also got off. Charges were dropped against one of the Shanahans — Diana — but her husband, Desmond, was sentenced to fifteen months in jail.

The case revealed that even in the frugal Ireland of those times there was plenty of spare money among the comfortable classes. And that they were greedy and gullible. It took nine years for the liquidator to sort out the chaos, selling assets and paying creditors. The liquidator himself earned fees of £55,000, a tidy sum for those days, and proof that not everyone lost out in the Singer scam.

See: Locke's Distillery.

Sleeping Judge

There is a legal tome titled *Archbold: Criminal Pleading, Evidence and Practice*. Lawyers find it comes in handy from time to time. Seldom did it come in as handy as it did in the Special Criminal Court in April 1978. Lawyers used to lift the volume several inches off the table in front of them and let it drop. Bang.

They were trying, as discreetly as possible, to wake up a judge. Up on the bench Mr Justice John William O'Connor was nodding off. It was happening with increasing regularity, usually after lunch.

On trial were Nicky Kelly, Brian McNally, Osgur Breatnach and Michael Plunkett, members of the Irish Republican Socialist Party, charged with robbing a mail train at Sallins in March 1976.

Judge O'Connor had run as a Fine Gael candidate in the 1941 general election and lost. He spent thirty-six years as a barrister and was made a judge in 1976. He was, though it was not known at the time, a sick man. He was on medication, and this may have been why he was falling asleep.

The fact that Judge O'Connor was falling asleep on the bench was first mentioned publicly in February 1978, when reporter Niall Kiely wrote in *Hibernia*:

> Judge John O'Connor seemed to fall asleep on Wednesday last: the courtroom is high-ceilinged but the well of the court is packed and very stuffy by mid-afternoon. At 2.42 his head was only inches above the bench but three minutes later he sat up and began to write; at 3.10 p.m. his head seems to be actually resting on the bench but two minutes later he again sits up.

And, on another day:

> By 2.25 p.m. Judge O'Connor seemed to be having difficulties staying upright in his chair, his eyes were closing and his head was slumped forward, D.J. Garavin appeared to nudge or signal Mr Justice McMahon who seemed to make an unsuccessful effort to rouse O'Connor. By 2.24 p.m., when [defence counsel Paddy] McEntee diplomatically requested a two-minute recess to 'take advice', the judge's head had dropped to within some 6–8 inches of the bench in front of him.

In order to create interruptions in which the judge might awaken, lawyers pretended to need a break 'for toilet purposes'; someone tugged at Judge O'Connor's robe. Another legal tome was picked up and dropped.

Members of the defence team privately approached Judge O'Connor and asked that the trial be stopped, because of his habit of falling asleep. The request was dismissed.

The trial dragged on through March and into April, and on 26 April, the fiftieth day of the trial, defence lawyers asked that the court discharge itself. The three judges of the Special Criminal Court, including Judge O'Connor, ruled on the matter, deciding that Judge O'Connor was awake all the time.

The issue went to the High Court; among the evidence offered were affidavits made by defence solicitors Pat McCartan and Michael White (both of whom were later themselves appointed to the bench), in which specific dates were given on which it appeared to them that Judge O'Connor fell asleep. Journalist Niall Kiely did likewise.

The High Court backed the decision of the Special Criminal Court. The defence appealed to the Supreme Court, which also backed the decision of the Special Criminal Court. Nine judges (O'Higgins, Henchy, Griffin, Kenny, Parke, Finlay, McMahon, Garavin and O'Connor himself) had now ruled that Judge O'Connor was wide awake and fulfilling his constitutional responsibilities.

The Sallins case went ahead, with more breaks for 'toilet purposes'. A month later, after sixty-five days of the trial, Judge O'Connor dropped dead. The trial was abandoned and a new trial arranged.

See: Kelly, Nicky.

Smyth, Fr Brendan

Very shortly after Fr Brendan Smyth began his religious life with the Norbertine Order, in 1945, his superiors realised that he had what Abbot Kevin Smith later described as a 'problem with children'. Over the years the order developed a system for working around Fr Smyth's problem. They moved him from parish to parish, country to country. And they kept the problem a secret. Thus the Norbertine Order, however unintentionally, facilitated Fr Brendan Smyth's stunningly successful career as a paedophile. For more than four decades he abused children all over Ireland, as well as children in Scotland, Wales and the United States.

He finally went to jail in Northern Ireland in 1994. The case caused the collapse of Albert Reynolds's government that year when it became known that the paedophile priest had evaded arrest in the North because the warrants for his extradition were allowed languish for seven months in the Attorney General's office in Dublin.

The Norbertine response to the proclivities of Fr Smyth was always to protect the priest. If the welfare of children was a consideration at all, it wasn't evident. Parishes were not told what to expect when they were offered the services of Fr Smyth. When he was caught abusing children in Rhode Island the local bishop put him on a plane back to Ireland and the crimes remained a church secret. Under the headline. 'Their Best Fan is Going Home' the local paper reported: 'He will . . . leave behind the memory of a man whose love of children . . . brightened the town and the lives of many in it . . . Recreation, especially children's recreation, has played a big part in his stay locally.'

Years later, when the Fr Brendan Smyth scandal broke, Abbot Kevin Smith responded, after much stonewalling, to questions put by UTV reporter Chris Moore. He admitted that even after three stints of treatment in psychiatric hospitals in Dublin, Belfast and Stroud in Gloucestershire, on the two occasions when Fr Smyth was assigned to parishes in the United States, the local bishop was not 'notified of his propensity to molest children'. In both cases he offended. When he came back from America in 1983 he was sent to Cork as a hospital chaplain. Again, there was no warning.

And all the while through the years he returned frequently to his native Belfast where he befriended families with young children. While trusting mothers prepared dinners in the kitchen, Fr Smyth abused their children in the sitting room. His visits to these children in their convent schools were further opportunities for abuse.

The RUC began investigating Fr Brendan Smyth in February 1990 after one of many victims came forward. In June 1994 Fr Smyth pleaded guilty to seventeen charges of sexual abuse and was sentenced to four years in Magilligan Prison.

He might have come before the court earlier, had the RUC been able to get their hands on him. But Fr Smyth was living in Cavan. On 30 April 1993 nine extradition warrants from the RUC were delivered to the Attorney General's office. And there they stayed.

The Attorney General at the time was Harry Whelehan and Albert Reynolds wanted to make him president of the High Court. Mr Whelehan was an enthusiastic supporter of the move, but not so the Tánaiste, Labour leader Dick Spring. The Labour–Fianna Fáil government was already teetering under the weight of mutual distrust. Dick Spring did not want Harry Whelehan in charge of the High Court. However, to keep the government together, he was willing to live with the appointment. That changed when he learned about the lack of action on the Brendan Smyth extradition warrants. The last thing Labour wanted was to be part of a government perceived to be soft on clerical child abusers.

Although, obviously, neither Harry Whelehan nor anyone else in the Attorney General's office acted out of sympathy for any alleged wrongdoer, inefficiencies within the office had left Ireland's most notorious paedophile free for an additional seven months. In fact, the extradition warrants were never processed. Fr Smyth returned to the North voluntarily. Labour held Harry Whelehan accountable for the debacle and would not support his move to the presidency of the High Court. Dick Spring and his ministers withdrew from cabinet as Albert Reynolds pushed through Harry Whelehan's appointment.

The justification from the Attorney General for the delay over the Brendan Smyth warrants was that, because the allegations went back several years, there was a legal point about the 'lapse of time' that had to be considered in an extradition case. Because there was no previous case that provided a precedent for this issue, the Fr Brendan Smyth case required a considerable amount of time-consuming legal work. This was the defence Albert Reynolds put to the Dáil. Labour continued to dither, not quite in government but not yet having resigned. Then an earlier case was revealed, the so-called Duggan case which involved another man extradited for abuse charges going back a few years. So the issues raised in the Smyth case had been considered before, and therefore, according to Labour's interpretation, there was no legitimate reason for the long delay.

The Duggan case removed Harry Whelehan's defence. Trying to keep the government together and himself in power, Albert Reynolds went into the Dáil and said if he had known then what he knew now he wouldn't have appointed Harry Whelehan president of the High Court. Neither would he have defended the appointment in the Dáil.

From then on it was who knew about Duggan and when they knew it. Labour and Fianna Fáil accounts differ. Labour came to the conclusion that Albert Reynolds knew about the Duggan case and its significance before he spoke in the Dáil in defence of Harry Whelehan. Now Labour was out of government unless Reynolds resigned. He did and Labour began a patch-up deal with the new leader of Fianna Fáil, Bertie Ahern. But then Geraldine Kennedy wrote a story in *The Irish Times* indicating that the entire Fianna Fáil cabinet, not just the Taoiseach, had been informed about the Duggan case. Labour immediately pulled out and the prospective Labour–Fianna Fáil deal was dead.

After he was released from prison in the North, Fr Brendan Smyth stood trial in Dublin where he pleaded guilty to seventy-four charges of indecent and sexual assault on children over a thirty-five-year period. A month later, in August 1997, he collapsed and died in the Curragh Prison. He was buried during a secret pre-dawn ceremony at the head-quarters of the Norbertine Order in Cavan.

See: Warrants: Matt Russell.

Spike, The

The *Spike* was a ten-part drama, produced by RTÉ. It was set in a Dublin post-primary school called St Aidan's, known in the neighbourhood as the Spike. The first episode of the drama was broadcast in January 1978.

The author, Patrick Gilligan, was himself a teacher and had strong views on the way in which the education system diverted working-class kids onto the scrapheap. His scripts dealt with such issues and touched on the clerical urge to maintain the Catholic church's grip on education.

Thus, *The Spike* was a ready-made target for the various conservative forces which sought to defend what used to be known as traditional values. The various liberal forces which might have been expected to defend such a drama were slow to do so. The series was more than a little ham-fisted, obvious and crude. Its heart was in the right place, but its scripts were pretty awful. The school and its pupils and teachers and assorted hangers-on and passers-by were not credible.

The series came under a sustained attack. County councils in Waterford and Limerick, and Fermoy Urban Council, had a lash at it and the Department of Education also had a go. The Christian Brothers complained that they ran a school called St Aidan's and it was getting a bad name from the TV show.

In the fifth episode actress Madeleine Erskine played a model in an evening class for art students at the Spike. She appeared posing nude. The scene was cautiously done, with the actress in long shot or shown from behind or the side, with no titillation and nothing you mightn't see in the average episode of *Dallas*. What was seen wasn't what mattered; the lack of titillation didn't count. What mattered was that RTÉ had made a drama in which an Irish woman was seen — however discreetly — to be naked. No matter how coyly the scene was shot, whether the scene was truthful or relevant, didn't matter. RTÉ was taking a step over an invisible line which had been drawn by the defenders of traditional values.

The nude scene provoked an almighty roar of anger and the RTÉ authorities, already feeling under threat from the complaints about *The Spike*'s attacks on the education system, backed down. Director General Oliver Maloney cancelled the remaining five episodes and *The Spike* was shelved, never to be heard from again.

Maloney justified his decision. The drama, he said, 'failed to achieve its programming objectives'. He didn't explain why RTÉ had noticed this only after half the series had been shown and the modelling scene had brought the wrath of Catholic Ireland down on the station.

RTÉ's Controller of Television, Muiris Mac Conghail, defended the drama, clashing with the Director General. Mac Conghail, while denouncing some of the wilder attacks on *The Spike* as 'hysterical', admitted that much of the criticism was well founded. He made the prophetic point that cancelling the series ensured that 'there is little prospect of RTÉ ever undertaking a project like it again'. And so it was. Had RTÉ stood by the programme, shown it whole, then learned from its failures, something positive might have emerged.

The Fine Gael spokesman on education, Eddie Collins, denounced *The Spike* as 'an indefensible and unjustifiable attack on the teaching profession and authorities'. Taoiseach Jack Lynch publicly approved the scrapping of the series, a stance somewhat weakened by the fact that Mr Lynch had never seen it. The fifth year class of St Joseph's Convent of Mercy, Tulla, County Clare, wrote to *The Irish Times*, demanding that the series be withdrawn. One of the actors in the drama was Jim Fitzgerald, who worked as a director in the early days of RTÉ and approached drama with a passion. He was accosted in the street by an elderly woman who asked if he was in *The Spike*. He said yes. She gave him a thump.

No organisation strove more mightily to scrap *The Spike* than the small but loud League of Decency. This outfit had first appeared in 1955 and campaigned against anything not in conformity with traditional Catholicism. Its founder, J.B. Murray, insisted on watching the episode with the nude scene, refusing to heed his family's entreaties that he spare himself the trauma. Mr Murray was incensed by what he saw. As the episode ended he began ringing around the newspapers to inform them of his anger. So angry was he, in fact, that in mid-phone call he had a heart attack and was rushed to hospital. He died a few weeks later, having lived long enough to declare himself 'jubilant' at the scrapping of *The Spike*.

Stagg, Emmet

Sensational allegations about a senior politician's personal life had been doing the rounds in Leinster House for several weeks in the spring of 1994. Scandalous rumours were not particularly unusual in Leinster House, but the time-honoured tradition of politicians and journalists held that this sort of Dáil bar gossip never made it into print. Private lives were to remain private. But this particular rumour was juicier than the usual infidelity tales that journalists discussed privately.

Eventually, the *Sunday Press* broke ranks and printed the story, albeit without naming the politician. RTÉ's *Morning Ireland* ran with it on the Monday and on the *News at One* the late Jim Kemmy, then chairman of the Labour Party, told presenter Shane Kenny that the politician should identify himself.

He did, and in the days that followed political commentators observed that it was unlikely that the story would have been made public at all had it not been for the homosexuality angle.

In the statement released at 8.30 p.m. on 7 March 1994, Emmet Stagg, the Labour TD and Minister of State at the Department of the Environment, said that on a night in November 1993 he had parked his car in a spot in the Phoenix Park which he knew to be a place where gay men met. A young man approached on a bicycle. They talked through the window, then the young man got into the car and they continued talking. 'No wrongful act occurred,' said the statement.

A garda car, patrolling the area which was also known for male prostitution, pulled up alongside the minister's car. After the minister identified himself, the garda told him 'in no uncertain terms' to leave.

Stagg said he realised through their conversation that the young man was gay but was unaware, and had no evidence to suggest, that he was a male prostitute. The statement was both sad and contrite. Emmet Stagg also gave an interview to Charlie Bird for the *Nine O'Clock News*. Stagg looked every bit the broken man and RTÉ's special correspondent sounded nearly as uncomfortable. This wasn't the kind of interview that normally featured on Irish television. Seeing the minister and hearing his story was shocking enough. Bird steered clear of the really hard questions and the viewing audience was probably grateful. He didn't ask the minister exactly what he was doing in the Phoenix Park, whether he had gone there on previous occasions or whether he was gay.

In his interview earlier in the day, Jim Kemmy had speculated that the career of the Phoenix Park politician might never recover. 'These things stick onto you. We're not a forgiving race at all.' As it turned out, he was wrong.

There were no immediate calls for the minister's resignation. His party leader Dick Spring, then Tánaiste in Albert Reynolds's coalition government, said the Phoenix Park incident was 'regrettable' but did not warrant resignation. He'd been given every reassurance by Stagg that there would never be another such incident.

Albert Reynolds said it was a personal tragedy for the minister and his family and it was now time for 'charity and restraint'. A cynical observer, wondering why the Taoiseach's response was so measured, might have pointed to Fianna Fáil's desire not to further test the fragile coalition with Labour. But this was also the same government that had introduced and passed a law providing for the decriminalisation of homosexual acts, in the face of considerable pockets of resistance within both opposition and government parties.

After he made his statement, Emmet Stagg was allowed get on with the business of being a minister. He was back in his office the next day and appeared on the government benches during the Order of Business in the Dáil. The Order of Business is the time when running public controversies are most likely to be raised by the opposition, but that day no one said anything about the story that was on the front page of all the newspapers and dominating the radio talk shows.

If there was outrage, it was directed at the gardaí. The question was asked: who leaked the story in the first place? After all, whatever Emmet Stagg was up to, there was no crime recorded. On RTÉ's *Questions & Answers* programme, an emotional Pat Cox MEP described as a 'merciless bastard' the person responsible for giving the details to the media. He wanted the garda commissioner to begin an inquiry to discover who the 'rat is who brought this out in the public in this demeaning and irresponsible way'. He said the journalists who 'went after' Stagg should now track down the source of the story. His party leader Mary Harney said it 'would appear there has been a breach of the Official Secrets Act if information on this matter was leaked by the gardaí'.

If the radio talk shows are any measure of public opinion, the initial response to Stagg and his family was one of sympathy. There was anger at the media for bringing the story to light in the first place and, after the first wave of compassion began to ebb, some criticism of Stagg for having put himself in such an appalling situation.

The furore over the Phoenix Park affair died down, Stagg continued on as a junior minister in the coalition government. Certainly, his profile was lower than in the years before he became a member of the government. He was a politician on the left who was 'proud to be socialist'. For years he was a thorn in the side of the coalitionist ascendancy within the Labour Party. Once he had resigned from the parliamentary party over the issue. After Labour's historic success in 1992 he became enthusiastically pro-coalition, arguing that they now had sufficient deputies to make an impact in government.

The chairman of Labour's constituency council in Kildare, John McGinley, told *The Irish Times* in 1994 that Emmet Stagg's future would be decided by his constituents. 'It may surprise the cynics but we are a compassionate nation.' Ultimately, he said, 'he will be answerable to the people of Kildare'.

The people of Kildare North re-elected Emmet Stagg in June 1997 in an election where Labour nationally lost fifteen seats. His first preference vote was down by 7.8 per cent but he was comfortably elected on the fifth and final count. Dick Spring appointed him to his front bench as spokesperson on public enterprise. Under the new leader of the Labour Party, Ruairí Quinn, Emmet Stagg became spokesperson on Transport, Energy and Roads.

Stardust Song

Christy Moore's album *Ordinary Man* was released on 29 July 1985. The most deeply felt song on the album was 'They Never Came Home', about the forty-eight young people who died in the Stardust fire on Valentine's Day 1981.

RTÉ's *Today Tonight* had weeks earlier screened a moving report on the bitterness of the survivors and the relatives of the victims of the fire, on the pain heaped on their pain as they watched the legal system string out their tragedy while their own wounds still gaped. Moore's song was a response to the programme, a sensitive mixture of compassion and anger.

Four days later, on Friday, 2 August, WEA Records received a letter from the legal representatives of the owners of the Stardust nightclub, complaining that Christy Moore's song was in contempt of court and asking what WEA, the label releasing the album, proposed to do about it. WEA began damage control measures, in case it should subsequently be found guilty of contempt. It froze the record, asking record shops not to sell it, radio stations not to play it. Then, to force a definite decision, one way or the other, it sought a High Court declaratory order on the issue.

A week later, Friday, 9 August, Mr Justice Frank Murphy decided in a special High Court sitting that Christy Moore's Stardust song was in contempt of court. The judge declared the song to be 'a real and serious threat' to a fair trial, referring to the litigation between the Stardust owners and the survivors and victims' relatives. This case had been pending for four years. The song said:

> In a matter of seconds confusion did reign
> The room was in darkness, fire exits were chained

Judge Murphy decided that what was said in the song was similar to a statement made in the Report of the Tribunal of Inquiry into the Stardust Tragedy, but 'it went further'.

Did it? The tribunal report, at paragraph 8.31, said that Stardust owner Eamonn Butterly's practice of keeping the emergency exits secured with chains and padlocks until midnight on disco nights was 'a recklessly dangerous practice which regularly endangered the lives of over one thousand people'.

Paragraph 9.39 of the tribunal report listed four principal reasons why 'a prompt and efficient evacuation of the building did not take place', one of which was the locked and obstructed condition of certain exits.

Potential jurors could read that in the tribunal report, or in newspaper reports of the tribunal's conclusions, but hearing about it in a Christy Moore song might prejudice them, so the song had to be suppressed.

(Around that time, *Magill* magazine published a story on the gagging. A lawyer vetted the story and advised that the words of the song could not be published. The magazine took out the lyrics and in their place inserted this sentence: 'The lines of the song which were found to be most in contempt were those which suggested that the Stardust doors were closed.' The lawyer advised that this too might be found in contempt. The magazine could only say: 'The lines of the song which were found to be most in contempt were those which expressed a fixed conclusion that the injuries were caused by one particular factor, relating to the condition of the exits.')

T

Taca

The efforts of business interests to influence politicians began shortly after the founding of the state. Kevin O'Higgins was Minister for Home Affairs in the Cumann na nGaedheal government of W.T. Cosgrave. Early in 1927 he was approached by a colleague, J.J. Walsh, Minister for Posts and Telegraphs. There were some businessmen, said Walsh, who wanted to help fund the party's campaign in the coming general election. They felt sure that the government would look favourably on protectionist measures behind which the businesses they were setting up could thrive.

Walsh gave O'Higgins a list of the businessmen's names. O'Higgins had been ruthless during the civil war, presiding over seventy-seven state executions and covering up twice that many unofficial killings. He had waded through blood in what he saw as the necessary task of preserving the infant state. He had not done so in order to act as a businessman's tout. He took the list and put it in the fire.

At the election in June, O'Higgins topped the poll in his Dublin County constituency. The following month he was murdered, a revenge killing by republican opponents.

The generation which founded the state was by and large free of financial scandal. Gerry Boland, brother of Michael Collins's friend Harry Boland, fought in the 1916 rising and the war of independence and was a government minister into the 1950s. As Minister for Justice he too was ruthless and had no problem presiding over the execution of IRA men. Like O'Higgins, who had stood on the other side of the civil war divide, Boland had seen too much blood and tears to lightly sell the favours of the state. When a cheque for £500 came in from outside interests, to be put into party funds, Boland returned it to the sender.

And Seán Lemass, future Taoiseach, who prided himself on his pragmatism, got it back again.

Although the parties which had run the state through the decades were socially and economically conservative, it wasn't until the late 1960s that the formal bonding between the parties and business interests began. It was Fianna Fáil that led the way, with the setting up in late 1966 of Taca, a low-profile outfit designed to gather money for the party. The friendly attitude towards wealthy people bearing gifts, begun under Seán Lemass, was formalised under Jack Lynch.

As a result of the post-1957 opening up of the economy, the country was experiencing for the first time a minor boom. A new generation of Fianna Fáil ministers — its principal characters including Charlie Haughey, Brian Lenihan and Donogh O'Malley — saw themselves as an elite group of achievers in a country ready to take its place among the nations of Europe. They were brash, flashy, arrogant. It was a time when sensitive cases — such as prominent politicians caught drunk driving — were heard after hours, when the reporters had gone home. The oppressive pub licensing laws didn't apply to such princes of the new Ireland. If a garda dared interrupt an after-hours drinking session he was invariably met with the invitation: 'Would you like a pint or a transfer?'

One story had Donogh O'Malley drunk, driving the wrong way down a one-way street in Dublin, being stopped by a garda who asked if he hadn't seen the arrows. 'I didn't even see the fucking Indians,' drawled the minister. It was all good fun, the lads brushing aside the fuddy-duddy conventions of the day. But the law was treated as optional for the elite. And it was in this arrogance that lay the roots of the scandals that would erupt in the 1990s.

The new Fianna Fáil saw no reason why the business interests which were benefiting from the improvement of the economy shouldn't pay to support the party which supported them. And you didn't leave such things to chance, as Lemass did, accepting the odd donation. You put the arrangement on a formal basis. You support us, as we support you. The word Taca, loosely meaning 'support', was given to the new organisation.

Selected businessmen, known for their closeness to the party, and some who might become close if properly coaxed, were invited to dine at the Gresham Hotel at £100 a plate. For that price, you got to rub shoulders with the new elite, to lobby ministers and make connections, to identify who was among the favoured, who could be depended on. It was all done on the quiet, by invitation only. The only ones who knew you were paying the party were the party people. No direct favours were sought or given. It was as Don Corleone, the Godfather, said: accept this gift; some day I may call on you for a favour.

When Taca's existence was revealed in an article in *Business and Finance* magazine, in February 1967, there was disquiet, not least among ordinary Fianna Fáil members. This wasn't what the party was supposed to be about. Fianna Fáil had been a national movement; it now seemed to be giving favoured status to a wealthy elite. For many in 1967, a hundred pounds was more than a month's wages. The secretive nature of Taca added to its sinister image. Taca supporters were derisively referred to as Tacateers.

There was nothing wrong with party supporters making donations, but this was the integration of the party with wealthy interests. Ordinary members complained; minister George Colley made a veiled attack on Taca. In a speech to the Kevin Barry Cumann of Fianna Fáil, at UCG, he said, 'Do not be dispirited if some people in high places appear to have low standards.' It was a phrase that would hover over the party through the decades.

There was a half-hearted effort by Taoiseach Jack Lynch to claim that Taca was set up to meet a cash shortage because the party coffers had been drained by the previous year's presidential election, but everyone knew what was going on. Mockery from outside the party, and unease from within, led to the winding up of Taca. First, at a party meeting in December 1968, the outfit was 'democratised'. Jack Lynch likened Taca's fund-raising to the Catholic church's recently inaugurated 'planned giving' system. You could become a Taca member for a donation of anything between £5 and £100. Since this defeated the purpose of Taca — the coming together of business and political interests — the organisation soon drifted into oblivion.

In its stead, the party perfected a system of canvassing wealthy interests which was Taca without the name, without the formality of an official organisation. Business people were wined and dined in private, while being stroked by party heavyweights, no favours were sought or given but a community of interests was built up between the politicians and their financial backers. The informal system was very much more effective than Taca ever was and the other parties followed suit.

The more clever seekers of influence spread their money around, giving to all the main parties. There was no commitment to any principles or politics, just a desire to keep in with all sides of the political establishment. When questioned, all agreed that this money was given not in the expectation of favours, but in a philanthropic wish to support the democratic system.

While still seeking to maintain Taca, Jack Lynch gave it this justification: 'It is an essential part of the machinery of democracy that people should be prepared to support in this voluntary way the party whose policy appears to them to be in the best interests of the country.'

This would be echoed thirty years later by Charlie Haughey: 'The capacity of businessmen to subscribe to political parties is closely related to the principle of free speech.' Haughey was speaking from the witness stand in the McCracken Tribunal on 15 July 1997.

See: Haughey, Charlie.

Tampons

In 1944 a new product became available to Irish women. The invention of the sanitary tampon, sold under the name Tampax, offered women what many considered a more convenient way of dealing with monthly periods than the traditional, bulky, uncomfortable sanitary towel. The Catholic bishops, upon learning of this invention, and of the manner in which it was used, became quite upset. The fact that the tampon had to be inserted into the vagina was considered scandalous. Having given this procedure some thought, the bishops concluded that a tampon 'could harmfully stimulate young girls at an impressionable age'.

The bishops got on to Dr Con Ward, parliamentary secretary to the Minister for Local Government and Public Health, who was effectively the Minister for Health in the Fianna Fáil government. Dr Ward had himself been giving the matter some thought and was just as concerned as the bishops were about the potential for female stimulation. Dr Ward and the bishops had a meeting of minds on the issue and the importation of tampons was solemnly banned.

See: Ward, Dr Con.

Tax Amnesties

When the Minister for Finance, Ray MacSharry, announced a tax amnesty in his budget of January 1988, it was expected that the Revenue would take in £30 million from repentant tax dodgers. However, as the 30 September deadline approached, it became clear there was lots more money coming in. The big accountancy firms in Dublin were reported to be either 'working around the clock' or 'burning the midnight oil'. At the offices of the Revenue Commissioners in the final week there were about 6,000 inquiries.

In the end, a staggering £500 million came in from the cold. Mostly everyone was delighted, for this was long before the arrival of the Celtic Tiger and buoyant tax revenues. The government needed the money, even if a handful of politicians on the left were critical of the method. Sure, the amnesty rewarded tax cheats, but, let's be practical here, it brought in more money than anyone could have hoped for. The advantage of having a bird in the hand was widely remarked upon.

It was said that the money came in because the scheme was forgiving: no interest or penalties, just pay what you owe. And anyone who didn't own up now would be threatened with truly tough action from the Revenue Commissioners. The 1988 tax amnesty was billed as the last chance saloon for evaders.

But as it happened, there was another tax amnesty around the corner and that offered an even better deal for the evaders. The person who had been evading tax for aeons had to pay only 15 per cent no matter how much money he or she had been hiding from the Revenue. It was a good deal. And it was a secret deal. The Revenue Commissioners collecting the 15 per cent from the cheats could not tell their colleagues in the Revenue's enforcement division just who was coming forward to declare hidden fortunes. So the evaders were safe in the knowledge that they wouldn't be marked down for future scrutiny.

The original target of the 1993 tax amnesty was money that had been illegally salted away abroad before exchange controls were abolished. This was 'hot' money which the government agreed to turn into legitimate money for a 15 per cent cut. In law enforcement circles this is called money laundering.

The idea was first mooted by Fianna Fáil deputy Noel Davern in 1991. Money was needed for job creation: 'The government can not continue to turn a blind eye to this option at this particular time.'

As far as Taoiseach Albert Reynolds was concerned this was a win-win situation. The country needed the money and this was a simple way of getting it. The ordinary taxpayer would benefit because there would be more money without having to raise taxes. 'Either we want to relieve pressure on the PAYE sector, or we want to get the economy to grow to create jobs, or we do not. So make up your mind, we have made up ours.'

There were conditions laid down to prevent the proceeds of crime being laundered through the government scheme, but they were largely unenforceable. Six years later it became apparent that Gerry Hutch, a well-known man being chased through the courts by the Criminal Assets Bureau, had availed of the tax amnesty.

For Fianna Fáil's coalition partners, Labour, the tax amnesty caused some hand-wringing. The chairman of the Parliamentary Labour Party, Toddy O'Sullivan, said they were being asked to choose between 'ethics and expediency'. He felt they were condoning a wrongdoing but: 'The pragmatic approach is that the country needs it. I have to go along with it at the end of the day, but it is something I don't condone.' But not everyone in Labour was against the amnesty. Jim Kemmy thought it was a great idea. If the 1988 amnesty had brought in £500 million, this one could bring in more. Those with worries about the ethics of what was going on he denounced as 'altar boys'.

In his political memoir, *Snakes and Ladders*, Labour adviser Fergus Finlay recalls the tax amnesty as a low point for the party in government. 'In accepting the idea of a tax amnesty, we were cementing the contrast between the high moral tone of our politics before the election and a sudden drop in standards afterwards.' At the time, Labour caved in because the revenue was needed and this seemed a painless way to get it. The irony, of course, was that it wasn't necessary, economic growth was just around the corner. 'Nobody would have suffered in the end if we'd declined the thirty pieces of silver,' wrote Finlay.

Interestingly, one man strongly against the tax amnesty was Albert Reynolds's finance minister Bertie Ahern. So were the officials of the Department of Finance and the Revenue Commissioners. Whatever happened around the cabinet table, the amnesty was approved by the government and implemented by Bertie Ahern.

Fine Gael raised hell in the Dáil. John Bruton told the Dáil it was a 'monster' write-off. 'It appears the government prefers Mafia votes to PAYE votes.' However, his righteous anger was undermined by the revelation that his spokesperson on finance, Ivan Yates, had tabled an amendment to the Finance Bill urging an amnesty for 'hot money'. Yates was suggesting an even better deal for crooks — under his scheme they would pay only 10 per cent to have the money laundered, 5 per cent less than the government plan.

In the end, about £200 million was collected and the state wrote off more than £1.3 billion in properly due taxes. Proof positive that 'only the little people pay taxes'.

Taylor, Tony

Tony Taylor was one of Ireland's best known and apparently successful independent investment managers. A divil for honesty, forever insisting on high standards, he was founding president of the Irish Brokers' Association, which aimed to keep the business on the straight and narrow. With a lovely three-storey office on Clyde Road, and a large home on Anglesea Road, Taylor was among the most highly regarded professionals in the financial services business.

In June 1996 the whole thing started falling apart. Investigators would later claim that money from seventeen clients' accounts had been diverted to a Jersey bank under the name Rolyat. Lesson: be wary when dealing with anyone who opens a bank account in his own name spelled backwards.

Taylor's firm, Taylor Asset Managers, had around 1,200 clients, who between them had given TAM between £30 and £40 million to manage. The allegedly missing money came from just a handful of valued clients whose accounts Taylor personally handled. Typically, such clients would have a spare £200,000 or £500,000 to invest, and they turned to Tony, a charming fellow who knew how to get the best return on the money.

Taylor had exclusive representation of Fidelity Investments, a US outfit. He would collect clients' money, pass it on to FI, which would invest it on their behalf. Around June 1996 FI apparently believed it had reason to doubt that all was well and quickly cut loose from Taylor. Clients began to inquire about their money. At least two went to the Irish Brokers' Association, the regulatory body Taylor helped found. The IBA wrote to Taylor, who hired a solicitor to send it a letter alleging defamation. This effectively shut up the association.

A Department of Enterprise and Employment inspector arranged to meet Taylor on 6 August. He requested company books and accounts and Taylor agreed to hand everything over at a further meeting the following Monday. That weekend, computer records of several accounts, totalling £880,000, were deleted. Among these was a Vincent de Paul account totalling £185,000. Estimates of the amount of money unaccounted for varied between £1.7 million and £2.5 million. It was believed that one reason it was hard to ascertain exactly how much was involved was that some wealthy people who lost money didn't report it, possibly because it was hot money.

Taylor was apparently broke at this stage and sold his Mercedes and his BMW. He reportedly asked a company employee to mind his terrier dog, Harvey. Then, Taylor and his wife, Shirley, did a flit and the company was put into liquidation.

Taylor remained out of sight until August 1999. Private detectives hired by Eddie Hobbs, a former associate of Taylor's, sent a copy of a newspaper article about Taylor to Taylor's son in the USA. Phone company records showed that the son made several calls to a number in Eastbourne, in Essex. The private detectives put the house in Eastbourne under surveillance and confirmed that the man living there under the name of Andrew Taylor was indeed the missing broker. Taylor was living with Shirley and his old, blind dog, Harvey.

The private detectives informed the Irish police; British police arrested Taylor and began the extradition process.

See: PD Fund-raising.

Telecom

Johnston, Mooney & O'Brien, the old bakery, had a 5.5-acre site in Ballsbridge for sale. Here's one version of what happened.

A company called UPH (United Property Holdings) bought the site in April 1989. UPH was a vehicle used by Dermot Desmond's stockbroking firm, NCB, for speculative property ventures. Selected wealthy people were invited to invest in UPH. These included Desmond himself, Michael Smurfit (heir to the international packaging company), and a man named Joe Lewis, who lived in the Bahamas.

Around the time the JMOB site came on the market, the chairman of Telecom Éireann set about searching for a site to build a corporate head-quarters for Telecom. The chairman of Telecom was Michael Smurfit.

So, we had UPH buying the JMOB site for £4 million, and looking for some wealthy client to sell it on to; and we had Telecom looking for a site.

The common ingredient in much of what followed was Dermot Desmond. No description of Desmond is complete without a reference to his northside origins, his flat Dublin accent and the fact that he didn't go to university. He is sometimes portrayed as a street urchin who fought his way to the top. In fact, his accent is not noticeably flat, he is from a comfortable background (his father was a senior customs official), and he went to boarding school. He didn't go to university because he knew right away that he wanted a career in finance. He went into banking, set up his own stockbroking firm, NCB, in 1981, and by the beginning of the 1990s was a very rich man who had forged useful connections in the financial and political worlds. It was he who convinced Charlie Haughey to back the International Financial Services Centre and he became close to Haughey. Haughey appointed him to the board of Aer Rianta.

According to this version of what happened, UPH now sold the JMOB site to a company called Chestvale, for £6.3 million. This was in July 1989. Chestvale was owned by a London-based property developer, Pat Doherty.

And in May 1990 Chestvale sold the site to Telecom for £9.4 million. The financing of this deal was done with the help of an Isle of Man company called Freezone, owned by a Guernsey businessman called Colin Probets. And the deal required a loan to Chestvale from an account in Jersey owned by J&N McMahon. Both of these entities — Freezone and the J&N McMahon account — made large chunks of money out of the deal.

All through these proceedings, Dermot Desmond helped Michael Smurfit, chairman of Telecom, find his way. He described himself at one point as Telecom's 'minder'. When Smurfit said he wanted to buy the JMOB site, Dermot Desmond told him: 'We [that is, UPH] disposed of the property to Chestvale and if I can influence the Chestvale people in any way I would be delighted to do so.' Smurfit now dealt with Chestvale through Dermot Desmond. Dermot wasn't representing Telecom, he was merely facilitating a deal.

Smurfit's method of operation was outlined later by a government-appointed inspector: 'Dr Smurfit neither sought nor obtained professional advice on value, planning, size of site, plot ratio, law or general feasibility before making his offer. His view was that all these matters would be done at a later stage.' Smurfit said, in the best entrepreneurial tradition: 'I kick-started the operation, which is my style, and got the train on the tracks.'

There was public unease at a site worth £4 million in 1989 being sold for £9.4 million in 1990, to a state company — and without planning permission to build offices. Charlie Haughey, usually very happy to engage in back-slapping with wealthy people, sought to distance himself from everyone involved. In a radio interview, he suggested people should 'step aside' from various duties involving state companies until everything had been cleared up. Smurfit resigned from Telecom; Desmond resigned from Aer Rianta.

A solicitor, John Glackin, was appointed by the government to inquire into the affair. His conclusions amounted to a very different version from the one given above.

It turned out that the simple deal (the site bought by UPH and sold to Chestvale and then to Telecom) was extremely complex. It involved companies and banks in Dublin, the Isle of Man, Jersey and Cyprus. Glackin's inquiries lasted twenty months and were slowed down by a number of legal actions. Dermot Desmond took the inspector to court, as did the owner of the J&N McMahon account in Jersey.

Inspector Glackin concluded that Joe Lewis, the Bahamas businessman, didn't own the shares in UPH, that he was holding them for J.P. McManus, the bookie and horse owner and friend of Dermot Desmond. He concluded that Desmond — and not Pat Doherty, the London developer — was behind Chestvale and that Desmond concealed that fact from Smurfit.

Effectively, that meant that Desmond (with J.P. McManus) was behind UPH, which sold the site to Chestvale; and Desmond was behind Chestvale, which sold the site to Telecom. And Desmond was helping Dr Smurfit buy the site for Telecom.

Solicitor and property speculator Noel Smyth (later to become well known through the Ben Dunne scandals) acted for Dermot Desmond in buying the JMOB site from UPH for Chestvale.

It got more complicated. Chestvale was moved from Dublin to Cyprus, to avoid tax. Ordinary people buy and sell property. Smart business people sell the company which owns the property: tax on the sale of shares is much lower than tax on the sale of property. An elaborate series of transactions was put in place: Chestvale was sold, as a company, to a Cyprus company called Delion, which sold on to a company called Hoddle, which sold on to Telecom. These transactions involved loan notes, 'mezzanine financing' and other assorted exotica from the world of high finance.

Inspector Glackin concluded that J.P. McManus was the beneficiary of the J&N McMahon account, in Jersey, which benefited from the sale; and that Dermot Desmond — and not Colin Probets — was the beneficial owner of Freezone, which also made a lot of money from the transactions. He concluded that a half-million pounds, which Desmond withdrew from a TSB account in Dublin, in cash, was part of J.P. McManus's cut. He concluded that Michael Smurfit had no financial interest in the sale, apart from his shares in UPH.

Dermot Desmond furiously contested Glackin's conclusions. The Minister for Enterprise, Ruairí Quinn, had the Glackin Report published at one o'clock in the morning, for fear another legal action might be mounted to stop it. He sent the report to various state agencies — the DPP, the Revenue Commissioners, the Stock Exchange and the Central Bank — but nothing came of any of that. Over the next few years Dermot Desmond became even richer, owning an airport in London, part of a football team in Scotland and a hotel in the Bahamas. No media reference to Desmond would henceforth be complete without reference to his flat Dublin accent and his patriotism and his charity.

J.P. McManus became an ever more successful bookie and horse owner, widely applauded as a thrusting businessman and philanthropist.

Tesco

The relentless encroachment of British retailers in the Irish market, from dress shops to supermarkets, was widely reckoned by consumers to be a good thing. Dublin's various shopping streets and out-of-town malls might look like replicas of their British equivalents, but if inefficient Irish retailers went to the wall, so be it. What many hadn't anticipated was that what was coming in wasn't always as good as what it was replacing.

When Tesco took over the Quinnsworth chain the outlets went from mediocre to dreadful. Poor management and empty shelves were bad enough, but in March 1999 Tesco was caught overcharging. RGDATA, the smaller retailers' outfit, systematically checked Tesco's prices and did a report. You bought a noodle sauce at 99p and when it went through the checkout it cost you £1.69. Most people don't check their receipts carefully enough to spot that they're being charged £2.09 for enchiladas priced at £1.59. When the scandal broke, Tesco explained that it had recently installed new automatic equipment, which was causing the problem. Then it emerged that the overcharging had been reported to the Office of Consumer Affairs months before the installation of the new machinery.

It didn't amount to much, just a tiny percentage of the bill. RGDATA found a 3 per cent increase. Just 60p on a bill of £20. But, claimed RGDATA, when this was calculated as a proportion of Tesco's overall takings, you were looking at an annual overcharge of £33 million. The Director of Consumer Affairs investigated the allegations and in July 1999 Tesco was fined £3,800.

Thundering Disgrace

During September and October 1976, in the wake of the IRA murder of the British Ambassador, Christopher Ewart-Biggs, Liam Cosgrave's Fine Gael–Labour coalition pushed through several repressive measures. These were sent to the president, Cearbhall Ó Dálaigh, for signature. Ó Dálaigh was a former Chief Justice, an expert in constitutional matters, with a strong sense of his own place in the scheme of things. He sent one of the bills passed by the government, the Emergency Powers Bill, to the Supreme Court for a ruling on its constitutionality.

It makes sense for a president to send to the Supreme Court a bill about which there are constitutional doubts. Otherwise, at a later stage, in the course of a trial, the constitutionality of the Act may be challenged, with consequences for the trial. Since it is likely that any such trial would involve crimes of violence, a Supreme Court judgment which caused the collapse of that trial might have serious consequences.

In that light, one can view the sending of a bill to the Supreme Court as a conservative act, checking for loopholes which can be closed before the bill becomes an Act. Others see such matters in a different light. Ó Dálaigh's action was seen by some as a liberal's distaste for, and attempt to scupper, a law and order bill.

No one believed himself more committed to law and order than Paddy Donegan, Minister for Defence. Donegan, a wealthy businessman, had been a TD since 1954. He was close to Taoiseach Liam Cosgrave. On Monday, 18 October 1976 Donegan had the less than glamorous job of declaring open a new cookhouse at Columb Barracks, in Mullingar. Addressing the troops, Donegan shared with them his view of the president: 'In my opinion,' said the Minister for Defence, 'he is a thundering disgrace. The fact is that the army must stand behind the state.'

There have been persistent claims that Donegan's words were subsequently cleaned up, that he actually described the president either as a 'fucking disgrace' or a 'thundering bollocks'. The only journalist present, Don Lavery then of the *Westmeath Examiner*, insisted that the term used was 'thundering disgrace'.

The remarks did not constitute the most coherently expressed   view on the subject of constitutional law. Donegan didn't seem to grasp the significance of a government minister denouncing the president, the nominal head of the defence forces, to members of those defence forces.

Paddy Cooney, Minister for Justice, who was present, certainly recognised that something regrettable had happened. He immediately phoned Taoiseach Cosgrave. Reporter Don Lavery was approached by an army officer but hurried away and wrote his story. An army officer rang the *Examiner*, looking for the editor, who was out of town. Lavery passed the story on to the national papers and the scandal erupted.

A showdown was under way between two stubborn men. For Ó Dálaigh the issue was simple: a minister had publicly attacked the head of state, and — even more seriously — had done so in front of the armed forces of the state. The minister had implied that the president was, unlike the army, somehow not standing behind the state.

Constitutionally, a minister holds office by virtue of the seal bestowed by the president. Ó Dálaigh considered the relationship between the minister and the president to be 'irreparably breached'. One of them had to go: Donegan or the president.

For Cosgrave the issue was simple: his minister had made a mistake, run off at the mouth, and that was wrong, the minister would apologise and that would be that. For Cosgrave, this was not a resigning matter. After all, as he saw it he was Taoiseach of a state under siege, the Provo vandals at the gates. This was a small incident, given the things he had to deal with.

For Ó Dálaigh, the preservation of proper procedure was paramount. To the legal mind, a thread out of place can lead to an unforeseen unravelling. Donegan's action did not just insult Ó Dálaigh personally, it threatened constitutional propriety.

That evening, Paddy Donegan did the decent thing. He offered his resignation to Liam Cosgrave. The Taoiseach rejected it. He wasn't going to sacrifice one of his closest political allies to constitutional niceties.

Donegan contacted Áras an Uachtaráin and asked to see Ó Dálaigh, to apologise. For Ó Dálaigh, an apology might be the appropriate response for the personal insult; for the constitutional breach there was only one remedy open to Donegan. Ó Dálaigh refused to see the minister.

Cosgrave rang the Áras and spoke to Ó Dálaigh, but the president wouldn't discuss the issue on the phone. It was open to Cosgrave to visit Ó Dálaigh. He chose not to.

That evening Ó Dálaigh wrote a formal letter of complaint to the Taoiseach. The next day, Cosgrave told the Dáil that while the minister had been disrespectful of the president, he had made a 'serious comment'. In short, Donegan had raised a valid point but might have done so in more diplomatic language. And that was that. Cosgrave had gone too far, there was no way back.

Next day, President Ó Dálaigh wrote a letter of resignation. He then left the Áras for a 2.30 p.m. appointment, after which he headed to his off-duty residence in Wicklow. Over two hours later Cosgrave was informed that a dispatch rider was on his way from the Áras. Cosgrave called in his ministers. It had to be a resignation.

Phone Donegan, said Garret FitzGerald, as told in his autobiography, *All in a Life*. Get his resignation and get onto the president before the dispatch rider gets here, tell him you've accepted Donegan's resignation.

Cosgrave reached for the phone, rang the Minister for Defence. Donegan agreed to resign. Cosgrave got onto the Áras. But Ó Dálaigh was out of reach. Cosgrave, doing what he should have done two days earlier, was too late.

Cosgrave played a tough game, facing down the president, and lost. It was Cosgrave who blinked, who tried to retrieve the situation, and it was Cosgrave who paid the political price, denounced as a man who put loyalty to his minister above loyalty to the president. Cosgrave couldn't win. Ó Dálaigh had accepted the job of president out of some sense of duty. Perhaps it appealed to his ego. Few believed he was happy in the job. Since he was quite prepared to lose the Áras, there was no possibility that he would back down.

The perception of an arrogant government prepared to stand over a gross insult to the president was one factor in the overwhelming defeat of the Cosgrave coalition at the general election eight months later.

Top People's Pay

There is a category of citizen that has assumed the media tag 'top people'. This category includes politicians, judges, heads of state companies, etc. It is a level of society where increases in pay can match the entire wage of others lower down in the pecking order. The outrageously unearned salaries and bonuses which 'top people' in the private sector arrange to pay each other are often a consequence of shareholder timidity and awe. In the public sector, whenever the Top People have their pay topped up the citizenry appears scandalised for a few days, then — with the citizenry having no say in the matter, except to foot the bill — things go on as before.

Take 1994. The Top People set up a group which conscientiously examined the issue before deciding to award large pay increases to the Top People. Barrister Dermot Gleeson performed a public service by heading the group. For this public service he waived his fee.

Gleeson would himself later become a Top Person when he served as a Fine Gael attorney general. When choosing a person to assess Top People's pay, the Top People perhaps inevitably pick someone who shares a background and a level of income at least as high as their own (in Gleeson's case, much higher). It would be instructive if the person assessing the value to society of the functions carried out by Top People was someone whose perspective on society and on income levels was somewhat different — say, for instance, Fr Peter McVerry.

In the Gleeson group assessment the then Taoiseach and Tánaiste each had their salary boosted to a level higher than that of British prime minister John Major. The head of Aer Lingus was awarded an extra 30 per cent.

Judge Liam Hamilton, who got an extra £12,000 per annum (£231 a week) as a result of Gleeson's report, presided over the Beef Tribunal at which so many lawyers, including Gleeson, got rich. Hamilton shortly afterwards got a further £10,000 per annum (£192 a week), under Gleeson's pay award, when Albert Reynolds appointed him Chief Justice.

Reynolds, who got a £14,000 (£269 a week) rise under Gleeson's recommendations, declared that he was 'vindicated' by the report Hamilton produced from the Beef Tribunal. Hamilton's promotion was okayed by Tánaiste Dick Spring (who got an extra £12,000, or £231 a week, on Gleeson's recommendation).

The Attorney General, Harry Whelehan, got a rise of £11,000 (an extra £212 a week).

In August 1999 Minister for Finance Charlie McCreevy began a debate by suggesting that TDs should receive an extra £200 a week, and that their rates of pay should be linked to other Top People, in the civil service.

The rationale for paying Top People so much is that if they get less they will leave the public service to make their fortunes in the private sector. There are, apparently, legions of companies queuing up to pay over £80,000 a year to the likes of Brian Cowen, Charlie McCreevy and John Bruton.

This theory was tested just once, when one of the state's most experienced and highly rated politicians, Des O'Malley, resigned the leadership of the PDs in October 1993 and announced he was leaving politics. He denied that he wanted to run for a seat in the European parliament. O'Malley said on RTÉ that he would accept a suitable offer from the private sector. Some time later O'Malley made a failed bid for a nomination for the Euro elections. He ran again for the Dáil in the 1997 general election and retained his seat, though his vote fell significantly. And as of 1999, six years after he said his goodbye to politics, he was still in the Dáil, and again announcing his retirement from politics.

Top People's pay is not determined by the market, drawing a premium for rare skills, or by reference to social value. It is set within a structure which is self-referential, narrow, interwoven, with a shared set of assumptions about the value to us all of Top People.

Publicity occasioned by Top People's pay rises causes brief expressions of public scandal. To avoid this, we have occasional efforts to create links and differentials within Top People's salary scales, so that pay will drift up automatically, without it appearing that anyone has made a decision, without any scandal-creating announcements.

See: Lawyers' Fees; Ministerial Pensions.

Tour de France

He was, they said, a prostitute. Paul Kimmage quit his career as a racing cyclist and became a highly regarded journalist. In 1990 he published *Rough Ride*, a tough, honest account of his cycling years, in which he wrote frankly about the extent to which drugs are used in the sport. Kimmage wasn't outing his fellow cyclists, he was exposing the cynicism of those who ran the sport and who budgeted for drugs and the doctors who administer them. In a *Late Late Show* appearance he refused to say that the great heroes of the sport had taken drugs — but he also refused to say they didn't. This, he insisted, was his story, not anyone else's.

When the book was published, former friends in the sport turned their backs on Kimmage. There was no rush from the mainstream of cycling or sports journalism to defend him. He had dared say in public what many knew to be true. The notion that the great Tour de France was contaminated by drugs was declared to be the fantasy of a prostitute journalist, a bitter loser. That was 1990. By 1997 the evidence of drug use was so abundant that only the terminally naive believed the official line. Riders being recruited to a team didn't ask first about money or conditions; they wanted to know who was the team doctor, who was the team lawyer.

And in 1998 Ireland was to have the privilege of hosting the starting stage of the 85th Tour de France. Those who questioned the use of taxpayers' money to host a festival of drug abuse were denounced as begrudgers and urged to think of the tourism spin-off.

Three days before the race began, in July, the façade of sporting achievement began to tear. A car from the Festina team, driven by masseur Willie Voet, was stopped at the Franco-Belgian border and the boot was found to contain 400 vials of such banned substances as erythropoietin (EPO) and steroids, along with a supply of syringes. The car was on its way to Ireland. Subsequently, eight of the nine Festina riders were found to have traces of EPO in their blood. The ninth had traces of amphetamines.

Festina said it was astonished, and threw Voet to the wolves. Voet said he was acting under orders. It eventually emerged that Festina routinely docked money from the cyclists' earnings to build up a £40,000 'war chest' of drugs. The team was thrown out of the race. Other teams quit, as the race moved to France and the police raided cyclists at their hotels. Cyclists went 'on strike', cycling slowly or tearing the race numbers off their jerseys, in protest at police activities. Only two-thirds of the twenty-one teams that started in Ireland finished the race in Paris.

Before the race, any mention of the drugs issue was dismissed. Six million pounds was spent on improving Irish roads to facilitate the race. We were so proud to have the Tour bless us with its presence that it was virtually unpatriotic to mention that the race was awash with drugs. After the 1998 Tour scandal, everyone was suddenly streetwise. Sports minister Jim McDaid — who had effusively welcomed the Tour — solemnly declared that he'd have second thoughts before inviting that crowd back.

Paul Kimmage took no pleasure in seeing his old sport brought to its knees; but events revealed just who was prostituting themselves in the cycling and journalism businesses.

Traynor, Des

Desmond Traynor was an old friend of Charlie Haughey. When the future Taoiseach was an accountant with Haughey Boland back in the 1950s, Traynor was 'articled' to Haughey. Traynor became a director of Guinness & Mahon (Ireland) Ltd in 1969 and deputy chairman in 1976. On reaching this position he was able to create the Ansbacher Deposits, through which he operated bogus 'offshore' accounts for members of the Golden Circle, including Haughey.

Traynor used companies such as Kentford, Amiens and Hamilton Ross to weave his money trails, juggling and concealing his dodgy transactions. Traynor left Guinness & Mahon in 1986 and became chairman of Cement Roadstone Holdings. However, he still operated the Ansbacher Deposits at Guinness & Mahon until he switched the racket to Irish Intercontinental Bank in 1992. Within a year of Traynor joining CRH, eight of the fifteen members of the CRH board were beneficiaries of the Ansbacher Deposits.

Traynor was Haughey's bagman, fronting for him in financial transactions. He died in 1994. This was, for Haughey, a somewhat fortunate development as he could implement a Dead Man Strategy. At the McCracken Tribunal he was able to claim complete ignorance of where the money came from to support his lavish lifestyle and state on oath that Des Traynor had absolute control of Haughey's finances from 1960 onward.

The Dead Man Strategy was demolished at the Moriarty Tribunal, where AIB documents were revealed which showed that Haughey had personally supervised his relationship with AIB from 1974 to 1980, and had called in Traynor only for specific functions. Traynor's reputation as one of the most prestigious men in financial and business circles was destroyed by his association with Haughey.

See: Ansbacher Deposits; Dead Man Strategy; Furze, John.

Trudder House

Anthony Cawley is probably the most famous graduate of Trudder House, the residential home for traveller children in Newtownmountkennedy, County Wicklow. He is, by his own admission, a dangerous man. In May 1999 he finished serving a sixteen-year sentence for rape and attempted murder and began serving a further eight years for the violent rape of a fellow prisoner.

Anthony Cawley was a disturbed child before he got to Trudder House. He was beaten at home, once tied naked to the wheel of a wagon, from the age of five or six left to roam the streets. Trudder House, as it turned out, was the worst possible place to send such a damaged child. There, in the words of one judge: 'He was repeatedly raped while in the custody of the People of Ireland.'

Trudder House was set up in the 1970s by a volunteer group, the Dublin Committee for Travelling People, and run with Eastern Health Board funding. At the time there were a number of traveller children living rough on the streets of Dublin, involved in petty crime and glue-sniffing. After some were convicted of burning down the APCK bookshop in Dawson Street, a judge asked that something be done to provide residential care for these troubled children. Trudder House was the response.

Rumours of beatings and sexual abuse in Trudder House surfaced by the late 1970s. But there were no court cases or public inquiries. More than a decade would pass before the abuse of children in Ireland was truly recognised as a crime. And if anyone was more vulnerable than a child left to institutional care, it was a traveller child left to institutional care.

In August 1985 *New Hibernia* magazine reported 'irregularities' at the home and allegations of beatings and homosexual child abuse. One staff member resigned, left the country and has since died. But the allegations of abuse continued.

It was not until January 1995 that gardaí launched a full investigation of what went on at Trudder House. They attempted to track down some two hundred former residents in halting sites throughout the country. At least nineteen of those contacted said they had been abused. The investigation centred on allegations against five men over a twenty-year period.

In 1998 Brendan Kelly from Drumvoughane, Moycullen, County Galway was sentenced to seven years for attempted buggery of two boys when he was a care worker at Trudder House in the 1980s. The court heard that he was not the most serious offender in the home. The main perpetrator was the man who had died abroad. He occupied a position of authority and was involved in violent sexual abuse. Kelly had come to work at Trudder House after this man had gone. He got the job through the assistance of a priest. He was just eighteen and had no formal training as a care worker.

As yet, there have been no other charges. Trudder House closed in April 1995 and residents were moved to a new centre in Clondalkin, County Dublin.

Anthony Cawley is just one former resident in whom the nightmare of Trudder House continues to live, and through Cawley's own crimes, to spread to further victims.

See: Madonna House.

Tuffy, Pat

In the summer of 1995, a bankrupt accountant, struck off, ill, decided to stir things up. Pat Tuffy wrote a series of anonymous letters to senior politicians of the Fine Gael–Labour–Democratic Left government. The letters alleged wholesale corruption within the state companies and provided enough credible detail to make the allegations worth looking into.

One of the letters alleged that Michael Lowry, Minister for Transport, Energy and Communications, had been placed under surveillance by corrupt businessmen. Private detectives had been hired, said one letter. Lowry's campaign against 'cosy cartels' had made him the target of ruthless Fianna Fáil gangsters. Lowry made a meal of this, eager to enhance the cool, clean hero image which had made him a potential Fine Gael Taoiseach. The 'fact' that he had been under surveillance was leaked. Lowry initiated a thorough search for corruption in the state companies (and found none).

The gardaí looked into the surveillance allegation, concluded there were no private eyes at work, and quickly backed off, using the excuse that it is not against the law to put anyone under surveillance.

RTÉ's *Prime Time* tracked down and exposed Pat Tuffy, a former Fianna Fáil candidate, as the author of the anonymous letters. Tuffy spun RTÉ a yarn about how he had been paid to write the letters. Off-screen, he lied that Lowry had paid him to write the letters.

Lowry was embarrassed when it was revealed that he had been making a big fuss, and throwing around baseless allegations, on the basis of hoax letters. This, however, was quickly covered over, now that he had been falsely accused of having himself been behind the creation of those letters. Within days, Tuffy withdrew his allegation that someone had paid him to write the letters and Lowry claimed vindication. Lowry issued writs to RTÉ and to a journalist who had discussed the matter on *Prime Time*: Sam Smyth.

Before too long, Smyth would be writing a story that put the hoax letters scandal in the ha'penny place.

See: Lowry, Michael.

Tully Allegations

Two Fianna Fáil deputies got the goods on Jimmy Tully, Minister for Local Government. Tully, they had discovered, while a member of the cabinet, had a business connection to a builder in his constituency, Robert Farrelly. For Fianna Fáil, repeatedly the target of corruption allegations, this was great news. To nail a minister in the Cosgrave coalition, and a Labour minister at that, would neatly reverse the usual way of things.

Trouble was, it wasn't true. Tully was not corrupt, there was no foundation to the allegations which FF's Bobby Molloy made in December 1974. And Tully said so.

That didn't stop Molloy, frontbench spokesman on Posts and Telegraphs, repeating the allegations six months later, in June 1975. Again, Tully denied them. On 2 July he made a personal statement in the Dáil, reiterating his denial.

Molloy repeated the allegations. And he was backed up by Brendan Crinion, FF TD for Meath, Tully's constituency.

Tully referred the matter to the Oireachtas Committee on Procedure and Privileges. The committee, however, couldn't do anything about the matter because Molloy and Crinion wouldn't make formal statements. It appeared that the lads were having second thoughts.

Next day, 3 July, Taoiseach Liam Cosgrave moved a motion setting up a tribunal of inquiry into the allegations. It was passed by the Dáil. On 4 July, just before the Seanad too passed the motion, Molloy and Crinion stood up in the Dáil, withdrew the allegations and apologised.

The result was devastating for Molloy and Crinion. To make the allegations in good faith was one thing, to persist in them after Tully had answered the allegations, and to do so without proof, was silly. Fine Gael and Labour mocked; Fianna Fáil, finally having got the knack of effective opposition, after two years out of government, had handed Cosgrave a stick to beat them with. On 7 July Molloy resigned from the FF front bench, acknowledging that his actions 'may be of some embarrassment to the Fianna Fáil party'.

That same day, Brendan Crinion failed to turn up to watch Jimmy Tully officially open a new housing estate in Meath. That evening, Crinion attended the annual general meeting of Meath County Council, wearing a large bandage over his right eye. He refused to answer reporters' questions and withdrew his name from the election for chairman of the county council.

Molloy would be out of favour for two years. However, in 1977 he would be made Minister for Defence and in the 1980s he left Fianna Fáil and became one of the founders of the Progressive Democrats.

The tribunal of inquiry went ahead and reported back to the Dáil by the end of the month, clearing Tully. Cosgrave took pleasure in pushing the matter as far as possible, rubbing Fianna Fáil's face in the mess. In February 1976 he moved a Dáil motion condemning Molloy and Crinion. Fianna Fáil protested that this was vindictive. Jack Lynch pointed out that when the Locke inquiry of 1947 found allegations against Fianna Fáil to be baseless the party didn't pursue the matter.

Standing to reply to the debate, Cosgrave said, dismissively: 'Res ipsa loquitur' — the thing speaks for itself. The motion was carried.

See: Locke's Distillery; Shaw Park.

Twink Ard-fheis

The traditional Fine Gael ard-fheis had become tired, boring. Party members still enjoyed going to Dublin for a weekend hooley in which they got to shake hands with their leaders, but the whole thing had become so stale that there was a danger that the all-important TV audience was tuning out. So, in May 1991, leader John Bruton decided to scale the ard-fheis down, design it as a television event, an entertainment show. Only a small audience would be allowed in and the proceedings were to take place over just the Saturday afternoon, and not the whole weekend.

The ard-fheis was handed over to media consultant Eoghan Harris, former Workers' Party activist, who had recently had great success remodelling Mary Robinson for the 1990 presidential election. Robinson's new hairstyle, her systematic nodding and her avoidance of controversy had paid off in votes. Harris staged the Fine Gael ard-fheis as a kind of Tops of the Towns variety show. It resulted in one of the most bizarre television events in political history, scandalising traditional Fine Gaelers.

The proceedings began with comedian Twink doing a ten-minute routine. The first five minutes dealt with a recent controversy involving Fianna Fáil TD Ned O'Keeffe. Twice O'Keeffe was referred to as an animal and once he was called a head case. Sample joke: 'The only kiss that Fianna Fáil wants from Europe is a French kiss.'

The camera cut away to the ranks of prominent Fine Gaelers laughing at this. Some of the more easily pleased were obviously enjoying it, others were plainly laughing because they had been told to laugh.

Unlike at other ard-fheisanna, there would be no spotty youths taking the podium to complain about the lack of a zebra crossing outside their home town's All Night Yankee Burger Emporium and Video Shop. Only TDs would be allowed speak. And when each was called to the stage they would be addressed by a made-up title. Phil Hogan, for instance, was declared to be 'Philip Hogan, The Tallest Man in the Dáil'.

'Paul Connaughton, That Mighty Man from the West'.

'Mr Dub Himself, Jim Mitchell'.

'The Mighty Man from Macroom, Michael Creed'.

Each time a TD came on stage there was a musical fanfare, played on a rather unimposing and very tinny-sounding electronic keyboard. Each time a TD said something which might be considered significant, dramatic chords were played: 'Den-de-den-den'.

The TDs had to engage in awkward attempts at scripted repartee. Ivan Yates ('The Big Man from Wexford') was introduced by Seán Barrett. As Yates approached the microphone Barrett addressed him in unnaturally loud tones.

'What's the news, Ivan?'

Ivan, The Big Man from Wexford, replied: 'Seán, the news is that Fine Gael want to improve the pace and quality of life in Ireland!'

Den-de-den-den.

This kind of thing went on for what seemed a very long time. Yates made great promises about Fine Gael's intention to develop Rapid Rail. He finished: 'With Fine Gael, we'll get you there on time!' Here were the descendants of the Blueshirts promising to make the trains run on time. It appeared that someone's tongue was in someone's cheek.

No one laughed more than Fianna Fáil, as the backlash against the ard-fheis came up from the Fine Gael grass roots. Prominent Fine Gaelers back-pedalled furiously, denouncing the comic capers and denying that they had in any way approved of this kind of carry-on. Unfortunately, the camera had caught them laughing at the show, or pretending to.

The experiment in political science was not repeated.

U

Uno Duce

When the New Ireland Forum Report was published in May 1984, Fianna Fáil was thrown into controversy again. Over the previous four years, since soon after the election of Charlie Haughey as party leader, various factions had been hacking at one another. One faction, led by Des O'Malley, would before long leave the party and found the Progressive Democrats.

On the issue of the Forum Report and the North, Haughey sought to shut up anyone who didn't agree with him. Party policy was framed so that no one but he, or someone he designated, could speak about the North.

When Des O'Malley was publicly critical of the limiting of party debate a parliamentary party meeting was held at twenty-four hours notice and Haughey proposed that O'Malley should have the whip withdrawn. This was carried by fifty-six votes to sixteen and O'Malley was thrown out of the parliamentary party.

Haughey's media handler, P.J. Mara, couldn't conceal his amusement at this turn of events and quipped to some journalists: 'Uno duce, una voce!', meaning: 'One leader, one voice'. Mara wisecracked: 'In other words, we are having no more nibbling at my leader's bum.' When word of the remarks got out, they caused a scandal that lingered. Although Mara's remarks were meant as an off-the-record joke, the 'Uno duce' slogan — which originated with Benito Mussolini's Italian fascist party — confirmed for those who feared or hated Haughey that he was a threat to democracy.

Upwardly Mobile

RTÉ's record with comedy and its efforts to create a funny sitcom have not met with universal approval. When, in the mid-1990s, the station produced *Upwardly Mobile*, a sitcom about a family of working-class Lotto winners moving to a middle-class area, hope was balanced with wariness. The programme achieved a certain notoriety for an unusual reason.

There was a song sung over the opening titles and repeated over the credits at the end. The lyrics of the song were about the Lotto winners moving from the inner city to an exclusive southside address, Belvedere. There were lines which said goodbye to Guinness and hello to Chablis. This was phrased in unfortunate terms.

> So it's goodbye to old J. Arthur
> And it's hello to fine Chablis
> For we're leaving behind the Ha'penny Bridge
> And it's Belvedere for me.

What no one seemed to notice was that the name of the founder of the Guinness brewery was not J. Arthur Guinness, but simply Arthur Guinness. This slight error held a significance somewhat greater than the addition of an inappropriate initial. Somehow, the *Upwardly Mobile* crew had mixed up Arthur Guinness and the founder of the British movie company and cinema chain J. Arthur Rank. Again, not a major mistake. However, the term 'J. Arthur' has a distinguished tradition in some areas of Dublin and beyond. For a long time Lord Rank's name has been used in rhyming slang: to 'have a J. Arthur' is to masturbate.

> So it's goodbye to old J. Arthur
> And it's hello to fine Chablis

RTÉ, then, at prime time each Friday evening, was informing viewers, through the medium of song, that the characters in its sitcom were abandoning masturbation in favour of a fine wine.

This created much scandalous merriment in certain circles until a sensitively phrased mention in a Sunday newspaper drew the attention of the producers to the error. The song had to be rerecorded, with the lyrics adjusted from J. Arthur to Arthur J.

Urlingford Sting

A man who is in a position to know what happened off the coast of Cork in the early hours of 4 November 1995 said it was 'like something out of *Apocalypse Now* out on the high seas'. A trawler out of Castletownbere, with an armed crew, kept a rendezvous with a larger ship some three hundred miles off the coast. The bigger vessel was lit up, music booming from within. On the decks were men in balaclavas armed with sub-machine guns. Some thirteen tonnes of cannabis were loaded from the supply ship onto the trawler before it headed back towards Castletownbere. In an area called Dinis Island, under the cover of darkness, the bales of cannabis were loaded onto a lorry.

On the following Wednesday, 8 November, the same lorry-load of cannabis was found by gardaí at the side of the road at Urlingford on the Kilkenny/Tipperary border. It was hailed as a great drugs seizure, the biggest ever in the history of the state. The television pictures were dramatic. The gardaí, viewers were told, had successfully intercepted drugs 'with a street value of £130 million'. The then Minister for Justice Nora Owen said the Urlingford operation was an example of the cooperation and coordination in the fight against drugs between the gardaí, the customs and the naval service. Of course, it was nothing of the kind.

The 'great drugs haul' story began to unravel straight away. Reporters wondered why there had been no arrests if, as the gardaí claimed, the drugs had been under surveillance since they arrived in the state. There was stalling, there was spinning, there was misinformation, but within a month, the game was up. The Urlingford drugs haul was not an interception, but a 'sting' operation that had gone badly wrong, not least because there was virtually no cooperation at all between the gardaí and the customs service. Indeed, by the time customs officers arrived in Urlingford, the RTÉ camera crew had been, had filmed the scene of the mighty victory, and had gone.

The garda sting was aimed at nobbling a major drug dealing gang. A garda informant set up the operation in Amsterdam when he met a Finglas drug dealer there and arranged for the importation of the cannabis into Ireland.

It was a trawler full of armed, undercover gardaí that travelled out from Castletownbere on 4 November. It was gardaí who loaded up a boat full of cannabis and later transferred it to a lorry. And it was gardaí who brought the drugs to Urlingford. If it had all gone according to plan, the criminals would have been arrested when they turned up to collect the drugs. But no one turned up and the gardaí decided they could no longer play a waiting game when a reporter from the *Cork Examiner* started asking questions about a major drugs operation.

The gardaí put a brave face on the fiasco and the story about the biggest drugs haul in the history of the state was born. The fact that the gardaí themselves had imported the drugs in the first place was a detail left out. Later, the Minister for Justice made it clear that the taxpayer had not paid for the drugs. The cannabis was burned at an ESB power station, presumably bringing smiles to the faces of all in the locality.

The most that could be said about the whole operation was that the criminal gang the gardaí had originally contacted lost their investment of about £250,000. And, while it represented a low point in relations between customs and gardaí, it was probably a turning point.

In the aftermath of the debacle, *Irish Times* reporter John Maher got his hands on a customs dossier on the operation. From that, it was apparent that customs officers — who are there to police whatever is brought into the country — knew very little about the operation. Indeed, suspicious that the captain of the trawler used in the sting seemed to have hired an entire unknown crew, they had started to investigate him, unaware that he was working for the gardaí.

The scandal was not in the fact that a garda operation went wrong, nor even in the lack of cooperation between police and customs, but in the attempt to portray a fiasco as a victory.

US Ambassador

In 1992 the US government had to appoint a new ambassador to Ireland. The George Bush administration chose William Henry Gerald FitzGerald, an 82-year-old Bush supporter. The way such things work is that people who pay large amounts of money to help get politicians elected to the White House get appointed to various positions, including ambassador to what's-its-name, green place, turn left when you leave England, it's on the tip of my tongue — Ireland, that's the one.

The position of US ambassador to Ireland was never considered terribly important and could safely be used as a thank-you for those on whom an administration looked with favour. Diplomatic work is done by the career diplomats. Politically, Ireland is comfortably in the US camp and in normal times the role of US ambassador is primarily one of smiling benignly. But these were changing times. A couple of years later, as the IRA ceasefire began and the various parties began to use the Clinton administration as a conduit, the career diplomats were locked into old ways and it was necessary that the US ambassador be capable of understanding the basic issues involved. By then, FitzGerald had departed and Jean Kennedy Smith had replaced him. It would not be productive to speculate on the possible course of developments had FitzGerald still been in place.

FitzGerald was born in Boston in 1909. It's not known exactly what it was that he did during the next eighty-two years which qualified him for the job of representing his country in Ireland. His first thirty-eight years were somewhat obscure. He spent the next thirty-five years as an executive of something called the Metallurgical Research and Development Company. Within that period FitzGerald spent some time as a director of various outfits. He was, for instance, chairman of the board of the National Metallizing Corporation. There seemed to be little about metal that FitzGerald didn't know.

It was during a hearing of a subcommittee of the Senate Foreign Relations Committee, at which FitzGerald's appointment was discussed, that his psychic abilities were first noticed. Apparently seeking some inkling of how close the new ambassador's ear was to the Irish ground, Senator Joseph Biden asked FitzGerald what he thought would be the likely outcome of the Maastricht referendum.

'It's already done,' said FitzGerald. 'It's a fait accompli,' he added with a flourish, showing off his command of French. 'On June 18th the referendum was held and 65 per cent of the people favoured it, 11 per cent opposed it.' FitzGerald continued, seemingly unaware that people's eyebrows were beginning to climb right up their foreheads. 'So, the Maastricht treaty,' he said, 'by referendum of the people of Ireland, who backed the Fianna Fáil party's opinion and decision to go along with the Maastricht treaty . . .'

Senator Biden had to interrupt. 'I thought the vote was due to take place on June 18th?' he asked.

You couldn't fool Ambassador-Designate FitzGerald. 'On June 18th,' he reiterated, 'the referendum was held.'

'But', said a puzzled Senator Biden, 'this is now June 3rd. Today is June 3rd.'

Perhaps annoyed at himself for letting slip his prophetic powers, FitzGerald glossed things over. 'Thank you for correcting me, I was in anticipation,' he said.

(The result of the referendum to ratify the Maastricht treaty, when it took place two weeks later, was 69 to 31 per cent in favour, so the ambassador wasn't all that far wrong.)

The 82-year-old demonstrated his command of the Northern Ireland conflict by telling the Senate subcommittee that he hoped the future would bring 'dialogue and cooperation between unionists and loyalists'.

Apparently impressed by the man's insights into the northern conflict, his ability to forecast referendum results, and not least his comprehensive knowledge of metal, the full Senate voted to ratify FitzGerald and send him as its representative to the land of his forefathers.

V

Voting Allegations

I t was general election day, 18 February 1982. Pat O'Connor had that morning gone to a polling station in Malahide, where he presented a polling card, received a ballot paper and put a ballot paper into the ballot box. He also drove to Kinsealy, where he again received a ballot paper.

Pat O'Connor was one of Charlie Haughey's oldest friends. He was a solicitor and had acted for Haughey during the Arms Crisis and was never far from his side in times of adversity. In this election he was Haughey's election agent.

O'Connor had received two polling cards, one for Malahide and the other for Kinsealy. He used them to obtain two ballot papers. Fine Gael party workers spotted this and complained to the gardaí, alleging personation. The police took statements in which election workers and officials described seeing O'Connor at both polling stations, applying for ballot papers.

Pat O'Connor was charged with election offences. It created quite a scandal: Charlie Haughey's election agent charged with voting twice. The fact that it happened in 1982, a period in which Haughey was under threat within Fianna Fáil and was reacting with his customary viciousness, made the Pat O'Connor scandal part of a bigger battle.

Before the case came to court, some witnesses made new statements in which they said that their earlier statements were incorrect. For example: 'I did not realise what I was really saying in my statement to the guards at Coolock on the night of the elections as I was too tired and hungry from work and newspaper men and all I wanted was to get out of the station and go home.'

The case came before District Justice Kearney in April 1982. Pat O'Connor faced up to a year in jail and a fine of up to £500 if found guilty. The judge said he had looked up the law and this required that a marked ballot paper, showing a first preference, would have to be produced in court and it would have to be proven that this was the defendant's ballot paper. Since it was impossible to do this the prosecution couldn't prove its case. Charges dismissed.

The Director of Public Prosecutions appealed this decision to the High Court, which in May 1983 dismissed the case on a technicality.

The following issue of *Magill* magazine christened the defendant Pat O'Connor Pat O'Connor and added:

> Too many people in these sorry days are contemptuous of the ballot box the ballot box and prefer to strike, protest or demonstrate instead of casting their vote casting their vote. What this country needs is twice as many Pat O'Connors Pat O'Connors.

The nickname haunted O'Connor thereafter.

W

Ward, Dr Con

Whatever else could be said about the generation that founded the state, they didn't tolerate even the appearance of financial impropriety, holding the state in too high a regard to lightly tarnish it out of personal greed. Therefore, the scandals of the type we have today were largely unknown among that generation.

Dr Francis Conor Ward was in the IRA in the war of independence, joined Fianna Fáil and was elected to the Dáil from Monaghan in 1927, through the 1930s and into the 1940s. He was Parliamentary Secretary for Local Government and Public Health for fourteen years, from 1932. He was effectively Minister for Health and in 1946 was preparing legislation for a bill that prefigured Dr Noel Browne's Mother and Child scheme.

Ward owned a bacon factory in Monaghan. A manager was dismissed. A brother of the manager, a Dr McCarville, sent a list of allegations against Ward to the Taoiseach, Eamon de Valera, who immediately set up a tribunal of inquiry. The tribunal did its work and reported within a month, clearing Ward of all the corruption allegations save one: he had dodged tax on some payments he received from the bacon factory. Ward seems to have initially had hopes that he could survive the scandal, but de Valera was insistent, and Ward resigned a week later and didn't stand at the next election.

Warrants: Matt Russell

'Compulsory retirement, although legally provided for, has never been successfully achieved.' That's what Taoiseach John Bruton told the Dáil on 31 May 1995. He was talking about the untouchable elite of the government's workforce: senior civil servants. And he was gloating because he had succeeded where Fianna Fáil had failed. He had got Senior Law Officer Matt Russell out of the Attorney General's office. 'Whereas Mr Russell was not prepared to go, quietly or otherwise, under the previous administration, my actions have resulted in his immediate retirement from the civil service. That speaks for itself.'

Matt Russell was the man who had the extradition warrants for the paedophile Fr Brendan Smyth on his desk for seven months. He later explained: 'I did not give it special priority because I did not identify it as a case which required that priority over other priority work.' Thus the case in the North against Fr Smyth was delayed, causing gratuitous added suffering for his victims. Politically, the impression given, of a less than urgent attitude towards clerical child abuse, hastened the collapse of the Labour–Fianna Fáil government and led to the resignation of Albert Reynolds as Taoiseach and leader of Fianna Fáil, and the resignation of the former Attorney General as president of the High Court just six days after his appointment.

It was a lot of collateral damage from one man's 'not special priority' in-tray. But Matt Russell was a very powerful man. Attorneys General came and went, but Matt was a permanent force. Attorney General Harry Whelehan didn't know about the warrants in the Brendan Smyth case because Matt Russell didn't tell him. Even a letter to the Attorney General from his British counterpart on the case got no further than Russell's desk. In an overworked office, Russell set the priorities and the Brendan Smyth case was not one of them.

He told the Dáil Committee on Public Accounts: 'In dealing with this volume of work priorities have to be applied . . . I worked on the Smyth file at intervals when there was an opportunity to do so.' He agreed that in retrospect his judgment was wrong. But he did not offer to resign: 'I was not made aware of any reason that I should.' Matt Russell stayed put and Harry Whelehan resigned, too damaged by the controversy to continue as president of the High Court.

There were promises of change in the Attorney General's office. An assistant secretary was brought in from the Department of Justice to lighten the workload. But Russell remained in charge and in another bout of insensitivity he failed to reply to two letters written by a solicitor on behalf of the victims of Fr Brendan Smyth. The letters stayed on his desk for six months and the new Attorney General, Dermot Gleeson, was not informed.

At this stage, you'd think that anything to do with the Brendan Smyth case would cause alarm bells to go off in the Attorney General's office. But, no. The letter — demanding compensation for the victims because of the suffering caused by the original extradition delay — was dealt with in the normal way of that office. It was opened by a junior civil servant. It was logged under the name of the solicitor. The envelope was stapled to the letter and it was placed in the post trolley which was brought to the Senior Law Officer's desk first. Because he was the top man, he selected his choice from the post before it was wheeled on to the next senior civil servant and so on down the pecking order. The first letter from the Fr Smyth victims was received in November 1994, the second on 10 January 1995. Russell decided there should be no answer for the time being. 'Furthermore . . . many more actions are threatened by solicitors' letters than are commenced, and in view of the tenuous nature of the claim I thought this might well occur in this case.'

In the Dáil John Bruton concluded: 'There is no one else in the Attorney General's office to whom blame attaches in this matter.' Matt Russell had not told the Attorney General about the letter. It was Matt Russell's fault, end of story. The original delay with the extradition warrants was also Matt Russell's fault. Harry Whelehan was as ignorant then as Dermot Gleeson was six months later, but for him that was no protection.

Matt Russell sent a letter of resignation to John Bruton on 29 May 1995. He received a lump sum of £138,500 and a pension of £33,700 per annum.

Wrong Man

The firm of Michael J. Staines and Co. was, on 8 July 1996, appointed, under the Legal Aid Scheme, to represent an Eric Monaghan at the Dublin District Court, in an upcoming case. Monaghan was to be tried for a robbery offence.

So, a couple of weeks later, 22 July, a solicitor from the firm attended at the District Court where Eric Monaghan was due to be tried. Eric Monaghan didn't turn up. A bench warrant was issued for his arrest.

The next day, Fiona Brennan, a solicitor at the firm, wrote a letter to Monaghan, informing him about the bench warrant. Eric Monaghan went to the solicitors' office a week later. He hadn't a clue what this was about, he said. He hadn't been charged with robbery. A few years earlier he had been done for supplying cannabis, and got twelve months probation, but he had nothing to do with this robbery.

What about the garda claim that he had been arrested and charged? Not me, he said.

Years back, Eric Monaghan had been notified that he had been fined for non-payment of bus fare. Someone had given his name and address when charged. And in 1994 someone gave his name and address and he was picked up for stealing a motorcycle. He knew nothing about that, but he had spent two weeks in jail until it was sorted out. Maybe this had happened to him because he was well known in the area, he said.

Now, it was happening again. Two guys had been done for a robbery and one gave Eric's name, the other gave the name of a neighbour of Eric's.

Fiona Brennan rang the garda named on the warrant and arranged for Eric Monaghan to go see him at the Dublin Bridewell garda station next day. There, the garda said, according to Eric Monaghan, that Eric certainly wasn't the man the garda had arrested. The charge would be struck out, not to worry.

And so Eric Monaghan went about his business.

Eight months passed.

On the night of Friday, 4 April 1997 Eric Monaghan was walking to his Finglas home from the pub when a garda van pulled alongside, gardaí jumped out, handcuffed him and threw him into the van. He was held in the Bridewell all night.

I'm innocent, he said.

There's a warrant out for you, they said.

What did I do? he asked.

There's a warrant and that's it, they said.

Someone gave my name, he said.

There's a warrant and that's it, they said.

Next day, Eric was taken from the Bridewell to Mountjoy and put in a cell with six others. He was held through Saturday and Sunday.

On the Monday, Eric got word of his plight to the firm of Michael J. Staines and Co. and solicitor Fiona Brennan went to Mountjoy and saw him. On Tuesday the matter was raised before Judge Kinlen in the High Court, who directed that it be dealt with immediately, and on

Wednesday, 9 April Eric Monaghan was brought before the High Court and ordered to be freed.

Eric was a bit miffed when nobody from the police or the state bothered to apologise to him. However, before he left the High Court no fewer than three barristers gave him their phone numbers and asked him to ring them if he wanted to sue the state.

X

X Case

The eighth amendment to the Constitution states: 'The State acknowledges the right to life of the unborn and, with due regard to the equal right to life of the mother, guarantees in its laws to respect, and, as far as practicable, by its laws to defend and vindicate that right.'

These words, proposed by Fianna Fáil, were put to the electorate by a reluctant Fine Gael government led by Garret FitzGerald. His Attorney General, Peter Sutherland, had advised that the wording was ambiguous and could lead to future difficulties. He imagined that these difficulties might compromise accepted medical treatment of pregnant women.

But the Dáil wouldn't back the Fine Gael wording which would have simply precluded a constitutional challenge to the law prohibiting abortion. Buoyed by the Pro-Life Amendment Campaign, which wanted the Irish constitution to include a positive statement asserting the rights of human life as it developed in the womb, four Labour and eight Fine Gael deputies voted with the opposition and the Fianna Fáil wording was carried.

Presumably, neither the Pro-Life Amendment Campaign nor its supporters imagined that the amendment would be turned on its head nine years later when a Dublin man sexually assaulted a neighbour's child. Because of the so-called X case, judges of the Supreme Court had cause to scrutinise the eighth amendment and they found that when the life of a mother is threatened by a pregnancy, abortion is permissible. Here. In Ireland.

On Monday, 27 January 1992, the parents of a fourteen-year-old Dublin girl discovered that she was pregnant, having been abused by a trusted middle-aged neighbour. The girl was referred to the Sexual Assault Unit of the Rotunda Hospital and the gardaí became involved in the case. Early in February the girl and her parents decided that she would have an abortion. They asked the gardaí about procedures for taking DNA evidence from the foetus to prove paternity in a criminal case against the neighbour. The gardaí referred the query to the DPP and the DPP, in turn, informed the Attorney General.

The X case family had no notion of the storm that was in the process of being unleashed. Certainly, it would have been aware of the constitutional guarantee to protect the life of the unborn, but it was an aspiration that had little to do with reality. The reality was that Irish women had their abortions in the UK. And, had Harry Whelehan not been the Attorney General at the time, the X case girl would have almost certainly become just one among the thousands of Irish women who check in to British abortion clinics each year.

In his memoir, Seán Duignan, then government press secretary, observed: 'but for Harry she would have become just another statistic under the prevailing nod and wink system. The trouble with Harry was that he refused to go along with the system . . . when presented with the X problem, as with any other case, he operated by the book.'

Acting with an independence that drove politicians mad, Harry Whelehan sought and obtained a High Court injunction preventing the girl having the abortion. No Irish solutions to Irish problems here. The Constitution said the state was to defend and vindicate the right to life of the unborn and that's what Harry Whelehan did. In later judgments, both High Court and the Supreme Court judges said he was right.

At this stage the X case family was already in England, but decided to return to Ireland to sort out the legalities. The case was heard by Mr Justice Declan Costello in the High Court. There was evidence that the pregnant girl was suicidal and that there was a danger she would kill herself if forced to continue with the pregnancy. But Justice Costello found that, in the balance of rights to life, 'the risk that the defendant may take her own life . . . is much less and is of a different order of magnitude than the certainty that the life of the unborn will be terminated' if she was not prevented from having an abortion. There was to be no abortion and the girl was not permitted to leave the jurisdiction for nine months.

A drawing by cartoonist Martyn Turner published in *The Irish Times* showed a map of Ireland with the Republic ringed in barbed wire. In the centre stood a little girl clutching a teddy bear. The caption read: '17th February 1992. The introduction of internment in Ireland . . . for 14 year old girls.'

It was a story that made international news. A German newspaper noted: 'This is no event from the previous century, or from the Romania of Nicolae Ceaucescu, or the Iran of the Ayatollah. No, it is much worse.

This unbelievable story comes from the EC member Ireland in the year 1992.'

At home, Justice Costello's decision raised the question: was this really what people had voted for when, by a two to one majority, they endorsed the anti-abortion amendment? It wasn't just the government who wished Harry Whelehan had let the X case file gather dust in his in-tray until it was too late to do anything about it.

It wasn't long after the story broke that rumours — later proven to be untrue — began to circulate about the girl at the centre of the case and the motivation of her family. On *The Late Late Show*, the late Fr Michael Cleary cast the first public smear. 'If a case was made, was planned deliberately, to test this amendment, this is it. It's the model. I honestly suspect a lot of organisation behind it.' It was rumoured that the middle-aged neighbour was innocent. The girl, who was said to be 'advanced', named the neighbour to deflect attention from her teenage boyfriend. All of this was later proven to be untrue in court when the man pleaded guilty to unlawful carnal knowledge and indecent assault.

The High Court's decision was appealed to the Supreme Court and overturned. By a four to one majority decision the Supreme Court found that because there was a real and substantial risk to the mother's life through the threat of suicide, the Constitution allowed for abortion. Here. In Ireland.

The injunction was lifted. The X case family travelled to Manchester where the victim suffered a miscarriage. DNA evidence was taken from the foetus and later it proved that the accused man was guilty. After two unsuccessful attempts to stop the criminal case on the grounds that the widespread publicity would preclude him receiving a fair trial, the case was finally heard in May 1994 and the unidentified man was sentenced to two seven-year sentences which were to run consecutively, making it a total of fourteen years imprisonment. The following year, Mr Justice Hugh O'Flaherty ruled that the sentences should be reduced to four years to run concurrently. The man at the centre of the X case was released in June 1997, having served three years.

Y

Yates, Ivan

Several Russian agricultural officials, including the director of the Russian Ministry of Agriculture's veterinary service, arrived in Dublin on Monday, 7 October 1996. The Russian authorities were concerned about the incidence of BSE, otherwise known as mad cow disease, in Irish herds. Only a tiny fraction of Irish cows had been infected, in contrast to the thousands of British cows who had the virus, yet foreign markets were nervous. The Russians, quite reasonably, wanted to attempt to ensure that the Irish beef exported to Russia would be BSE-free. They wanted to limit imports of Irish beef produced in those areas of the country where the reported infection was greatest.

Over the next few days, Russian and Irish officials engaged in intense negotiations. Minister for Agriculture Ivan Yates took the Russians to dinner on Wednesday, Taoiseach John Bruton did the same on Thursday. Civil servants do the work, politicians organise hospitality and say yes or no when the civil servants come up with a proposal.

The discussions between the officials appeared to be winding up on the Friday, and the Russians were insisting that imports from the seven Irish counties most affected by BSE should be banned. The Irish officials contacted Ivan Yates and gave him the news, and he contacted John Bruton, then Yates got back to his officials and said no, we can't agree to that.

The next morning, Saturday, the Russians were going home. The Irish officials went out to Dublin airport to see them off. Ivan Yates was down in Kavanagh's pub in Enniscorthy, running a 'clinic' and attending to his constituents' worries. Meanwhile, back at Dublin airport, in the VIP lounge, the Irish officials were beating the Russians down from a seven-county ban to a three-county ban and a last-minute deal was agreed. The Irish officials rang Ivan Yates in Enniscorthy with the proposal: beef from the three most affected counties — Tipperary, Cork and Monaghan — would be banned. Yates okayed the deal, and that was that.

It was as good a deal as could be got. The farmers from the three affected counties, of course, accused the government of betrayal. The fact that four counties which the Russians had wanted included in the ban — Donegal, Limerick, Longford and Wexford — had been saved had little effect on farmer anger. In the course of defending the deal, the following weekend, Yates went on RTÉ television's *The Week in Politics*, where he claimed that the deal was done under pressure, when the Russians had a gun to his head: 'I did the deal with the Russians last Saturday week at 1 p.m. in the VIP lounge of Dublin airport.'

Thus began the scandal of the minister with the legendary power of bilocation.

The following Wednesday, PD Des O'Malley slapped in a parliamentary question asking where Yates had been at lunchtime on that Saturday. Yates was forced to admit that he had not been at Dublin airport. 'Any gun to the head', said O'Malley, 'was a very long-range weapon indeed.'

The next day, Yates had to undergo the ritual humiliation of apologising to the Dáil for misleading deputies. For an hour he was questioned and taunted about his bilocation. He was paying the price for throwing macho shapes, for giving the impression of a hard-nosed minister personally locking horns with the bolshie Russians.

Catching politicians out in such matters is part of the sport of politics as practised in Ireland. The point was not the extent to which Irish beef was infected; or the wholly understandable wish of the Russian authorities to defend their people from a dangerous disease; or whether meat which is not good enough for the Russians should be allowed on sale to the rest of us. Such matters are of little import in comparison with the sport of poking a minister who has made a fool of himself. Once Yates stood up in the Dáil and took his punishment the whole thing was allowed fade, apart from the occasional bilocation crack.

Z

Zoe Developments

James Masterson was working alone on the roof of an apartment building being constructed by Zoe Developments in Ringsend, Dublin. It was Monday, 3 November 1997. The roof was almost flat, apparently safe enough for a man who earned his living working at heights. There were other workers elsewhere on the site but no one saw or heard what happened when James Masterson walked onto a piece of plastic sheeting that was covering a skylight opening.

No one knows for sure what time it happened, but Masterson was found on the third-floor landing at 4 p.m., by other workers who came along. The plastic sheeting had come through the skylight after him, along with some of the concrete blocks that had been holding the sheeting in place. Masterson had fallen thirty feet. An ambulance was called, he was brought to the Meath Hospital, but he was dead on admission.

James Masterson was one of seven born to a Mayo couple. He worked the small family farm at Tullaghan, Ballina, with his father, Donal. He was twenty-four.

A Health and Safety Authority inspector noted thirteen breaches of health and safety regulations on the Ringsend site. A garda sergeant noted that there was no protective barrier around the opening through which James Masterson had fallen.

Zoe epitomised the no-nonsense full-speed-ahead ethos of the new Ireland that gave birth to the much-vaunted Celtic Tiger. It built a third of the apartments that saturated Dublin in the mid-1990s. Zoe specialised in building small apartments in areas where sites were cheap and urban renewal tax incentives were available.

The site where James Masterson died was closed down while safety measures were looked at. As part of this process, Zoe came before Judge Peter Kelly in the High Court on Monday, 17 November 1997. The judge said the evidence was 'very disquieting'. He wanted the three directors of Zoe — Liam Carroll, Roisin Carroll, Liam's wife, and David Torpey — in court. He called Liam Carroll to the witness box and launched a stinging attack on Zoe. The company, he told Carroll, 'that you are responsible for is a criminal, and a recidivist criminal at that, and is so thanks to you'.

Zoe had made handsome profits, 'but the workers on whose sweat you make your money are treated with contempt. And so are the laws.' Carroll had happily paid 'fleabite' fines but he was no longer in the lower courts, said the judge.

> This court has wider powers and can make orders to close you down. And close you down I will, on every site where I find conduct of that sort. You will stay closed until you comply with your regulations. You are entitled to make profits on the sweat of your workers but you are not entitled to make a profit on the blood and lives of your workers. You are a disgrace to the construction industry and ought to be ashamed of yourself.

Judge Kelly asked if Liam Carroll had anything to say. The builder remained mute. The judge said, 'Would you not think of apologising at all? Would it not strike you or cross your mind that you might apologise?' After this blunt prompting, Carroll said he'd like to apologise for not having the regulations fully in force when James Masterson died. The judge asked if Carroll bore any contrition.

'I bear a lot of contrition for what has gone on.'

The judge told him he could demonstrate that contrition in a tangible form. Carroll didn't get it. He asked for an explanation. There were charities which could do with a contribution, he was told. It was just over a month to Christmas.

Carroll and his barrister had a quick consultation. The judge was told Mr Carroll would donate a hundred thousand pounds. Fifty thousand to the Vincent de Paul night shelter at Back Lane, and the same again to Temple Street Children's Hospital, said the judge. A week later, on Monday, 24 November, the judge allowed Zoe reopen the Charlotte Quay site.

In 1998 Zoe's profit jumped from £5 million to £9.3 million. Liam Carroll's personal worth was estimated at £50 million.

Zoe was just one element of the roaring Celtic Tiger, in which investors needed somewhere to put their money and apartment builders obliged as fast as they could. Thirteen building workers died in accidents in 1995, fourteen in 1996 and thirteen in 1997, of which one was James Masterson. In 1998, twenty-two building workers were killed, a 70 per cent increase on 1997.

Select Bibliography

Books

Adams, Michael, *Censorship, The Irish Experience*, University of Alabama Press 1968

Arnold, Bruce, *What Kind of Country*, Jonathan Cape 1984

Arnold, Mavis and Heather Laskey, *Children of the Poor Clares*, Appletree 1985

Bloch, Jonathan and Patrick Fitzgerald, *British Intelligence and Covert Action*, Brandon 1983

Bowers, Fergal, *Hep C, Niamh's Story*, Marino Books 1997

Brady, Séamus, *Doctor of Millions*, Anvil Books 1975

Broderick, Joe, *Fall from Grace*, Brandon 1992

Brown, Terence, *Ireland, A Social and Cultural History*, Fontana 1985

Browne, Vincent (ed.), *The Magill Book of Irish Politics*, Magill 1981

Byrne, Gay, with Deirdre Purcell, *The Time of My Life: An Autobiography*, Gill & Macmillan 1989

de Búrca, Marcus, *The GAA: A History*, Cumann Lúthchleas Gael 1980; Gill & Macmillan 1999

Donnelly, Seán, *Partnership: Election '92*, Seán Donnelly 1993

Donnelly, Seán, *Elections '97*, Seán Donnelly 1998

Downey, James, *Brian Lenihan*, New Island Books 1998

Duignan, Seán, *One Spin on the Merry-Go-Round*, Blackwater n.d.

Dunne, Derek and Gene Kerrigan, *Round Up the Usual Suspects*, Magill 1984

Dwyer, T. Ryle, *Charlie: The Political Biography of Charles J. Haughey*, Gill & Macmillan 1987

Farmar, Tony, *A History of Craig Gardner & Co.: The First 100 Years*, Gill & Macmillan 1988

Farrell, Brian, *Chairman or Chief*, Gill & Macmillan 1971

Farrell, Brian, *Seán Lemass*, Gill & Macmillan 1983, 1991

Farrelly, Jim, *Who's Who in Irish Politics*, Blackwater 1990

Finegan, John, *Honor Bright*, Elo

Finlay, Fergus, *Snakes and Ladders*, New Island Books 1998

Fisk, Robert, *In Time of War: Ireland, Ulster and the Price of Neutrality 1939–45*, Gill & Macmillan 1983

FitzGerald, Garret, *All in a Life: An Autobiography*, Gill & Macmillan 1991

Gallagher, Michael, *The Irish Labour Party in Transition 1957–82*, Gill & Macmillan 1982

Gray, Tony, *Ireland this Century*, Little Brown 1996

Hermon, Sir John, *Holding the Line: An Autobiography*, Gill & Macmillan 1997

Hussey, Gemma, *At the Cutting Edge: Cabinet Diaries 1982–1987*, Gill & Macmillan 1990

Joyce, Joe and Peter Murtagh, *The Boss*, Poolbeg 1983

Keogh, Dermot, *The Jews in 20th Century Ireland*, Cork University Press 1998

Kerrigan, Gene, *Nothing But the Truth*, Tomar 1990

Kerrigan, Gene, *Hard Cases: True Stories of Irish Crime*, Gill & Macmillan 1996

Kimmage, Paul, *Rough Ride*, Yellow Jersey Press 1990

Lee, George and Charlie Bird, *Breaking the Bank*, Blackwater 1998

Lee, J.J., *Ireland 1912–1985*, Cambridge 1990

Lenihan, Brian, *For the Record*, Blackwater 1991

MacDermott, Eithne, *Clann na Poblachta*, Cork University Press 1999

McDonald, Frank, *The Destruction of Dublin*, Gill & Macmillan 1985

McKay, Susan, *Sophia's Story*, Gill & Macmillan 1998

MacManus, Francis, *The Years of the Great Test*, Mercier 1978

Mitchell, Arthur, *JFK and His Irish Legacy*, Moytura 1993

Moore, Chris, *Betrayal of Trust: The Father Brendan Smyth Affair and the Catholic Church*, Marino Books 1995

Morrissey, James, *Hot Whiskey*, The Kerryman 1989

Murphy, Annie, *Forbidden Fruit*, Little Brown 1994

O'Brien, Conor Cruise, *Memoir — My Life and Themes*, Poolbeg 1998

O'Farrell, Padraic, *Tales for the Telling*, The Collins Press n.d.

Ó hEithir, Breandán, *The Begrudger's Guide to Irish Politics*, Poolbeg n.d.

O'Leary, Olivia and Helen Burke, *Mary Robinson*, Hodder & Stoughton 1998

Rafter, Kevin, *The Clann*, Mercier 1996

Sheehan, Helena, *Irish Television Drama*, RTÉ 1987

Siggins, Lorna, *Mary Robinson*, Mainstream 1997

Smyth, Sam, *Thanks a Million Big Fella*, Blackwater 1997

Spray, Glenys, *Blood, Sweat and Tears: The Hepatitis C Scandal*, Wolfhound 1998

Tobin, Fergal, *The Best of Decades: Ireland in the 1960s*, Gill & Macmillan 1984, 1996

Touher, Patrick, *Fear of the Collar: Artane Industrial School*, The O'Brien Press 1991

Whyte, J.H., *Church and State in Modern Ireland 1923–1979*, Gill & Macmillan 1980

Newspapers and Magazines

Business and Finance

Evening Herald

Hibernia

Irish Independent

Irish Times

Magill

Sunday Business Post

Sunday Independent

Sunday Tribune